The Complete Guide to
Blender Graphics
Computer Modeling
& Animation

FIFTH EDITION

The Complete Guide to
Blender Graphics
Computer Modeling
& Animation

FIFTH EDITION

JOHN M. BLAIN

CRC Press
Taylor & Francis Group
Boca Raton London New York

CRC Press is an imprint of the
Taylor & Francis Group, an **informa** business

AN A K PETERS BOOK

CRC Press
Taylor & Francis Group
6000 Broken Sound Parkway NW, Suite 300
Boca Raton, FL 33487-2742

© 2019 by Taylor & Francis Group, LLC
CRC Press is an imprint of Taylor & Francis Group, an Informa business

No claim to original U.S. Government works

Printed on acid-free paper

International Standard Book Number-13: 978-0-367-18475-9 (Hardback)
International Standard Book Number-13: 978-0-367-18474-2 (Paperback)

Visit the Taylor & Francis Web site at
http://www.taylorandfrancis.com

and the CRC Press Web site at
http://www.crcpress.com

Contents

Introduction

The Program and the Book

The Book – The Complete Guide to Blender Graphics - 5th Edition

The Complete Guide to Blender Graphics - 5th Edition provides instruction in the use of the Computer Graphics 3D Program **Blender** version **2.80**. The manual is for those who wish to undertake a learning experience and discover a wonderful creative new world of computer graphics. The book also serves as a reference for established operators.

Instructions throughout the book introduce Blender's features with examples and diagrams referenced to the **Graphical User Interface (GUI).**

The Complete Guide to Blender Graphics originated when Blender's Graphical User Interface was transformed with the release of Blender version 2.50. Subsequent editions of the book have kept pace with developments to the program and have included new material. With the release of Blender 2.80 and its' new interface and operational philosophy, the Fifth Edition of The Complete Guide to Blender Graphics provides current instruction.

For new users this book provides a fantastic learning experience in **Computer Graphics** using **Blender,** by introducing the operation of the Blender program through the use of its' Graphical user Interface. The book is intended to be read in conjunction with having the program in operation, with the interface displayed on a computer monitor screen.

Instruction is presented using the tools displayed in the Graphical User Interface, with basic examples demonstrating results. It is not intended to provide explicit tutorials on any particular topic. Understanding where tools are located, their uses and how they are implemented will allow the reader to more easily follow detailed instruction in the many written and video tutorials available on the internet.

The Program - Blender

Blender is a 3D Computer Graphics Program with tools for modeling and animating objects and characters and creating background scenes. Scenes may be made into still images. Animated sequences may be used for video production. Models and Scenes are enhanced with color and texture producing brilliant realistic effects. The still images and video may be for artistic appreciation or employed as architectural or scientific presentations. There are also tools for 2D animation production. Stand alone models may be used for 3D Printing.

The Blender program is maintained by the **Blender Foundation** and released as **Open Source Software** which is available for download and **FREE** to be used for any purpose.

The program may be downloaded from:

www.blender.org

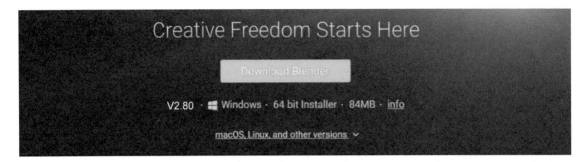

Blender Features

A comprehensive display of the Blender features is available at:

www.blender.org/features/

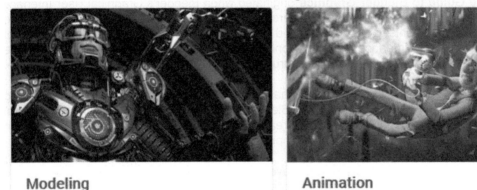

Modeling   **Animation**

Blender Platforms

A **computing platform** or **digital platform** is the environment in which a piece of software is executed. It may be the hardware or the operating system (OS)

Blender is a cross platform application for **Windows Vista and above, Linux** and **Mac OSX 10.6 and above** operating systems.

The operation of Blender in this manual is applicable to all operating platforms but operations ancillary to the program, such as, saving work to the computers hard drive, have been described exclusively using a Windows operating system.

System Requirements

Graphics

Blender 2.80 requires OpenGL 3.3 or above, with recent graphics drivers from your graphics card manufacturer.

Hardware

Minimum (basic usage) hardware

- 32-bit dual core 2Ghz CPU with SSE2 support.
- 2 GB RAM
- 1280×768 display
- Mouse or Trackpad

Recommended hardware

- 64-bit quad core CPU
- 8 GB RAM
- Full HD display with 24 bit color
- Three button mouse

Optimal (production-grade) hardware

- 64-bit eight core CPU
- 16 GB RAM
- Full HD displays
- Three button mouse and graphics tablet

OpenGL - Open Graphics Library (Version Number) is a cross-language, cross-platform application programming interface (API) for rendering 2D and 3D vector graphics. The API is typically used to interact with a graphics processing unit (GPU – Graphics Card), to achieve hardware-accelerated rendering.

Program Evolution

Blender is continually evolving. New versions of the program are released as additions and changes are incorporated, therefore, it is advisable to check the Blender website, from time to time.

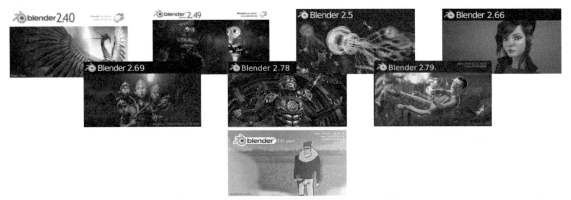

Earlier versions of the program and documentation may be obtained which provide valuable information when you are conversant with the current release of the program. Video tutorials available on the internet also provide valuable information but may not strictly adhere to the current user interface or work flow. Major transformations occurred when the program changed from version 2.49 to 2.50 and again at the change from version 2.79 to the current version 2.80. Being aware of this evolution will allow you to consider anomalies when viewing online tutorials.

Starting the Program

How you start Blender depends on how you have installed the program (see Download & Installation at the front of the book). If you have used the **MSI installer option** for Windows, Blender will be in the Program Files directory on your C: Drive and a shortcut icon will have been placed on your desktop. If you have installed to a Window 10 operating system, Blender will be listed under, Program Files\ Blender Foundation\ Blender.

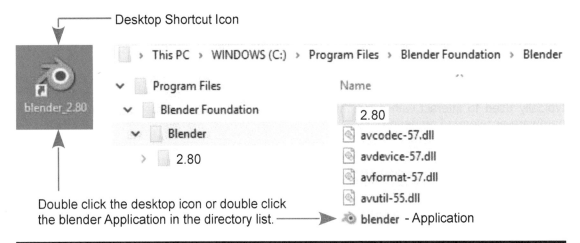

If you have downloaded and unzipped the compressed (ZIP) file for Blender the **blender.exe** application file will be located in the folder where you unzipped the compressed file. Open the folder and double click **blender.exe** or right click and select **Open**.

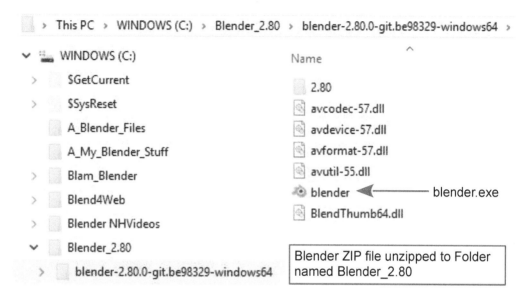

Note: By having one version of Blender installed via the Installer(.msi) option and another using the ZIP method you can have more than one Blender version installed on your computer at the same time. This is useful for version comparison or for development purposes.

Shortcut

In the directory containing the **blender.exe** file create a shortcut and place it on the desktop.

The Manual Compilation

This manual has been compiled as the experimental builds of Blender 2.80 have been released. During that time numerous subtle changes improving the program's interface have been implemented. Every effort has been made to incorporate these changes in images which demonstrate operational features of the program.

Images used to construct diagrams may differ to what you see on your computer screen. The Blender screen display may be customized or modified to suit individual user preferences. There are several in built display themes which you can choose. In some cases the screen display has been altered to facilitate the construction of diagrams (Figures). When alterations have been made they do not detract from the instruction presented.

Download & Installation

Download Blender

Download Blender from: **www.blender.org**

Select the current Blender version which is applicable to your operating system. Blender is available for Windows, Mac OSX and GNU/Linux in 64 bit and 32 bit versions.

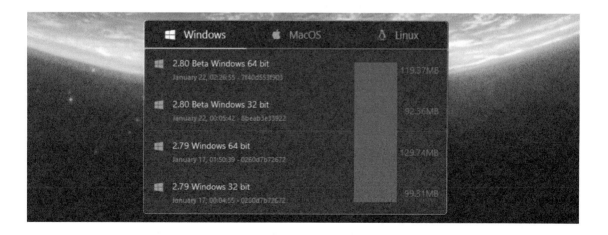

The download options shown in the previous diagram present a download window for a compressed zip file of the program.

You have chosen to open:

blender-2.79-0260d7b72672-win64.zip

which is: WinRAR ZIP archive (130 MB)

from: https://builder.blender.org

Alternative download options can be for a msi installer file.

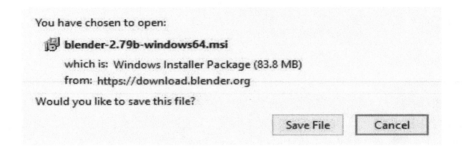

You have chosen to open:

blender-2.79b-windows64.msi

which is: Windows Installer Package (83.8 MB)

from: https://download.blender.org

Would you like to save this file?

Save File | Cancel

Installation on a Windows Operating System

Installing with the Installer(.msi) Option

Double click on the file name in the Downloads folder, follow the prompts and Blender will be automatically installed to the **Program Files** folder on your computer and an icon will be placed on your **Desktop**.

Installing with the ZIP Option

With a ZIP file you have to unzip the file. You first create a new folder on your computers hard drive then use a program like 7-Zip or Win-Zip to unzip (decompress) the zip file into the new folder (see the note at the end of the chapter).

When the file is unzipped into the new folder you will see **blender.exe** as one of the entries. You double click on this to run Blender or you create a shortcut which places an icon on your desktop.

When using either installation option you double click the **blender.exe** file to run the program. Shortcuts on the Desktop are shortcuts to the blender.exe file.

Note: By having one version of Blender installed via the Installer(.msi) option and another using the ZIP method you can have more than one Blender version installed on your computer at the same time. This is useful for version comparison or for development purposes.

Installing Blender on a Linux Operating System

Ubuntu

http://www.wikihow.com/Install-Blender-3D-on-Ubuntu

Fedora

https://wiki.blender.org/index.php/Doc:KO/2.6/Manual/
Introduction/Installing_Blender/Linux/Fedora

Debian

https://www.howtoinstall.co/en/debian/jessie/blender

Installing Blender on Mac OS X

https://wiki.blender.org/index.php/User:Greylica/Doc:2.6/Manual/
Introduction/Installing_Blender/Mac

The Author

John M. Blain was born in 1942 in Swindon, Wiltshire in England and emigrated to Canada with his family in 1952. He now lives in Coffs Harbour, New South Wales in Australia.

Drawing and painting were skills John developed from an early age and while attending school on Vancouver Island he became interested in wood sculpture inspired by the work of the indigenous west coast people. Artistic pursuits were curtailed on graduating from high school when he returned to England to undertake a technical engineering apprenticeship. Following his apprenticeship he worked for a short period in England then made the decision to return to Vancouver, Canada. On the voyage between Southampton and Vancouver he met his wife to be and Vancouver became a stopover for a journey to Sydney Australia. In this new country he began work as an engineering draughtsman, married, had children and studied engineering . The magic milestone of seven years saw John with his young family move out of the city to the coastal town of Coffs Harbour, New South Wales.

Coffs Harbour was a center for sawmill machinery and John became engaged in machinery design and manufacture. He acquired a sound knowledge of this industry acting as installation engineer then progressing to sales. This work afforded travel throughout Australia, Canada, the United States and New Zealand.

On retirement, artistic pursuits returned with additional interests in writing and computing. Writing notes whilst learning computer animation using Blender resulted in **The Complete Guide to Blender Graphics**. The first edition, published in 2012, was well received and encouraged John to compile a second edition inline with the latest version of the Blender program. This afforded the opportunity to include new material. Subsequent editions have followed until this new reformatted fifth edition.

Acknowledgments

Helen's assistance and patience have made this Fifth Edition of the book possible.

Continued thanks to Neal Hirsig for his encouragement without which **The Complete Guide to Blender Graphics** would not have been created.

A thank you goes to Kevin Hayes for his permission to use his art work on the book cover.

- John M. Blain

Preamble

Basic Objective

The fundamental objective in using a computer graphics program such as Blender is to produce a display on a computer Screen which converts (**Renders**) into a digital image or series of images for an animation sequence. The display may only contain a single inanimate model such as that used for 3D printing but will will usually contain multiple 3D models of animate and or inanimate Objects. The arrangement of **Objects** constitutes a **Scene**. Animate Objects (animated Objects) are the moving characters in animation sequences. Inanimate Objects are the components of a Scene with which the characters interact. These may be obstacles in a Scene such as, ground planes, terrain and background.

Before you begin to read this book it is assumed you know how to operate a computer. In the past this assumption meant you knew how to operate using a keyboard and mouse. Today many of you will be more familiar with touch screens or laptop touch pads, therefore, although this may appear to be a retrograde step the first instruction will be to familiarise you with Mouse and Keyboard operations.

Blender has been designed to be operated using a Keyboard and Mouse and instruction will be provided using these devices.

Formats Conventions and Commands

In writing this book the following format conventions have been adopted:

Paragraphs are separated by an empty line and have not been indented.

Key words and phrases are printed in **bold text** with the first letter of a component name specific to Blender capitalised.

Headings are printed in Bold Olive Green.

The following conventions will be used when giving instructions.

When using a Mouse connected to a computer, the commands will be:

Click or **Click LMB** – In either case this means make a single click with the left mouse button with the Mouse Cursor positioned over a control displayed on the computer Screen. In some instances it is explicit that the left mouse button should be used.

A Control: Is a designated area on the computer Screen represented by an icon in the form of a button or bar, with or without text annotation.

Double Click – Make two clicks in quick succession with **LMB** (the left mouse button).

Click, Hold and Drag – Click the left mouse button, hold it depressed while moving the mouse. Release the button at the end of the movement.

Click RMB – Click the right mouse button.

Click MMB – Click the middle mouse button (the middle mouse button may be the scroll wheel).

Scroll MMB – Scroll (rotate) the scroll wheel (MMB).

Clicking is used in conjunction with placing the Mouse Cursor over a button, icon or a slider which is displayed on the Screen.

The Graphical User Interface (GUI)

When Blender is first opened what you see on the computer Screen is the **Graphical User Interface (GUI)** for the program. This arrangement of panels is the interface which allows you, the user, to communicate with the program by entering commands (data) using the Keyboard and Mouse, previously described. The panels that you see are called **Editors**.

Editors

Editors (the panels in the **GUI**) are so named since the basic philosophy in operating the program is; You are presented with a set of default data producing a Screen display. You Edit or modify the default data to create what you want.

There are numerous Editors for selection depending on the particular feature of Blender you wish to use. The different Editors will be introduced as features of the program are encountered.

Controls - Buttons, Icons and Sliders

Each Editor in the **GUI** is a separate panel comprising a **Header** at the top of the panel and sub-panels which display within the Editor. The Header and sub-panels contain buttons which you click to activate functions or display menus for selecting functions. The buttons are displayed as text annotation, icons and panels. Each of these, relay data to the program to perform an action.

Example 1 : The 3D View Editor (the default Screen display – **Upper LH Side**)

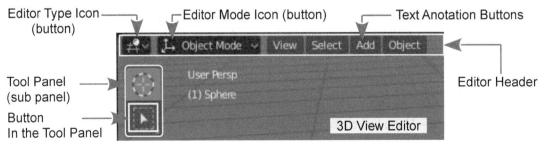

Editor Type Icon (button) ─── Editor Mode Icon (button) ─── Text Anotation Buttons

Tool Panel (sub panel)

Button In the Tool Panel

Editor Header

User Persp
(1) Sphere

3D View Editor

> **Note:** The buttons shown in the previous diagram can be seen in the panel at the left hand side of the **default** Blender Screen arrangement. A detailed description of the Screen Arrangement with its Editors and panels constituting **Blender's GUI** (Graphical User Interface) is presented in **Chapter 1**.

A Button in Blender can be a small square or rectangular area on the screen or an elongated rectangle in which case it may be referred to as a bar. Some buttons display with icons.

An Icon is a pictorial representation of a function. In the diagram the icons show the Editor panels that are opened and also act as buttons for selecting alternative Editors.

A Slider is an elongated area, usually containing a numeric value, which is modified by clicking, deleting and retyping the value, or clicking, holding and dragging the Mouse Cursor that displays on **Mouse Over**, left or right to decrease or increase the value. Some sliders have a small arrow at either end which display when the Mouse Cursor is positioned over the Slider (Mouse Over). Click on an arrow to incrementally alter the value. Some sliders directly alter the display on the computer Screen.

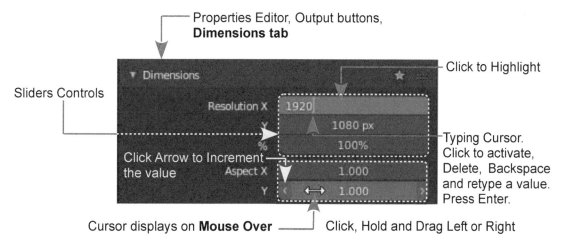

Properties Editor, Output buttons, **Dimensions tab**

Sliders Controls

Click to Highlight

Click Arrow to Increment the value

Typing Cursor. Click to activate, Delete, Backspace and retype a value. Press Enter.

Cursor displays on **Mouse Over** — Click, Hold and Drag Left or Right

For the Keyboard input, a command is; to press a specific Key or a series of Keys. Press **Shift + Ctrl + T Key** means, press and hold both the **Shift** and **Ctrl** Keys simultaneously and tap the **T Key**.

Num Pad (Number Pad) Keys are also used in which case the command is Press **Num Pad 0** to **9** or **Plus** and **Minus**.

Having established this basic and perhaps, obvious nomenclature, you are good to go.

> **Note:** In giving instructions, **Default** means, that which is displayed on the computer Screen before any action is taken.

The default display shows the content of the Properties Editor with the **Object button** active displaying the controls for the default Cube **Object** in the 3 View Editor.

Properties Editor
Icon

Properties Editor Header
(RHS of Screen)

Editor Display Selection
buttons

Cube Object
(in the 3D View Editor)

Object button
(Display contents of the
Editor Panel)

Editor Panel showing the
Object button display

Slider Controls
(Adjust Numeric Value)

Button
(Click to display a Selection
Menu)

Tabs
(Click to Open Panel)

Tab Closed

Tab Open

Panel Opened

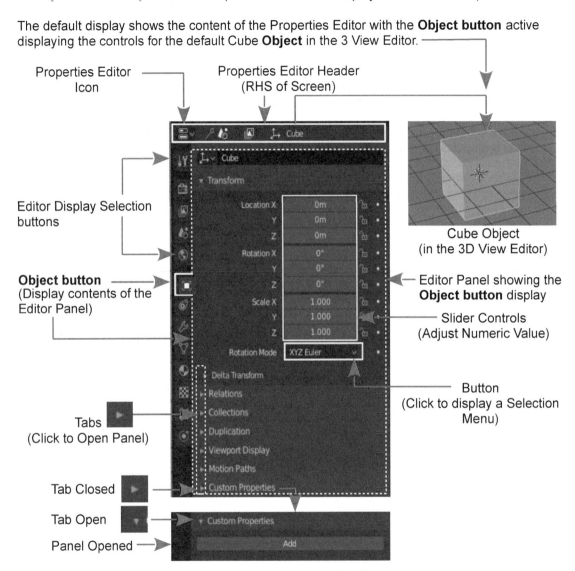

Note: Previous versions of Blender displayed the Editor selection buttons in the Properties Editor Header in a **horizontal configuration at the top of the Editor panel**.

Properties Editor, **Object button**

To assist those of you transitioning from earlier versions and to facilitate the arrangement of diagrams in this manual the horizontal configuration will be employed in some figures.

The following diagram shows the correlation between the horizontal and vertical.

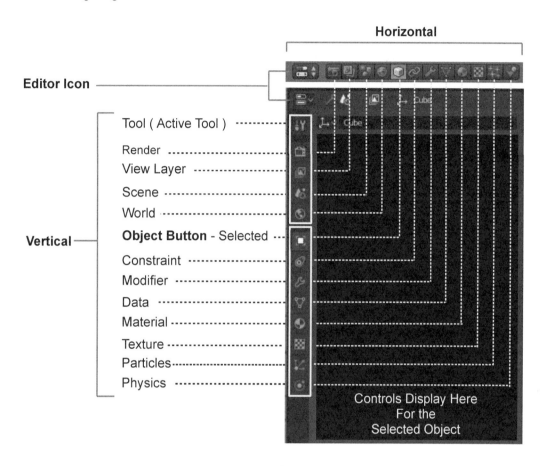

Horizontal

Editor Icon

Tool (Active Tool)

Render
View Layer

Scene

World

Vertical

Object Button - Selected

Constraint

Modifier

Data

Material

Texture

Particles

Physics

Controls Display Here
For the
Selected Object

Command Instruction Example:

Go to the **Blender Screen Header, Render button,** click **Render Image:**

Remember: A control button, icon or slider which is displayed, indicates a specific location on the computer Screen. Positioning the Mouse Cursor at this location and clicking the Mouse button or depressing a keyboard button, inputs a signal to the computer. The interpretation , made by by the computer is; signal received at specific location = perform explicit computation and export result.

The example above means, in the **Blender Screen Header,** position the **Mouse Cursor** over the **Render image** and click the left mouse button, clicking once. In this case the signal received by the computer with the Mouse Cursor at the position of the Render Button tells the computer to display the **Render Options Sub Menu**. Positioning the Mouse Cursor over **Render Image** in the sub menu and clicking once renders an image of **Camera View** (what the camera sees). The rendered image is displayed in a new Editor panel, the **Image Editor**. The image may be saved from this location but for the time being press **Esc** on the Keyboard to cancel the render and return to the 3D View Editor.

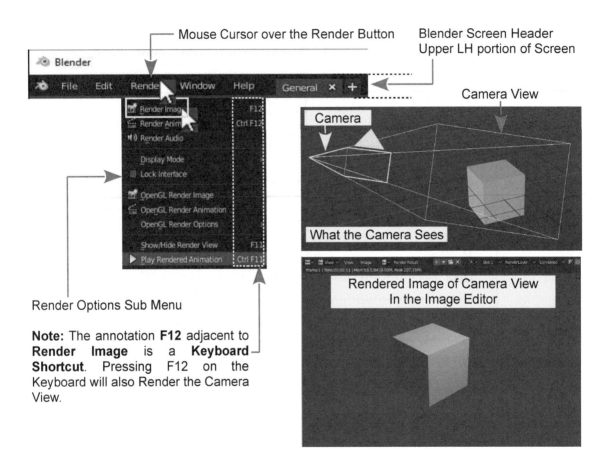

Mouse Cursor over the Render Button

Blender Screen Header
Upper LH portion of Screen

Camera View

Camera

What the Camera Sees

Rendered Image of Camera View
In the Image Editor

Render Options Sub Menu

Note: The annotation **F12** adjacent to **Render Image** is a **Keyboard Shortcut**. Pressing F12 on the Keyboard will also Render the Camera View.

Book Work Flow

The initial work flow in the book will introduce the Editors and panels which make up the **Graphical User Interface (GUI)** and familiarise you with basic control operations. During the initial introduction detailed explanation of the Blender processes will be limited to a need to know basis. To start with, you will have to blindly follow along without understanding why. Explanation will be given as you progress and are made aware of the different Blender features.

In demonstrating one of the previous **Command Examples** the command was; **Click the Render button**.

Rendering

Rendering: Definition from the Wiki when specifically applied to computer graphics. The Wiki? The Free Encyclopedia Wikipedia.

Https://en.wikipedia.org/wiki/Rendering_(computer_graphics)

Rendering or **Image Synthesis** is the automatic process of generating a photo realistic or non-photo realistic image from a 2D or 3D model (or models in what collectively could be called a Scene file) by means of a computer program. Also, the results of displaying such a model can be called **Rendering**. A Scene file contains objects in a strictly defined language or data structure; it would contain geometry, viewpoint, texture, lighting, and shading information as a description of the virtual Scene. The data contained in the scene file is then passed to a rendering program to be processed and output to a digital image or raster graphics image file. The term "rendering" may be by analogy with an "artist's rendering" of a Scene.

Render Engines - GUI Versions in Blender

Render Engines are the parts of the Blender program that convert the display into an image or sequence of images. Image sequences generate animations which in turn produce a movie files.

In Blender 2.8 there are three **Render Engine options**. With the selection of each Render Engine type the Graphical User Interface (GUI) is displayed in a slightly different manner. Which option you chose depends on the particular process, to which the engine type is suited.

The Render Engines in Blender 2.80 are named; **Eevee Render, Cycles Render, Workbench Render.**

Eevee Render

The default Render Engine presented when Blender starts is **Eevee**. This is an acronym for *"Extra Easy Virtual Environment Engine"*. Eevee displays a real time rendered view. In other words, what you see on the Screen as you make changes, is a good approximation of what you get in your final image view. Eevee quickly renders the Scene as you work but the quality of the render can incur a time disadvantage in the advanced stages of modeling.

Cycles Render

Cycles Rendering is specifically designed to produce a photo realistic high quality display of an image or frame in an animation incorporating colors, textures and special lighting. The quality of the display is adjustable since high resolution rendering comes at a cost with respect to time.

Workbench Render

Workbench Rendering uses the 3D View's drawing for quick *preview* renders. This allows you to inspect your animation (for object movements, alternate angles, etc.). This can also be used to preview your animations – in the event your Scene is too complex for your system to play back in real-time in the 3D View. You can use Workbench to render both images and animations.

> **Note: Workbench Render** was formerly **OpenGL Render**. The definition
> has been taken from the Blender Manual. Each Render Engine type
> displays the view in the computer Screen in different ways depending on the
> **Viewport Shading** method that you select. This will be explained as you
> progress through the book.

Workspaces

A **Workspace** is the arrangement or configuration of **Editor** panels on the computer Screen. Blender includes numerous Editors for specific functions and these Editors are selected and arranged to facilitate particular operations.

Several Workspaces (Editor arrangements) are provided and may be selected in the Blender Screen Header. There is also the facility for users to build and save specialised arrangements of Editors to suit their working environment for specific tasks.

Layout displays the default **Workspace** in the default Screen Arrangement

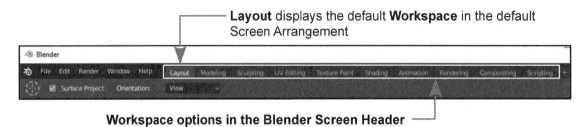

Workspace options in the Blender Screen Header

Although not designated as Workspaces there are five other Screen arrangements for specific tasks. In the Header at the top of the Screen, click on **File** then New to display the option menu.

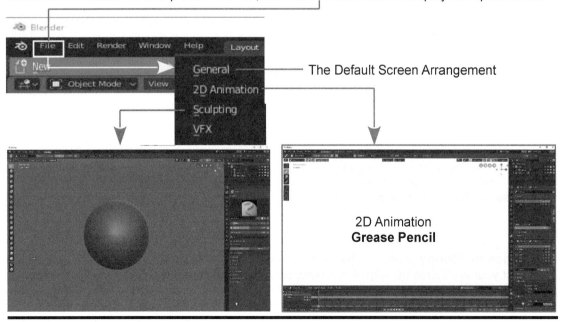

The Default Screen Arrangement

2D Animation
Grease Pencil

Notes

Book Content

The contents of the book introduce the components and features of the Blender version 2.80 program. Many of the features are similar, if not identical, to those found in version 2.79 but the Graphical User Interface and the method of operation has been modified and improved.

When you are conversant with the operation of the new interface you will discover that there is a vast array of information available on the internet written for earlier versions, which is relevant and adaptable to current work.

This book shows you the tools for performing operations. The examples and tutorials on the internet provide ideas and inspiration. Combining the two with your imagination, will allow you release your creative genius.

Supplements

Blender is a comprehensive application and while learning and using Blender you will discover many subjects which have not been included in the book. While it is tempting to add material there is only so much room between the covers. It is the author's intention, as new features are discovered, to write instruction and make this available as a supplement to the book, on the authors website at:

tamarindcreativegraphics.com

Comment

The author welcomes comment and constructive criticism which may be directed to:

silverjb12@gmail.com

1

Understanding the Interface

The Interface

When you start Blender you are presented with a Screen arrangement displaying multiple windows. This arrangement is called the **Graphical User Interface (GUI)** (Figure 1.1). The **GUI** connects you to **Blender**. Windows in **Blender** are called **Editors.** The main **3D View Editor** filling most of the **Screen** is where you create **Models** and **Scenes**. The **Outliner Editor** and **Properties Editor** at the right hand side of the Screen contain controls for operating the program to affect what occurs in the 3D View Editor. The **Timeline Editor** at the bottom of the Screen is where animations are set up. Becoming familiar with Editors and how to input data is the key to understanding how the program operates. Each Blender Editor contains tools for creating a multitude of effects, which when combined, produce fantastic visual displays. Being aware of the tools available and understanding what they do is paramount to understanding Blender.

To get you started using Blender, this chapter will describe the Editors that you see when Blender is first opened. This arrangement of Editors and panels is the **Default Workspace**. You will be introduced to each Editor and instructed in using a sample of the Blender controls. This introduction will make you familiar with the Editors, entering command using the controls and seeing how the different Editors interrelate.

Be aware that there are more Editors and controls other than what you see in the default Screen arrangement and that a Screen arrangement may be fully customised.

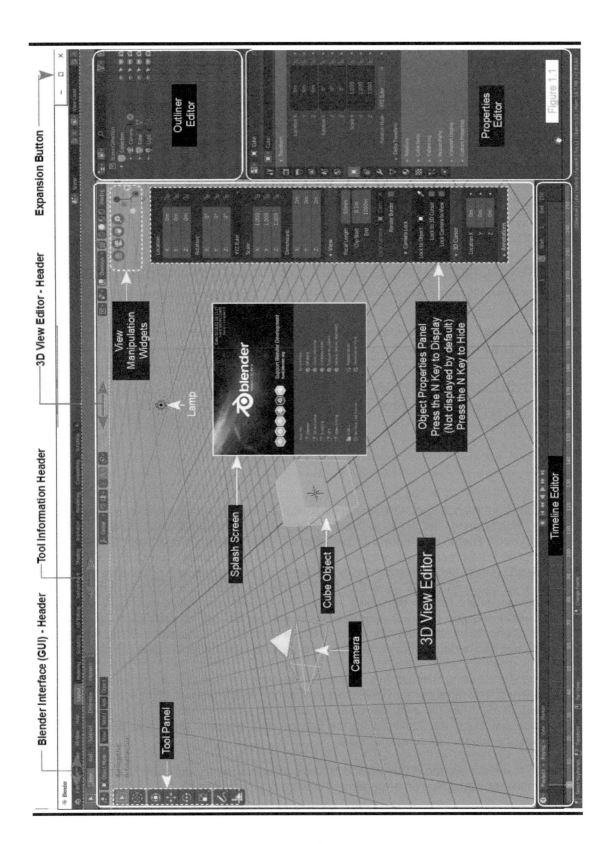

Blender Interface (GUI) - Header — Tool Information Header — 3D View Editor - Header — Expansion Button

Outliner Editor

Properties Editor

Figure 1.1

View Manipulation Widgets

Lamp

Object Properties Panel
Press the N Key to Display
(Not displayed by default)
Press the N Key to Hide

Splash Screen

Cube Object

Camera

3D View Editor

Tool Panel

Timeline Editor

2

1.1 Understanding the Interface

When Blender first opens, the Screen displays the **Graphical User Interface (GUI)** as shown in Figure 1.1. The default arrangement shows the **Screen** with the **Eevee Render Engine** active (see **Rendering** in the Preamble).

The Blender **GUI** opens with the **Splash Screen** panel in the center, showing which version of Blender you have opened (Figure 1.2). There are web page links included in the **Splash Screen**.

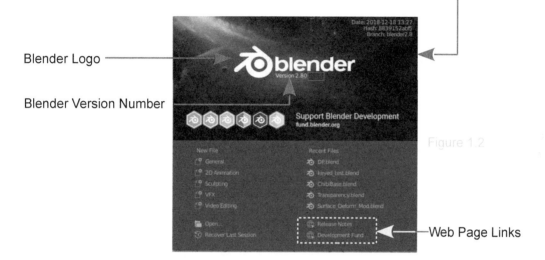

Figure 1.2

- Blender Logo
- Blender Version Number
- Web Page Links

> **Note:** You can have more than one version of Blender open at the same time.
>
> **Note:** In Figure 1.1 borders have been added to distinguish the Editors.
>
> **Note:** As features are introduced, detailed instruction will be deferred until you have acquired sufficient knowledge to understand the usage. In the early stages of learning Blender this will occur frequently, therefore, a reference will be given to detailed explanation.

Blender is continually being amended and revised with improvements and new releases of the program being made available. Check the Blender website to keep up to date with new releases.

With the **Mouse Cursor** positioned anywhere in the **Screen**, click the Left **M**ouse **B**utton (LMB) or press **Enter** on the **Keyboard** to remove the **Splash Screen** panel.

Before you can explore the Blender interface you have to know the fundamental procedures for entering commands to the program via the Keyboard and Mouse. Refer to the section titled **Formats Conventions and Commands** in the Preamble.

1.2 The Blender Screen (GUI)

The **Default** Screen arrangement comprises four individual panels or windows as shown in Figure 1.1. The panels are called **Editors**.

> **Note: Default** means that which is displayed before any changes are made. The basic process in Blender is to start with default data producing a display on the computer monitor Screen and modify or edit the data to display what you require. You modify the data in an **Editor** window or panel.

The default Editors displayed are: The **3D View Editor**, the **Outliner Editor,** the **Properties Editor** and the **Timeline Editor**. Each has an icon representing the Editor Type in the upper left hand corner of the panel. Clicking LMB on this icon displays a menu for changing the Editor to a different Editor Type.

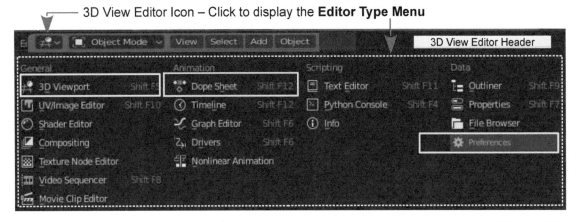

Figure 1.3

As an example; click on the **3D View Editor** icon in the upper left hand corner of the Editor panel (Figure1.3) then in the **Editor Type Menu** click on **Dope Sheet**. The 3D View Editor changes to the **Dope Sheet Editor.**

The icon representing the Dope Sheet Editor in the new panel is located in the upper left hand corner. Click on this icon, select **3D View** in the Editor Type menu and the 3D View Editor will be reinstated.

The Editor types will be explained, when required, as you progress through the book.

When you start Blender you may find that the Blender interface does not fill the entire computer screen. There may be a narrow strip exposing the desktop around the edge. If this occurs click the expansion button located in the upper RH corner of the Screen .

Expansion Button

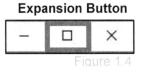

Figure 1.4

On starting Blender you may also find that some buttons in the interface are hidden from view causing text to be partially obscured. This will depend on the size of your monitor screen.

Editor panels in Blender may be resized by dragging the panel edges. Place the Mouse Cursor over (Mouse Over) the edge of an Editor panel and it turns into a double headed arrow (Figure 1.5). This applies to vertical and horizontal edges. Click LMB (left mouse button), hold the Mouse button depressed and drag the Mouse to move the edge.

Figure 1.5

1.3 Headers

The Blender Screen and each Editor in Blender has a **Header** (strip) across the top of the panel which contains buttons for displaying selection menus. The menus allow you to select functions which performing operations.

The **Blender Program Header** is the strip across the very top of the Screen (Figure 1.6) containing buttons for minimising, expanding and quitting.

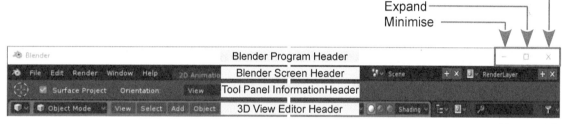

Figure 1.6

The **Blender Screen Header** contains buttons for displaying selection menus with functions that affect the program in a general sense.

The **Tool Panel Information Header** displays information about the Tool that is selected in the 3D View Editor, Tool Panel.

The **3D View Editor Header** has buttons for selecting functions and menus affecting operations within the 3D View Editor.

Example

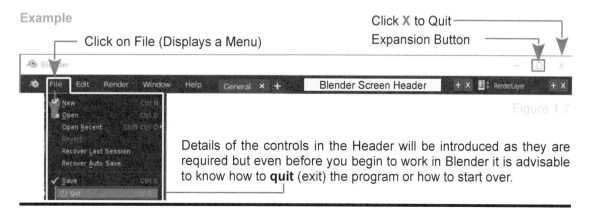

Figure 1.7

Details of the controls in the Header will be introduced as they are required but even before you begin to work in Blender it is advisable to know how to **quit** (exit) the program or how to start over.

5

1.4 How to Quit Blender

As you try different functions you will inevitably mess up, maybe want to take a break or begin with a fresh start and try again.

The simplest way to quit Blender is to click the **X** button in the upper right hand corner of the Screen (Figure 1.7).

Alternatively click on **File** in the **Blender Screen Header** then click **Quit** at the bottom of the menu that displays.

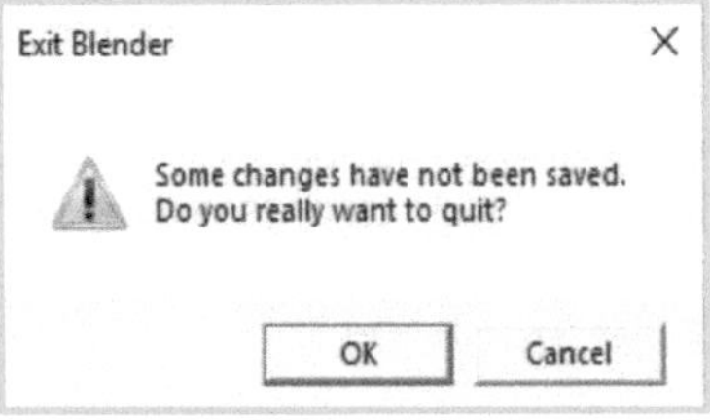

Figure 1.8

In either case Blender will display a warning about saving (Figure 1.8): Click **OK** to Quit or Cancel, save your work then Quit.

The menu that displays when you click **File** contains numerous options, two being; **Save** and **Save As**. How to save work in a Blender file and recover your work saved in the file, is explained in Chapter 3.

1.5 How to Start Over

To simply start over in a fresh default Screen arrangement, click **File** in the **Screen Header** and select (click on) **New** in the menu. A sub menu opens with options.

After clicking on **New,** position the Mouse Cursor over **General** to Open the Default File and click LMB.

Figure 1.9

Selection options in the Screen Header will be introduced as you work through the book but in the early stages of learning how to use the program it's nice to know where to get help.

Clicking the **Help** button in the **Screen Header** displays a menu.

Figure 1.10

Selecting **Manual** in the menu will open your web browser and direct you to the **Blender Manual**.

(https://docs.blender.org/manual/en/dev/)

The remaining options in the menu are links to websites with the exception, **Splash Screen**. Clicking on this entry reinstates the **Splash Screen** panel.

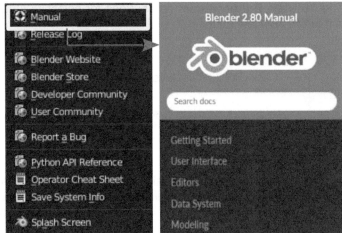

1.6 3D View Editor

The **3D View Editor** filling the majority of the Screen, represents an artificial three dimensional world. The world contains three **Objects**. The Objects are; a **Cube**, a **Camera** (to the left of the Cube) and a **Lamp** positioned above the Cube to the right (Figure 1.11).

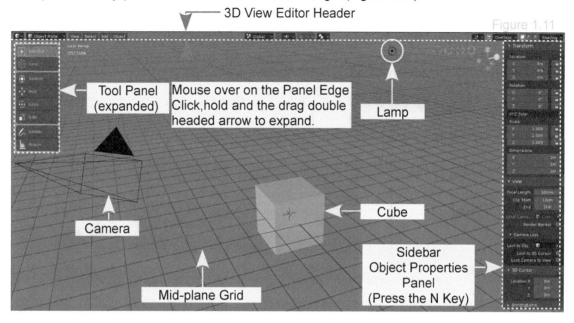

3D View Editor Header

Figure 1.11

Tool Panel (expanded)

Mouse over on the Panel Edge Click,hold and the drag double headed arrow to expand.

Lamp

Cube

Camera

Sidebar
Object Properties
Panel
(Press the N Key)

Mid-plane Grid

> **Note:** If you fail to see one of the Objects described, zoom out on the Editor panel. Place the Mouse Cursor in the Editor and scroll the Mouse Wheel or press the **Minus Key** in the keyboard **Num Pad**.

The 3D View Editor is the working area where Models and Scenes are created.

The 3D View Editor has a **Tool Panel** <u>inside the Editor</u> at the left hand side of the Screen.

Note: Tools in Blender are buttons which activate functions. For example; clicking the **Move** button in the Tool Panel allows you to move an Object in the Scene but before you can use a Tool with an Object, the Object must be **selected**. The Cube Object in the default Screen is selected as indicated by the orange outline (Figure 1.12). Press **Alt + A Key** to deselect. In Figure 1.11, the Cube Object is shown unselected (**NOT** selected). Cick **LMB** on the Cube to select. The Cube displays with an orange outline (Figure 1.12). With the Move Tool active (highlighted red) a **Manipulation Widget** displays on the Cube. Clicking, holding and dragging LMB on one of the Widget's handles (arrows) moves the Cube in the Scene.

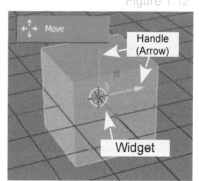

Figure 1.12

Handle
(Arrow)

Widget

7

1.7 3D View Editor - Header

The 3D View Editor Header is the strip across the top of the Editor panel containing buttons for displaying menus. The menus contain functions that perform actions in the 3D View Editor.

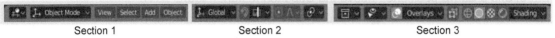

Section 1   Section 2   Section 3

Buttons in the Header have been categorised into three sections. The options will be explained on a need to know basis as topics are discussed but for the moment the organisation of the selection menus will be demonstrated.

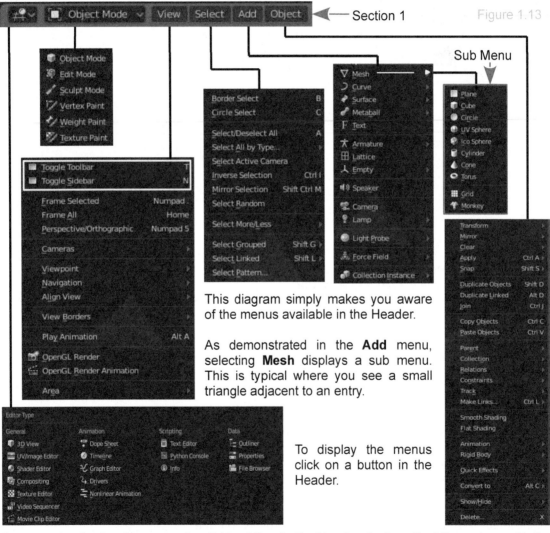

This diagram simply makes you aware of the menus available in the Header.

As demonstrated in the **Add** menu, selecting **Mesh** displays a sub menu. This is typical where you see a small triangle adjacent to an entry.

To display the menus click on a button in the Header.

An example of using the menus is; clicking **View** in the Header displays the **View menu** with the two entries at the top, **Toggle Toolbar – T** and **Toggle Sidebar – N**. T and N refer to the Keyboard keys for **toggling** hide and display of the **Tool Panel** and **Object Properties Panel** .

Toggling

Toggling is the process of pressing a Key, alternating the display and hiding of a panel or to change from one display mode to another and back again. Press the **T Key** to hide the **Tool Panel** at the left of the 3D View Editor. Press the **T Key** again to show the panel.

It is fruitless to list all the options in the Headers and provide explanations unless you have a photographic memory. Options will be referred to and explained as and when required.

1.8 3D View Editor Tool Panel   Figure 1.14

The **Tool Panel** at the left hand side of the 3D View Editor contains buttons which activate Tools. The Tools perform operations in the 3D View Editor.

Note: Mouse over on the edge of the panel, click and drag the arrow to expand the Tool Panel.

Tool Panel Header – Information displays when a Tool is activated

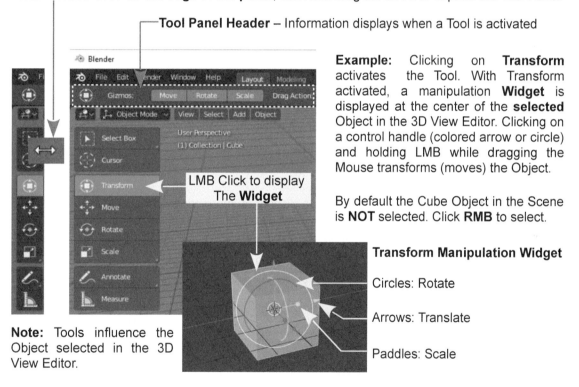

Example: Clicking on **Transform** activates the Tool. With Transform activated, a manipulation **Widget** is displayed at the center of the **selected** Object in the 3D View Editor. Clicking on a control handle (colored arrow or circle) and holding LMB while dragging the Mouse transforms (moves) the Object.

By default the Cube Object in the Scene is **NOT** selected. Click **RMB** to select.

Transform Manipulation Widget

Circles: Rotate

Arrows: Translate

Paddles: Scale

LMB Click to display
The **Widget**

Note: Tools influence the Object selected in the 3D View Editor.

1.9 Sidebar - Object Properties Panel

Pressing the **N Key** with the Mouse Cursor in the 3D View Editor displays the **Sidebar** or **Object Properties (Side) Panel**. By default this panel is hidden from view to save space in the 3D View Editor. Press the **N Key** a second time to hide the panel. You may also toggle display and hide the panel in **View** menu in the 3D View Editor Header. The Sidebar displays information (Properties) which relate to the Object that is selected in the 3D View Editor.

Alternative Display-Hide Methods

In Blender there are, sometimes, more ways than one to perform an operation. When both the **Tool Panel** and **Sidebar** (Object Properties Panel) are hidden in the 3D View Editor you will see a small cross icon in the upper corners of the Editor panel. Placing the Mouse cursor over either of these (Mouse Cursor changes to a double headed arrow) and clicking LMB (left mouse button) will display the respective hidden panels.

3D View Editor Header Figure 1.15

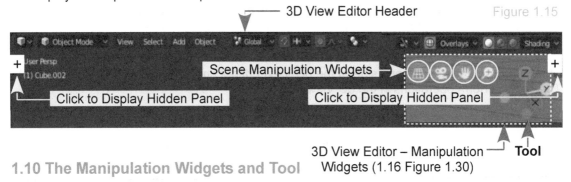

3D View Editor – Manipulation **Tool**

1.10 The Manipulation Widgets and Tool
Widgets (1.16 Figure 1.30)

The **Manipulation Tool** is mentioned here since it displays prominently in the 3D View Editor and you will be wondering what it is. This **Tool** is a widget for manipulating the Scene in the 3D View Editor. Be aware that the Scene in the 3D View Editor may be seen from different angles and perspectives and that Objects in the Scene can also be rotated within the Scene for different viewing angles. There are four other Widgets for Scene manipulation.

1.11 Outliner Editor (upper right hand side)

The **Outliner Editor** (Figure 1.16) provides a display of information relating to the Scene in the 3D View Editor. The default display is **View Layer** which lists the Objects in the Scene.

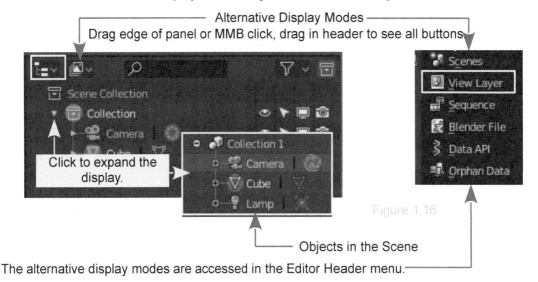

The alternative display modes are accessed in the Editor Header menu.

The Objects are listed in **Collections** which allow you to organise Objects into groups. This assists when working in complicated Scenes. Collections will be discussed in detail later. The alternative display modes will be introduced as their functions are encountered.

1.12 The Properties Editor (lower right hand side)

The Properties Editor is the panel below the Outliner Editor which extends to the bottom of the Screen. This Editor is the engine room for Blender containing controls for actions in the 3D View Editor. The controls will be explained as you progress through the book and encounter the different features of the program. What you see in the Properties Editor depends on which selection button is activated (Figure 1.17). As you can see there are fourteen buttons from which to choose, each will present a different display of controls. The buttons are arranged in two categories (Scene Controls and Object Controls).

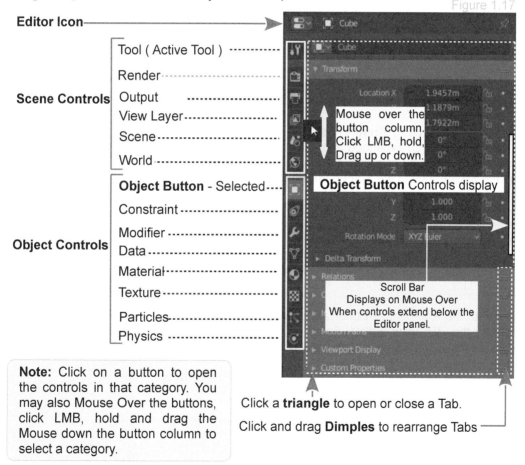

Figure 1.17

Editor Icon

Scene Controls
- Tool (Active Tool)
- Render
- Output
- View Layer
- Scene
- World

Mouse over the button column. Click LMB, hold, Drag up or down.

Object Button Controls display

Object Controls
- **Object Button** - Selected
- Constraint
- Modifier
- Data
- Material
- Texture
- Particles
- Physics

Scroll Bar
Displays on Mouse Over
When controls extend below the
Editor panel.

Note: Click on a button to open the controls in that category. You may also Mouse Over the buttons, click LMB, hold and drag the Mouse down the button column to select a category.

Click a **triangle** to open or close a Tab.

Click and drag **Dimples** to rearrange Tabs

Figures 1.17 shows the Properties Edit with the **Object button** selected. The Object buttons control the properties of **the Object that is selected** in the 3D View Editor Scene. The default Object is the Cube. The Object button displays controls and information about any Object which you have selected in the 3D View Editor.

In the Properties Editor the controls are segregated into sections or **Tabs** in a vertical stack. Tabs are opened and closed by clicking the little triangle adjacent to the Tab name. When the Tabs in the Editor extend below the lower edge of the Editor panel a **Scroll Bar** displays at the right hand edge of the Editor panel, when the Mouse Cursor is positioned over the edge of the panel (**Mouse Over**). Tabs may be rearranged vertically in the stack by clicking on the dimpled area in the upper RH corner of a tab and dragging the Mouse vertically.

1.13 Editor Types

At the beginning of the chapter (Ref 1.2) how to change an Editor panel to a different type of Editor was explained. This is revisited in Chapter 2 (Ref 2.1) when splitting and dividing Editor panels to create specialised Workspaces is discussed. One Editor of particular importance, found in the Editor Type menu, is the **Preferences Editor**.

1.14 The Preferences Editor

The **Preferences Editor** is not displayed in the default Screen, but you should be aware of its existence and importance. The Editor can be opened by selecting in the **Editor Type menu** or by clicking **Edit** in the Blender Screen Header and selecting **Preferences** at the bottom of the option list.

Clicking Edit and selecting Preferences opens the Editor as a panel in the upper LH of the Screen. The panel may be expanded to full Screen by clicking the expansion button in the upper RH corner but since many of the control options in the User Preferences are concerned with modifying the appearance of the Screen arrangement, it is advantageous to have it displayed at a reduced size.

The Preferences Editor contains settings which allow you to customise Blender and add functionality to the program. To save space in the interface some features are disabled and can be activated in the Preferences Editor. There are additional features to Blender (Add-ons) available on the internet which can be downloaded and activated. This is also performed in the Preferences Editor.

To demonstrate the Preferences Editor and how it allows you to modify the interface, the 3D View Editor Scene background color will be changed. The default is the sombre dark gray color.

Click on **Edit** in the Blender Screen Header and select **Preferences** in the menu that presents (Figure 1.18).

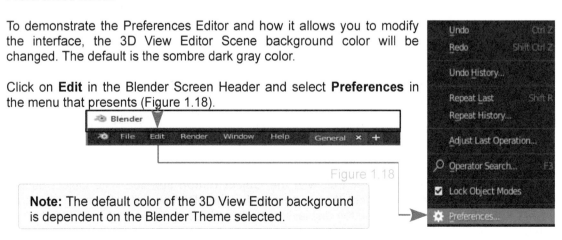

Figure 1.18

Note: The default color of the 3D View Editor background is dependent on the Blender Theme selected.

In the new Editor Header click on the **Themes Tab in the panel at the LHS.**
In the adjacent column at the left hand side click **3D View.**

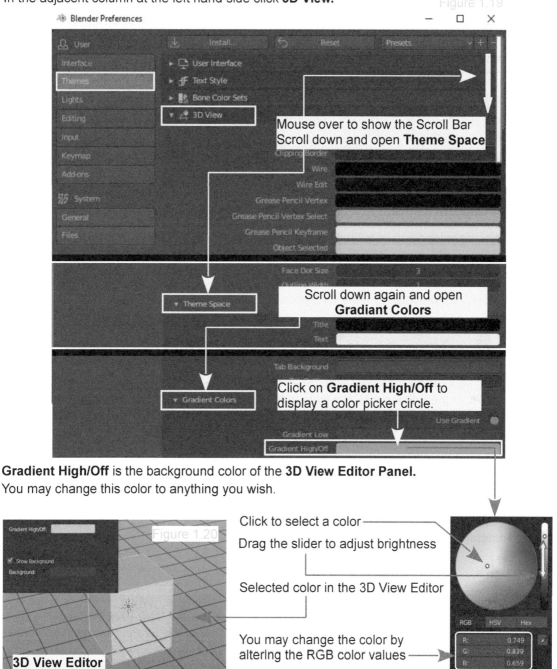

Figure 1.19

Mouse over to show the Scroll Bar
Scroll down and open **Theme Space**

Scroll down again and open
Gradiant Colors

Click on **Gradient High/Off** to
display a color picker circle.

Gradient High/Off is the background color of the **3D View Editor Panel.**
You may change this color to anything you wish.

Figure 1.20

Click to select a color

Drag the slider to adjust brightness

Selected color in the 3D View Editor

3D View Editor

You may change the color by
alterIng the RGB color values

The Preferences Editor contains many options in the Themes Tab category alone and
more when you consider each of ten categories at the top of the panel.

It is realised that the default Screen display is probably not to everyone's taste. By changing values in the Preferences Editor you can modify the interface to your personal preference (User Preferences) but Blender has three Themes built in from which you may choose.

Have **Themes** Selected   Click to display the Presets menu.   Figure 1.21

You may also download and install themes from the internet. One example is found at:

https://blenderartists.org/t/theme-awesome-theme-for-blender-2-8/1120656

Download [Theme] Awsome – Theme for Blender 2.8 XML File from:

With the XML file saved to your computer, open the Preferences Editor and click on Install Theme at the lower left of the Editor panel. Navigate to the XML file in the File Browser, select the file and click Install Theme. The **Awesome** Theme will be available in the **Theme Preset** menu.

> Note: See Navigate and Save Chapter 3

Saving Changes: When changes to Blender are made in the Preferences Editor click on **Save User Settings** in the **Header at the bottom of the Preferences Panel**. This applies the setting for the next time Blender is opened. Without saving, the program will reopen with the default Theme. When changes are made you can always go back to the default arrangement by clicking **Reset To default Theme** in this Header.

1.15 Overlays in the 3D View Editor

Overlays give control over what displays in the user interface. When a Scene becomes complicated it can be advantageous to turn off displays such as the User Perspective and Object notification in the upper left hand corner of the 3D View Editor or the Scene manipulation Widget at the right hand side or perhaps the background grid in the 3D View Editor panel.

The Overlay controls are in the 3D View Editor Header at the right hand side of the Screen. The controls for Object Mode and Edit Mode are different.

Note: The 3D View Editor has several different Modes. Overlays are only relevant to Object Mode and Edit Mode. You switch between the Modes by clicking on the Object Mode button in the 3D View Editor Header and selecting Edit Mode or vice versa. You may also toggle between Object and Edit Modes by pressing the **Tab Key**.

You set Overlay preferences in the relevant Overlay panels. The preferences are then toggled on / off by clicking the **Toggle Button** in the Header.

Hide/Display presents options for showing or hiding elements in the 3D View Editor.

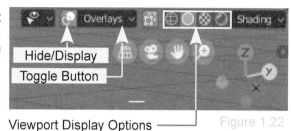

Viewport Display Options ———— Figure 1.22

Overlay Preferences
◀ Edit Mode   Object Mode ▶

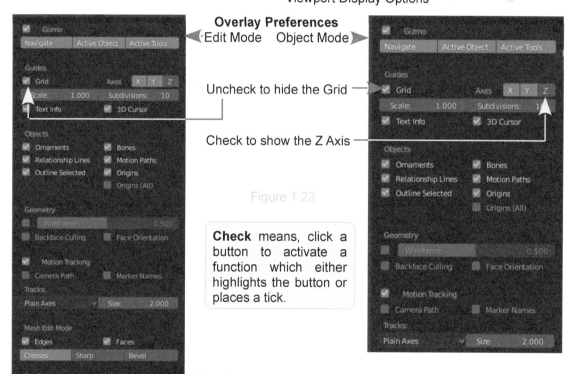

Uncheck to hide the Grid ——→

Check to show the Z Axis ——

Figure 1.23

Check means, click a button to activate a function which either highlights the button or places a tick.

The foregoing has introduced the Editors and given a small insight to how they are employed. By far the majority of work will be carried out in the 3D View Editor where Models and Scenes are created. That being the case you should understand how the View in the Editor is manipulated.

1.16 Scene Manipulation

Before adding new Objects and creating a Scene you should be conversant with how the 3D View Editor may be viewed and how to move in the three dimensional world.

Moving in 3D Space

In a 3D (Three Dimensional) program, not only do you have to consider where you are in two dimensions (height and width), but you also need to consider depth (how close or far away).

Moving around in the 3D View Editor is controlled by the Mouse and the Keyboard Number Pad.

User Perspective and Orthographic View

The Blender default Scene in the 3D View Editor, opens in the **User Perspective** view as indicated in the upper LH corner of the Editor. The Scene contains a Cube Object located at the center. There is also a Camera and a Lamp in the Scene. All three Objects are positioned relative to the center of the Scene which is the center of the 3D World, or if you like, a central point in 3D Space.

The Blender Scene may be viewed in either **Perspective** or **Orthographic** view.

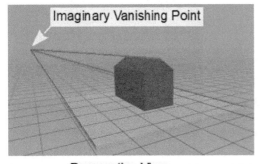
Perspective View   Figure 1.24

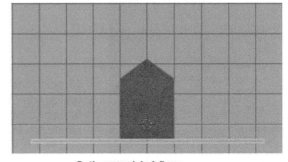
Orthographic View   Figure 1.25

A **Perspective View** projects parallel lines to a single vanishing point somewhere in the distance.

An **Orthographic View** is seen looking square on to a face.

The position of Objects relative to each other is important when considering 3D Space especially with Lamps (lighting) and the Camera (seeing). When taking a photograph with a camera, the position of the camera relative to what you want to photograph and where the lighting is located determine what you get in your snapshot. This is the same in a Blender Scene.

By default the Camera in the default Scene is positioned such that it points towards the Cube and with the default settings for the Camera captures an image of the Cube in its viewport. This is the image that will render (convert what the Camera sees to an image). To understand this perform the following demonstration.

With the default Scene press the Keyboard **Num Pad 0** which places the 3D View Editor in **Camera View** (what the Camera sees). Press **F12** on the Keyboard to **Render (Esc to Quit)**.

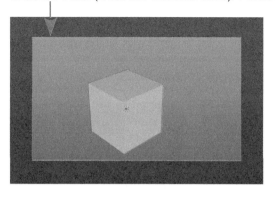
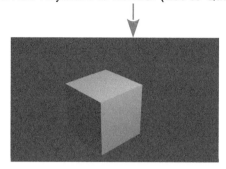

Figure 1.26

Pressing **F12** Renders (converts) the Camera view to a format that may be saved as an image file. Note that the rendered view has been opened in a new Editor panel – the **Image Editor**.

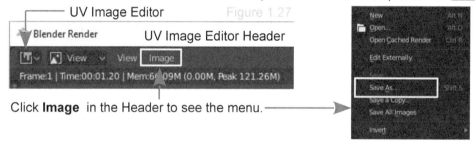

Figure 1.27

Click **Image** in the Header to see the menu.

At this point you could save the display as an image. To save an image you have to understand how to save a file into a folder (see Chapter 3).

Press the **Esc Key** to cancel the UV Image Editor window and return to Camera View in the 3D View Editor. Press the **Num Pad 5** Key to enter **User Orthographic** view, then press the **Num Pad 5** Key a second time for **User Perspective** view.

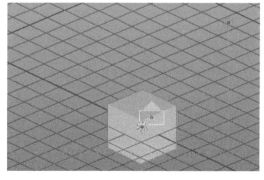

Note: This User Perspective is a little different to the default User Perspective.

User Orthographic View   Figure 1.28   User Perspective View

Pressing Num Pad 5 a second time displays a User Perspective view but it isn't the same as the original view in the 3D View Editor. To return to the origional view place the Mouse Cursor in the 3D View Editor, click the Midle Mouse Button (MMB), hold the button depressed and drag the Mouse to rotate the view.

Clicking, holding and dragging MMB is one of several methods for manipulating the Scene in the 3D View Editor . Clicking **View – Navigation** in the Header gives a menu with all the **options**.

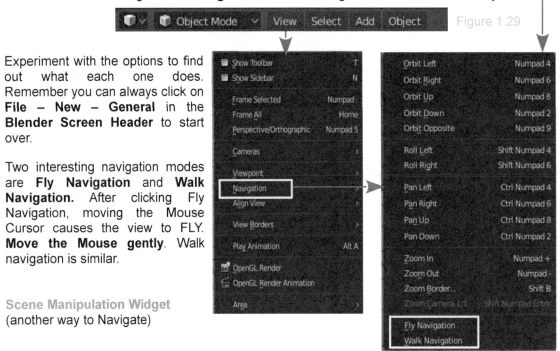

Experiment with the options to find out what each one does. Remember you can always click on **File – New – General** in the **Blender Screen Header** to start over.

Two interesting navigation modes are **Fly Navigation** and **Walk Navigation.** After clicking Fly Navigation, moving the Mouse Cursor causes the view to FLY. **Move the Mouse gently**. Walk navigation is similar.

Scene Manipulation Widget (another way to Navigate)

Place the Mouse Cursor on the circle (changes to a white **+**), click, hold and move the Mouse to rotate the view.

The Circle represents a Sphere.

Click the Cube to toggle User Perspective/User Orthographic

Axis Manipulation

Click on the Camera to toggle Camera View On/Off

Confine Manipulation to a Plane

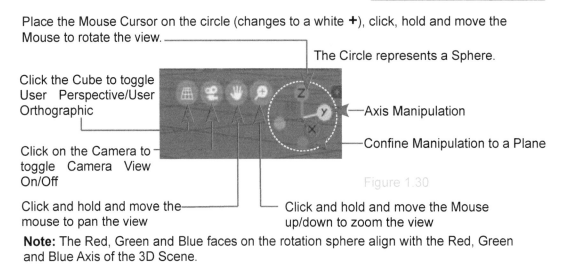

Figure 1.30

Click and hold and move the mouse to pan the view

Click and hold and move the Mouse up/down to zoom the view

Note: The Red, Green and Blue faces on the rotation sphere align with the Red, Green and Blue Axis of the 3D Scene.

2

Editors and Workspaces

Windows – Editors – Workspaces - Scenes

The **Windows** of the Blender interface are called **Editors** since they contain the controls for editing data. Everything initially displayed in the 3D View Editor (Window) is generated by a set of default data which you modify using the controls in the various Editors.

The Blender **GUI** opens with four separate Editors displayed. This arrangement constitutes a **Workspace** (working space) where you model characters and create Scenes and Render images . The 3D View Editor is the main working area for modeling while the other Editor types provides the tools and controls for performing other works.

Rendering an image of Camera View (press F12 on the Keyboard) changes the 3D View Editor to the **UV Image Editor**. In this particular instance, pressing **Esc** on the keyboard changes back to the 3D View Editor. This simple exercise shows that there are other Editors for use other than what you see in the default GUI. There are 18 Editor Types available each of which provide controls for different functions.

Editors and panels within Editors may be resized and arranged to suit your personal preference and saved for future use. These arrangements are labelled **Workspaces**.

2.1 Editor Types

The default Blender GUI displays with four different Editors opened (Chapter 1 Figure 1.1). The main Editor is the 3D View Editor, showing a view of three dimensional space with a Cube object located at its centre.

The Preferences Editor was introduced and opened in the Screen space occupied by the 3D View Editor (Chapter 1.14). There are, in fact, twenty (20) different Editor types available.

Any one of the default Editors can be changed to a different type by clicking on the Editor icon in the upper or lower left hand corner of the Editor panel (Figure 2.1). Clicking the icon displays the Editor Type selection menu. Select (click) one of the Editors and the current Editor changes to that selected.

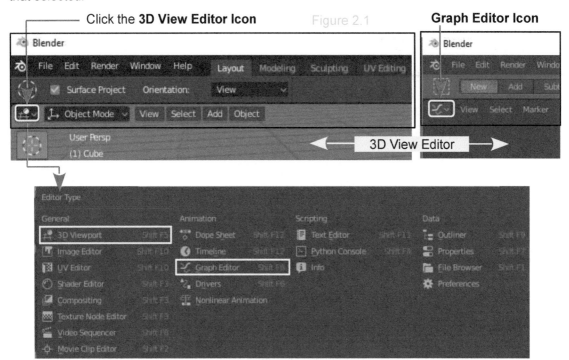

Here's an example; In the upper LH (Left hand) corner of the 3D View Editor, position the mouse cursor over the **Editor Icon** and click the left mouse button to display the Editor Type selection menu. Select (click on), **Graph Editor**, in the menu and the 3D View Editor changes to the **Graph Editor**. Click on the **Graph Editor** icon and select **3D View**—the window reverts to the 3D View Editor. Any Editor may be changed to a different Editor type in this way.

The use of the Editors will be described as you progress through the manual. You have been introduced to Blender's default GUI with the four default Editors displayed. It's time to recap on the Editors that you will require to progress and expand on the description of their uses.

To describe every control in every Editor would require a massive encyclopaedia and would prove confusing. It is not recommended that you attempt to memorise the application of controls without understanding when and how they are applied. Many controls are used over and over, therefore, you will become familiar with their application which will become second nature. In using obscure controls it is a good idea to record when and where you had occasion to use them and compile a reference diary.

2.2 Resizing Editors

Figure 2.2

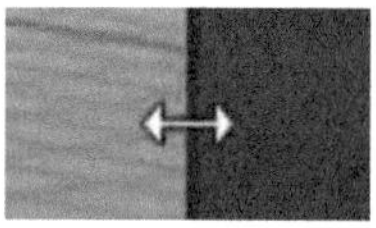

Most Editors and panels may be resized. Place the mouse cursor on an Editor or panel border and it changes to a double headed arrow (Figure 2.2). Click and hold with the LH mouse button and drag the arrow to resize the Editor panel. This works on both horizontal and vertical borders.

2.3 Splitting Editors

Figure 2.3

Editors may be divided to initially form a duplicate then changed to a different Editor type. When the mouse cursor is placed in the corner of an Editor panel it changes to a **white cross** (✛ Figure 2.3). Click, hold and drag into the Editor to be divided to drag the edge of the Editor forming a duplicate. This works in the horizontal and vertical directions.

Alternativly to split an Editor, mouse over in the corner of an Editor panel (mouse icon becomes a cross), RMB click and select Split Area in the Area Options menu. A dividing line displays in the Editor (Figure 2.5). Position the line where you want the split and click LMB.

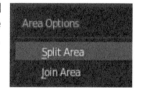

Figure 2.4

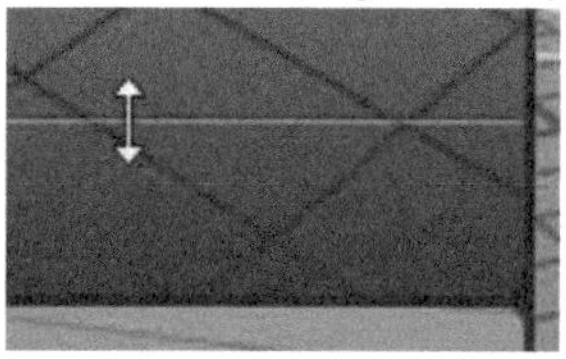

If you want to cancel before Splitting click RMB. You may drag the split line into an adjacent Editor.

Figure 2.5

Alternativly, click on View in the Header, select Area (at the bottom) then choose Horizontal or Vertical Split.

With an Editor split in two one copy may then be changed to another Editor type (Figure 2.6).

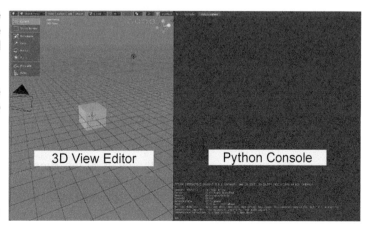

3D View Editor   Python Console

Figure 2.6

2.4 Cancel an Editor

To cancel or join an Editor panel, position the Mouse cursor in the Editor corner (cursor becomes a cross). Click RMB and select **Join area** in the menu that displays (Figure 2.4). **Replace the Mouse Cursor in the corner of the Editor**. While holding **LMB** drag the Mouse Cursor into the Editor to be cancelled. A large arrow displays pointing into the unwanted Editor. Release LMB to cancel the Editor.

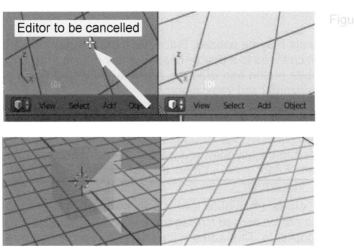

Figure 2.7

Editor to be cancelled

Note: While holding LMB with the large arrow displayed you may reverse the direction of the arrow from one Editor to the other.

2.5 Workspaces

Workspaces are the arrangements of Editor panels configured for specific working procedures. You may select a pre-assembled Workspace in the Blender Screen Header or arrange Editor panels to suit your personal requirements.

Pre-Assembled Workspace: Click on one of the Workspace options in the Blender Screen Header (Figure 2.8).

Layout is the Default Workspace

Figure 2.8

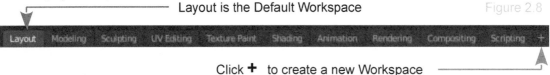

Click **+** to create a new Workspace

Selecting an option in the Header rearranges the Blender Screen. **Note:** The option **Layout** is the default Workspace Arrangement.

Creating a New Workspace: Click the cross in the **Blender Screen Header** at the RHS of the Workspace options. Click **Duplicate Current** in the menu. Duplicating Current generates a copy of the current Screen arrangement and automatically names it Layout.001. The new name is displayed in the Header.

Obviously, clicking on Layout or Layout.001, does not change the Screen arrangement since they are identical copies.

Click on **Lay0ut.001** in the Blender Screen Header to ensure you have Layout.001 displayed in the Screen. You may now reconfigure the Screen arrangement to suit your working requirements.

With **Layout.001** configured, selecting **Modeling** in the Screen header changes the Screen back to the default Screen arrangement.

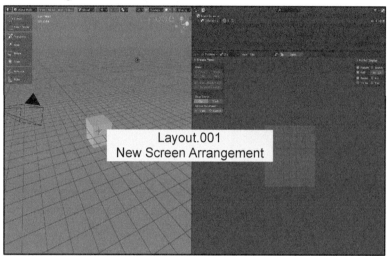

Figure 2.9

Layout.001
New Screen Arrangement

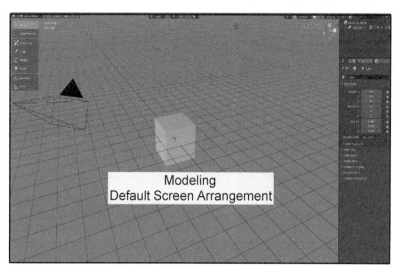

Modeling
Default Screen Arrangement

Renaming Workspaces

You may create as many Workspaces as you like but remembering which is which from a list such as: Layout, Layout.001, Layout.002, Layout.003, Layout.004 could be confusing.

You rename a Workspace by double clicking on the name in the Screen Header, backspace and retype a new name. Alternatively in the **Outliner Editor**.

The default **Outliner Editor** display is **View Layer**.

Click for **Display Mode Options**

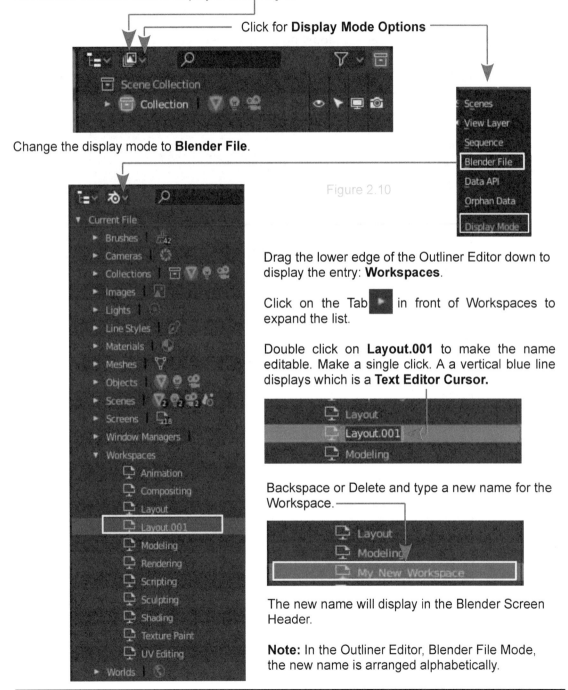

Change the display mode to **Blender File**.

Figure 2.10

Drag the lower edge of the Outliner Editor down to display the entry: **Workspaces**.

Click on the Tab ▶ in front of Workspaces to expand the list.

Double click on **Layout.001** to make the name editable. Make a single click. A a vertical blue line displays which is a **Text Editor Cursor.**

Backspace or Delete and type a new name for the Workspace.

The new name will display in the Blender Screen Header.

Note: In the Outliner Editor, Blender File Mode, the new name is arranged alphabetically.

Having created a new Workspace you will want it to be available for future use.

> **Note**: Creating a Workspace (Working Environment) in the default Blender Screen arrangement is, in fact, modifying the default Blender File. This procedure occures whenever you change anything in the default Screen. This means, whenever you model something, change a color or create an animation. The changes are, therefore only available in the Blender file that is open when the changes are made.
>
> To use changes in future work you have to save the Blender File, as a new file, then reopen it when you want to use something contained in the file. This applies to Workspaces.

How to save a Blender file is discussed in Chapter 3.

2.6 Multiple Scenes

Workspaces are Screen Arrangements of Editors for working at specific tasks. The default Screen arrangement is the **Layout Workspace** as seen in the **Screen Header**.

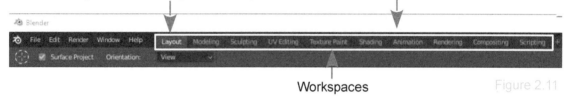

Workspaces
Figure 2.11

The main portion of the Layout Workspace is the 3D View Editor which shows a 3D View of the default Blender Scene. The Scene has a Cube Object at the center of the 3D World.

The Outliner Editor displays Scene Collection which lists the Objects in the Scene in the 3D View Editor. At this point there is one single Scene in this Blender file.

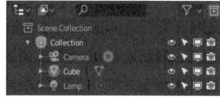

At some stage you may wish to have more Scenes which is like having different sets on a stage or different sets for filming different parts of a movie.

Figure 2.12

In the Screen Header (upper RH side) you will see Scene displayed. Clicking on the Scene button shows a single entry **Scene** (highlighted blue).

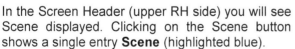

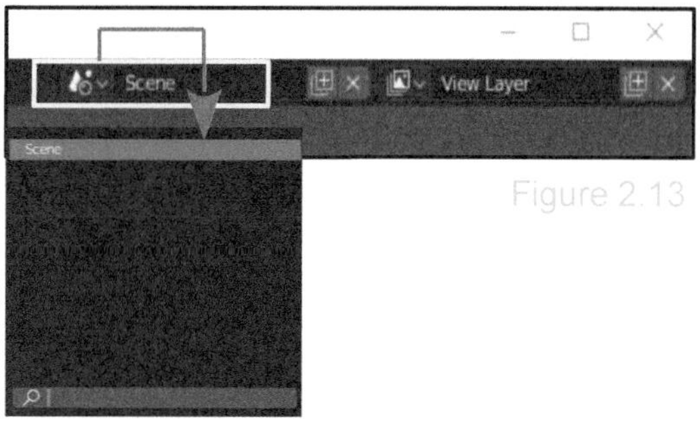

Figure 2.13

To add additional Scenes click the **Add Scene button**.

Click **New** in the options menu.

The 3D View Editor shows a new empty Scene.

Scene.001 is entered in the Header.

If you add a Monkey Object in the new Scene in the 3D View Editor you have the option to select the default Scene or the new Scene with the Monkey.

Figure 2.14

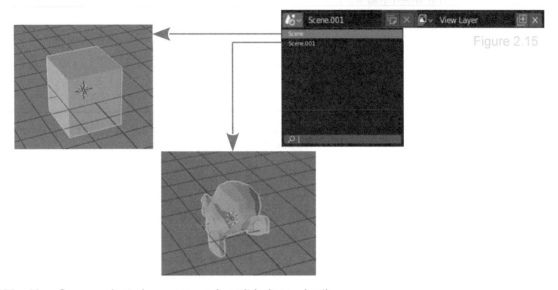

Figure 2.15

With either Scene selected you can work on it independently.

3

Navigate and Save

Saving Work

When you work in Blender you edit (modify) the default file which opens when you start Blender or a file that has been previously saved. Blender file names end with a **.blend** suffix and are peculiar to the Blender program. Saving work means you save the modifications or editing, that has been performed in a Blender file. You save the file, in a folder of your choice on your computer's hard drive. You should understand how and where to create a folder and how to retrieve a file when it has been saved. In other words you need to know how to navigate your file system. Files are saved on your computer using the **File Browser Editor**.

Navigation

Navigation is the science of finding the way from one place to another. If you can see where you are going it's an easy process to head over to that place but sometimes where you want to go is hidden from view. In Blender you create files and store them away for future use. You can reuse the files and build on to them and then save the new material. Saved files are your library of information from which you can extract elements and insert into future work. The saying is, **"There is no point reinventing the wheel"**. If you have created something that works use it again. But where did you put the wheel? That's where navigation comes in. You need to find the place where you safely stored that wheel or, in the case of Blender, where you saved a file containing the wheel. Navigation in Blender is performed in the **File Browser Editor**.

3.1 Files and Folders

Definition (from the internet)

A file is a common storage unit in a computer, and all programs and data are "written" into a file and "read" from a file. A folder holds one or more files, and a folder can be empty until it is filled. A folder can contain other folders (sub folders). Folders provide a method for organising files much like a manilla file folder contains paper documents in a file cabinet. In fact, files that contain text are often called documents.

Folders are also called "directories," and they are created on the hard drive (HD) or solid state drive (SSD) when the operating system and applications are installed. Files are always stored in folders. In fact, even the computer desktop is a folder; a special kind of folder that displays its contents across the entire screen.

File Extensions

A file extension or suffix, is the bit at the end of a file name preceded by a dot or period. For example, My_Photo.JPEG, would be a JPEG image (photograph). The .JPEG extension tells the computer which application (App) or program to use when opening the file. With a .JPEG extension the computer would look for an image editor or viewer to open the file. With a .TXT extension signifying a text file the computer would use a text editor.

When writing file extensions to a file name they are usually written in lower case letters such as .jpeg or .txt.

Blender files have a **.blend** extension which tells the computer to open the file in the Blender program.

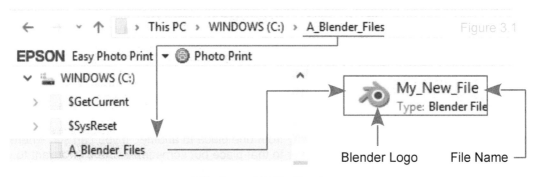

Windows 10 File Explorer

Figure 3.1 show a Blender file saved in the **C: Directory** (Hard Drive) in a Folder named **A_Blender_Files**. The Blender file is named **My_New_File**. Blender file names usually display with the Blender logo preceding the file name but the **.blend** file extension does not display.

3.2 Saving a File

Outliner Editor ⎯⎯⎯ ⎯⎯⎯ Blender File Mode

On a computer, when you save a Blender file (.blend) you are saving the data which is producing the display on the computer screen. This set of data includes not only what you see but all the settings which control all the effects that will be displayed in the various Editors. The Blender file may be considered as a complete package. Saving a file for the default arrangement saves everything.

Figure 3.2 shows the data listed in the Outliner Editor which would be saved for the default Blender Scene. Even before any editing has taken place the list is extensive. All this data is saved to a single file.

Figure 3.2

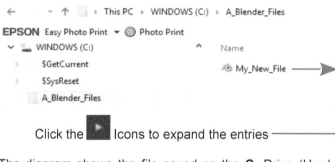

Click the ▶ Icons to expand the entries ⎯⎯⎯⎯⎯⎯➤

The diagram shows the file saved on the **C:** Drive (Hard Drive) of the computer in the Directory Folder named **A_Blender_Files**. The file has been named **My_New_File**. Although not shown, in this Windows file system the file does have a **.blend** suffix.

> **Note:** Placing an **A** in front of the Directory Folder name ensures that it is located at the top of the alphabetical directory list.

In Blender the **File Browser Editor** is used to navigate through the file system on your computer. On a Windows operating system, **Windows Explorer** or **Windows File Explorer** is used. Blender's File Browser is a little different to the Windows system in appearance but uses the same work flow.

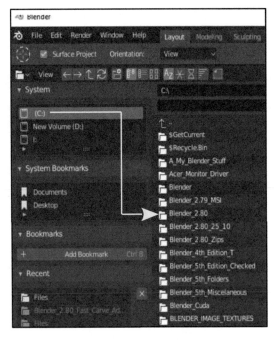

| Blender – File Browser | Figure 3.3 | Windows – File Explorer |

3.3 Windows File Explorer

Take a short refresher to analyse what you do when you save something when using a Windows operating system.

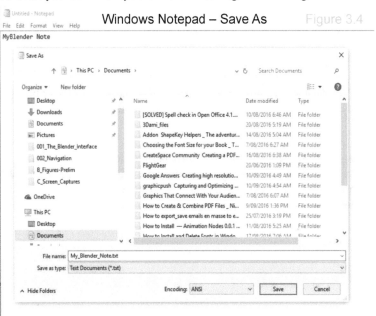

Windows Notepad – Save As   Figure 3.4

As an example, it is assumed you have written a note using **Windows Notepad** and you are about to save the file. You simply go to the top of the Notepad window, click on File, click on Save and the Save As window displays. In the panel at the top of this window you will probably see a panel showing **This PC > Documents** which is telling you that your file will be saved to the Documents folder on your computer (Figure 3.4). You enter a name for your file (**My_Blender_Note.txt**) and click **Save**. Simple!

The problem with this is; the file gets saved amongst your letters to your mother, the tax man, pictures of your pet dog and holiday snaps all saved in the Documents folder. You should make a special folder for your **Blender Stuff**. You can create new folders in File Explorer by Right clicking on a folder or sub folder, selecting **New** then clicking **New Folder** and entering a name. You probably know how to do this but it is more important for you to understand how to do this is in Blender.

3.4 Windows File Explorer Diagram

Figure 3.5

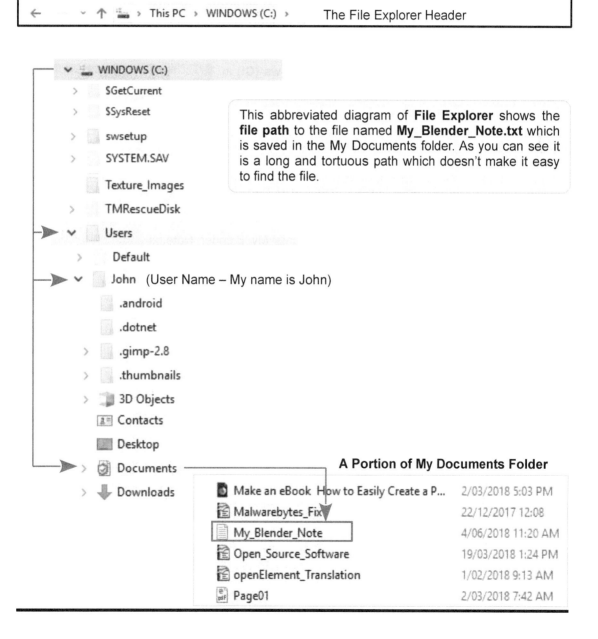

The File Explorer Header

This abbreviated diagram of **File Explorer** shows the **file path** to the file named **My_Blender_Note.txt** which is saved in the My Documents folder. As you can see it is a long and tortuous path which doesn't make it easy to find the file.

Users

Default

John   (User Name – My name is John)

A Portion of My Documents Folder

3.5 Blender File Browser

Blender's File Browser is the **File Browser Editor**. Click on the 3D View Editor icon (upper left) and select **Editor type: File Browser** in the menu. The 3D View Editor is replaced by the **File Browser Editor** (Figure 3.7 opposite). This is where you navigate to find things and save things. You save your Blender files and rendered images and animation files and you search for pre-saved files from which you obtain data to use in new work. You can also create a new folder for your **Blender Stuff**.

To navigate the File Browser is very simple. As an example, go find the file named **My_Blender_Note.txt**. The **.txt** bit (suffix) on the end of the name tells you that the file is a Text file.

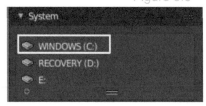

Figure 3.6

In the File Browser Editor click on **(C:)** or **Windows (C:)** in the **System Tab** panel in the upper LH part of the Editor panel. This is the C: drive on your PC. The PC used in this demonstration is a HP computer running Windows 10. The name on your computer is probably different but you will have something that tells you it is your C: Drive.

When you click on the C: Drive the main panel (in the File Browser Editor) to the right displays the list of folders that you have in the C: Drive. The list is displayed in columns and by default is in alphabetical order. To follow the file path that was shown in Windows File Explorer:

C:\ Users\ John\ Documents\ My_Blender_Note.txt

My name is John. This will be your **User Name**.

Click on the folder name **Users**. The panel will display the list of sub folders in the Users directory. In **Users** click on the sub folder named **User Name** (your name). The panel displays the list of folders in that directory one of which is named, **Documents**. Click on the **Documents** folder to see the directory list of folders and files and somewhere in amongst the multitude of stuff you will see the file named **My_Blender_Note.txt**.

> **Note:** When using Windows Ten there is sometimes a folder named **My Documents**. In either case you **cannot** open a Text (.txt) file from this location.

Blender opens different types of files in different windows (see Chapter 04 Objects in the 3D View Editor). **My_Blender_Note.txt** is a text file therefore you would open it in the **Text Editor**. Blender files with the **.blend** extension open in **Blender** from the **Blender Screen Header, File button**. Image files (pictures) with file extensions such as .jpeg or .png will open in the UV/Image Editor. The File Browser Editor merely allows you to search for files and folders to see where they are saved. You can make a new folder but that will be discussed later.

For now take a look at some of the other features of the File Browser Editor. You have navigated down the file path to the Documents folder but what about going back?

Simple! Click one of the **Back Arrows** (Figure 3.7) to go back to the previous directory folder.

3.6 Navigation in the File Browser

Having made your way down the file path Blender remembers where you have been. To move from where you are on the path you can click on the **Previous Folder** arrow or the **Next Folder** arrow to go forward or back.

Previous Folder – Next Folder
Back Arrows

Folders and Files on the C: Drive

Figure 3.7

The File Path

C:\Users\John\Documents\File Name

3.7 File Browser Editor Features (Figure 3.7)

Refresh the File List

Create a NewDirectory

Make the List Short or Long

Display Image Files as Pictures

Sort the File List Methods

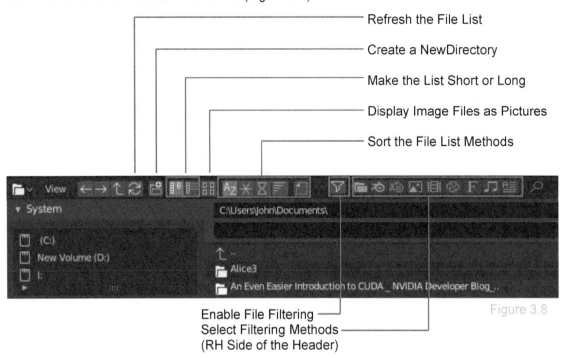

Enable File Filtering
Select Filtering Methods
(RH Side of the Header)

Figure 3.8

3.8 Make a New Folder

At some stage you will want to make a new folder to store your Blender stuff. In the File Browser navigate to an existing folder in which to create a sub folder or perhaps make a new folder in the C: Drive. When you have selected your location simply click on the **Create New Directory** button. A folder is created with the name **New Folder** highlighted. Click the entry see a blue cursor at the end of the name. Backspace or delete and type a new name. Press **Enter**.

Display Images

Click to display Image Files as Thumbnail Pictures

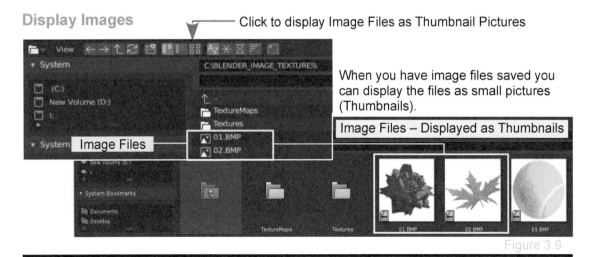

When you have image files saved you can display the files as small pictures (Thumbnails).

Image Files – Displayed as Thumbnails

Figure 3.9

3.9 Saving Your Work

Besides being able to navigate the File Browser to find things that have been saved you will inevitably want to save your work. It's a good idea to be organised and create folders for different things. Let's assume you have made a folder and named it **A_My_Blender_Stuff** and the folder is located on your C: Drive. In fact, using the default Blender Scene, make the folder.

The next assumption is; you have Blender opened and you have created work that you wish to save for future use.

To save the Blender file click on **File** in the **Blender Screen Header.**

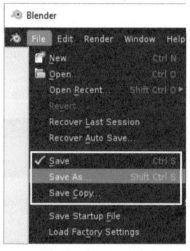

When **saving a file** you will have noticed that there are three options;

Save: This option will save the Blender file that you have open. If the file is one that you have previously created and opened for modification, clicking **Save** will save the file with modifications to the directory where previously saved.

If you have been working in the default Blender file (the file that opens when you first start Blender) clicking **Save** will open the **File Browser Editor**. Click where you see **untitled.blend** and enter a name for your new file. When you have typed the name press **Enter** then click **Save Blender File** in the upper RH corner of the File Browser Editor.

Figure 3.10

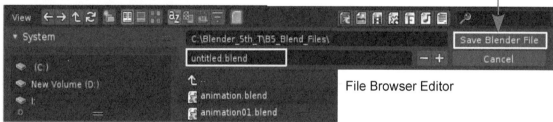

File Browser Editor

When saving the file with the modifications or as a new file with a new name, the file remains open (active) in Blender.

Save As: This saves a copy of the file that is opened. You can give the file a new name which will distinguish it from the original. When saved this file is open (active) in Blender.

Save a Copy: This saves a copy of the file but the file will not be active. The file is saved but the original file is the file which remains open in Blender.

To recap, you have created work in Blender and wish to save the work in a Blender file (.blend). You wish to save the Blender file in the folder (directory) named **A_ My_Blender_Stuff** previously created. You have clicked **File** in the Blender Screen Header then **Save** in the menu that displayed. The File Browser Editor opens.

Since **A_My_Blender_Stuff** was placed on the C: Drive and it was named beginning with the letter **A** it will be somewhere near the top of the first column. Click on the folder name. You will be presented with an empty File Browser Editor. At the top of the Editor you will see the file path <u>**C:**</u> **A_My_Blender_Stuff** and immediately below the name **untitled.blend** (Figure 3.11).

Blender has automatically named your Blender file **untitled.blend**. Note the **.blend** suffix. All **Blender files** end in **.blend**. Click where you see untitled.blend and a blue cursor will display at the end of the name. Backspace or delete and retype a new name for your file. Don't forget the **.blend** suffix. Press **Enter.** With your new file name in place click **Save Blender File** in the top RH corner of the Editor. The 3D Editor is reinstated. When you open the File Browser Editor you will see your file in C:\A_My_Blender_Stuff\ . Using the default Blender Scene save a file and name it **Stuff.blend**.

Retype a New Name – Press Enter – Click Save Blender File

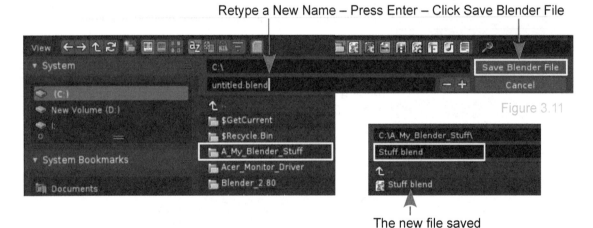

Figure 3.11

The new file saved

Important: If you close a Blender file without saving, your work will be lost.

3.10 The Concept of Files

To save a file? What does this mean? It's easy to say, save a file but what are you actually doing when you save? The chapter started by discussing saving a file created in Windows Notepad. This was a simple text file. A text file contains data which displays letters and words on your screen i.e. Text. An image file contains data which displays a picture. A music file plays music. Each file type uses a different application (App) or program to generate the display or, in the case of a music file, play the music. Sure! You know all this but the point is; a Blender file contains a combination of data organised into separate parts or elements.

When you save a blender file you save all the elements.

To show you what this means in practical terms, open Blender with the default Scene. Click on **File** in the **Blender Screen Header** then click on **Append**. The **File Browser Editor** opens. Navigate to the file you previously saved named **Stuff.blend** (Figure 3.12).

Parts of the File Browser Editor

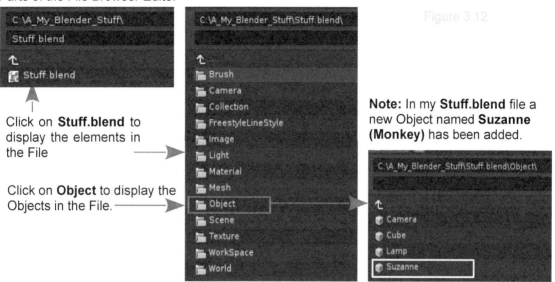

Figure 3.12

Click on **Stuff.blend** to display the elements in the File

Click on **Object** to display the Objects in the File.

Note: In my **Stuff.blend** file a new Object named **Suzanne (Monkey)** has been added.

3.11 The Append or Link Command

You can insert elements from one Blender (.blend) file into another Blender file. To do this you select the **Append** or **Link** commands from the **File** pull-down menu in the **Blender Screen Header** (Figure 3.13). An element could be a model you have created.

Figure 3.13

Append takes data from an existing file and adds it to the current file. **Link** allows you to use data from an existing file in the current file but the data remains in the existing file. In the latter case the data cannot be edited in the current file—if the data is changed in the existing file, the changes show in the current file the next time it is opened.

At this stage the foregoing is probably somewhat difficult to understand, therefore working through an example will help to clarify the meaning. You will have to jump the gun a little and follow some procedures without explanation. The detail of the procedures will be covered later but at the moment only be concerned with the file system navigation involved.

Selecting **Append** or **Link** opens the File Browser Editor allowing you to navigate to the Blender file you wish to select elements from. You can **Append** anything, including cameras, lights, meshes, materials, textures, scenes, and objects. By appending objects, any materials, textures and animations that are linked to that object will automatically be imported with the object. Clicking the LMB on an object will select it. Pressing the A key will deselect.

To clarify this procedure start a new Blender file (open Blender) with the default Scene containing the Cube object. Select the **Append** command as previously described and navigate to the file **Stuff.blend**. Open the Objects directory (the Objects folder, Figure3.14). Click on the Object named **Suzanne** to highlight it, then click on the **Append from Library** button in the upper RH corner of the Editor (Figure 3.14).

Figure 3.14

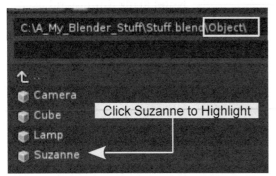

Click Suzanne to Highlight

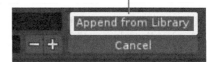

Click Append from Library

Figure 3.15

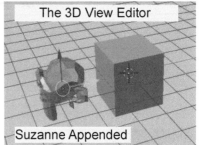

The File Browser Editor reverts to the 3D Editor and you will see the object named Suzanne in the Editor. **Suzanne is a Monkey** object (monkey's head Figure 3.15).

You can Append any object from any Blender file.

3.12 Importing Objects

One of Blender's strong points is its ability to accept several generic types of 3D files from other programs. Two examples are:The **.dae Collada** file format used by the **Make Human** program, which creates models of the human figure.

The **Make Human** program is freely available. Other programs save files in one format but also give the option to export in another format. You will have to find the **Export** command in the program and match up the file type with one of the file types in Blender's import menu .

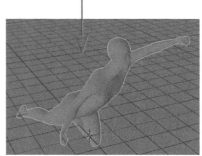

Collada File Imported

Figure 3.16

Note: There are only a few file type options shown in the default selection menu (Figure 3.16). Collada (.dae) is shown while Pointcache (.pc2) is not. To conserve space in the GUI, Blender has limited the file type display. Other file types are available as **Add-ons** in the **Preferences Editor** in the **Import-Export** category.

3.13 Activating Import File Types

To import a DXF file into a Blender scene, open the **Preferences Editor** and click on **Add-ons** at the LHS of the Editor. In the list to the right select an **Import-Export** Add-on. Find the file you require and check (tick) the box adjacent to the file name. The checked file type will display in white text and be available in the **Import** or **Export** selection menu.

Note: When importing Blender files into other Blender files, remember to use the **Append** command instead of Import. In the **Append** command, select the file, then select what you would like to bring into the current file. You will usually use the objects option.

The Preferences Editor – Add-ons – Import-Export   Figure 3.17

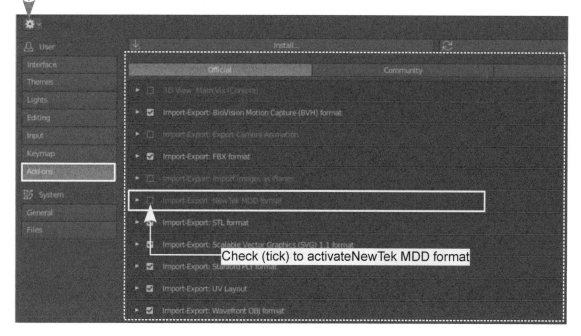

To import a particular file type click on the type in the list.

Clicking the file type opens the File Browser Editor where you navigate to the file containing the Object you wish to import. As an example, a model of a human figure has been created using the **Make Human Program**. The model has been exported as a **Wavefront.obj** file. You will see that this type of file is included in the default Import file list, **Wavefront OBJ.** Click on this file type to display the **File Browser Editor**.

> **Important:** When you export a model from another program, know where it is saved on your computer and what the file name is.

The model exported from the **Make Human** program is named **Running_Man.obj.** The model was exported to:

C:\A_My_Blender_Stuff

Figure 3.18

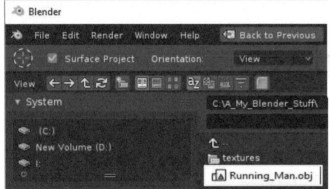

In the File Browser Editor navigate and find your file. Click on the file name to select it (highlight) then click on **Import OBJ** in the upper RH corner

The Object Running_Man (Figure 3.19) is entered into the Blender 3D View Editor. Note: You will probably have to scale the model to suit.

3.14 Packing Data

If you plan to open a Blender file on other computers, you will need to select the **Pack All into .blend file** option in the **File** menu under **External Data**. Textures and sounds are not automatically included in your Blender file in order to keep the file size down. Every time your file opens, the textures and sounds are placed into your file. If the files can't be found, you won't have any textures and sounds. If you **Pack the Data**, those files are included with the .blend file so they can be opened anywhere. Remember, your file size may become very large. You can also unpack data to bring the file size back down.

You may alternatively check **Automatically Pack Into .blend**.

Objects in the 3D View Editor

This overview of Blender will introduced the Editors in the default Screen arrangement and demonstrated how they interrelate. The fundamental concept in using Blender is to create a model, place the model in a Scene and perhaps animate the model to move creating an animation sequence. In the creation process the models and components of the Scene may be colored and textured and the Scene illuminated for effect.

To model an object or character, or a component of a Scene such as a landscape, a simple shape is placed in the 3D View Editor and modified (modeled). The simple shape is called a **Primitive**. Blender has ten primitives from which to choose, which one you select will depend on what you want to create.

Instruction will be given with the default Screen Arrangement (GUI) with the **Eevee Render Engine** active.

Bear in mind that you have the options to use the **Cycles** or **Workbench** Render Engines. Workbench provides a simplified working environments for modeling when a Scenes become complicated. Cycles allows you to work in a viewport that continually renders a **photo-realistic** view.

4.1 Modeling Workflow Philosophy

Blender has been introduced by studying the Graphical User Interface (GUI) with its arrangement of Editors and panels and having Keyboard and Mouse input commands explained. Knowing how to work the interface allows you to create something by Modeling.

Before you begin to Model you should understand the philosophy of the Blender process.

When you open Blender you are presented with the default 3D View Editor showing a Scene containing a Cube object. The Scene also has a Lamp and a Camera in place. To create something new, you start by saving this arrangement with a **new file name**. The new file is a starting point for developing a new Scene with new Models. You modify the default Scene in the new file to whatever you require. Modifying a Scene will involve such things as moving and repositioning objects, reshaping objects, adding new objects, applying color, arranging lighting effects, positioning the camera etc.

4.2 Starting a New File

When beginning a new project it is advisable to start a new file with a new name. Start Blender and before changing anything in the default Scene, save the file in your **Blender_Stuff** folder with a meaningful name. Write down the name. You can save your work wherever you like as long as you remember what you named the file and where you saved it. Be familiar with saving and creating files and folders, so go back and review Chapter 3 if necessary.

> **Note:** Depending on the version of Blender you have, the program may not prompt you to save your file when closing . Remember to always save your work often and don't forget the .blend suffix!

After saving the default Scene as a new file, the new file is open in the Screen ready to be modified. The new Blender file will display the default arrangement of Editors and the 3D View Editor will display the default Scene. If you have closed Blender after saving you will have to reopen the new file.

When you restart Blender the default Screen arrangement is displayed. To reopen the file that you saved, click on **File** in the **Blender Screen Header** and click on **Open** in the **File** menu. The **File Browser Editor** opens (Figure 4.1) where you navigate to where you saved your file. Click on your file name then click **Open Blender File** in the upper RH corner of the Editor ┐

Figure 4.1

4.3 Modifying the Scene

Any changes you make to the Scene will be construed as modifying the Scene. For example, changing the shape of an Object is a modification. Changing the shape of an Object is called modeling. Another basic modification would be to move an Object in the Scene. Another Scene modification is to add an Object. There are many modifications that can be made.

4.4 Object Mode and Edit Mode

In the **3D View Editor** there are two basic display modes, **Object Mode** and **Edit Mode**. With an Object selected in the 3D View Editor in Object Mode you Translate (move), Rotate and Scale the Object. In Edit Mode you change the shape of the Object. Note: This is a simplistic description of the operations, there is more to it than that. Look at the Cube Object in the default Scene.

Switching Modes: Click to display the menu and select **Edit Mode** in the 3D View Editor Header.

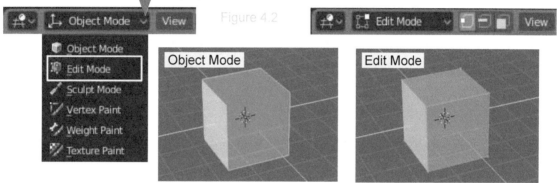

Figure 4.2

Alternative: Press the **Tab Key** on the Keyboard to toggle between modes.

In **Object Mode** the Cube displays as a solid gray Object with an orange outline. The orange outline indicates that the Cube is **selected**. Being selected means that the Cube may be manipulated in the Scene (Translated (Moved), Rotated or Scaled).

In Edit Mode, when the Cube is selected, it is shown with an orange tint with orange edges and with little orange dots at each corner. The orange dots are called Vertices, the orange edges are Edges while the orange tinted surfaces are Faces. In Edit Mode you select either of these elements individually and manipulate them to change (model) the shape (REF: Chapter 5).

4.5 3D View Editor Cursor

3D View Editor Cursor ⟶  ⟵ Mouse Cursor   Figure 4.3

When working in the 3D View Editor there are two Cursors; the **Mouse Cursor** and the **Editor Cursor**. By default the **Editor Cursor** is located at the center of the Scene. The center of the default Cube Object is also at the center of the Scene. Objects may be positioned by using the Editor Cursor. To understand positioning using the Editor Cursor you must first understand selecting, deselecting and adding Objects.

4.6 Selecting – Deselecting Objects

In the default Scene the **Cube Object is selected as shown by the orange outline.** To deselect the Cube press **Alt + A Key** on the keyboard (the orange outline cancels) or **LMB click** (left mouse button) an empty space in the Editor. To **select** the Cube again, click **LMB** on the Cube.

> **Note:** If you deselect then press the **A Key** all Objects in the Scene will be selected. If you inadvertently select all Objects press Alt + A Key or LMB click an empty space to deselect all Objects. Click LMB on a single Object to select.

B Key Selection

An alternative selection method is to press the **B Key** on the Keyboard with the Mouse Cursor in the 3D View Editor panel. In this case, pressing the B Key displays cross hair lines in the Editor panel which you drag, forming a rectangle, around an Object **or multiple Objects**. Release the mouse button to select.

Press the B Key to display the cross hairs - Position the Mouse Cursor
Click LMB, hold and drag a rectangle – release the Mouse button   Figure 4.4

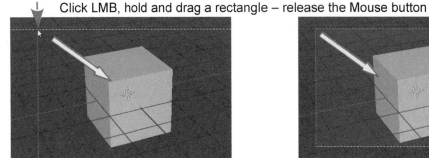
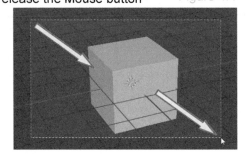

Border Select Tool

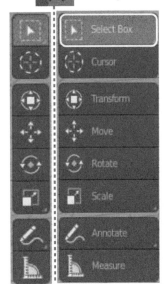

Note: The default Tool Panel is minimised. Mouse over, click, hold and drag the double headed arrow to expand and display the names.

Another method of selection is to use the **Border Select Tool** in the **Tool Panel** at the LH side of the 3D View Editor. In this case, click the **Select Box** button, position the Mouse Cursor, click LMB, hold drag the mouse, drawing a rectangle around the Object or Objects to be selected. Release the Mouse button to select (as previously described).

Click the **Select Box** button, position the **Mouse Cursor.**   Figure 4.5   Click, Hold and Drag a Rectangle

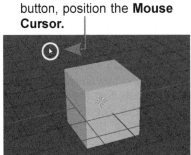
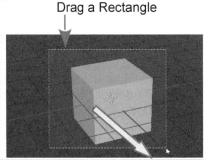

C Key Selection

Yet another method of selection is to position the Mouse Cursor in the 3D View Editor and press the **C Key**. In this case the Mouse Cursor becomes a **Selection Circle** which you position over the Object or Objects to be selected. When first displayed the circle is relatively small.

Unless the circle encapsulates a whole Object the Object will not be selected. To increase or decrease the size of the circle **Scroll MMB**. With the circle surrounding the Object click LMB to select.

Selection Circle

Figure 4.6

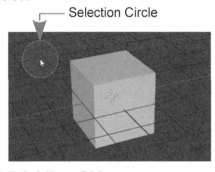

Scroll MMB to increase the size of the Circle.

Position over the Cube and click LMB to select. Click **Esc** to cancel.

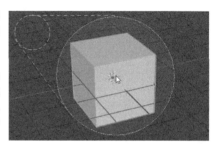

4.7 Adding Objects

The default Blender Scene contains three Objects, a Cube, a Camera and a Lamp. The Camera and Lamp are special Objects which perform functions but do not render as part of an image or animation. The Cube, on the other hand, does render. The Cube is one of ten Objects called **Primitives**, which are the starting point for modeling. You modify the shape of a primitive into a model of a character or as part of the Scene background.

4.8 Object Primitives

3D Manipulation Widget shown on the Circle Primative

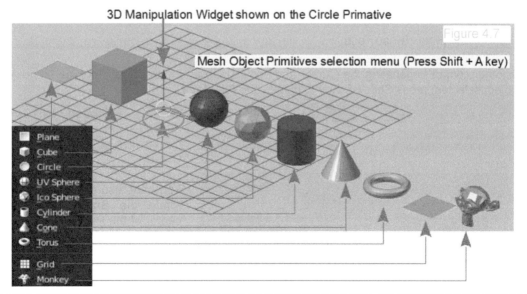

Figure 4.7

Mesh Object Primitives selection menu (Press Shift + A key)

Plane
Cube
Circle
UV Sphere
Ico Sphere
Cylinder
Cone
Torus
Grid
Monkey

Figure 4.7 shows the ten default **Primitives** available for selection. They have been colored to distinguish them. When added to a Scene they are entered with the default gray color. A **Primitive** shape entered into the scene it is referred to as an **Object**. Blender automatically names Objects according to the shape i.e. **Cube**, **Sphere**, **Cone** etc. When you reshape (modify) the primitive Object to make a model you will rename it. Primitives are entered in the 3D View Editor with the Editor in **Object mode.**

To add a new Object into a Scene you click on **Add** in the **3D View Editor Header** then click **Mesh** to add a new Object. This displays the **Add Mesh menu**.

An alternative way to display the **Add** menu is to press **Shift + A Key**.

In either case, with the Add menu displayed you click **Mesh** to display the selection menu where you click to select one of the **Primitives**. Selecting a Primitive enters it in the Scene at the location of the 3D View Editor Cursor.

4.9 Locating the 3D View Editor Cursor

By default the **3D View Editor Cursor** is located at the center of the Scene which is the center of the 3D World. Also by default, the Cube Object is located at the same point.

Remember; Objects added (entered) in the Scene are located at the position of the 3D View Editor Cursor, therefore, you will wish to relocate the Cursor to position Objects.

Hold Shift and **click RMB** to position the Cursor. Alternatively activate the Cursor Tool in the Tool Panel. With the Tool activated you can click LMB anywhere in the 3D View Editor to position the Cursor. With the Tool activated you can click LMB, hold and drag the Cursor to a new location.

Don't forget to deactivate the Cursor Tool so you can LMB click to select and deselect Objects. To deactivate the Cursor Tool click on the Select Box Tool.

The Cursor Pie Menu (Snap Tool)

Yet another control for locating the Cursor and positing Objects is the Snap Tool Pie Menu. With an Object selected, press Shift + S Key to display the Pie Menu (Figure 4.8).

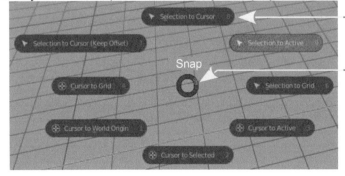

—Clicking **Selection to Cursor** relocates the selected Object to the position of the 3D View Editor Cursor.

You may also drag the Mouse to rotate the **Snap Ring** at the center of the Pie Menu to make a selection. With the orange segment located as shown, **Selection to Active** is selected.

4.10 Deleting Objects

To Delete (remove) an Object from the Scene, select the Object then press the **X Key**. The **OK Delete** panel displays. Click **OK** to delete or press **Esc** to cancel.

Note: You may select multiple Objects for deletion.

Figure 4.9

4.11 Duplicating Objects

When you want to **duplicate an Object** (make an identical copy), select the Object and press **Shift + D Key**. A new Object is created occupying the same space as the original. The new Object is in Move Mode (able to be moved by dragging the Mouse) as indicated by a white outline. To reposition in the Scene, drag the Mouse and click LMB when in place.

4.12 Object Mode Manipulation

The three basic manipulation controls are: **Translate, Rotate and Scale**.

Translate: To move an object freely in the plane of the view, press the **G Key** (Grab Mode) with the object selected and drag the Mouse or click **RMB,** hold and drag the Mouse. In Grab mode the outline turns white. To lock the movement to a particular axis, press the G Key + X, Y, or Z. G key + Y restricts the movement to the Y (green) Axis (Figure 4.10).

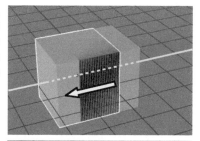

Figure 4.10

Scaling: To scale an object (make larger or smaller), press the **S Key** and drag the mouse. To lock the scale to a particular axis, press S Key + X, Y, or Z. To scale by a specific value press S Key + Number Key (S + 2 + Y = Scale twice on the Y Axis (Figure 4.11)

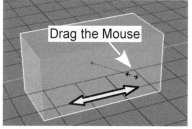

Drag the Mouse

Figure 4.11

Rotating: To rotate an object, press the **R Key** and move the mouse about the **Object's center**. To lock the rotation to an axis, press the R Key + X, Y, or Z. To rotate a set number of degrees, press R + the number of degrees of rotation, R+30 rotates the object 30 degrees. R + Y + 30 rotates the object 30 degrees about the Y-Axis (Figure 4.12).

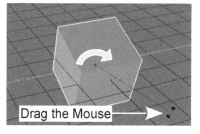

Drag the Mouse

Figure 4.12

4.13 The Last Operator Panel

When the Object was manipulated in the preceding demonstrations, a panel displayed at the lower left hand side of the 3D View Editor. This panel shows information relating to the last operation performed in the Editor. The panel also allows values to be adjusted, providing a means of fine tuning or correcting the operation.

Consider Translation of the default Cube Object along the Y Axis.

The Cube Translated 2.50 m on the Y Axis
The Last Operator panel displays at the lower LH side of the 3D View Editor. **Click to expand**.

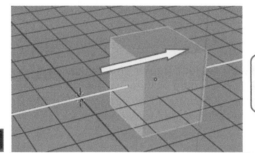

Note: The Panel displays for all operations in Object Mode and Edit Mode.

▶ Move

Click to hide the panel
Last Operator Panel
Shows the distance moved

Figure
4.13

Properties Editor, Object Button
The Properties Editor shows the new Location

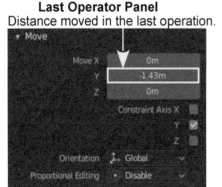

You may alter the value to move the Cube in the 3D View Editor

Restricted to the Y Axis

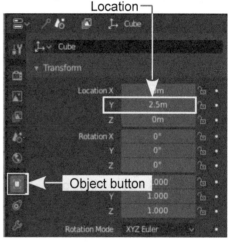

Translating the Cube to the left in the 3D View Editor by 1.41m (negative 1.41) locates the Cube at -0.34005m

Last Operator Panel
Distance moved in the last operation.

Object button

The new location

Properties Editor, Object Button
Shows the new location

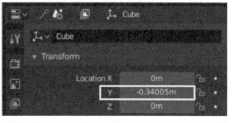

4.14 Tool Panel – Widgets Expand the Tool Panel to display the Tool Names
Tool Panel

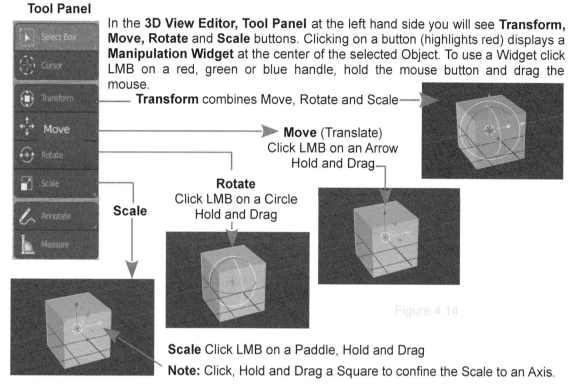

In the **3D View Editor, Tool Panel** at the left hand side you will see **Transform, Move, Rotate** and **Scale** buttons. Clicking on a button (highlights red) displays a **Manipulation Widget** at the center of the selected Object. To use a Widget click LMB on a red, green or blue handle, hold the mouse button and drag the mouse.

Transform combines Move, Rotate and Scale

Move (Translate)
Click LMB on an Arrow
Hold and Drag

Rotate
Click LMB on a Circle
Hold and Drag

Scale

Figure 4.14

Scale Click LMB on a Paddle, Hold and Drag

Note: Click, Hold and Drag a Square to confine the Scale to an Axis.

4.15 Manipulation Units

By default Translation and Scaling units are expressed in **Metric** values and Rotation is in **Degrees**. You can change the values in the **Properties Editor, Scene buttons, Units tab.**

When using Metric values the Background Grid in the 3D View Editor is considered to represent One Meter by One Meter divisions.

Properties Editor – Scene Buttons

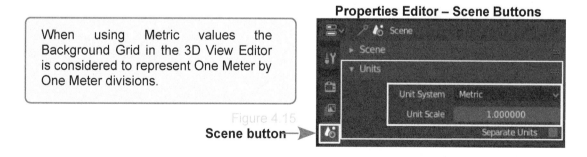

Figure 4.15

Scene button

Scale Units: By default the size of an object is expressed in **Metric Units**. You may elect to change this. In the **Properties Editor, Scene buttons, Units tab** you will see **Unit System** and **Rotation**. Clicking either unit bar will display option menus (Figure 4.16 over).

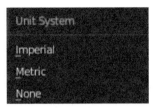

Figure 4.16

Unit System – Metric is the default setting, in which case the mid plane grid in the 3D View Editor is considered as representing 1M x 1M units.

To demonstrate: With the Mouse cursor in the default 3D View Editor press the G Key (Grab) and move the mouse translating the Cube (the Cube must be selected). In Figure 4.18 the Cube has been translated + 45.89**cm** on the X axis, +1.8844 **M** on the Y axis and +64.109**cm** on the Z axis.

You can see the exact values in the **Editor Header** while you have the Cube in Grab mode. You will also see the values in the **Object Properties Panel** (Press the **N Key** to display, Figure 4.17).

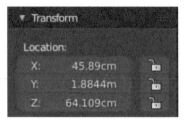

Note: Values change from Meters to Centimetres to Millimetres depending on the scale.

Figure 4.17

Values in the 3D View Editor Header display during Manipulation.

Figure 4.18

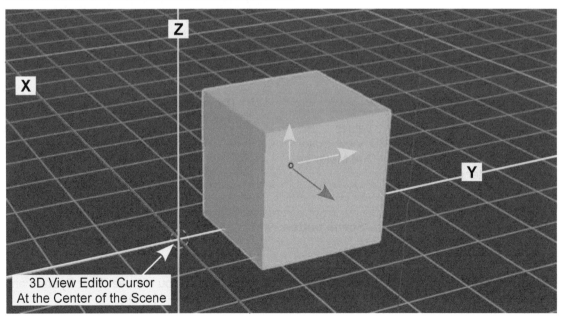

None: Changing the **Unit System – Unit Preset** to **None** means you chose to work in Blender units as represented by the division of the mid plane grid (each grid segment = 1 Unit by 1 Unit)

Rotation or Angle: Changing the Unit Preset **Degrees** to **Radians** means you are choosing the measurement where there are **2π Radians** in a circle (Figure 4.18). Angular values are, therefore, given in Radians instead of Degrees.

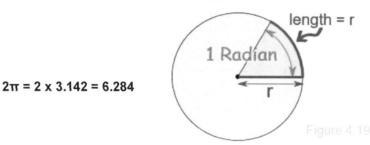

The angle made when the radius is wrapped round the circle:

length = r

1 Radian

2π = 2 x 3.142 = 6.284

r

Figure 4.19

4.16 Measuring - Ruler/Protractor

At the bottom of the Tool Panel you will see the **Measure button** (Figure 4.20). This button allows you to take liner and angular measurements in the 3D View Editor.

Tool Panel	**Linear Measurement** Figure 4.20	**Angular Measurement**
	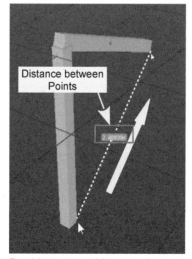	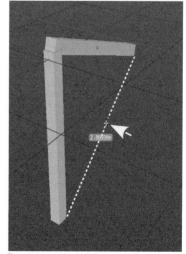
	Distance between Points	
	Position the Mouse Cursor, click, hold and drag from Start point to Finish.	Position the Mouse Cursor, (Cross) mid way between points.

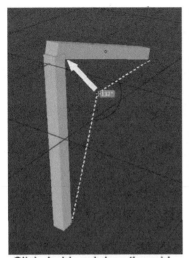

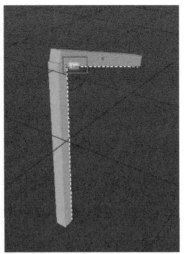

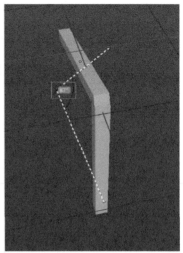

Click, hold and drag the mid point to the Apex.	Read the angle.	Plane of the Screen rotated showing where measurements were taken (see Note).

Figure 4.21

Note: When using the Measure Tool measurements are taken on the plane of the computer Screen. True measurements can only be made in Top, Front and Side Orthographic Views.

4.17 Precision Manipulation

Precise Manipulation, precise Translation (location), Rotation and Scaling can be performed in the **3D View Editor, Object Properties Panel** (press the N Key to display). Remember, the values shown in this panel are for the Object that is selected in the 3D View Editor.

In Figure 4.22 the values are for the default Cube Object in its default position at the center of the Scene. The location is, therefore, X, Y and Z = 0m.

Figure 4.22

To move the Cube a precise distance away from the center, position the Mouse Cursor over a value. The cursor changes to a double headed arrow.

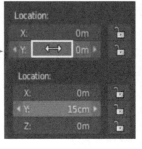

Click LMB and drag left or right to change the value. The value bar displays the value as you drag the cursor. Release the Mouse button to set the value. The Cube is moved in the 3D View Editor as the value alters.
Clicking the little arrows incrementally alters the value.

You may also click LMB on the value bar to display a typing cursor

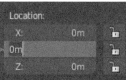

Backspace to delete the existing value and retype a new value.

Figure 4.23

Note: When Translating an Object in the 3D View Editor you may be moving the Object out of Camera View. When you render an image your model may not be included. Press **Num Pad 0** to see what is included in the shot.

To return to the original User Perspective View press Num Pad 5 twice, click and hold RMB to rotate the Viewport.

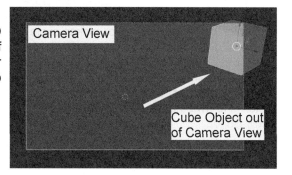

Camera View

Cube Object out of Camera View

4.18 Coloring Objects

Figure 4.7 shows the Object Primitives displayed in different colors. Adding color to an Object in Blender is referred to as; **Applying a Material**. Materials are discussed in Chapter 16 in detail but for the moment consider Material as simply meaning Color.

Color is how you see something in a certain lighting condition. A white ball in the sunlight will look completely different under a colored street lamp at night. This phenomena is true in Blender. How something appears on the computer screen is determined by the simulated lighting effects that are generated, the Material color that is applied and the **Viewport Shading Mode** that is being employed. For the present, how to color an Object in the default Screen arrangement will be demonstrated. The default **Viewport Shading Mode** is; **Solid** with **Studio Lighting** (see Chapter 14)

For the demonstration, add a UV Sphere Object (Primitive) to the Scene (Figure 4.24).

When the UV Sphere is entered into the Scene it is selected as shown by the **orange outline.**

Press **Alt + A Key** to deselect or LMB click an empty part of the Editor.

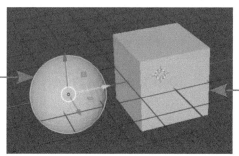

LMB Click to select the Cube.

Figure 4.24

Have the Cube selected in the 3D View Editor then go to the Properties Editor and click on the Material button (Figure 4.25). In the Properties Editor panel Note: Use Nodes highlighted red.

Note: With the Cube Object selected the controls in the Properties Editor apply only to the Cube.

Figure 4.25

The red highlight indicates that the **Blender Node System** for applying the Material is active. The Base Color shows a color bar with the default gray color of the Cube. Clicking on the color bar displays a color picker circle where you may select a different Material (color). **BUT:** If you are reading this book for the first time and are progressing chronologically you have not encountered **Nodes** (Chapter 16) or **Viewport Shading** (Chapter 14) both of which determine whether a new Material will display in the 3D View Editor.

To enable you to add Material color at this point, click on the **Use Nodes** bar. This disables the Node System and allows a basic Material to be added to an Object and to display in the default 3D View Editor.

Material Button

Properties Editor, Material Button

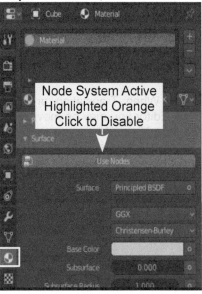

Node System Active
Highlighted Orange
Click to Disable

In the **Surface Tab** click on the **Base Color bar** to display the **Color Picker**, click in the circle to select a color. The color is applied to the Cube in the 3D View Editor. Note that the brightness slider at the side of the color picker is towards the top making the applied color comparatively bright.

Brightness Slider

3D View Editor

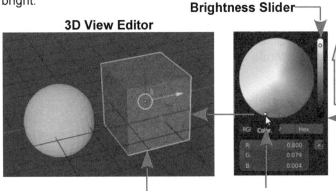

Selected color applied to Cube   Click to select a Color

Figure 4.26

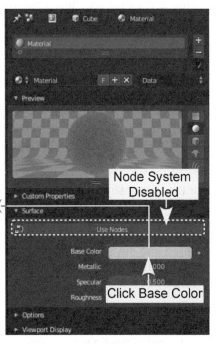

Node System
Disabled

Click Base Color

With color applied to the Cube, deselect the Cube and select the UV Sphere.

When you select the **UV Sphere** the **Properties Editor, Material buttons** change showing a minimal display containing only the **New** button (Figure 4.27).

Figure 4.27

Click the **New** button to open Material (color) controls for the UV Sphere.

In the default Scene, the default Cube Object was displayed with a gray Material color. This color is a default Material which shows on all new Objects entered into a Scene. In the case of the default Cube the Material is considered to be pre-applied. In the foregoing exercise, coloring the Cube has modified the pre-applied gray Material.

When a new Object is entered into a Scene it displays with the default gray color but the Material **HAS NOT** been applied. Blender needs something to show, therefore, the default gray is used.

You click the **New** button in the **Properties Editor, Material buttons** to apply the default gray Material. You then modify the Material. With the UV Sphere selected, clicking New, again, activates the Node System, reverting to the **Base Color** used previously.

In the new **Properties Editor, Material buttons** click in the bar where you see **Use Nodes** to cancel the Node System. The Editor will display the arrangement similar to that employed for the Cube Object.

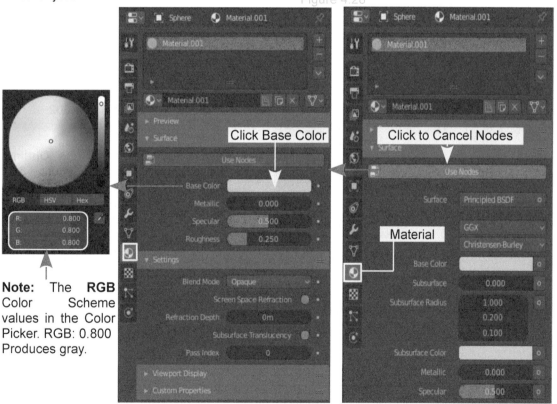

Figure 4.28

Note: The **RGB** Color Scheme values in the Color Picker. RGB: 0.800 Produces gray.

Material Buttons – Nodes Canceled   Material Buttons – Nodes Active

Clicking **Base Color** and selecting a color applies it to the UV Sphere (the selected Object).
Note: The Material buttons apply to the selected Object only. With a different Object selected a different button panel is displayed.

4.19 Other Types of Objects

Figure 4.29

Besides **Object Primitives** there are other types of Objects which can be introduced into a Scene. These have a variety of uses and are accessed by clicking the **Add** button in the **3D View Editor Header** or by pressing **Shift + A Key** on the Keyboard (Figure 4.29).

How the different types are used will be explained as you progress through the book but you see the **Mesh** option at the top of the Add menu which opens the list of Primitives previously discussed.

From the menu you will see that you may add additional Cameras and Lamps into a Scene. These influence how you see Objects. For one type of special Object see 4.21 Metashapes.

4.20 Naming Objects

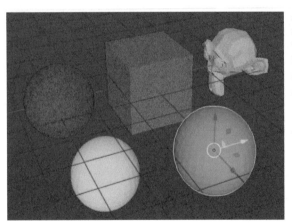

Figure 4.30

As you enter Objects to a Scene Blender automatically assigns a name. In Figure 4.32 the Cube Object has been named **Cube**, the Monkey Object has been named **Suzanne** and the UV Spheres have been named **Sphere, Sphere.001** and **Sphere.002**.

The names are displayed in the **Outliner Editor** under **Scene Collection** (Figure 4.31).

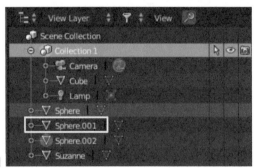

You will also see an Object's name in the **Properties Editor** with the **Object button** selected (Figure 4.32).

Figure 4.31

Figure 4.32

The automatic names are all very well, but as you build a Scene and add many Objects, it is obvious that automatic names could become meaningless and confusing. For example; **UV Spheres** are named **Sphere, Sphere.001** and **Sphere.002**.

Blender has a monkey head that's affectionately referred to as **Suzanne**, a reference to the ape in two of Kevin Smith's films: *Jay and Silent Bob Strike Back* and *Mallrats* (close to the end). Many 3D modeling and animation suites have a generic semi-complex primitive that is used for test renders, benchmarks, and examples that necessitate something a little more complex than a cube or sphere.

The name **Suzanne** will definitely distinguish Monkey unless you add more Monkeys, in which case they will be named Suzanne, Susanne.001, Suzanne.002 etc. Even though the UV Spheres have been colored the question arises, *which one is which?*

Obviously it is preferable to name Objects with meaningful names especially when they have been reshaped into Characters or components of a complex Scene.

You rename Objects in the **Properties Editor, Object buttons** or in the **Outliner Editor** by double clicking on the Object name, backspacing or deleting the name and retyping a new name.

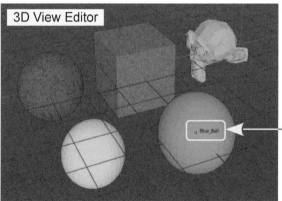

Figure 4.33

A handy way of identifying Objects in the 3D View Editor is to check (tick) **Name** in the **Properties Editor, Object buttons, Viewport Display Tab**. The name of the Object is displayed in the Editor (Figure 4.33).

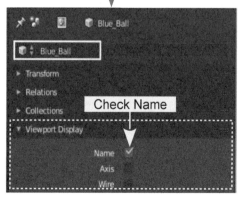

Note: Objects in the 3D View Editor are listed in the Outliner Editor in groups called **Collections**. The arrangement and management of Collections are detailed in Chapter 12.

4.21 The Header Button Menus

The 3D View Editor **Header** Buttons provide menus for selecting a variety of functions. The individual functions will be called upon as required in specific instructions. Some functions have already been covered such as switching between Object Mode and Edit Mode, Object selection (Select button) and adding Objects (Add button). The menus allow you to activate a function by clicking the function name and in many cases provide a Keyboard shortcut. For example; in the Select button menu you will see Border Select and Circle Select with the Keyboard shortcuts B Key and C Key. You either click the select type name in the menu or press the Keyboard shortcut with the Mouse cursor in the 3D View Editor panel. The Add button displays the Object Add Menu which is the same as pressing Shift + A Key. The Object button displays a comprehensive menu with sub menus. As you progress in Blender you will become familiar with the functions in the menus but for now, the following are worth mentioning:

Join (Ctrl + J Key)   Selecting two or more Objects at the same time (Hold Shift + RMB Click) then clicking Join in the menu or pressing Ctrl + J Key joins the selected Objects into a single Object.

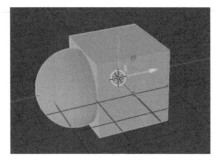

Figure 4.34

Copy and Paste - Objects may be copied from one Blender file and pasted into another file.

Smooth and Flat Shading

In the previous diagrams describing naming and coloring Objects you will observe that the surface of the UV Sphere is made up from a series of rectangular flat surfaces (FlatShading). In the **3D View Editor Header** selecting **Object – Shade Smooth** in the menu produces a smooth spherical surface which is much nicer for coloring the sphere. Alternatively RMB click to display the **Object Context Menu** with the shading options.

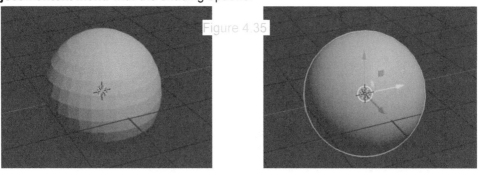

Figure 4.35

4.22 Meta Shapes

Meta Shapes are described as *mercurial, or clay-like forms that have a rounded shape.*

When two Meta Objects get close, they begin to interact with one another. They merge, as water droplets do. When they are moved apart, they restore their original shape.

There are several Meta Shapes you can use in Blender (Figure 4.36). Meta Shapes are added to a Scene in Object mode like any other shape: press **Shift + the A key – Add – Metaball** and select either Ball, Capsule, Plane, Ellipsoid, or Cube. Be sure to deselect one shape before adding another, or they will be automatically joined. When **Meta Shapes** get close to one another, they begin to pull and flow together like droplets of liquid (Figure 4.37). The shapes can be animated and textured, and reflection and transparency can be applied to create some stunning effects.

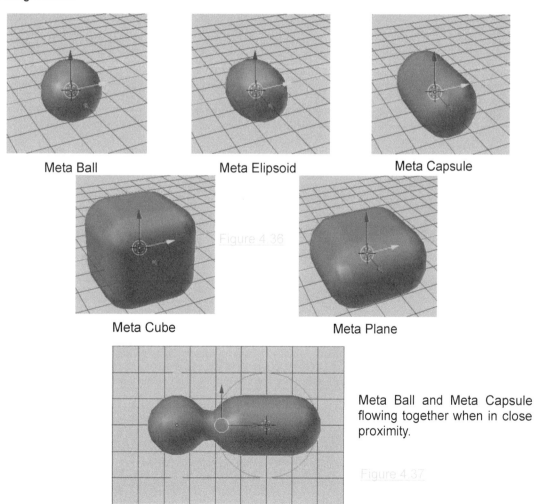

Meta Ball   Meta Elipsoid   Meta Capsule

Meta Cube   Meta Plane

Meta Ball and Meta Capsule flowing together when in close proximity.

Editing Objects

Editing Objects

Editing or modifying one of the basic shapes (Primitives) in Blender is the process of Modeling.

Creating a model begins by introducing a Primitive to the Scene. Blender's Primitives are Mesh Objects, that is to say, they are constructed with surfaces formed by a mesh. The mesh can be imagined as a fishing net or a piece of chicken coop wire with strands of twine or wire criss-crossing and joined where they intersect. The spaces between the strands are filled in forming a surface.

The shape of a primitive is altered by manipulating the mesh. This is achieved by selecting (grabbing) the intersection points (**Vertices**) or the strands (**Edges**) or the filled in pieces (**Faces**) and moving them in 3D Space.

Vertices, Edges and Faces can be extruded to build onto a Primitive. Edges and Faces may be scaled and rotated to twist the shape of the Primitive.

Several Primitives can be joined together to shape a single Object.

5.1 The Mesh Object

The default Blender Scene contains a **Cube Mesh Object** which by default is selected in **Object Mode**. With the Cube selected (orange outline) press the **Tab key** to enter **Edit Mode** to see the basic components of the Cube Mesh (Figure 5.1).

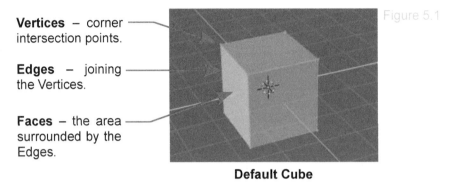

Vertices – corner intersection points.

Edges – joining the Vertices.

Faces – the area surrounded by the Edges.

Figure 5.1

Default Cube

5.2 Edit Mode Selecting

In **Edit Mode**, you work with the individual Vertices (mesh intersections) to Model the shape. You know you're in Edit Mode when you see orange lines and dots on the selected Object (Figure 5.1). When you tab into Edit Mode, the whole of your selected Object is in Edit Mode with all the Vertices selected. By default, Edit mode is in **Vertex Select Mode**.

Selection Options

In **Edit Mode**, the default selection Mode is **Vertex** which means you may select Vertices. You can elect to enter **Edge** or **Face** select Mode (Figure 5.2). These options are available in the 3D View Editor Header.

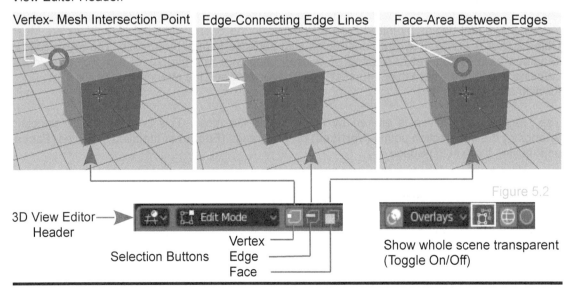

Vertex- Mesh Intersection Point   Edge-Connecting Edge Lines   Face-Area Between Edges

Figure 5.2

3D View Editor Header

Selection Buttons

Vertex
Edge
Face

Show whole scene transparent (Toggle On/Off)

Also, by default, only visible Vertices, Edges or Faces are available for selection. This means that you can only select the Vertices, Edges or Faces that you actually see in the Editor. Blender has a **Limit Selection to Visible** function, which allows you to only select Vertices, Edges or Faces on the front (Figure 5.3). This function is toggled on and off in the 3D View Editor Header by clicking the **Show Whole Scene Transparent** button (Figure 5.2).

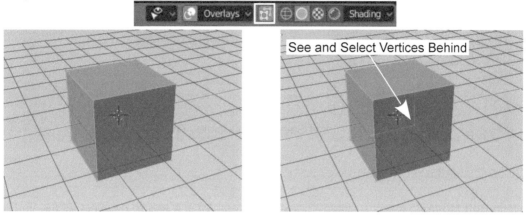

Limit Selection to Visible - On   Figure 5.3   Limit Selection to Visible - Off

In introducing the Limit Selection to Visible option, allowing you to see Vertices in Edit Mode which are hidden behind front Faces, you should be aware that a similar feature exists for Object Mode. You can not select Vertices in Object Mode but there are occasions when you may wish to see hidden geometry.

The 3D View Editor displays Objects in several different Display methods referred to as Viewport Shading Modes (see Chapter 14 – Viewport Shading). The default display is Solid Viewport Shading. The options are accessed in the 3D View Editor Header.

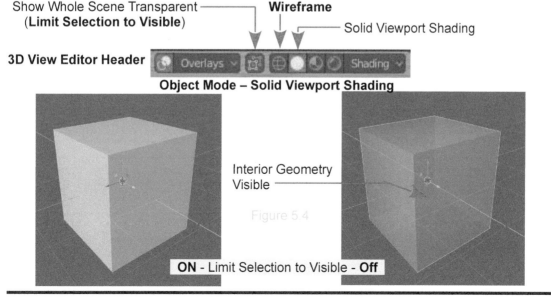

Show Whole Scene Transparent ———— **Wireframe**
   (**Limit Selection to Visible**)   Solid Viewport Shading

3D View Editor Header

Object Mode – Solid Viewport Shading

Interior Geometry Visible ————

Figure 5.4

ON - Limit Selection to Visible - **Off**

Object Mode – Wireframe Display

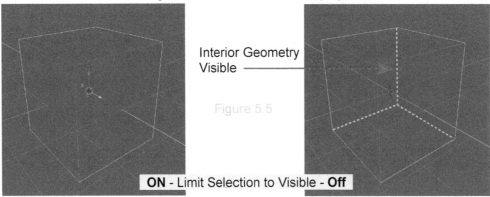

Interior Geometry
Visible ————

Figure 5.5

ON - Limit Selection to Visible - **Off**

5.3 Selecting Vertices, Edges and Faces

While in **Edit Mode**, to select a single Vertex, first press **Alt + A key** to deselect all the Vertices. In **Edit Mode** this does not deselect the Object, only the Vertices. Click with the right mouse button (RMB) on a single Vertex to select it. To select multiple Vertices, hold down **Shift** while using the RMB to click. You can also drag a rectangle around the Vertices. Press the **B Key**, hold and drag a rectangle to select a group of Vertices. Pressing the **C Key** will bring up a circle selection tool. Holding the LMB and dragging the circle, selects Vertices on the move. The circle can be sized by scrolling the center Mouse Wheel (MMB). Pressing **Esc** will get you out of the circular selection tool. In order to deselect all Vertices or deselect those currently selected, press the **Alt + A Key** or **RMB** click on an empty space in the **3D View Editor.**.

The selection and de selection procedures are the same for Vertices, Edges and Faces.

5.4 Manipulating Selected Vertices, Edges and Faces

After selecting Vertices, Edges or Faces, you can use the basic manipulation controls used for manipulating Objects (**G Key** to grab or move (Translate), **S Key** to scale, and **R Key** to rotate) (Figure 5.6). Obviously you cannot scale a single vertex but you can scale two or more selected Vertices which constitute a **Vertex Group**. **Note:** The **Edit Mode Tool Panel** at the LHS of the 3D View Editor provides **Manipulation Widgets** for Translating, Scaling and Rotating (see Chapter 6 - Editing Tools).

Examples of Translation (Move), Scale and Rotation   Figure 5.6

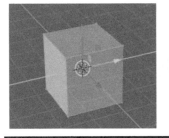 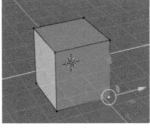 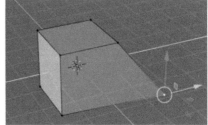

Default Cube – All Vertices
Selected

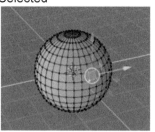

Single Vertex Selected

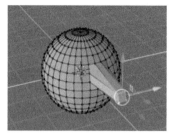

Single Vertex Moved (Translated)

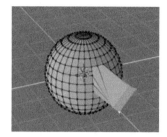

Four Vertices Selected
Hold Shift – Click RMB

Vertex Group **Translated**
Using the Widget

Vertex Group Scaled and Rotated
S key Scale – R key Rotate

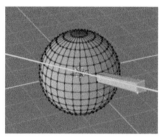

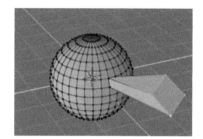

Vertex Group **Extruded** Along
the Axis Normal to the Face

Vertex Group Scaled and Rotated

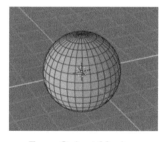

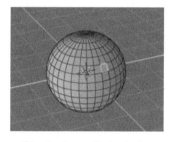

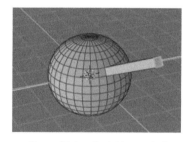

Face Select Mode

Single Face Selected

Face Extruded Along Axis

Note the difference between **Translating (Moving)** a **Vertex Group** and **Extruding** a **Vertex Group**. Extrusion creates new Vertices (see Chapter 6- 6.5 Editing Tool – Extrude Region). The figures show the Move (Translate) Tool, Widget being used.

5.5 Creating Vertices by Subdivision

There are occasions when you need to add more Vertices to part or **all of the mesh** in order to create detail. To do this, you must be in **Edit Mode** with Vertices selected. To add Vertices to a specific area select Vertices surrounding the area where you wish to add detail. Click **RMB** in the Screen to display the **Mesh Context Menu** and select **Subdivide.**

Selecting **Subdivide** cuts (divides) the surface Faces of the Mesh inserting Vertices at the intersection of the Edges. Opening the Last Operator **Subdivide Panel** shows **Number of Cuts = 1**. Each Face has been cut once producing four Faces.

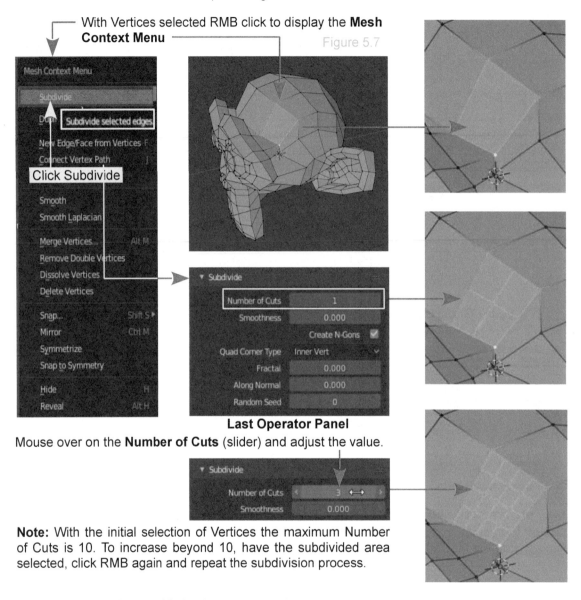

With Vertices selected RMB click to display the **Mesh Context Menu**

Figure 5.7

Last Operator Panel

Mouse over on the **Number of Cuts** (slider) and adjust the value.

Note: With the initial selection of Vertices the maximum Number of Cuts is 10. To increase beyond 10, have the subdivided area selected, click RMB again and repeat the subdivision process.

Alternative Subdivision Method

Note: With the initial Vertices selected you may also click Edge in the 3D View Editor Header and click Subdivide for the same result.

5.6 Adding and Deleting Vertices, Edges, or Faces

Deleting: If you want to make a hole in a mesh, enter **Edit mode** and select the vertices, edges or faces you wish to remove, then hit the **X Key or Delete Key**. Select (click) the item from the menu that displays (Figure 5.8).

Figure 5.8

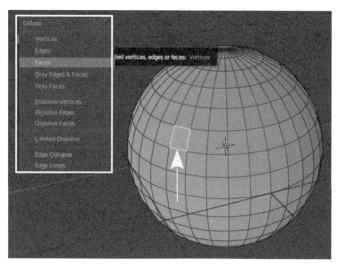

Adding Vertices and Faces: Place the Object in **Edit Mode**. Deselect all Vertices. **Press Ctrl** and click **LMB** where you wish to place a new Vertex. Shift select three or more Vertices. Press the **F key** to **Face** (fill in between the selected Vertices Figure 5.9).

Figure 5.9

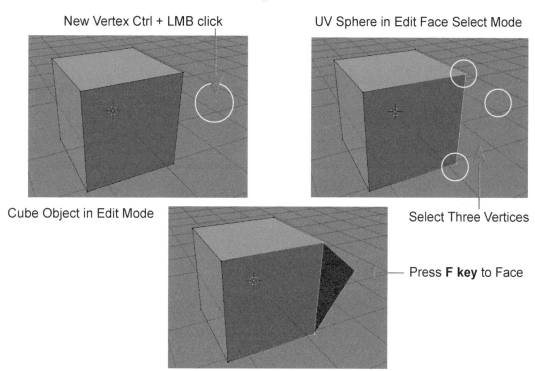

New Vertex Ctrl + LMB click

UV Sphere in Edit Face Select Mode

Cube Object in Edit Mode

Select Three Vertices

Press **F key** to Face

Adding Faces – User Perspective View

Be aware that when you add a new Vertex in **User Perspective View** the Vertex is placed on the mid plane of the view. This means it is placed on an imaginary plane located at the center of the 3D World. The plane is normal to your computer screen.

Top Orthographic View

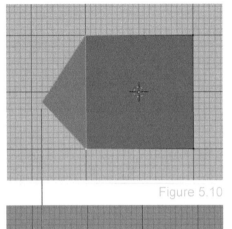

Figure 5.10

New Vertex added. Three Vertices are selected then Faced (Figure 5.10).

All Vertices are located on the same plane in elevation.

Front Orthographic View (Figure 5.11)

Side Orthographic View (Figure 5.12)

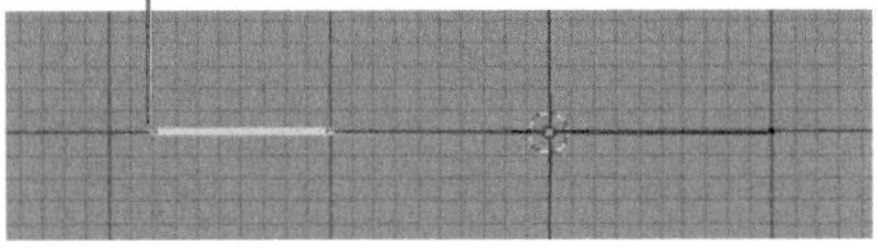

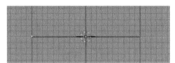

Figure 5.11

Figure 5.12

User Perspective View

Figure 5.13

New Vertex added. Three Vertices are selected then faced (Figure 5.13).

The new Vertex is displaced in elevation.

Front Orthographic View (Figure 5.14).

Side Orthographic View (Figure 5.15).

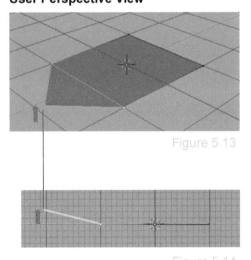

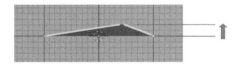

Figure 5.14

Figure 5.15

5.7 Center Points

Every Object you create in Blender has a small dot somewhere in the center (by default, usually at the center of geometry of the Object). This is the Object's center, or pivot point (Figure 5.16).

With the Object selected in **Object Mode**, moving the Object moves the center point at the same time. In **Edit mode** the center point does not move when Vertices are moved.

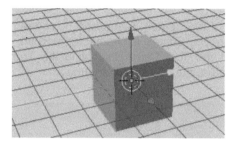

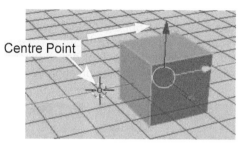

Center Point at Center of Geometry   Figure 5.16   Vertices Moved in Edit Mode

It is easy to move center points to locations other than where you want them. This happens because all the Vertices of the Object are moved in **Edit mode.**

If you ever need to relocate an Object's center point, move the 3D View Editor Cursor to the new center location. In **Object Mode**, click on **Object** in the Editor Header. Click **Origin** followed by **Origin to 3D Cursor** (Figure 5.17). This will move the center point to the Cursor. Repeat the process selecting **Geometry to Origin**, which moves the Vertices to the center.

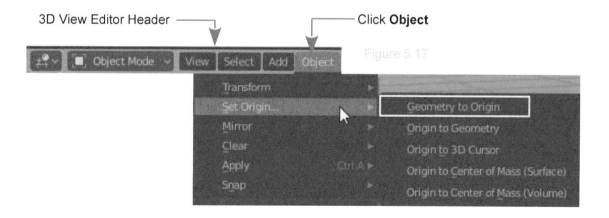

Figure 5.17

5.8 Joining and Separating

Individual Objects can be joined together to make a single Object. The Objects may be separated under certain conditions or parts of a mesh can be separated from the main Object.

Joining in Object Mode

In Figure 5.18, a UV Sphere Object has been added to the default Scene and positioned such that it intersects with the default Cube. After positioning, the Sphere is deselected and the Cube selected. **Note:** The Move Tool has been selected in the Tool Panel displaying the Translate Manipulation Widget. The Manipulation Widget is located at the center of the Cube.

Figure 5.18

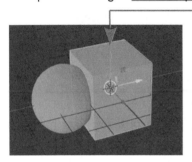 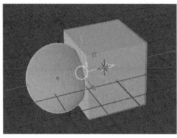 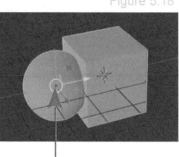

Cube Selected After Positioning   Widget Locates Mid Way   New Center of Rotation

To join the two Objects, have the Cube selected and shift select the UV Sphere. Note: The Sphere was the last Object selected and the Manipulation Widget is located mid way between the center of the Sphere and the Cube. Press **Ctrl + J Key** to join the two Objects. Note: There is an orange outline encapsulating both the Sphere and the Cube which indicates they are a single Object. Note Also: The Widget has located at the center of the Sphere, the last Object selected. The center of geometry for the combined Object is at the center of the Sphere. Rotation of the combined Object will be about this center.

Joining in Edit Mode

Consider the following with the default Blender Scene; The Cube Object is selected in Object Mode. Press **Tab** to enter Edit Mode. Press the **Alt +A Key** deselecting the Vertices. The Cube remains selected since it is the active Object selected in Object Mode. While remaining in Edit mode, add a UV Sphere Object to the Scene.

> Objects added to a Scene in **Edit Mode** are automatically joined to the last object that was selected while it was in **Object Mode**.

When the UV Sphere is added all its Vertices are selected and may be manipulated (translated and scaled). Press **Alt + A** Key to deselect the Sphere's Vertices. Press the A key again to select the UV Sphere plus the Cube. They have been joined and form a single Object (Figure 5.19 over)

When the UV Sphere is added it is positioned at the location of the 3D View Editor Cursor which by default coincides with the center of the Scene and the center of the default Cube Object. The UV Sphere is, therefore, fully encapsulated inside the Cube and not visible. Selecting the Move Tool in the Tool Panel displays the Translate Widget for the UV Sphere and allows you to move the Sphere's Vertices.

Tip: To see the UV Sphere inside the Cube click the **Show Whole Scene Transparent** button in the 3D View Editor Header

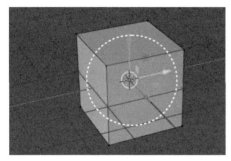
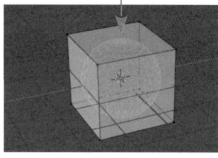

Figure 5.19

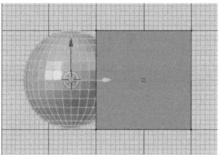
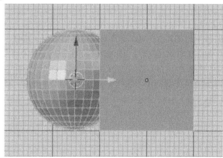

UV Sphere added in Edit Mode
The Sphere May Be Repositioned

Pressing A key Twice Joins the Mesh

Separating in Edit Mode

To demonstrate separation in Edit Mode, use the same Cube – Sphere arrangement as shown in Figure 5.19. Have the Cube and the Sphere joined into a single Object.

Figure 5.20

Place the **3D View Editor** in **Right Orthographic view** and with the combined Object selected, **Tab** to Edit mode. Press **Alt + A key** to deselect all Vertices. Press the **B key** (Box Select) and drag a rectangle around the LH side of the spherical part. **Don't forget to have Show Whole Scene transparent turned Off.**

The selected Vertices will be displayed orange.
(Figure 5.20)

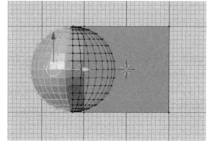

With the selection made, press the **P key** to display the **Separate Menu** and in this case click on the **Selection** option. The selection option separates the selected Vertices creating a new Object as shown by the orange outline. (Figure 5.21).

Figure 5.21

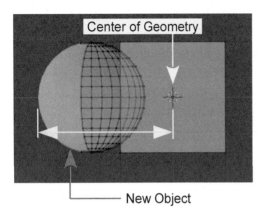
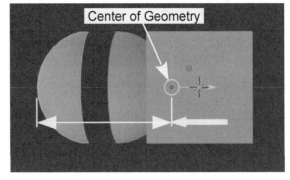

New Object   New Object Moved

Tab back to Object mode. With the Manipulation Widget turned on, move the new Object along the Y Axis. You can move the object anywhere you like, rotate it, scale it etc.

Note: In joining the Sphere to the Cube in Object Mode by pressing **Ctrl + J**, in this case the Cube was the last Object selected, therefore, the center of geometry of the combined Objects was at the center of the Cube. After separating part of the Sphere mesh, its' center of geometry is also located, coinciding with the center of the Cube. When moving the separated part of the Sphere you see the center of geometry, i.e. center of rotation, displaced from the mesh.

The Separate Menu Options

In the previous example you used the **Selection option** in the **Separate** menu. There are two alternatives (Figure 5.22):

Separate by Material: When joined objects have different Materials (Color) applied they will be separated into single Objects according to their color.

Figure 5.22

Material (Color) is discussed in Chapter 16

Separate by Loose Parts: Consider the Objects automatically joined in Edit Mode (Figure 5.22).

With the UV Sphere and Cube joined in Edit Mode, and displayed in Edit Mode, press the **P Key** to display the **Separate** menu and select **By Loose Parts**. Immediately one of the Objects will display a red outline. **Tab to Object Mode**. You may now select either part as a separate Object. Note the center of Geometry.

5.9 Creating Vertex Groups

On occasion you will want to manipulate a group of vertices. You can select multiple vertices on an Object and manipulate them, but once deselected you could have trouble selecting the exact same group the next time. To assist with this you can assign multiple Vertices to a designated group for re-selection. Working through the following example will show you how.

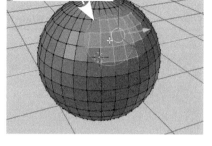

Circle Selection

Figure 5.23

Start the default Scene and replace the Cube with a **UV Sphere**. Zoom in on the Scene to give a better view (press the Number Pad **+** sign). Tab to **Edit mode** and then press **Alt + A key** to **deselect** all the Vertices. Press the **C key** for circle select (scroll the mouse wheel to adjust the circle size) and click, hold and drag the circle over the Sphere to select a group of Vertices (Figure 5.23). Press **Esc** to cancel the circle selection. The Vertices remain selected.

In the **Properties Editor, Data button, Vertex Groups tab**, click on the **+** sign to create a **Vertex Group Data Slot**. By default, this will be named simply **Group** (Figure 5.24). If you wish you can change the name to something meaningful by clicking on **Group** in the **Name** slot, deleting it, and retyping a new name.

Properties Editor

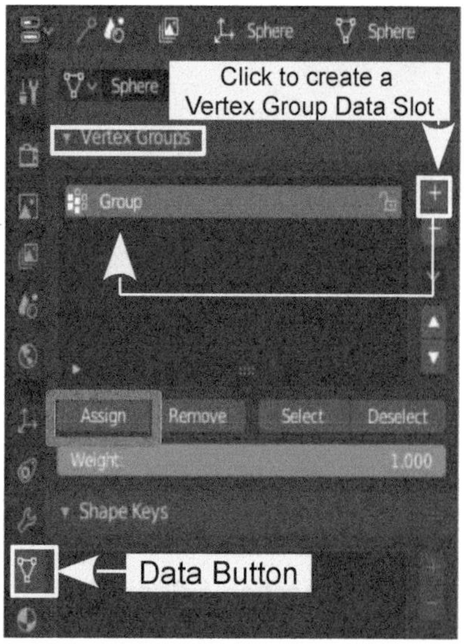

Figure 5.24

With the group of vertices still selected on the Sphere, click on the **Assign button** in the **Vertex Groups Tab** - this assigns the selected vertices to **Group**.

By clicking on the **Select** and **Deselect** buttons, you will see the vertices on the Sphere being selected or deselected, respectively.

Deselect the Vertices and repeat the circle select with a different group. Click on the **+** sign again in the **Vertex Groups Tab** and you should see a new data block created named **Group.001**. Click the **Assign button** to assign the new group of vertices to **Group.001**. Deselect the Vertices on the Sphere in the 3D View Editor, and you can now select **Group** or **Group.001** (Figure 5.25).

Weigh Paint Method

Figure 5.25

An alternative method for selecting Vertices for assignment to a Vertex Group is to use Blenders, **Weigh Paint Tool.**

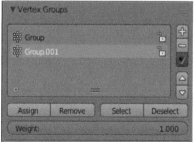

With a **UV Sphere** selected in the **3D window** go to the **Properties Editor, Data buttons**. In the **Vertex Group Tab** click the **Plus** sign to create a new **Vertex Group**. The Vertex Group will be named simply **Group** (Figure 5.27).

Place the 3D View Editor in **Weigh Paint Mode** (Figure 5.26).

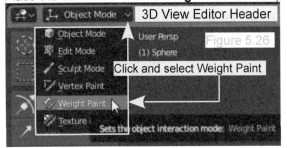

In the **Weigh Paint Mode Tool Panel** click on **Draw.**
The 3D Editor cursor becomes a red circle which is the paint **Brush** (Figure 5.28).

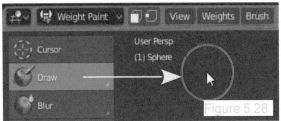

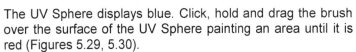

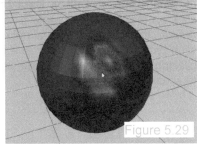

The UV Sphere displays blue. Click, hold and drag the brush over the surface of the UV Sphere painting an area until it is red (Figures 5.29, 5.30).

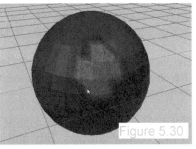

Press the **Tab Key** to place the 3D window in **Edit Mode** and **deselect all Vertices** (press Alt + A Key).

In the **Properties Editor, Data buttons, Vertex Groups Tab** with the new Vertex Group named Group highlighted blue, click the **Assign button** (Figure 5.31).

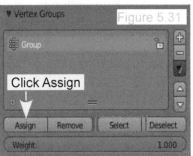

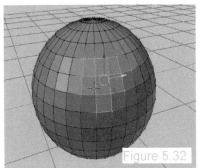

Click the **Select button** to see the painted vertices assigned to the **Vertex Group** (Figure 5.32).

Note: Clicking **LMB** while holding **Ctrl** with a Vertex Group selected duplicates the group at the position on the Screen where you click.

5.10 Proportional Vertex Editing

Proportional Vertex Editing is used to create a flow in the shape when editing Vertices. To turn **Proportional Vertex Editing** on, in **Edit mode**, click the **Proportional Editing** button in the **3D View Editor Header** (Figure 5.33) .

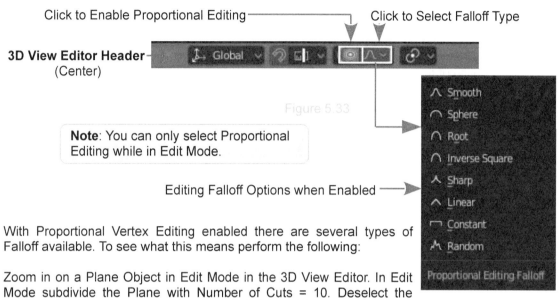

Click to Enable Proportional Editing

Click to Select Falloff Type

3D View Editor Header
(Center)

Figure 5.33

Note: You can only select Proportional Editing while in Edit Mode.

Editing Falloff Options when Enabled

With Proportional Vertex Editing enabled there are several types of Falloff available. To see what this means perform the following:

Zoom in on a Plane Object in Edit Mode in the 3D View Editor. In Edit Mode subdivide the Plane with Number of Cuts = 10. Deselect the Vertices then re-select and repeat the subdivision with Number of Cuts = 2. Select a single Vertex and Translate up on the Z Axis (Figure 5.34).

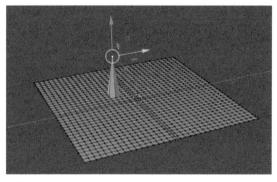

Plane Subdivided – Single Vertex Translated
Note: Proportional Vertex Editing has **NOT** been activated.

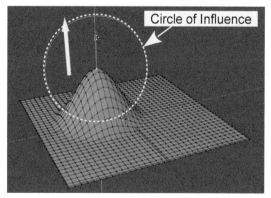

Single Vertex Translated on the Z Axis
Proportional Vertex Editing Activated

Figure 5.34

When a single Vertex is selected and Translated with Proportional Vertex Editing activated a **Circle of Influence** determines how many surrounding Vertices are influenced in the Translation.

The diameter of the circle is adjustable. Select the Vertex to be Translated. Press the G Key (places the Vertex in Grab Mode) to display the circle. Without moving the Mouse, scroll the mouse wheel or tap the Num Pad Plus and Minus Keys. Click LMB. The circle display is cancelled but the influence is retained. Pressing the G Key and moving the Mouse moves the selected Vertex. Pressing the Grab button in the Tool Panel displays the Manipulation Widget and allows Translation of the Vertex. Although not displayed the Circle of Influence previously set is in effect. Experiment with the different types of Falloff.

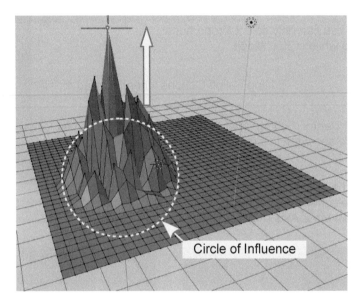

Figure 5.35

Circle of Influence

Single Vertex Translated with Random Falloff Selected

It doesn't take much imagination to see that Proportional Vertex Editing as seen in Figure 5.33 can be employed to create a landscape (see Chapter 11 – 11.1 Editing Techniques and Examples).

5.11 Inset Faces

The **Inset Faces** command causes new Faces to be created inside or outside a selected geometry.

To demonstrate, delete the default Cube in the 3D window and add a **Plane** object. Zoom in (Scroll MMB), Tab into **Edit** mode and Subdivide the Plane twice. Deselect the Vertices (A key). Change from **Vertex select** mode to **Face Select** mode.

Select a single Face and with the Mouse Cursor in the 3D View Editor press the **I Key** and move the Mouse Cursor towards the center of the Face.(Figure 5.36). Alternatively click **Face** in the 3D View Editor Header and select **Inset Faces** or press **Inset Faces** in the **Tool Panel**. With either method, move the **Mouse cursor** towards the center of the selected Face and you see new Faces created. Click LMB to set the new Faces in position.

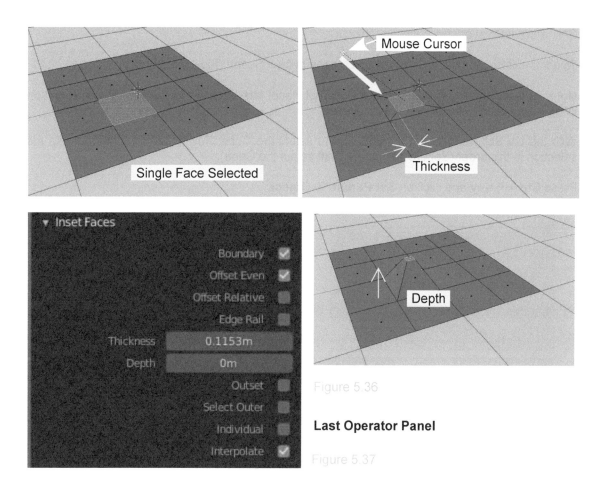

Figure 5.36

Last Operator Panel

Figure 5.37

Note: Inset Faces displays in the **Last Operator Panel** (Figure 5.37). While this panel is displayed you can make adjustments. The **Thickness Slider** controls the size of the new Face. The **Depth Slider** displaces the face normal to the Plane. Positive values above the Plane, negative values below the Plane.

Note: The procedure can be processed in both **Vertex Select Mode** and **Edge Select Mode** by selecting the perimeter of an area on the surface of the plane. The principle can be applied to the surface of any mesh Object.

5.12 Parenting

In 5.80 it was demonstrated how two Mesh Objects may be joined together to form a single combined Object. There are, however, occasions when you will want two or more Objects to act as a single unit but not actually have the mesh joined. For example, you may want one Object to follow another when the first Object is moved. This can be achieved by Parenting or creating a Child Parent Relationship between Objects.

To demonstrate, add a UV Sphere Object to the default Scene (Figure 5.38).

Note: In the diagram the Move Tool in the Tool Panel has been activated and the Manipulation Widget employed to position the UV Sphere.

With the UV Sphere selected press Shift and select the Cube. For the demonstration make the selection in this order (Sphere selected – Shift select the Cube).

Press **Ctrl + P Key** and click on **Set Parent To Object.**

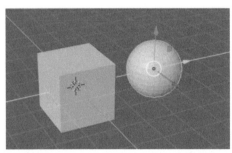

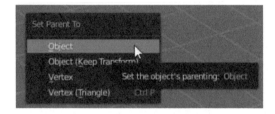

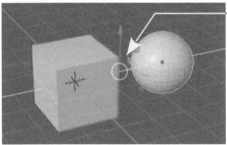

With the Move Tool activated displaying the Manipulation Widget, you will observe that the **Widget relocates mid way** between the two Objects. This indicates that Parenting is in place. Using the Widget to move along the Y Axis will demonstrate that the Objects are Parented. They both move together.

Note: The selection order in the Parenting operation is important.

Having the UV Sphere selected then selecting the Cube has made the UV Sphere the child of the Cube. Selecting the Cube individually and moving, will see the UV Sphere follow. If the UV Sphere is selected individually it can be moved independently.

6

Editing Tools

Editing Tools

In the previous chapter some of Blender's basic mesh editing techniques were introduced which allowed you to manipulate and reshape Primitives. These techniques are the beginning of the process and are essential for mastering more sophisticated practices. Blender incorporates many techniques for performing a variety of functions some of which are automated. The automated techniques may be considered as **Tools**.

Like any trades person, mechanic or engineer, knowing what tools are available, how each functions and most importantly what tool to use for a particular application is the key to success. And, yes! where to find the tool.

As you have seen many editing techniques are simple Key and Mouse commands applied to an Object or to an Object's mesh surface. Other tools automate some fantastic and complex operations. In this chapter some of the Tools will be introduced with examples showing how they are employed.

Other Tools will be introduced in context with specific operations as you progress through the book.

6.1 The Edit Mode Tool Panel

The **Tool Panel** at the left hand side of the **3D View Editor** in **Edit Mode** contains a variety of tools for automating editing processes (Figure 6.1).

The top eight Tools are identical to those found in the Object Mode Tool panel and function in the same way when applied to a selection of Vertices, Edges or Faces. The Tools are activated by clicking (LMB) on a Tool (highlights red – see **Select Box Tool** at the top of the Tool Stack).

Figure 6.1   Figure 6.2

By default the Tool Panel displays as shown in Figure 6.2. Mouse over on the panel edge and drag the double headed arrow to expand. First expansion created a two column display. Second expansion displays names as shown in Figure 6.1.

To gain Screen space you may mouse over at the side of the Tool Panel to reveal a double headed arrow, click, hold and drag **to the left** to reduce the size of the panel (Figure 6.2).

Two Columns

> **Note:** You cannot apply the Rotate, Scale or Ruler Tools to a single Vertex.
>
> **Remember:** Pressing the **T Key** on the Keyboard toggles hide and show the Tool Panel.

6.2 The Add Cube Tool

The Add Cube Tool (click to activate – highlights blue), click in the 3D View Editor, drag the Mouse, does just what it says, **Add a Cube Object** or rather, a **Cuboid Object**, to the Scene (Figure 6.3). Remember this is in Edit Mode. You can add a new Cube Object by pressing **Shift + A Key** and selecting Cube from the Mesh Menu.

The Cuboid's shape is adjustable by moving the Mouse when entered. When you have the desired shape, deselect (Alt + A Key) to fix it.

Remember: Adding in Edit Mode makes it part of the Object in Object Mode, previously added to the Scene.

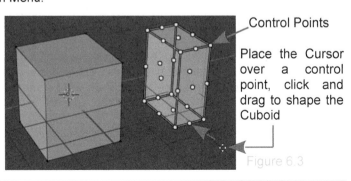

Control Points

Place the Cursor over a control point, click and drag to shape the Cuboid

Figure 6.3

6.3 Last Operator Panels

Figure 6.4

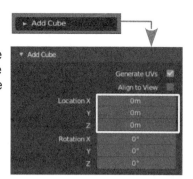

When an action has been performed in the 3D View Editor, the **Last Operator Panel** is displayed in the bottom LH corner of the Editor. **Click to Expand**, allowing values in the panel to be adjusted affecting the action (see Chapter 01 – 4.13)

The Last Operator Panel (Figure 6.4) showing that a Cube Object was added at the center of the Scene (Location X, Y, and Z = 0 m)

6.4 Extrusion

Before examining the **Extrude Region Tool** consider Extrusion in general.

Extrusion means, taking a shape and stretching such that the shape is altered. Shapes can be altered by selecting either a single Vertex or a group of Vertices then Translating, Rotating or Scaling. You may also select Edges or Faces and apply the same processes (Figure 6.5).

Vertices are selected with the Object in Edit Mode. The selected **Vertices are duplicated**, then Moved, Scaled or Rotated. The new Vertices remain attached to the original Object's surface mesh thus altering the shape of the Object.

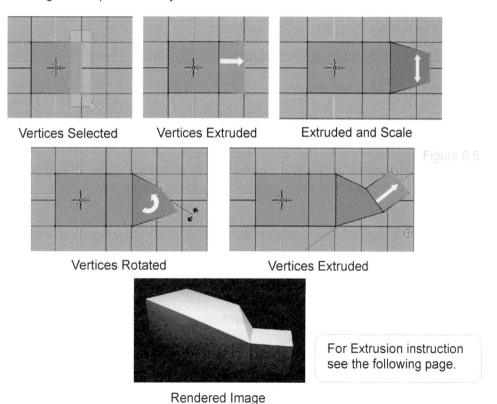

Vertices Selected   Vertices Extruded   Extruded and Scale

Figure 6.5

Vertices Rotated   Vertices Extruded

For Extrusion instruction see the following page.

Rendered Image

In Figure 6.5 the RH Vertices of a Cube (Top Orthographic View) are selected in **Edit Mode** by pressing the **B Key** (Box Select) and dragging a rectangle (don't forget to have **Show whole Scene transparent** turned off - Chapter 5 – 5.1). With the Vertices selected press the **E key** (Extrude) + **X Key** (confines Extrusion to the X Axis) and drag the Mouse. The Vertices are duplicated and repositioned. With the Vertices remaining selected the Extrusion process is repeated, and the selection Scaled down by pressing the **S Key** and moving the Mouse in. The selection is Rotated by pressing the **R Key** and moving the mouse. Finally, the selection is Extruded again.

6.5 The Extrude Region Tool

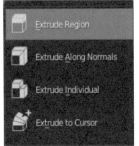 Activating the **Extrude Region Tool** displays a manipulation Widget located at the center of the selection. In Figure 6.6 the selection is the top Face of the default Cube. Click, hold and drag the Widget to Extrude the selection.

The Tool has four options. Click on the lower RH corner of the Tool and drag down to expand the panel.

Figure 6.6

Extrude Region ⟶

Extrude Along Normal means Extrude at right angles to the selected Face.
Extrude Individual allows Extrusion of an individual Face.

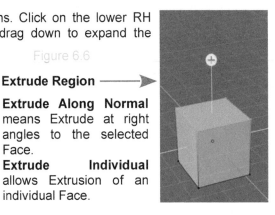
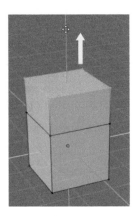

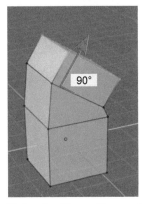
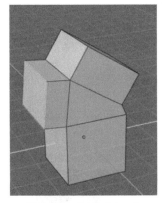
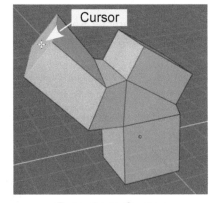

Extrude Along Normal **Extrude Individual** **Extrude to Cursor**

With **Extrude to Cursor** selected. Click LMB in the 3D View Editor and the selected Face will be Extruded to wherever the Cursor has been placed.

Note: The Extrusion methods can be applied to Faces, Edges and Vertices.

6.6 Inset Faces

Inset Faces creates new Faces inside a selected geometry.

Figure 6.7

To demonstrate, select the top Face of the default Cube while in Edit Mode. Press the **I Key** (Insert Figure 6.7) and move the **Mouse Cursor** towards the center of the selected Face. You see new Faces created. Click LMB to set the new Faces in position.

Note: The **Inset Faces Last Operator Panel** displays (Figure 6.8). While this panel is displayed you can make adjustments. The **Thickness slider** controls the size of the new Face. The **Depth slider** displaces the Face normal to the surface (positive values above the surface, negative values below). Note: The procedure can be processed in both **Vertex Select Mode** and **Edge Select Mode** by selecting the perimeter of an area on the surface. The procedure can be applied to the surface of any mesh Object.

Figure 6.8

6.7 The Inset Faces Tool

Activating the **Inset Faces Tool** replicates the above procedure. Click the Tool to activate, place the Mouse Cursor in the 3D View Editor, click and drag. While the Tool is activated you can select any Face in the 3D View Editor and apply the procedure.

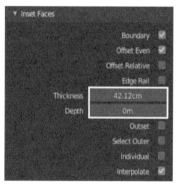

6.8 The Bevel Tool

The **Bevel Tool** bevels the Edges of a selected Face.

Figure 6.9

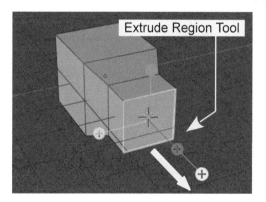

The default Cube with the front face Extruded and Scaled down then Extruded a second time.

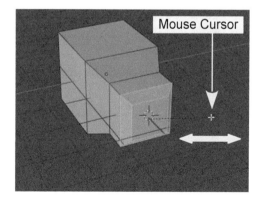

With the face selected activate the Bevel Tool. Place the Mouse Cursor, click hold and drag to bevel the edges of the Face.

6.9 Edge and Loop Selection

When working with Vertices, it is sometimes useful to select a group of Vertices which form an Edge or a Loop.

Cylinder Object in Edit Mode

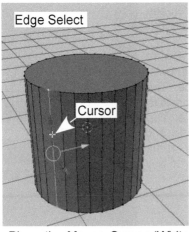

Figure 6.10

Edge Select

Cursor

Loop Select

Cursor

Place the Mouse Cursor (White Cross) over an Edge – Press and Hold Alt – Click RMB

Place the Mouse Cursor (White Cross) over a Loop – Press and Hold Alt – Click RMB

6.10 The Loop Cut Tool

The **Loop Cut Tool** allows you to create new Edges and Loops. In Edit Mode (Vertices deselected).

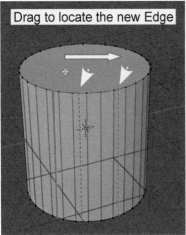

Drag to locate the new Edge

Figure 6.11

Create an Edge

Position the Mouse Cursor and click LMB. Hold LMB and drag the Mouse to locate the new Edge. Click LMB.

Drag to locate the new Edge On the Face

Clicking LMB sets the Edge on a Face. Drag the Mouse to locate the new Edge on the Face then click LMB again.

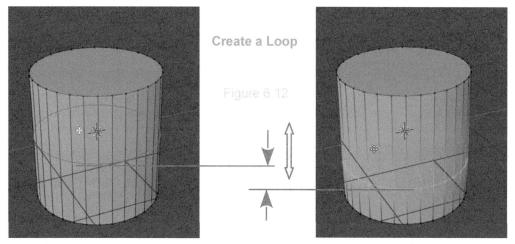

Create a Loop

Figure 6.12

Position the Mouse Cursor and click LMB.
Hold LMB and drag the Mouse to locate
the new Loop. Click LMB.

Clicking LMB sets the Loop in place.
Drag the Mouse to locate the new Loop
then click LMB again.

Adjust the number of Loop Cuts in the **Last Operator Panel.**

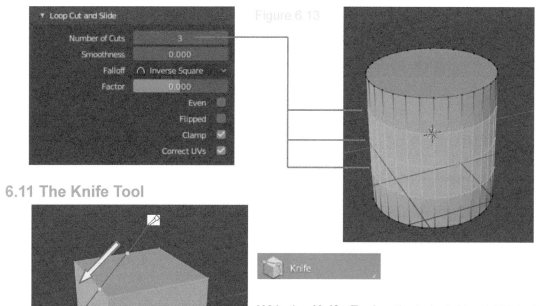

Figure 6.13

6.11 The Knife Tool

Knife

With the **Knife Tool** activated clicking LMB in the
Editor displays the Mouse Cursor as a knife. Hold
and drag across Edges creating Vertices and
Edges. Release the Mouse button and press Enter.

Figure 6.14

6.12 The Poly Build Tool

 **Poly Build** allows you to create Polygon Surfaces generating shapes by simply clicking LMB in the 3D View Editor.

At the position where you click a **Vertex is entered**, connected by Edges to the nearest existing Face.

Figure 6.15

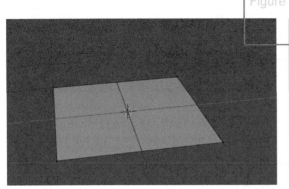 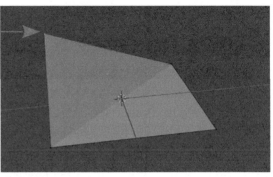

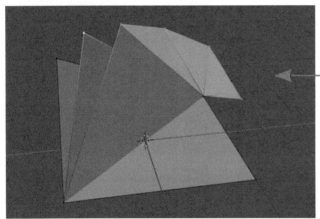

Clicking and entering a series of Vertices produces Polygon Shapes

The view rotated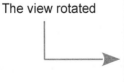

86

6.13 The Spin Tool

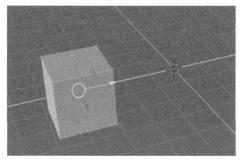 To see what the Spin Tool accomplishes, have the default Cube Object in Edit Mode displaced from the center of the Scene (Figure 16.16).View Editor Cursor is located at the center of the Scene. The Cursor is the center of rotation for the Spin Action. Click on the Spin Tool in the Tool Panel. The Spin Arc displays.

Figure 6.16

Figure 6.17

At this point there are two options. Click and release LMB on a cross to Spin the Cube 360° about the center of rotation (the 3D View Editor Cursor) (Figure 16.18) or click and hold LMB and drag the Mouse to create a partial Spin (Figure 16.19).

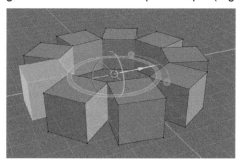

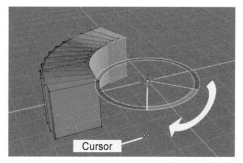

Figure 6.18

Figure 6.19

Continue dragging the Mouse to increase the Spin. Release the Mouse button then click on the manipulation Widget that displays and skew the Spin profile (Figure 16.20).

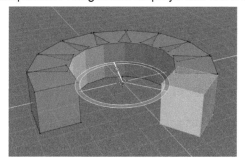

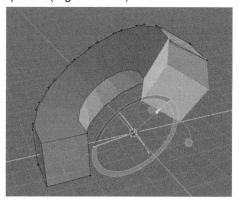

Figure 6.20

6.14 Creating a Spin Profile

To create a Spin Profile you start two vertices in Edit Mode in the 3D View Editor. One way to do this is having a **Plane Object** in a new Scene and deleting two Vertices in Edit mode.

Have the Plane in **Front Orthographic View**. A Plane Object is always added to a Scene laying flat in Top Orthographic View, therefore, flick it on edge by pressing R Key (Rotate) + X Key + 90 (rotate about the X Axis 90 degrees). In Front Orthographic View, in Edit Mode select one vertical edge and delete two Vertices. This leaves the remaining two Vertices from which you build your profile.

In Front Orthographic View have the two Vertices just to the left of the centerline of the Scene. Check that the 3D View Editor Cursor is on the centerline of the Scene (Shift + S Key – Cursor to World Origin). Still in Edit Mode press Alt + A Key to deselect the Vertices then **LMB click** on one Vertex. **Hold Ctrl and RMB click** to place a series of new Vertices in the shape that you want. Select the other Vertex and repeat. Finish by placing a Vertex on the centerline.

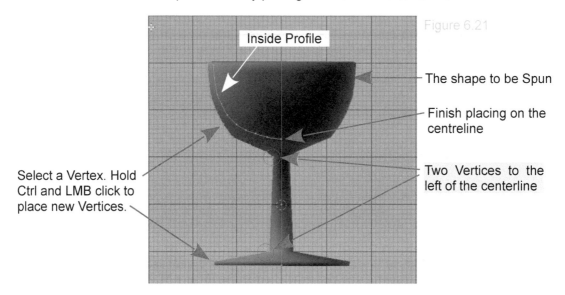

Figure 6.21

Inside Profile

The shape to be Spun

Finish placing on the centreline

Select a Vertex. Hold Ctrl and LMB click to place new Vertices.

Two Vertices to the left of the centerline

With the profile complete, place the Scene in **Top Orthographic View**. Remember the 3D View Editor Cursor remains at the center of the 3D Scene and in this case it is also the center of rotation (Spin). With the new Vertices selected activate **Spin** in the **Tool Panel** then click **LMB** in the Editor. Increase **Steps** to 32 and change **Angle** to 360° . **Remove the Double Vertices** (in the 3D View editor Header, click Vertex and select **Remove Double Vertices**) .

Tip: If you fail to see the Last Operator Panel after performing the Spin, look for a small arrow icon at the lower left of the Editor window. Click on the arrow to expand the Operator Panel.

Rotate the view to see your shape (Figure 6.22 over).

Vertices before removing Doubles   Figure 6.22

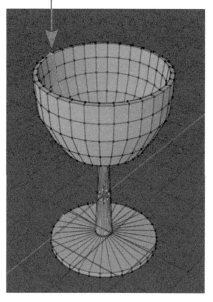
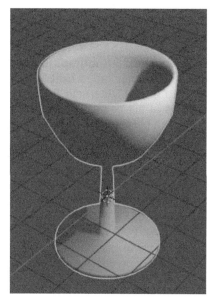

Edit Mode Showing the Spin
Profile

Rendered Viewport Shading

Rendered Viewport Shading with a Material color and the surface smoothed begins to show what can be achieved. Materials and Textures combined with Scene lighting effects produce fantastic results.

Figure 6.23

A Quick Spun Shape Example

6.15 Spin Duplication

The Spin Tool may be used to duplicate an Object around a circular path. The Spin is always about the Z Axis on the XY Plane, therefore, place the 3D View Editor in Top Orthographic View. The Spin uses the location of the 3D View Editor Cursor as the center of rotation.

In a new Scene in **Top Orthographic View** with the default **Cube Object** selected and located at the centre of the Scene, Tab to **Edit Mode**. Place the 3D View Editor Cursor off to one side (Shift + RMB click to place). Alternatively, with all Vertices selected move the Cube away from the Cursor which is at the center of the Scene. Activate the **Spin Tools** and click **LMB** on either of the crosses in the blue circles that are displayed. (Figure 6.24).

By default the Spin creates eight duplications of the Cube spaced in a circle around the 3D View Editor Cursor. The Vertices of the original Cube are selected (in Edit Mode). You may press the G Key and move the Vertices but if you Tab to Object Mode you will discover that although you appear have separate Cubes, they are in fact joined as one Object. Tab back to Edit Mode. Press the P Key and select Separate by Loose Parts. In Object Mode you may select individual Cubes and move them but note where the center of each Cube is located. With one Cube selected Tab to Edit Mode and reposition the individual Vertices of the Cube over the center point.

Top Orthographic View
Click LMB on a Blue Cross   Figure 6.24

Eight Duplication
Nine Steps in the Last Operator Panel

Last Operator Panel

Original Cube
Moved from the Center

6.16 The Screw Tool

Figure 6.25

Previous versions of Blender included a Screw Tool which spun vertices and at the same time generated duplications at right angles to the spin producing a Screw effect. This procedure is now accomplished by the Screw Modifier (see Modifiers Chapter 7). You may, however, use the Manipulation Widget of the Spin Tool to skew the Spin Duplication.

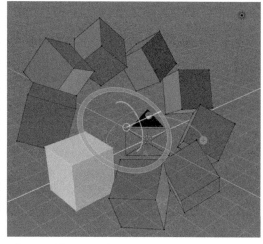

6.17 The Smooth Tool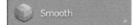

The effect of the **Smooth Tool** is to smooth or round transitions at the corners of a mesh. It is best demonstrated with an Object that has been Extruded and Subdivided.

In the **3D View Editor Header** select **Edge** and click **Subdivide**.

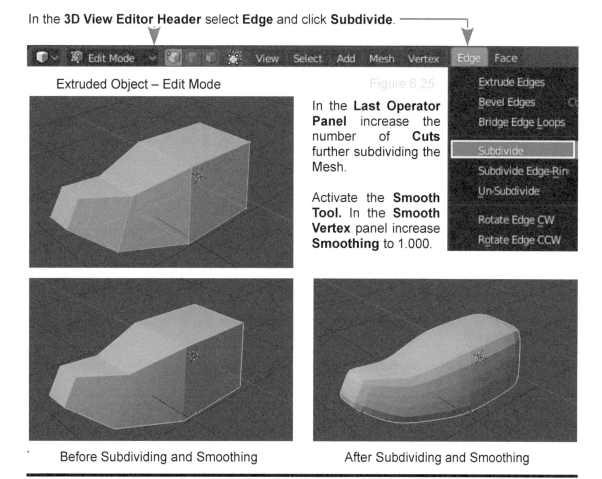

Extruded Object – Edit Mode

Figure 6.25

In the **Last Operator Panel** increase the number of **Cuts** further subdividing the Mesh.

Activate the **Smooth Tool.** In the **Smooth Vertex** panel increase **Smoothing** to 1.000.

Before Subdividing and Smoothing

After Subdividing and Smoothing

6.18 The Edge Slide Tool

Figure 6.26

Select an Edge on an Object. Activate the Edge Slide Tool. Click in the Editor and drag the Mouse. The Edge will be translated within the space occupied by the Object.

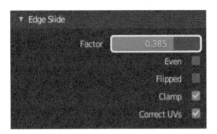

Adjust the position of the Edge in the Last Operator Panel, Factor Value

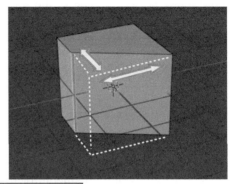

6.19 The Shrink Fatten Tool

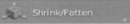

The **Shrink Fatten** Tool allows you to expand (fatten) or shrink a selection.

Figure 6.27

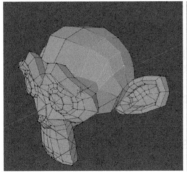

Normal Selection

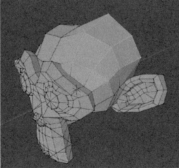

Fatten

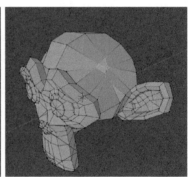

Shrink

6.20 The Rip Region Tool

Select an Edge (Edit Mode – Edge Selection Mode). Activate the **Rip Region Tool**.

With the Mouse Cursor in the Editor, click, hold and drag to translate the selected Edge.

Figure 6.28

7

Modifiers

Modifiers, in Blender, are pre assembled code that apply a process or algorithm to an Object, changing the Object's properties and affecting the way the Object behaves or how it is displayed. Modifiers may, therefore be considered as Editing Tools.

The Modifiers are designed to automate some of the otherwise tedious processes involved in shaping Objects and controlling their behaviour. Some Modifiers can only be used in conjunction with other processes.

The following chapters are offered as a guide. You will be shown how a Modifier is added to an Object and provided with examples showing the Modifier's basic features.

Modifiers are found in the **Properties Editor, Modifiers buttons**.

The Object Modifiers button is only displayed when an object to which a Modifier can be applied is selected in the 3D View Editor. Some objects can not have Modifiers applied.

> **Note:** If there are Objects in the 3D View Editor to which Modifiers may be applied (not necessarily selected), clicking the **Add Modifier** button and selecting a Modifier will apply the Modifier to the last Object that was selected. This occurs even though that Object is not selected at the time.

7.1 Modifiers in General

Figure 7.1

Properties Editor, Modifier button

Modifiers are found in the **Properties Editor, Modifiers button** 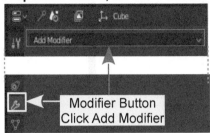 (Figure 7.1).

> **Note:** The Modifiers button is only displayed when an Object to which a Modifier can be applied is selected in the 3D View Editor. Some Objects cannot have Modifiers applied.

In this chapter **Modifiers in general** will be briefly described. Some Modifiers are complex and beyond a basic introduction and will be better understood having undergone further studies. New Modifiers are continually being added to the program and the selection menu changes accordingly. Click on the **Add Modifier** button to view the menu (Figure 7.2).

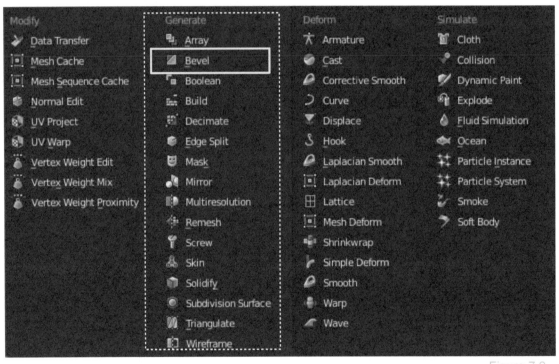

Figure 7.2

The menu is divided into four categories to aid selection.

To demonstrate the basic procedure for adding a **Modifier** the **Generate – Bevel Modifier** will be used. Begin by having the default Cube Object selected in the **3D View Editor**. In the **Properties Editor, Modifier buttons**, click the **Add Modifier** button to display the selection menu (Figure 7.2).

> This instruction has been purposely repeated

Under the **Generate** heading select **Bevel**.   Figure 7.3

The **Bevel Modifier panel** opens in the **Properties Editor** and the Cube object in the 3D View Editor displays with its edges bevelled (Figure 7.4).

Figure 7.4

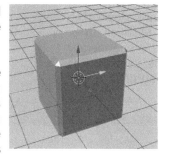

Values in the Modifier panel may be adjusted to affect the bevel.

Before adjusting values make note of the **Apply button** in the Modifier panel. At this point the Modifier has been added to the Cube (the selected Object) but it has **NOT been applied**. If you Tab to Edit Mode you will see the Cube displayed without bevels, as it was before adding the Modifier (Figure 7.8).

Change the Width value (Width: 30cm – 0.3m) and Segments value (Segments: 3) to increase the width of the bevel (Figure 7.6) and divide the bevel, rounding the edges (Figure 7.7)

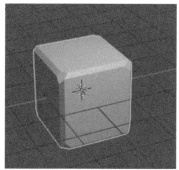

Bevel Added   Figure 7.5

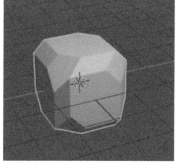

Width: 0.3710   Figure 7.6

Segments: 3   Figure 7.7

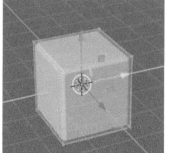

Figure 7.8

Having adjusted values in the Modifier panel, be in Object mode and click the **Apply** button.

Tab back to Edit mode to see that additional Vertices, Edges and Faces have been created (Figure 7.9).

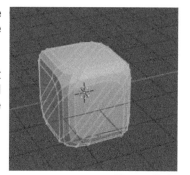

Figure 7.9

95

7.2 The Modifier Stack

Figure 7.10

In some cases it is appropriate to apply more than one Modifier to an Object. The modifiers are placed in a stack in order of priority. A Modifier at the top of the stack takes precedent over Modifiers lower down. The priority can be changed by moving a Modifier up or down in the stack. Although Modifiers are generally applied in Object mode, some may be used in Edit mode. Figure 7.10 shows an **Array Modifier** and a **Bevel Modifier**.

Click to move the Modifier up or down in the Stack

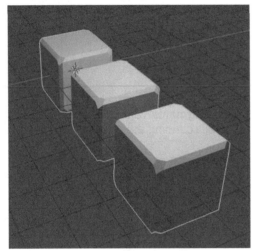

Figure 7.11

The Bevel Modifier has been added first followed by the Array.

The Array modifier has been moved to the top of the stack.

The Bevel Modifier bevels the edges of the Cube and the Array modifier duplicates the Cube in the 3D View Editor.

In the following pages you will be shown how some of the Modifiers are used. The full listing of Modifiers available are shown in the Modifier selection menu (Figure 7.2).

Where Modifiers are used in conjunction with other processes they will be described in the chapter which relates to that process. For example: Armatures (Chapter 20), Particle Systems (Chapter 22), Fluid Simulation and Smoke Simulation (Chapter 23).

7.3 The Modify Group

The Modifiers under the heading **Modify** do not directly affect the shape of an object but rather other data such as Vertex Groups and appearance. The demonstration of this group will be left in abeyance at this point since you will have to study some of Blender's more advanced features before being a position to understand what they do.

7.4 The Simulate Group

The **Simulate** group of modifiers, activate simulations. In most cases, these modifiers are automatically added to the Modifiers stack whenever a Particle System or Physics Simulation is enabled. Their role is to define the place in the modifier stack used as base data by the tool they represent. Generally, the attributes of these modifiers are accessible in separate panels.

This group of Modifiers is discussed in Chapter 23 Physics and Simulation.

7.5 Generate and Deform Modifiers

The Generate and Deform Modifier Groups are discussed in Chapters 8 and 9.

8

Editing with Generate Modifiers

Modifiers

Modifiers are described as automatic operations that affect an object in a non-destructive way allowing effects to be generated which would otherwise be tedious to do manually.

Modifiers work by changing how an Object is displayed and rendered in the Viewport. The underlying geometry of the mesh is maintained until the Modifier is Applied. This means that the underlying geometry of the mesh may be edited to suit, before permanently applying the Modifier.

You can add several modifiers to a single Object combining effects. This forms a Modifier Stack.

Modifiers are accessed in the **Properties Editor, Modifiers Button**.

Modifiers Button ———▶

The **Generate** group of Modifiers are construction tools that change the general appearance of a shape or add new geometry to an Object

8.1 Modifiers - Generate

Note: When an Editing Modifier is activated it immediately affects the Object that is selected in the 3D View Editor but initially it is not a permanent effect. The Modifier has to be Applied.

Clicking the **Modifiers button** in the **Properties Editor Header** displays the **Add Modifier** button. With an Object selected, clicking **Add Modifier** displays a selection menu listing the available Modifiers.   Figure 8.1

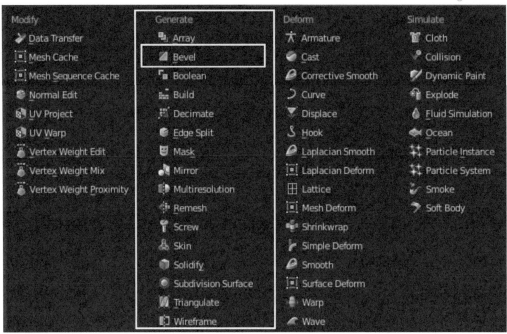

The Modifiers for Editing an Object, by and large, are listed in the **Generate** category. This group of Modifiers are building tools that change the general appearance of or automatically add new geometry to an Object.

Some Modifiers duplicate processes which are encountered in Editing Tools. For example; the Bevel Modifier performs the same action as the Bevel Tool.

To demonstrate the procedure for selecting and applying a Modifier to an Object the Bevel Modifier will be used.

In the 3D View Editor have the default Cube Object selected in **Object Mode**.

> **Note:** Modifiers can only be used with the selected Object in **Object Mode**

In the **Properties Editor** click the **Modifiers** button then in the selection menu under **Generate** click on **Bevel**.

Clicking on **Bevel** displays the **Bevel Modifier Tab** in the **Properties Editor** and at the same time you will see that a bevel has been created on the Edges of the Cube in the 3D View Editor. ⎯⎤

Figure 8.2

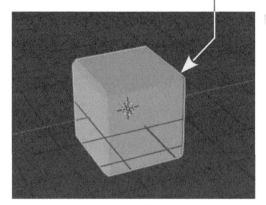

If you increase the Width value to 38cm and the Segments value to 2 the bevel in the 3D View Editor will be increased in size and rounded.

If you press the **Tab Key** and enter **Edit Mode** you will find that the Cube Object retains its original geometry with the default eight Vertices. You may alter the shape of the Object in Edit Mode and the bevel will still be displayed in Object Mode.

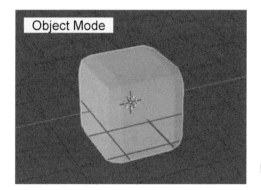

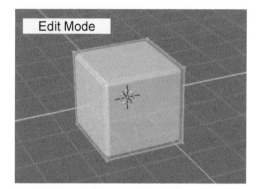

Figure 8.3

To permanently apply the bevel click the **Apply** button in the Modifier tab. In **Edit Mode** you will see that additional Vertices, Edges and Faces are created.

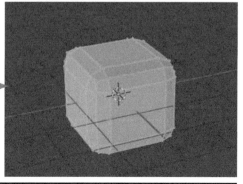

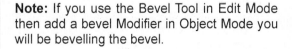

Note: If you use the Bevel Tool in Edit Mode then add a bevel Modifier in Object Mode you will be bevelling the bevel.

8.2 Array Modifier

Figure 8.4

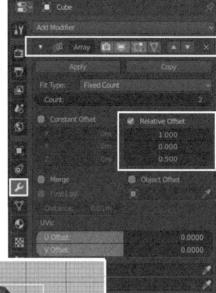

The **Array Modifier** creates copies of an Object, placing the copies in an array with each copy offset from the original. Figure 8.5 shows a **Monkey** Object in **Front Orthographic** view duplicated using an Array Modifier. To add the modifier select the Monkey in the 3DView Editor then in the **Properties Editor, Modifier buttons** click on **Add Modifier** and select **Array** from the menu.

To produce the arrangement shown in Figure 8.5 enter the **Relative Offset** values shown in Figure 8.4. The **Count: 3** value tells Blender to produce three Monkeys in the array (the original plus two).

Figure 8.5

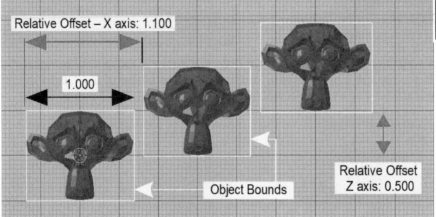

Relative Offset – X axis: 1.100

1.000

Object Bounds

Relative Offset Z axis: 0.500

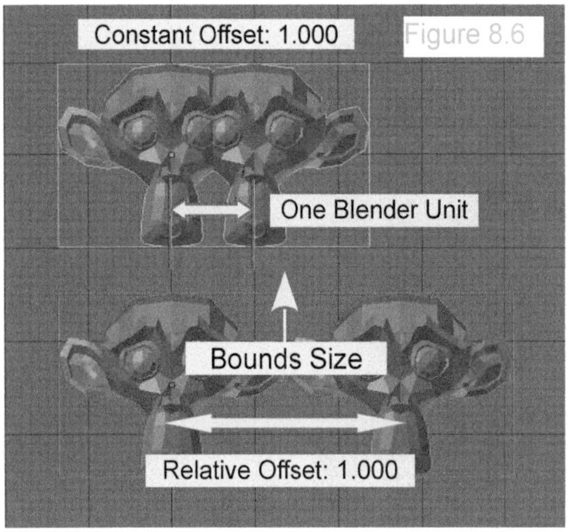

Constant Offset: 1.000

Figure 8.6

One Blender Unit

Bounds Size

Relative Offset: 1.000

The Offset is calculated using the Object's bounds. Every Object has a **Bounding Volume** which encapsulates its shape. You may view the Bound Volume by checking (tick) **Bound** in the **Properties Editor, Object buttons, Viewport Display Tab**. The Bound Volume may be viewed in a variety of ways. In the image above the **Bound Volume** is **Type: Box**.

The difference between relative and constant offset is shown in Figure 8.6. Constant offset one (1) means offset one Blender unit irrespective of the Object's size. The Monkey's center is offset one Blender unit which overlaps the display. Relative offset uses the **Bound** size (overall size) of the Object.

Object Offset: Uses the relative displacement of one Object to influence the displacement of another.

To use **Object Offset** position the **Control Object** in the 3D View Editor (you can Translate, Rotate and Scale after adding the modifier if you wish). By default **Relative Offset is** checked (ticked) in the **Properties Editor, Modifier panel**. Uncheck and check Object Offset. Click in the bar below Object Offset and select your **Offset Object** (the Sphere) from the menu that displays (Figures 8.7, 8.8).

Monkey Object in the 3D View Editor

UV Sphere positioned and scaled to affect the Array Offset

Properties Editor, Modifier button.

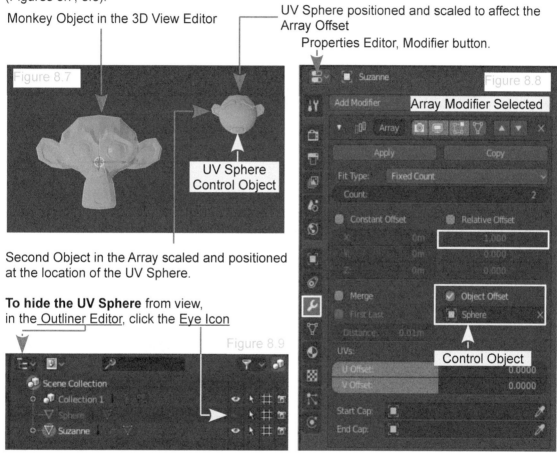

Second Object in the Array scaled and positioned at the location of the UV Sphere.

To hide the UV Sphere from view, in the Outliner Editor, click the Eye Icon

Increasing the Count Value in the Array Modifier panel duplicate Objects. As demonstrated, when using Object Offset, the duplicated Object is positioned and Scaled accordingly. Increasing the Count Value in the Modifier will replicate the original Object, repositioning and Scaling exponentially. Any modification made to the Control Object will be reflected in the duplications. (see Figure 8.10 over).

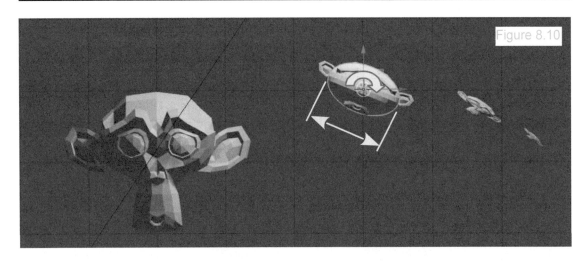

Figure 8.10 shows the Array with the Count Value in the Modifier increased to 4 and with the UV Sphere Control Object Scaled on its' X Axis and Rotated.

8.3 Boolean Modifier

Boolean Modifiers are used to create shapes by adding or subtracting one Object from another. In the Modifier panel there are three options: **Difference**, **Intersection**, and **Union.**

To demonstrate the different operations position a UV Sphere Object with the default Cube as shown in Figure 8.11. Scale the sphere down to fit inside the top face of the cube.

The arrangement of cube and sphere will be used for all three Boolean operations.

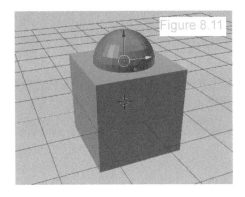

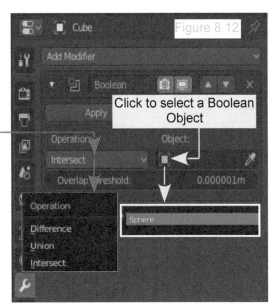

Click to select an Operation Type.

The procedure for a Boolean Operation is as follows; select the Cube. Add the Modifier. Select the Operation Type. Select the Boolean Object. Click Apply (Figure 8.12)

The part of the Cube intersected by the Boolean Object (the Sphere) is separated as a New Object

Figure 8.13

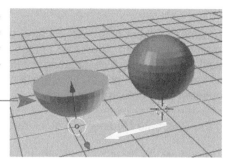

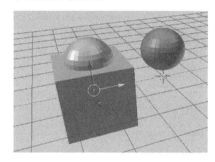

Union: The surfaces of the two Objects are joined.

Note: The lower part of the Sphere inside the Cube does not exist after Union.

Figure 8.14

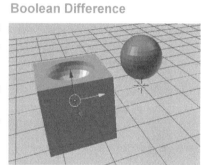

Difference: The part of the Boolean Object (the Sphere) overlapping the Cube forms a dish in the surface of the Cube.

8.4 Build Modifier

The **Build Modifier** creates the effect of something building linearly over a period of time. Any Object can have a build modifier, but to see a nice effect, a high vertex count is required.

In the 3D Editor, Scale the default Cube on the Y axis, Tab to **Edit mode** and Subdivide the surface (select Edge in the 3D View Editor Header and click Subdivide – Increase the Number of Cuts value in the Last Operator Panel).

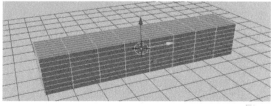

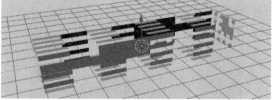

Figure 8.15

Tab back to **Object mode** and add a Build Modifier. **The Object disappears from view**. RMB click and hold on the blue Cursor in the **Timeline Editor** and Drag (Scrub) to see the elongated Cube being reconstructed (Figure 8.15). When you have the build where you want it apply the Modifier. Checking (ticking) **Reversed** in the Modifier panel reverses the build process.

8.5 Decimate Modifier

When a mesh Object has been created using complex modeling, you may well have an Object with many vertices and , therefore, a high Vertex Face count. Blender uses the Vertex/Face count to calculate such things as shading effects. This should not be confused with the Vertices and mesh Faces in the actual construction of a model. The Vertex/Face count is, in effect, triangulation within mesh Faces.

Using the Decimate Modifier is a quick and easy way of reducing the Vertex/Face count.

To demonstrate Decimation start with the default blender Scene, delete the Cube Object and add a **Monkey**. The Monkey is a reasonably complex shape consisting of numerous Faces and Vertices.

Figure 8.16

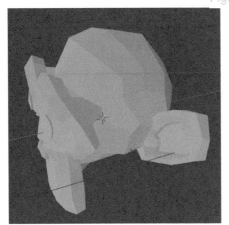 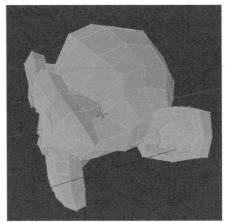

Object Mode   Edit Mode

In Object Mode the shape of the Monkey is representative of the Vertices you see in Edit Mode.

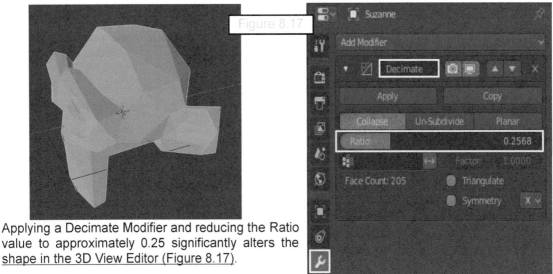

Applying a Decimate Modifier and reducing the Ratio value to approximately 0.25 significantly alters the shape in the 3D View Editor (Figure 8.17).

Subdividing the Mesh in Edit Mode with <u>Number of Cuts 10 creates many Vertices</u>.

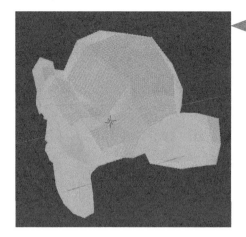

Figure 8.18

Last Operator Panel

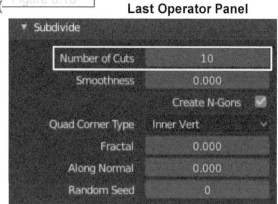

Reducing the Ratio Value to 0.255 in the Decimate Modifier when there are many Vertices reduces the Face Count for generating Shading Effects.

Reducing the Face Count in this case has no appreciable effect on the display in the **3D View Editor** or in a rendered image.

Figure 8.19

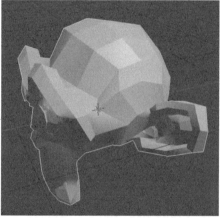

8.6 Edge Split Modifier

The **Edge Split Modifier** allows you to split an Object apart by selecting Vertices, Edges, or Faces.

In **Object Mode** with the Cube selected, add an **Edge Split Modifier** and click **Apply**

Make sure you click Apply   Figure 8.20

Tab to **Edit mode.** Select a **Face**. Use the **Movex Tool Widget** to pull the Face away from the Cube.

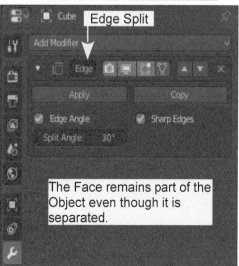

Edge Split

The Face remains part of the Object even though it is separated.

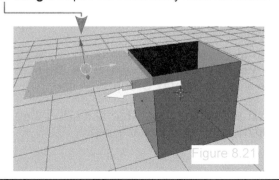

Figure 8.21

Selecting an <u>Edge</u> will open a face like the lid on a box (see **Rip Region Tool** Chapter 6 - 6.20)

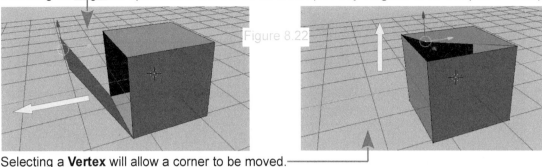

Figure 8.22

Selecting a **Vertex** will allow a corner to be moved.

8.7 Mask Modifier

The **Mask Modifier** allows you to limit what part of a mesh displays in the 3D View Editor or renders. The part of the mesh is defined by a **Vertex Group** (see Chapter 5 – 5.8). Add a **UV Sphere** to the Scene. In **Edit Mode** select Vertices (Figure 8.20). Leave the V ertices selected.

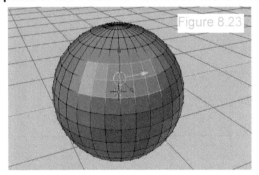

Figure 8.23

Click the Plus Sign

Vertex Group

Object Data

Figure 8.24

In the **Properties Editor, Object Data buttons, Vertex Groups Tab** (Figure 8.24) click the **Plus sign** to create a Vertex Group

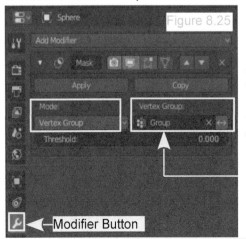

Figure 8.25

Modifier Button

Click the **Assign button** to assign the vertices to the Group. **Note:** The vertex group is named **Group**.

Switch to the **Modifiers buttons** (Figure 8.25) click **Add Modifier** and select the **Mask Modifier**. The **Mode** should be **Vertex Group**.

Click in the **Vertex Group bar** and select the Vertex Group named **Group** from the menu.

In the **3D View Editor** in **Object Mode** only the part of the Cube defined by the Vertex Group is displayed (Figure 8.26).

In the bottom right hand corner of the Mask Modifier panel click the **double headed arrow** button and the complete Object less the area defined by the Vertex Group is displayed (Figure 8.27).

By using the modifier, visibility can be controlled without removing any Vertices from the UV Sphere.

Figure 8.26

Figure 8.27

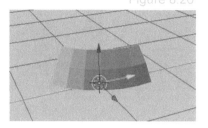

3D Window – Object Mode

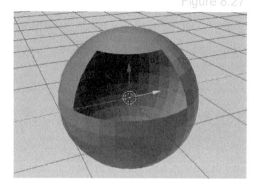

8.8 Mirror Modifier

The **Mirror Modifier** allows the construction or deformation of a mesh on one side of a centre point to be duplicated (mirrored) on the opposite side.

Add a **UV Sphere** to the Scene in **Top Orthographic View**. Tab to Edit Mode, deselect the Vertices (Alt + A Key) then B key (Box select) and drag a rectangle to select one half of the Sphere's Vertices (Figure 8.28, 8.29). Press **X Key** to delete the selected Vertices (Figure 8.30).

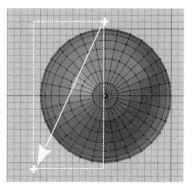

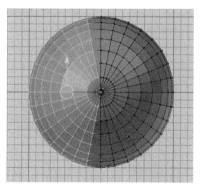

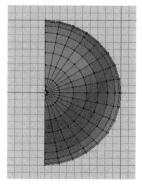

Figure 8.28

Figure 8.29

Figure 8.30

Tip: Don't forget to turn **Show Whole Scene Transparent** on   in the 3D View Editor Header before dragging the rectangle.

In **Object Mode** (with the half sphere selected), in the **Properties Editor, Modifier buttons** add a **Mirror Modifier**. The deleted half of the UV Sphere will be reinstated in the 3D View Editor (Figure 8.29).

In **Edit Mode** you will see that vertices exist only on one side of the sphere (Figure 8.32).

Single vertex translated with Proportional Editing ON.

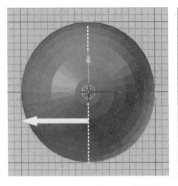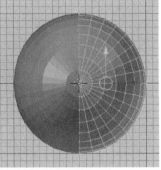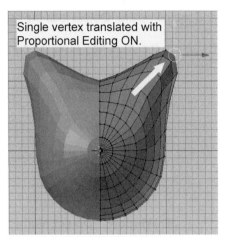

Figure 8.31   Figure 8.32   Figure 8.33

Select and Translate a single Vertex and you see that the mesh on the opposite side is duplicated (mirrored) (Figure 8.33).

When the Modifier is applied (click **Apply** in the Modifier Panel) Vertices are created on the mirrored side (Figure 8.34).

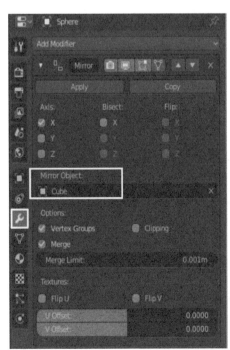

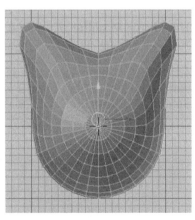

Note: By default the mirror takes place either side of the X Axis. You may elect to mirror on the Y or Z Axis.

Figure 8.34

Figure 8.35

In the center of the Mirror Modifier panel you will see **Mirror Object**. Placing an object in the Scene and entering this Object in the Mirror Object Bar causes the mirror to be about the centerline of the new Object instead of the centerline of the original object (Figure 8.35, 8.36, 8.37).

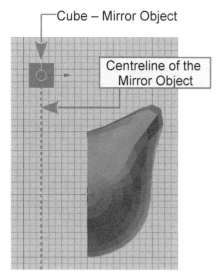

Cube – Mirror Object

Centreline of the Mirror Object

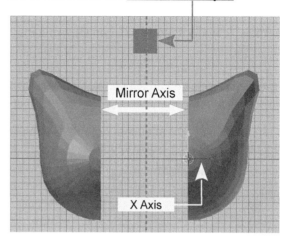

The shape is mirrored along the X Axis about the centerline of the Cube Mirror Object.

Mirror Axis

X Axis

Figure 8.36

Figure 8.37

8.9 Multiresolution Modifier

The **Multiresolution Modifier** is designed to be used with the **Sculpt Tool** (Chapter 11 –11.4, 11.5).

8.10 Remesh Modifier

The **Remesh Modifier** allows you to recalculate how a Mesh Surface is constructed. Some basic mesh shapes do not provide sufficient Vertices, Edges and Faces to allow detailed modeling.

To demonstrate, use a Cylinder Object to cut a hole through the default Cube Object by applying a **Boolean Difference Modifier**.

Figure 8.38

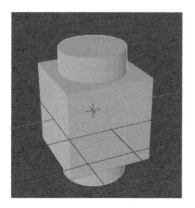

Cylinder scale down and extended on the Z Axis.

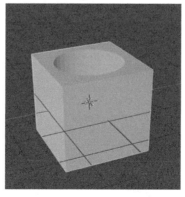

The Boolean Difference Modifier Applied.

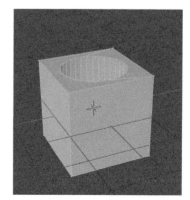

Edit Mode showing the Mesh construction

When the Boolean Modifier is applied you see a minimal mesh construction which limits any detailed modeling. To increase the Vertex count apply a **Remesh Modifier.**

Remember: To apply a **Modifier** to an **Object** it must be in **Object Mode.**

Figure 8.39

With the Cube selected in Object Mode add a Remesh Modifier.

Note: In the Modifier Panel the default **Octree Depth** value is **4** and the **Scale** is **0.900**.

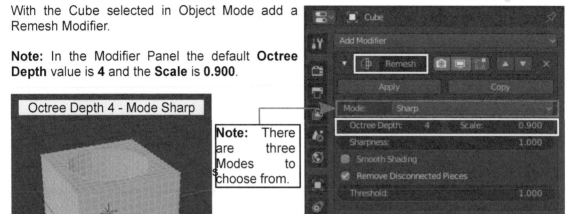

Octree Depth 4 - Mode Sharp

Note: There are three Modes to choose from.

Figure 8.40

With the default values, when the Modifier has been Applied (click the Apply button) the Mesh surface of the Cube in Edit Mode shows a significant increase in the number of Vertices, Edges and Faces (Figure 8.40).

When the Modifier is Applied the Modifier Panel is cancelled. To adjust the Octree and Scale values press **Ctrl + Z Key** to undo and step back through the operations until the panel is reinstated. Increasing the Octree Depth significantly increases the number of Vertices on the Mesh. Even increasing from 4 to 5 has a dramatic effect.

Be Warned: Increasing to 6 - 7 - 8 will exponentially increase the Vertex Count and seriously affect computer speed.

Figure 8.41

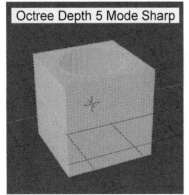

Octree Depth 5 Mode Sharp

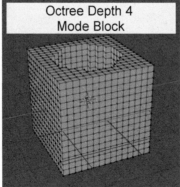

Octree Depth 4
Mode Block

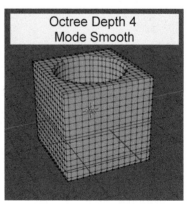

Octree Depth 4
Mode Smooth

8.11 Screw Modifier

The **Screw Modifier** generates a spiral shape by revolving a profile around an Axis. To demonstrate, construct a coil spring from the default Cube object.

All operations are conducted in the default **3D View Editor, User Perspective view**. Follow the steps below.

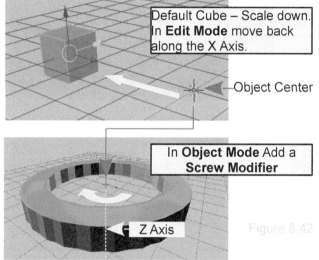

Default Cube – Scale down. In **Edit Mode** move back along the X Axis.

Object Center

In **Object Mode** Add a **Screw Modifier**

Z Axis

Figure 8.42

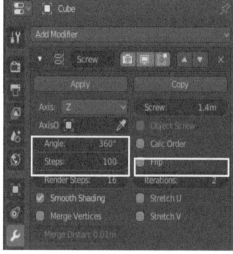

Screw Modifier Panel

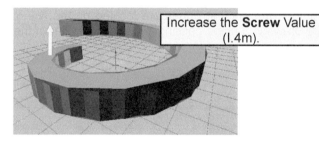

Increase the **Screw** Value (I.4m).

By default the Screw Modifier is set to revolve about the Z Axis. You may change this to either the X or Y Axis.

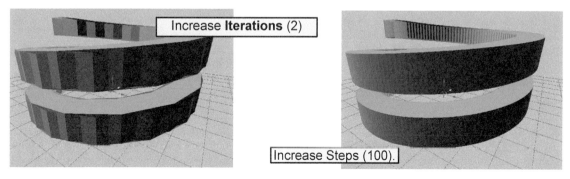

Increase **Iterations** (2)

Increase Steps (100).

8.12 Skin Modifier

The **Skin Modifier** allows you to create a three dimensional shape from a basic stick arrangement consisting of a minimal number of Vertices. To demonstrate how this is achieved have a Plane Object in the 3D View Editor. The Plane is a simple Object with four Vertices, four Edges and one Face.

Rotate the Plane about the Z Axis. This simply moves the Edges of the Plane away from the background grid lines to improve visibility when in Edit Mode.

Figure 8.43

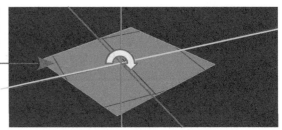

Background Grid Line

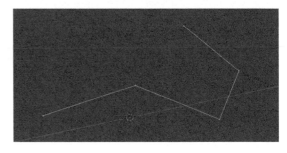

In **Edit Mode** delete one Vertex leaving two Edges (the basic stick arrangement).

Select one Vertex and extrude twice. Remember; the original Edges are located on the X – Y Axis of the Scene. The two new Edges will be drawn in a plane passing through the center of the Scene normal to the computer Screen.

Figure 8.44

In Object Mode, with the stick figure selected, add a Skin Modifier and click Apply to produce the solid shown in Figure 8.45.

Figure 8.45

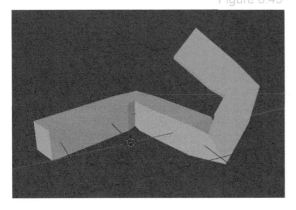

114

In essence the procedure entails Extruding Vertices from a simple Object to form a rudimentary stick shape in Edit Mode. The Skin Modifier is then added to the shape in Object Mode. The Modifier creates a cage around the stick which converts to a Mesh Object when the Modifier is applied.

At this point, note the distinction between **Adding the Modifier** and **Applying the Modifier**. You add the Modifier in the Properties Editor, Modifier buttons by clicking the Add Modifier button and selecting from the menu. The Modifier panel displays where you adjust values to affect the selected Object in the 3D View Editor. When adjustments are complete you Apply the Modifier by clicking the Apply button in the Modifier panel.

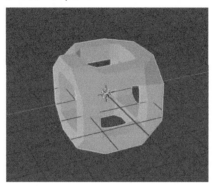

Figure 8.46

Skin Modifier Applied to the default Cube

8.13 Solidify Modifier

Figure 8.47

The **Solidify Modifier** provides a tool for creating solid Objects from thin-walled Objects. To demonstrate this, begin with a simple Plane Object selected in the 3D View Editor. Add a **Solidify Modifier** in the **Properties Editor.**

Look closely at the plane and you will observe that it now has a thickness (Figure 8.48).

In the Modifier panel you will see **Thickness** 1cm and **Offset** -1.0000.

Thickness is the thickness of the surface. Increasing this to 10 cm will give a better view (Figure 8.49).

The Offset value range is -1.0000 to +1.000 which places the Thickness below or above the mid-plane. Offset 0.0000 has the Thickness straddling the mid-plane.

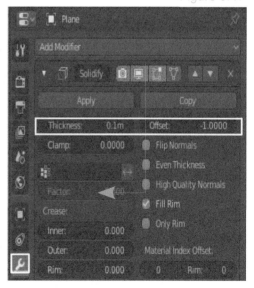

Tab to **Edit mode** and see that the original vertices of the plane object remain on the mid-plane of the Scene.

Figure 8.48

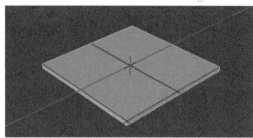
Figure 8.49

For a practical demonstration of how to use the **Solidify Modifier**, create a new Scene with a **Cylinder** object instead of the default Cube. Delete the upper face of the Cylinder. You now have a thin-walled container (Figure 8.50). In Object mode add a Solidify Modifier and increase the thickness value to 10 cm (0.1m). The container will have wall thickness (Figure 8.51).

With Offset -1.0000 the wall thickness is created inside the original surface of the Cylinder. Offset +1.0000 creates the thickness outside the original surface.

In Edit Mode you see the original Vertices, Edges and Faces are unchanged until you click Apply in the Modifier Panel with the Cylinder in the 3D View Editor in Object Mode

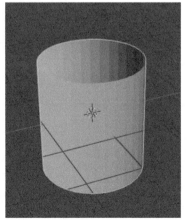
Figure8.50

Figure 8.51

Original Cylinder – Top Face Deleted

Cylinder – Solidify Modifier Added

8.14 Subdivision Surface Modifier

The Subdivision Surface Modifier subdivides the surface of an Object adding Vertices, Edges and Faces giving the surface of the Object a smoother and rounded appearance. The additions also allow more detail to be modeled.

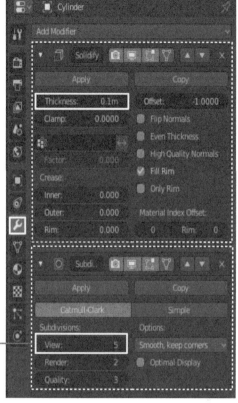

Figure 8.52

To demonstrate, use the container created in the previous exercise (Figure 8.51) and with the Solidify Modifier in place (**NOT Applied**) add a Subdivision Surface (Subserf) Modifier.

In the Subserf Modifier panel increase the Subdivisions – View value to: 5 (Figure 8.53).

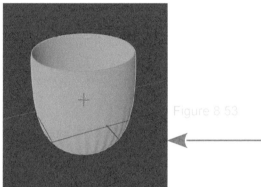

Figure 8.53

Note: At this point neither the Solidify Modifier or the Subserf Modifier have been applied. The Apply button, in both cases, has **NOT** been activated. The Modifiers display their effects in the 3D View Editor but placing the Cylinder Object in Edit Mode shows that the original Vertices, Edges and Faces remain.

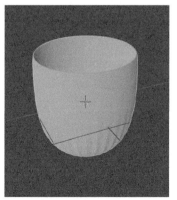

Figure 8.54

To demonstrate the previous statement a little cheating has taken place. A new Cylinder has been added to the Scene superimposed over the original.

The new Cylinder has been placed in **Edit Face Select Mode** then, **Overlays** in the 3D View Editor Header have been activated and **Hidden Wire** checked.

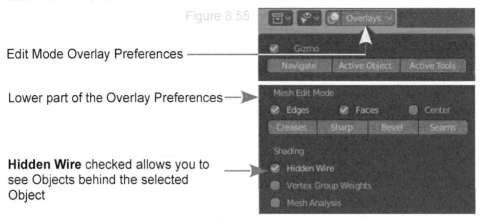

Figure 8.55

Edit Mode Overlay Preferences —————

Lower part of the Overlay Preferences ——▶

Hidden Wire checked allows you to see Objects behind the selected Object ——▶

Another simple example using the Subserf Modifier forms something like a whale's tooth (Figure 8.56).

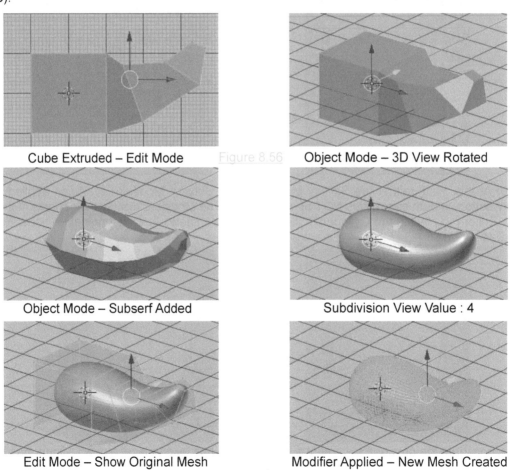

Cube Extruded – Edit Mode   Figure 8.56   Object Mode – 3D View Rotated

Object Mode – Subserf Added   Subdivision View Value : 4

Edit Mode – Show Original Mesh   Modifier Applied – New Mesh Created

8.15 Triangulation Modifier

A **Triangulation Modifier** is added when a mesh model has been subdivided and Vertices added producing fine detail in a model. The Modifier ensures that triangulation will remain consistent when exporting or rendering.

If the model is animated using armatures the modifier should be placed in the modifier stack before (above) the armature modifier.

The Triangulation Modifier is also used when baking prior to exporting and importing.

8.16 Wireframe Modifier

The **Wireframe Modifier** converts a solid display as seen in **Solid Viewport Shading** to **Stick** or **Wireframe** display.

With the modifier added to a **Cube** object, instead of a solid Cube, you see a frame where the edges of the Cube have thickness (Figure 8.57).

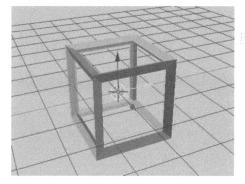
Figure 8.57

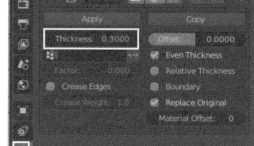

The Whale's Tooth from the previous example with a Wireframe Modifier added (Figure 8.58).

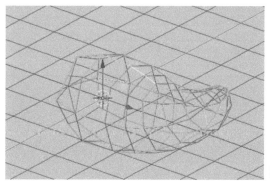
Figure 8.58

9

Editing with Deform Modifiers

The Deform group of Modifiers change the shape of an Object without adding new geometry, and are available for meshes, texts, curves, surfaces and/or lattices.

9.1 Modifiers for Editing - Deform

Figure 9.1

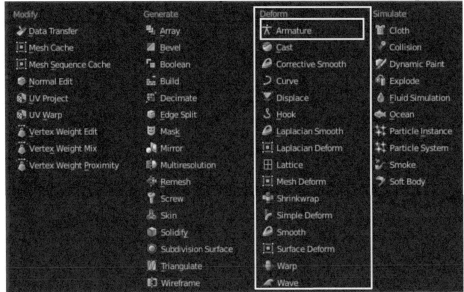

The Deform group of Modifiers generally provides tools for modifying or deforming a mesh Object as a whole. Some of these modifiers require a knowledge of other Blender features and will, therefore, be described in conjunction with the feature as it is encountered.

9.2 Armature Modifier

Armatures in Blender are Objects used for manipulating and posing other Objects such as models of characters. Posing is the technique used when animating figures. The **Armature Modifier** is discussed in conjunction with Armatures and Character Rigging in Chapter 20
.

9.3 Cast Modifier

Figure 9.2

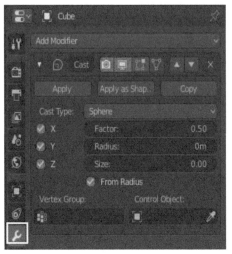

The **Cast Modifier** is used to deform a primitive Object such as the Cube Object in the default Scene.

Select the Cube Object. In **Edit Mode,** Subdivide (number of cuts 4) (Chapter 5 – 5.4) then **Tab** back to **Object mode**.

In the **Properties Editor, Modifier button** add a **Cast Modifier** (Figure 9.2). By changing the **Cast Type**, altering the **Factor**, **Radius** and **Size** values and or limiting the effects to the X,Y and Z axis the deformation of the cube may be controlled.

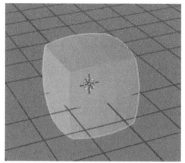
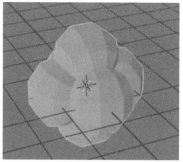
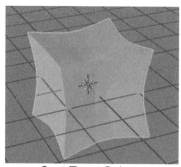

Default Cube
Subdivided Four Times
Cast Modifier Added
Type Sphere Factor: 0.50

Cast Type: Sphere
Factor: 2.000

Cast Type: Sphere
Factor: -2.000

Figure 9.3

The deformation may also be controlled by introducing a **Control object** (Figure 9.4).

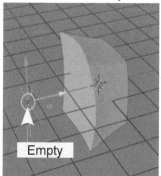
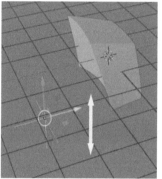

Figure 9.4

With the default Cube subdivided, deselect the Cube and place an **Empty Object** in the Scene. Add a **Cast Modifier** to the **Cube** and then click on the **Control Object** (cube icon) and select **Empty** from the menu to enter the **Empty** as the **Control Object**.

Move the Empty in the Scene to see the Cube being deformed.

Experiment with the Cast Type, the X,Y and Z axis settings and Factor, Radius and Size values. Keep in mind that the Empty Object may be animated to move in the Scene thus animating the deformation of the Cube.

9.4 Corrective Smooth Modifier

The **Corrective Smooth Modifier** is primarily designed to smooth incorrect mesh deformation which can occur when Armatures are used to deform a mesh. See Chapter 20.

9.5 Curve Modifier

The **Curve Modifier** uses the shape of a Curve to deform a mesh. Figure 9.5 shows the default Blender Scene with the Cube Scaled down, then Scaled along the Y Axis (S Key + Y Key) and Subdivided in Edit Mode with Number of Cuts = 10.

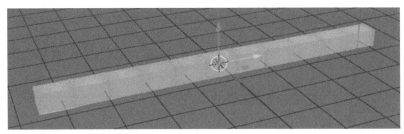

Figure 9.5

In **Object Mode** the elongated Cube is deselected and a **Bezier Curve** added (Chapter 10 – 10.2). The **Curve** is rotated and scaled up to match the length of the Cube (Figure 9.6).

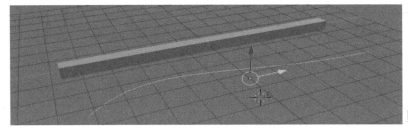

Figure 9.6

Deselect the Curve and **select the Cube**. Be in **Object Mode** and add a **Curve Modifier.** Enter **BezierCurve** as the name in the **Object** panel (Figure 9.7).

Figure 9.7

Click and select **Bezier Curve** in the menu. ──────

Manipulate the Curve in Edit Mode. Change its shape and position to affect the shape of the Cube (Figure 9.8).

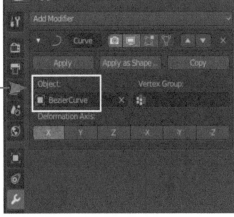

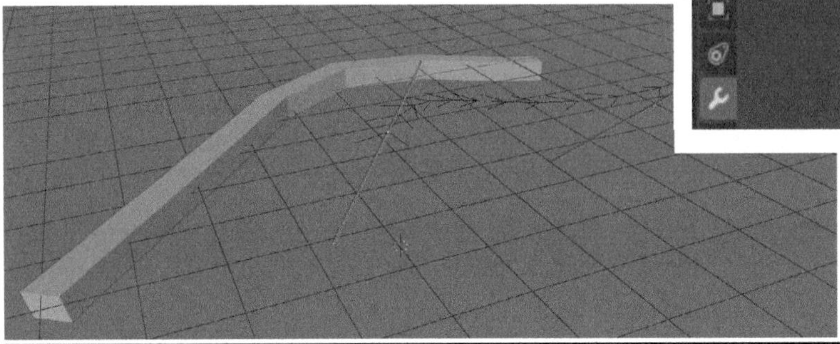

Note: in the Curve Modifier panel the **Deformation Axis** is the **X Axis**.

Figure 9.8

9.6 Displace Modifier

The **Displace Modifier** displaces the Vertices of a Mesh Object. If Vertices are assigned to a **Vertex Group** and the group is entered in the Modifier, only the Vertices belonging to the group will be affected. Incorporating a Texture displaces Vertices according to the dark and light values in the Texture.

Start with the default Blender Scene and replace the **Cube** with a **Plane**. Have the Plane selected in **Edit Mode** and subdivide sixteen times. Select a group of Vertices and create a **Vertex Group** in the Properties Editor, Object Data buttons, see Chapter 5 - 5.8 (Figure 9.9, 9.10) .

Figure 9.9

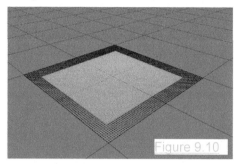

Figure 9.10

Tab back to **Object Mode.** Add a Material (default gray is OK) and in the Texture Buttons add a Noise Texture (Textures are discussed in Chapter 16 but for now, click the Texture button, click **New** and where you see **Type: Image or Movie**, click the bar and select **Noise** in the menu that displays. **Note** the Texture Name in this example is: Texture) (Figure 9.11).

Figure 9.11

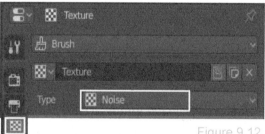

In the Properties Editor, with the Plane selected , go to the Modifier buttons and add a **Displace Modifier** (Figure 9.12).

In the Displace Modifier panel enter the Texture and the Vertex Group to <u>displace the Vertices</u> (Figure 9.13).

Figure 9.12

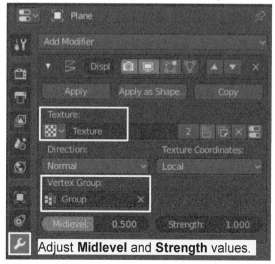

Adjust **Midlevel** and **Strength** values.

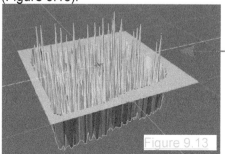

Figure 9.13

9.7 Hook Modifier

The **Hook Modifier** allows you to manipulate or animate selected vertices of a mesh while in Object mode. Vertices are assigned (hooked) to an **Empty** Object which is moved in Object Mode pulling the selected vertices with it. This can be used for a static mesh deformation or the movement can be animated.

Start with the default Scene with the Cube Object selected. Tab to **Edit mode** and select one Vertex (corner) only.

Press **Ctrl + H key** and select **Hook to New Object**. An **Empty Object** is added to the Scene. In the **Properties Editor, Modifiers button**, you will see that a **Hook Modifier** has been added named **Hook-Empty** (Figure 9.14).

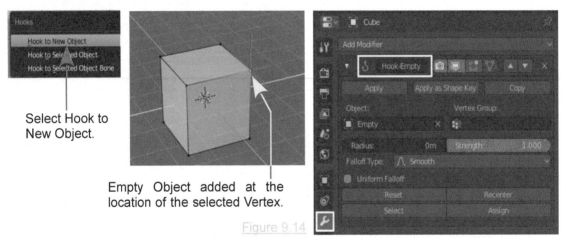

Select Hook to New Object.

Empty Object added at the location of the selected Vertex.

Figure 9.14

Select and move the **Empty** in **Object Mode** to move the Vertex (Figure 9.15, 9.16).

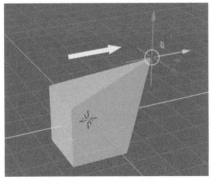

In Edit Mode you will see the Empty in the new location but the selected Vertex remains in its original position.

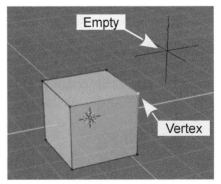

Object Mode   Figure 9.15

Edit Mode   Figure 9.16

In Object mode click **Apply** in the Modifier panel and the Cube deformation is made permanent. You may delete the Empty object.

With the default **Cube object** in the default Scene, **Tab** to **Edit Mode** and select one Vertex only. In the **Properties Editor, Object data buttons, Vertex Groups Tab** click on the plus sign to add a Vertex Group and click **Assign.** This creates a Vertex Group consisting of the one Vertex.

In **Object Mode** deselect the Cube and add an **Empty Object**. Position the **Empty** away from the Cube (Figure 9.16).

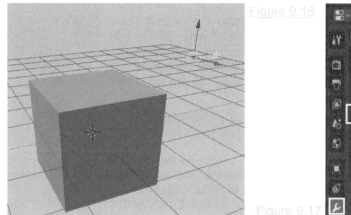

Figure 9.16

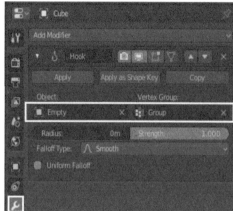

Figure 9.17

Deselect the Empty and select the Cube. In the **Properties Editor, Modifiers buttons** add a **Hook Modifier**. In the **Hook Modifier** panel click on the **Vertex Group panel** and select **Group**. This is assigning the Vertex Group consisting of one single Vertex to the Modifier. Click on the **Object panel** and select **Empty** to assign the Empty Object to the Modifier (Figure 9.17).

By selecting the **Empty** Object in the 3D View Editor and moving it about, the single Cube's Vertex in the Vertex Group will follow the movement (Figure 9.18).

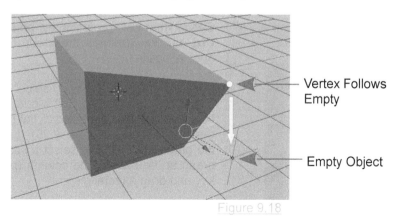

Vertex Follows Empty

Empty Object

Figure 9.18

9.8 Laplacian Deform Modifier

The **Laplacian Deform Modifier** allows you to pose a mesh while maintaining the geometry of the surface. Posing is accomplished by assigning **Hooks** to **Vertex Groups**. You must also assign **Anchor Vertex Groups. Note:** You must define an **Anchors Vertex Group.** Without a vertex group the modifier does nothing.

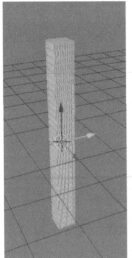

Hook Empty Assigned

To demonstrate the process Scale the default Cube down in size and elongate on the Z Axis. Tab to Edit Mode and Subdivide (eleven times) to create plenty of Vertices (Figure 9.22). Deselect the Vertices (press Alt bb+ A Key). Place the 3D View Editor in Front Orthographic View.

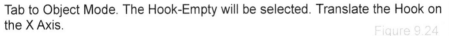

Activate Show Whole Scene Transparent in the Header. Select a group of Vertices at the top. Press **Ctrl + H key** and select **Hook to New Object** in the menu that displays. This assigns a Hook-Empty to the group of Vertices (Figure 9.23).

Figure 9.22   Figure 9.23

Tab to Object Mode. The Hook-Empty will be selected. Translate the Hook on the X Axis.

Figure 9.24

You see the group of Vertices moved with the connecting Edges and Faces stretched between the group and the main body of the Object (Figure 9 .24). This may be what you require but on the other hand you may wish for a more elegant result.

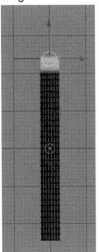
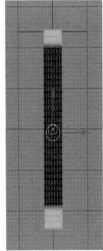

Cancel the last operation by pressing **Ctrl + Z key** (returns the group to its original position).

Deselect the Hook and select the column (Cube). Tab to Edit Mode. The group of Vertices connected to the Hook remains selected (Figure 9.25). Leave the group selected and select a second group at the base of the column (press key and drag a rectangle).

Figure 9.25

With both groups selected go to the Properties Editor, Data buttons, Vertex Group Tab. Click the Plus sign to create a Vertex Group and Assign the selected vertices to the Group.

Note: The Vertex Group is named **Group**.

Tab back to Object Mode and add a **Laplacian Deform Modifier.**

Note: A Hook Modifier was added when you assigned the Hook-Empty.

Figure 9.26

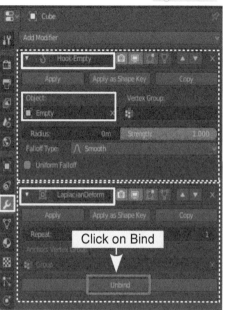

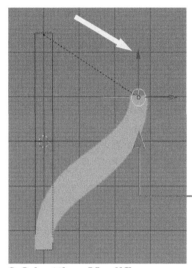

In the Modifier panel enter **Group** in the **Anchor Vertex Group panel** then click on **Bind** (Figure 9.26).

Figure 9.27

Deselect the column and select the Hook-Empty. Grab the Hook and translate to see the top group of vertices moved with the connecting mesh following in a smooth transition.

Click on Bind

9.9 Lattice Modifier

The **Lattice Modifier** is used to deform a mesh Object or to control the movement of Particles (Chapter 22). By using the Modifier, it is easy to shape a mesh Object that has many Vertices. A Lattice is a non-renderable grid of Vertices, therefore, it does not render in the Scene. You can use the same Lattice to deform several Objects by giving each Object a Modifier pointing to the Lattice.

To demonstrate deforming a **UV Sphere** Object with a **Lattice Modifier,** delete the default Cube, add a UV Sphere to the Scene. **With the UV Sphere selected** add a **Lattice** (Shift + A key – Add - Lattice).

Figure 9.28
Figure 9.29

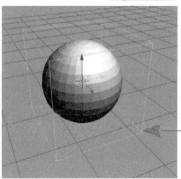
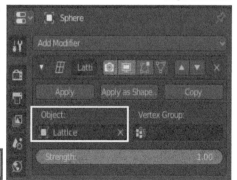

Change to **Wireframe Display Mode**. You will see the Lattice mesh as a Cube inside the Sphere. **Scale the Lattice up** (S Key + drag the mouse). The Lattice is entered as a simple mesh cube (Figure 9.28).

Select the **UV Sphere** and add a **Lattice Modifier** . Enter **Lattice** under **Object** (Figure 9.29).

Select the Lattice, go to the **Object Data buttons** in the **Properties Editor**, and alter the *u*, *v*, and *w* values in the Lattice Tab to subdivide the Lattice mesh (Figure 9.30).

In **Edit Mode**, select a single lattice Vertex and move it to deform the UV Sphere mesh (Figure 9.31).

Figure 9.30

You may select multiple vertices on the Lattice then scale, translate or rotate to deform the sphere.

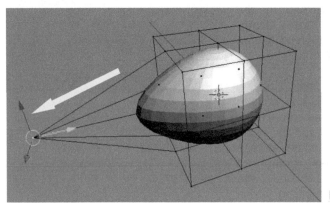

Figure 9.31

9.11 Mesh Deform Modifier

The **Mesh Deform Modifier** deforms a mesh with **Cage Mesh**. This is similar to a Lattice Modifier but instead of being restricted to the regular grid layout of a lattice, the cage can be modeled to fit around the mesh Object being deformed. The Cage Mesh must form a closed cage around the part of the mesh to be deformed, and only vertices within the cage will be deformed. Typically the cage will have far fewer Vertices than the mesh being deformed.

After modeling a UV Sphere Object as shown in Figure 9.32, surround it with a simple cage mesh by scaling a Cube to fit around the elongated Sphere, then select Vertices in **Edit mode** and extrude (Figure 9.32).

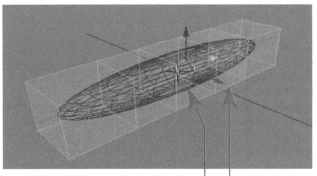

UV Sphere Scaled on the Y Axis
Cube Extruded to form a Cage

Figure 9.32

Add a **Mesh Deform Modifier** to the scaled UV Sphere. Enter the name of the cage mesh (Cube) and press **Bind** to link the two meshes. The Bind operation may take several seconds to calculate depending on the complexity of your model. Wait until Bind changes to Unbind before selecting Vertices on the cage (Figure 9.33). By Moving, Scaling and Rotating the selected Vertices, the Sphere mesh will be deformed . The proximity of the cage to the original Object has an influence on how the deformation reacts.

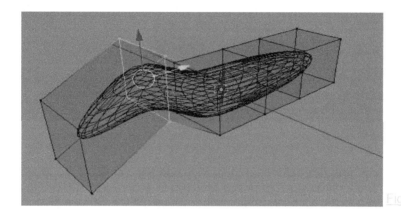

Figure 9.33

Note: The cage mesh will render in the scene; Apply the Modifier and delete the Cage.

9.12 Shrinkwrap Modifier

Shrinkwrap Modifier added to the UV Sphere

The **Shrinkwrap Modifier** takes a mesh and shrinks it down, wrapping the mesh around another object. The deformed mesh can then be offset to produce shapes in between the original shape and the deformed shape.

Delete the Cube in the default Blender Scene and add a **UV Sphere** and a **Cone** mesh Object. The Cone should be located inside the UV Sphere, which is easy to see when both objects are viewed in **Wireframe Mode** (Chapter 5 – 5.2) (Figure 9.34). Add a **Shrinkwrap Modifier** to the UV sphere, and enter **Cone** in the **Target panel** (Figure 9.35). Change the **Offset value**; notice how the shape changes when you increase the value (Figure 9.36 over).

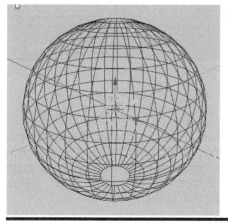

Figure 9.34

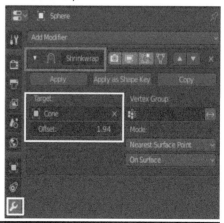

Figure 9.35

131

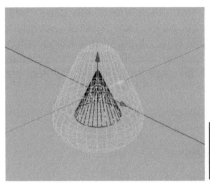

Figure 9.36

**Altering the Offset value in the Modifier panel
changes the size of the modified UV Sphere.**

9.13 Simple Deform Modifier

The **Simple Deform Modifier** deforms a mesh by changing values in the Modifier and having a second Object with an influence. To see this Modifier in action, add a UV Sphere in the default Scene with a scaled down Cube located in the center of the Sphere (Figure 9.37). Activate **Wireframe Display Mode** and add the Simple Deform modifier to the UV Sphere with Cube entered as the origin (Figure 9.38, 9.39). Drag the Limits slider to see the change to the Sphere (Figure 9.40). Select the Cube with the RMB and manipulate it on an axis to deform the Sphere (Figure 9.41).

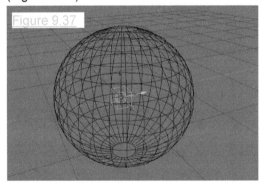

Figure 9.37

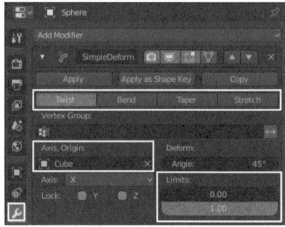

Figure 9.38

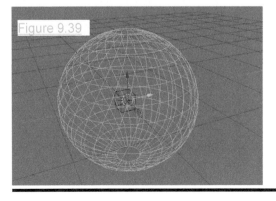

Figure 9.39

Note the skew in the mesh when the Modifier is added to the UV Sphere. Adjust the **Deform: Angle** slider and the **Limits** sliders to change the skew. Experiment with the Twist, Bend, Taper and Stretch buttons.

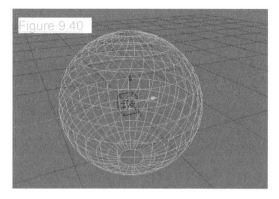

Figure 9.40

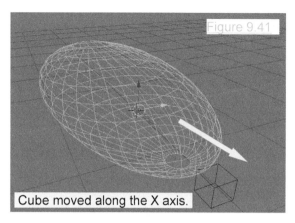

Figure 9.41

Cube moved along the X axis.

9.14 Smooth Modifier

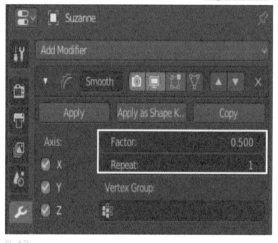

Figure 9.42

The **Smooth Modifier** smooths the mesh Object by softening the angles between adjacent Faces; this shrinks the size of the original Object at the same time. **Note:** The smoothing effect is only applied to how the Objects surfaces are drawn in the 3D View Editor. In smoothing, no additional Vertices, Edges or Faces are added to the Object. To use the Smooth Modifier select an Object in the 3D View Editor then Add the Modifier in the **Properties Editor, Modifier buttons.**

Adjust the **Factor slider** to increase or decrease smoothing. The **Repeat value** multiplies the Factor value. The **X, Y** and **Z** axis confine the smoothing to a particular axis.

Figure 9.43

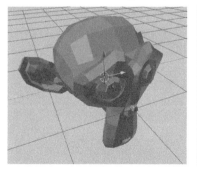

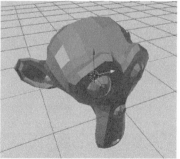

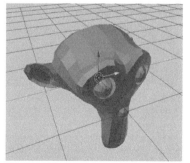

Factor: 0.500 – Repeat: 1   Repeat: 5   Repeat: 10

In applying the **Factor** and **Repeat** values the logic of the operation is to first set a value (the Factor) then perform the calculation (repeat) several times to achieve the desired smoothing. When the desired smoothing is achieved Apply the Modifier.

Note: An Object should have a reasonable number of Faces before the Modifier is effective. For example; the Monkey Object with its default Faces will shrink in size as **Repeats** are applied. When subdivided three or four times it will show a completely different effect.

Figure 9.44

Repeat: 1 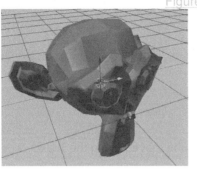 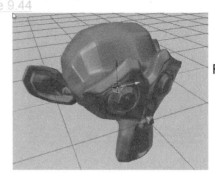 Repeat: 10

9.15 Smooth Corrective Modifier

Figure 9.45

The Smooth Corrective Modifier is used to Smooth and Correct imperfections in a model which occur when the surface is deformed. Figure 9.45 shows a model of an arm which has been posed and in doing so creates an imperfection.

Imperfection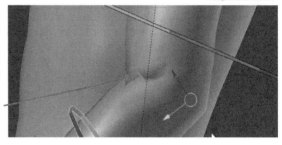

9.16 Smooth Laplacian Modifier

The Laplacian Smooth Modifier is used to smooth a mesh which has become irregular when Vertices have been manipulated during detailed modeling (Figures 9.46, 9.47).

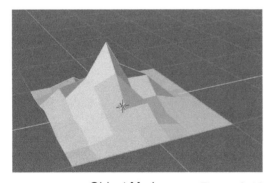 

Object Mode   Figure 9.46   Object Mode   Figure 9.47

Plane Object, Subdivided – Number of Cuts: 7   Smooth Laplacian Modifier added in Object
One Vertex moved up with Proportional Editing   Mode. Repeat Value: 5, Factor: 1.100.
enabled and Random Falloff.

With the Modifier added (NOT Applied) Edit Mode shows the Vertices in their original state (Figure 9.48).

To permanently set the surface smooth, Apply the Modifier.

Figure 9.48

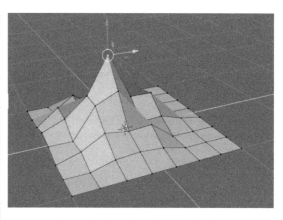

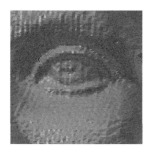 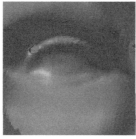

Practical application of the Smooth Laplacian Modifier.

9.16 Surface Deform Modifier

The Surface Deform Modifier is similar to the Mesh Deform Modifier in that one mesh is used to shape another. The difference being, the controlling mesh does not have to surround the Object being shaped.

Figure 9.49

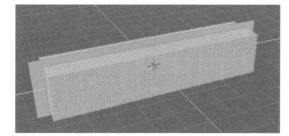 

In Figure 9.49 a Cube Object has been Scaled along the Y Axis in Object Mode. In Edit Mode the Cube has been Subdivided with Number of Cuts: 10. A Plane Object has been added to the Scene, Rotated on the Y Axis and Scaled to bisect the elongated Cube. The Plane has also been Subdivided in Edit Mode, Number of Cuts: 10.

Figure 9.50

In Object Mode select the elongated Cube and add a **Surface Deform Modifier** (Figure 9.50). Enter **Plane** in the **Target Panel** as the controlling Object. **To set the Plane as the control click on Bind**.

Deforming the Plane will deform the elongated Cube (Figure 9.51 over).

Proportional Editing Circle of Influence
(see Chapter 5 – 5.10) ————

Figure 9.51

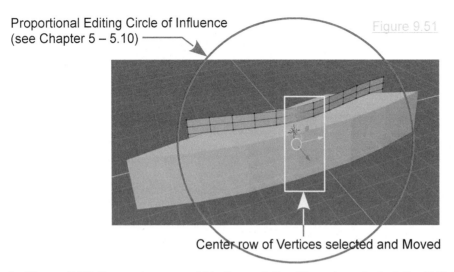

Center row of Vertices selected and Moved

In Figure 9.52 the center row of Vertices of the Plane is selected (in Edit Mode) and Moved forward deforming the Cube. In performing this operation Proportional Editing has been activated with Smooth Falloff and a Circle of Influence expanded to encapsulate the entire Plane.

After using this method to shape the Cube, Apply the Modifier and delete the Plane.

Animating the vertices of the Plane to move is an effective way of introducing lifelike characteristics to a Model. Figure 9.52 shows a Plane being animated to make the tail of a fish model move. (Reference: YouTube Video by yojigraphics.

https://www.youtube.com/watch?v=EJLIaNhoSSs

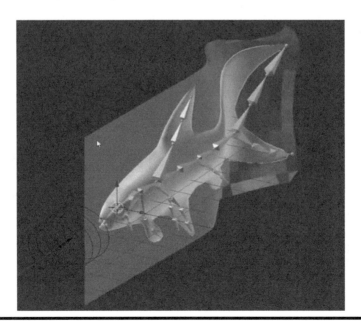

Figure 9.52

9.17 Warp Modifier

The **Warp Modifier** allows you to deform a mesh surface in Object mode by manipulating Target Objects. If you do not want the Targets to render in the Scene use Empty Objects. The deformation of the mesh takes place in a gradient between the two Targets.

This description requires clarification by a simple exercise.

In a new Blender Scene add a **Plane** Object, zoom in and **Subdivide** in Edit Mode (Cuts 10).

In Object Mode add two **Empty objects** and position as shown in Figure 9.53. Make note of the Empty names in the **Outliner Editor**; **Empty** and **Empty.001** (you may rename if you wish).

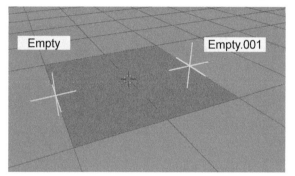

Figure 9.53

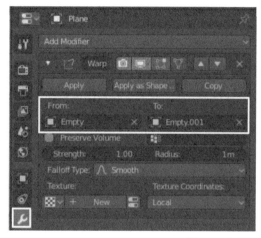

Select the Plane and in the Properties Editor, Modifier buttons add a **Warp Modifier** (Figure 9.54).

Figure 9.54

In the Modifier panel enter the names of the Empty Target Objects in the **From** and **To** panels (From: Empty and To: Empty.001). You will immediately see the Plane deform in the 3D View Editor (Figure 9.55).

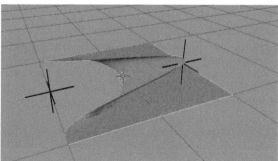

Figure 9.55

You may consider the Modifier as saying; deform the mesh From Empty to Empty.001.

By selecting either Empty in the 3D View Editor and translating the deformation of the Plane is affected (Figure 9.56).

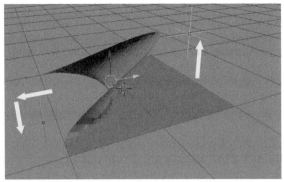

Figure 9.56

In the Modifier panel you may choose a different **Falloff Type** by clicking the bar to display a selection menu (Figure 9.57) and adjust the **Strength** and **Radius** sliders to modify the deformation (Figure 9.54).

When the Modifier is Applied the shape of the Plane is permanently set.

Figure 9.57

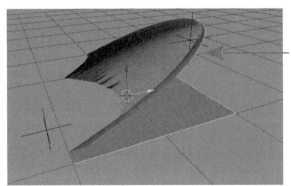

Spherical Falloff

Figure 9.58

Note: In Figures 9.58 ans 9.60 the position of the Empty target objects have NOT been moved.

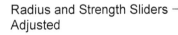

Radius and Strength Sliders Adjusted

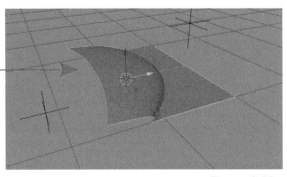

Figure 9.59

The **Wave Modifier** applies a deformation and creates an animation in a wave form. To demonstrate, in the default Blender Scene, delete the Cube and add a **Plane**. Scale the Plane up six times, Tab into **Edit mode**, and Subdivide the Plane by clicking **RMB - Subdivide** in the **Mesh Context** menu. In the **Subdivide** panel, make **Number of Cuts** 15. **Tab** back to **Object Mode**.

With the Plane selected, in the **Properties Editor, Modifiers buttons** add a **Wave Modifier** (Figure 9.60).

Figure 9.60

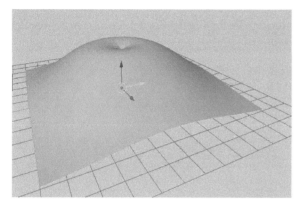

Figure 9.61

You immediately see the plane deform in the 3D View Editor, pulled up in the middle and punched in at the top of the bulge (Figure 9.61).

The Wave Modifier has been applied on both the **X** and **Y** axis. In the Modifier panel you see **X**, **Y**, and **Cyclic** ticked. **X** and **Y** refer to the axis and **Cyclic** means that an animation of the wave will repeat over and over.

Figure 9.62

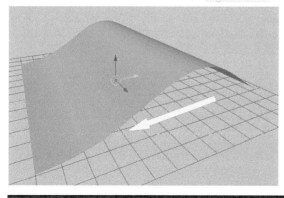

Press the **Play** button in the **Timeline Editor Header** to see the animation play.

Untick the **X Axis** in the Modifier panel and play again. A wave along the **Y** axis results Figure 9.62). At the bottom of the Modifier panel, change **Speed** to 0.09, **Width** to 1.08, and **Height** to 0.34 and Narrowness to 4.40 (Figure 9.60). You can change these values to whatever you want . Play the animation again and experiment with the values.

10

Editing Using Curves

Introduction

In Blender a Curve is a line or a path used to control the shape of a mesh in modeling or the movement of an Object in animation.

In Blender there are three types of curves: **Bezier Curves, Nurbs Curves and Paths**. Bezier types are subdivided into Curves and Circles.

Each type of Curve entered in the Blender Scene as a basic line with control handles which allow the shape of the Curve to be modified. The curve can also be Scaled and Extruded and additional control handles may be added.

A Curve does not Render. It merely acts as a control for editing a Mesh Object. The Object renders but the curve is invisible to the Render process.

Bezier and Nurbs Curves can be circular (circles) in which case they form a closed loop.

10.1 Curves, Circles and Paths

In Blender, **Curves, Circles and Paths** are lines giving a graphical representation of data or a line representing a path which controls direction or movement. Do not be confused with the Circle Object.

Curves are editable, which means that the shape of the curve may be altered to suit a particular application. An Object can be made to follow a Curve in an animation or it can be extruded along a Curve to affect its shape or it can be duplicated along a Curve. **Curve Circles** are merely circular Curves joined at the ends forming a continuous loop.

Figure 10.1

In Blender there are five basic Curve options which are accessed by the **Add menu in the 3D View Editor Header** or by pressing the **Alt + A Key** with the Mouse Cursor in the 3D View Editor (Figure 10.1).

To examine the options place the 3D View Editor in Top Orthographic View and delete the default Cube. Press **Alt + A Key**, select **Curve**, then **Path**.

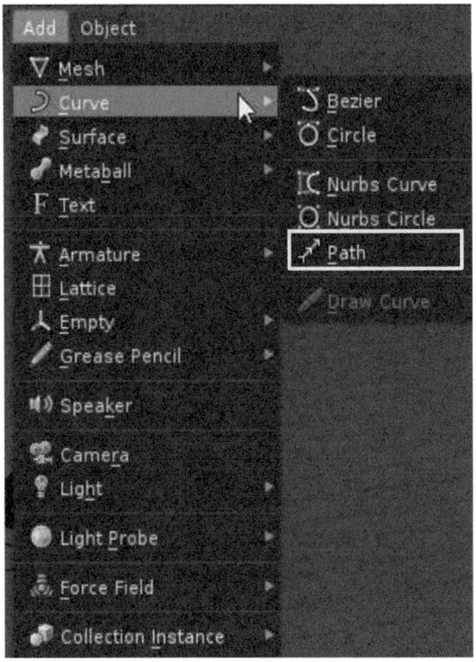

Path: Entered in **Object Mode** in **Top Orthographic View.**

Figure 10.2

To improve visibility in the demonstration lighten the background in the 3D View Editor (Chapter 1 -1.14)

Path: In Edit Mode.

Figure 10.3

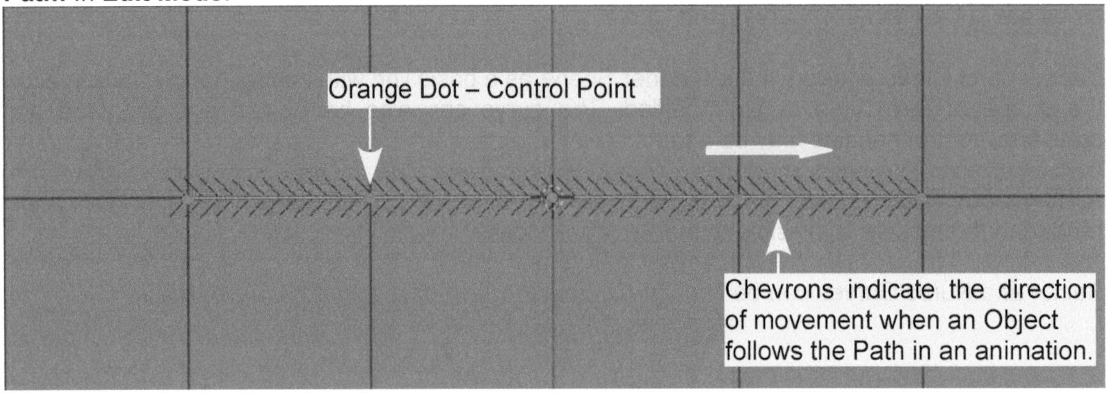

Orange Dot – Control Point

Chevrons indicate the direction of movement when an Object follows the Path in an animation.

RMB click a Control Point and translate (move) to edit the Path shape.

Figure 10.4

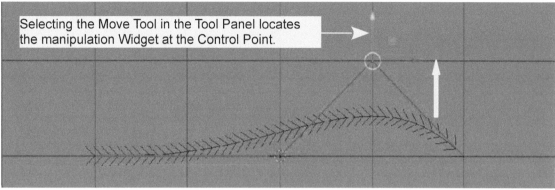

Selecting the Move Tool in the Tool Panel locates the manipulation Widget at the Control Point.

10.2 Bezier Curve

Bezier Curve entered in **Object Mode** in Top Orthographic View.

Figure 10.5

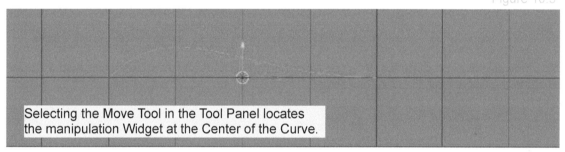

Selecting the Move Tool in the Tool Panel locates the manipulation Widget at the Center of the Curve.

Bezier Curve in **Edit Mode** showing **Control Handles** (red lines) at the ends of the curve.

Figure 10.6

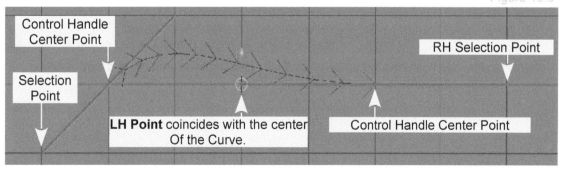

Control Handle Center Point

RH Selection Point

Selection Point

LH Point coincides with the center Of the Curve.

Control Handle Center Point

By default the Control Handles are **NOT** selected. The Control Handles have a Selection Point at the center, coinciding with the center of the Curve, and Selection Points at either end. In the default arrangement the LH Selection Point of the RH Handle coincides with the center of the Curve.

Selecting a Control Handle's center point (RMB click) and Moving alters the shape. Figure 10.7

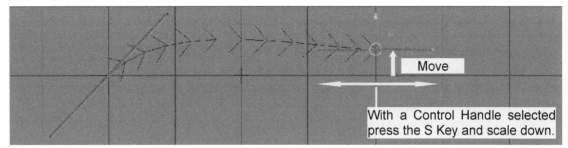

With the Control Handle selected press the **R Key** and rotate to shape the Curve. Figure 10.8

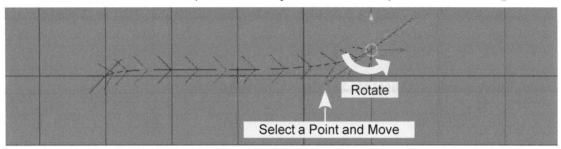

You may also click on a Handle Selection Point and Move (G Key) to rotate and shape the Curve. Extrude the Curve from the Control Handle.

Figure 10.9

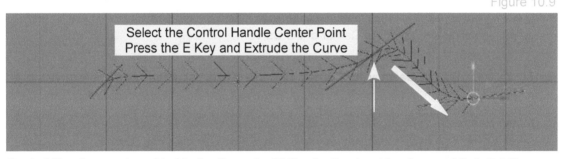

Control Handles can be added to the Curve by Shift selecting two Handles and **Subdividing**.

Figure 10.10

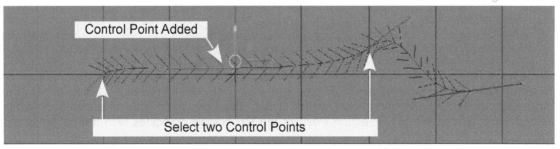

10.3 Bezier Circle

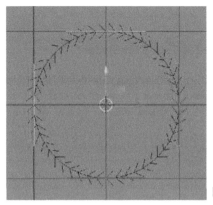

The **Bezier Circle** is similar to the Bezier Curve with control handles at the four cardinal points.

Click RMB to select a handle. **G Key** to grab and move to reshape the path. **R Key** to rotate and flatten the curve.

> Note: The Bezier Circle, Nurbs Path and Nurbs Circle are shown in Edit Mode.

Figure 10.11

10.4 Nurbs Path

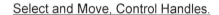

Select and Move, Control Handles.

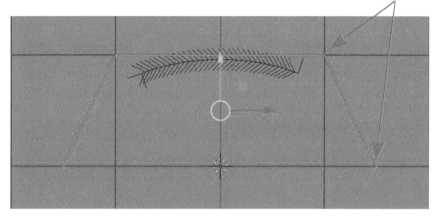

Figure 10.12

10.5 Nurbs Circle

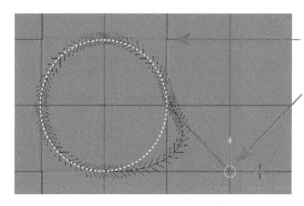

The **Nurbs Circle** with control handles external to the Path.

Control Handle Moved reshaping the Circle Curve.

Note: The diagrams serve only to show you what the different Curves look like and how to Edit their shape.

Figure 10.13

10.6 Modeling from a Curve

Any Curve Path or Circle may be used to create a Mesh Object by Extrusion.

Enter a **Bezier Curve** in **User Perspective View,** zoom in and **Tab into Edit Mode**.

Note: The following is **NOT** the way to create a Mesh Object but to demonstrate what happens when the Curve is Extruded in Edit Mode. When Edit Mode is entered the Control Handles at both ends of the Curve are selected. Extrude down on the Z Axis (E Key+Z Key, drag the Mouse).

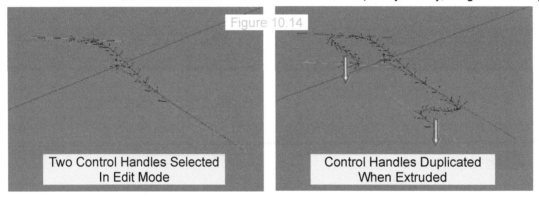

Figure 10.14

Two Control Handles Selected In Edit Mode

Control Handles Duplicated When Extruded

To create a Mesh from a Curve be in Object Mode with the default Curve selected (NOT Extruded). In the **Properties Editor, Data buttons, Geometry Tab** change values as shown (Figure 10.16). Rotate the 3D Editor Viewport (Figure 10.15)

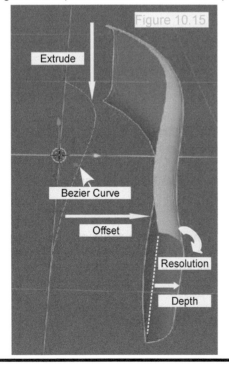

Figure 10.15

Extrude

Bezier Curve

Offset

Resolution

Depth

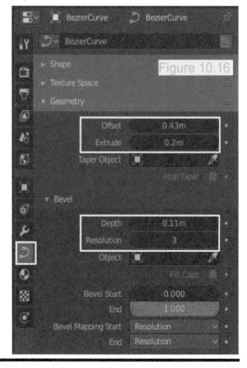

Figure 10.16

With the shape of the Mesh created, go to the **3D View Editor Header**, click on **Object** and select **Convert to Mesh from Curve**. In Edit Mode you will see that Vertices, Edges and Faces have been created.

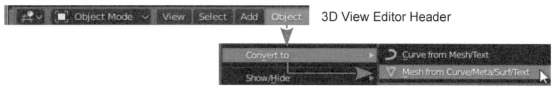

3D View Editor Header

Note: Before converting to a Mesh, in Edit Mode, you can select the Control Handles on the original Bezier Curve and reshape the Object. Once converted to a Mesh the original Curve is deleted.

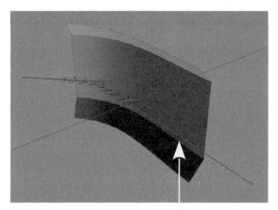

Figure 10.17

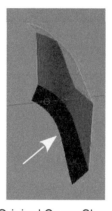

Select Control Handles and reshape before converting

Original Curve Shape

10.7 Closed Loops

Bezier and Nurbs Circles are Closed Loops which means they can be used to create tubular Objects or form a continuous path for an animation. Any Curve or Path may be converted to a Closed Loop.

The following shows a **Curve Path** entered in **Edit Mode** with the RH Control Point Moved then Extruded three times. **In Edit Mode**, click **Curve** in the Header and select **Toggle_Cylic** to form a closed loop.

Figure 10.18

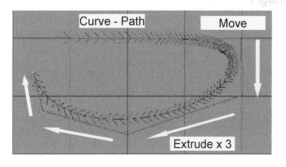

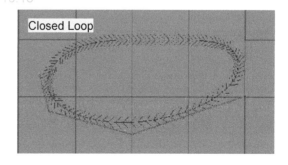

10.8 Using Nurbs Curves

Nurbs Curves are entered in the 3DView Editor by pressing **Shift + A Key** or clicking **Add** in the 3D View Editor Header and selecting from the menu that displays. There are two options; **Nurbs Curve** and **Nurbs Circle** (Figure 10.19). **Place the 3D View Editor in Top Orthographic View**.

Menu   **Nurbs Curve**   **Nurbs Circle**

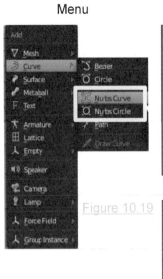

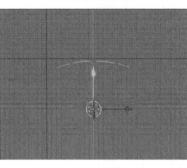

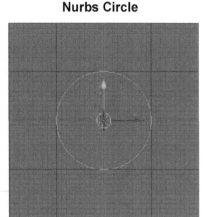

Object Mode

Figure 10.19

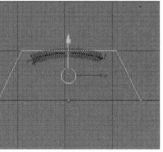

Edit Mode

Object Mode

In Edit Mode, Nurbs Curves and Circles have control handles attached with which you manipulate the shape (Figure 10.20). In both cases you see chevrons spaced on the Curve indicating that they may be used as Paths for animation.

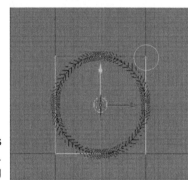

Edit Mode

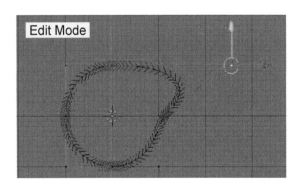

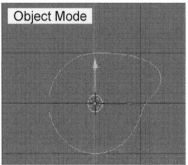

Figure 10.20

10.9 Nurbs Circle

Figure 10.21 shows a **Nurbs Circle** with a Control Point selected and Moved on the X Axis.

With the Nurbs Circle selected in **Object Mode** the shape may be expanded by changing settings in the **Properties Editor, Data buttons, Geometry tab** (Figure 10.22). To demonstrate, skew the 3D View Editor into a User Orthographic View as shown in Figure 10.21 (MMB Drag).

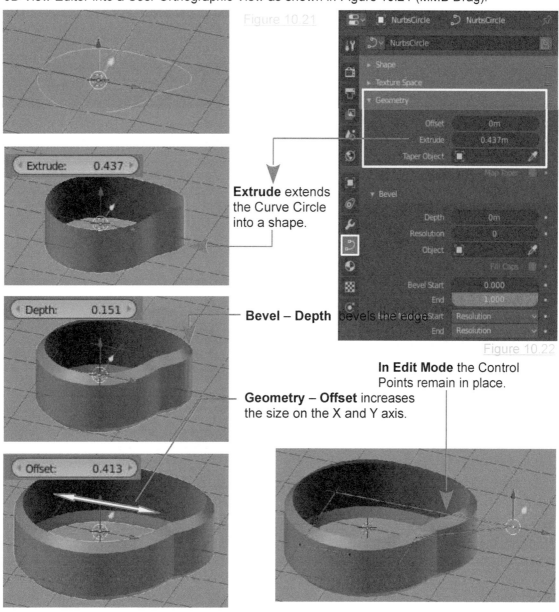

Figure 10.21

Figure 10.22

Extrude extends the Curve Circle into a shape.

Bevel – Depth bevels the edge.

Geometry – Offset increases the size on the X and Y axis.

In Edit Mode the Control Points remain in place.

With the Circle expanded then selected in **Object Mode** you may convert the shape into a **Mesh Object** (in the Header, click Object, select Convert to – Mesh from Curve). You see the Object in Edit mode with vertices, edges and faces (Figure 10.23).

Note: When you convert to a Mesh Object the ability to use the settings in the Properties Editor, Data buttons, Geometry tab is no longer available.

Press **A Key** to deselect then select individual vertices for manipulation.

A key - Deselect

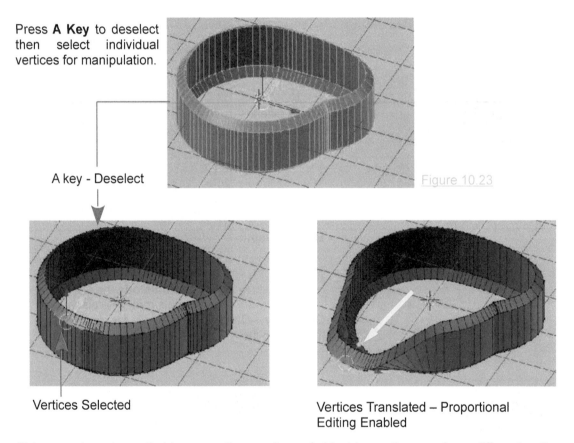

Figure 10.23

Vertices Selected

Vertices Translated – Proportional Editing Enabled

This procedure shows that by converting one type of object to another, you have different options for shape manipulation.

10.10 Nurbs Curve

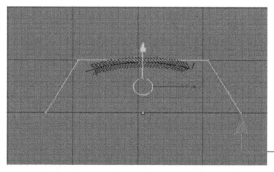

The **Nurbs Curve** is the another starting place for creating shapes, objects or animation paths.

Edit mode shows the Curve surrounded by Control Handles (orange lines) with control points (orange dots)

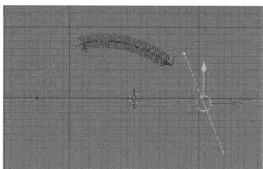

You may select a single point or multiple points then Move, Rotate or Scale to shape the Curve.

Figure 10.24

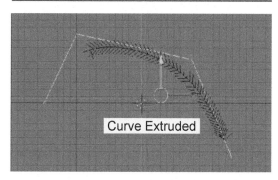

Curve Extruded

Select an end control point (RMB click). Press the **E Key** and drag the Mouse to extrude the Curve.

In the Header, click **Curve** and select **Toggle Cyclic** to form a closed loop Path.

In **Object Mode** try settings in the **Properties Editor, Data buttons, Geometry tab** starting with **Extrude**.

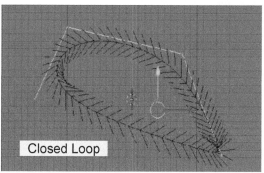

Closed Loop

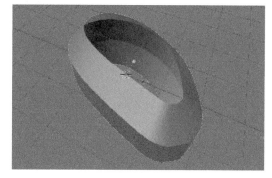

10.11 Lofting

Lofting is sometimes referred to as **Lathing** which is the process of generating shapes using Curves. The shape is generated then converted to a Mesh Object.

To demonstrate the process a **Bezier Circle** will be used in conjunction with a **Bezier Curve**.

Begin a new Blender Scene, delete the default Cube then add a Bezier Circle. Deselect the circle and add a Bezier Curve. Zoom in on the 3D View Editor (Figure 10.25).

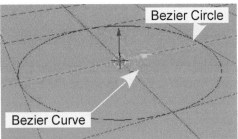

Figure 10.25

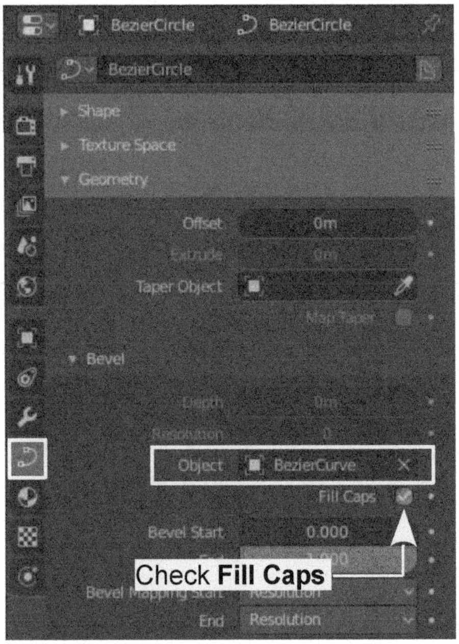

Deselect the Curve and select the Circle. In the **Properties Editor, Data buttons, Geometry Bevel tab,** click on **Object** and select **Bezier Curve** (Figure 10.26). Check **Fill Caps**.

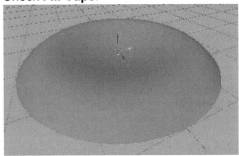

Figure 10.26

Figure 10.27

A shape is generated in the 3D View Editor (Figure 10.27).

To understand what has occurred place the 3D View Editor in **Wireframe Viewport Shading** Mode. Select the **Bezier Curve** by clicking on the name in the **Outliner Editor** (Figure 10.29).
To see more clearly turn off the grid display in the **Overlays**.

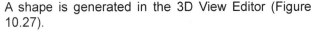

Figure 10.28

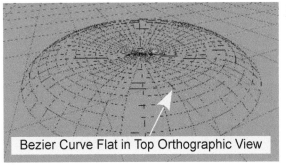

Bezier Curve Flat in Top Orthographic View

Figure 10.29

The profile of the Bezier Curve is presented flat in **Top Orthographic View** (Figure 10.25). With the curve selected press R + X + 90 to flip it on edge. Go into **Front Orthographic View** and translate the Curve to align with the profile of the generated shape (Figures 10.30 & 10.31.

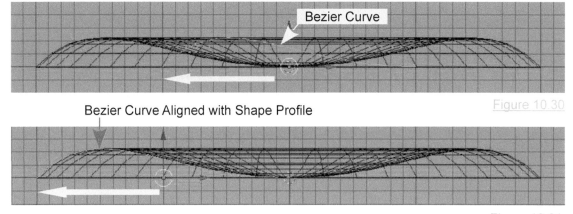

Bezier Curve

Figure 10.30

Bezier Curve Aligned with Shape Profile

Figure 10.31

By skewing the 3D View Editor you will see that the shape has been generated by extruding the Curve profile through 360° (Figure 10.32).

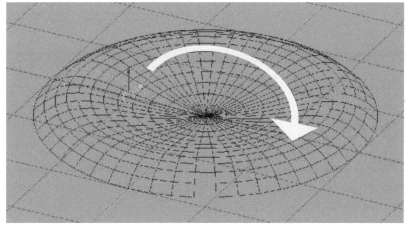

Figure 10.32

With the Bezier Curve still selected Tab to Edit Mode to see the **Control Handles** at each end of the Curve (Figure 10.33).

By selecting the Control Handle at the center of the shape and translating it along the **X Axis** towards the outside, you will see that it increases the inner diameter of the shape. Similarly translating the Control Handle at the outer diameter alters the outer diameter.

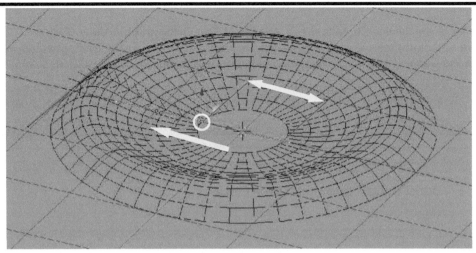

Figure 10.33

Shift select both Control Handles then press **R + Y + 90**. Doing this flips the Bezier Curve up on edge and changes the shape into something resembling a pot (Figure 10.34).

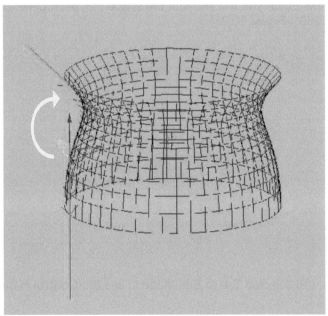

Figure 10.34

By manipulating the Control Handles you can modify the shape. Selecting both Control Handles and Subdividing (Click RMB in the Editor and select Subdivide in the Curve Context Menu) adds a third Control Handle (Figure 13.16). With the Control Handle selected, press the **V Key** to display the Handle type menu. Type **Vector** allows you to produce sharp corners when the handle is rotated.

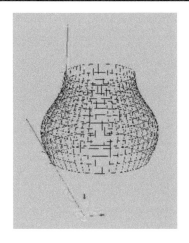 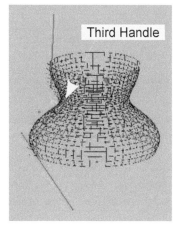

Third Handle

Figure 10.36

When you have completed shaping, Tab to Object Mode, deselect the **Bezier Curve** and select the shape itself. Change to **Solid Viewport Shading Mode** (Figure 10.37).

In the **Properties Editor, Object buttons (NOT Object Data), Viewport Display Tab** check (tick) **Wireframe** to view to see the subdivisions that will be created when the shape is converted to a Mesh Object (Figure 10.38). You may modify the subdivisions by altering values in the **Properties Editor, Object Data buttons, Geometry Tab.**

  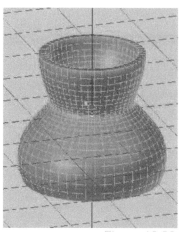

Figure 10.37   Figure 10.38   Figure 10.39

Finally, with the shape completed, click Object in the Header and select Convert to Mesh from Curve.

Add a **Solidify Modifier** (see Chapter 8 – 8.13) and increase the **Thickness value** to give the shape <u>wall thickness</u> (Figure 10.39).

11

Editing Techniques - Examples

Introduction

Becoming proficient at Modeling requires a knowledge of the tools that are available and how to combine the use of tools to create what you want. There are no hard and fast rules concerning which tool is used for any particular application. You use whatever suits what you are doing.

This chapter shows a very brief sample of how different tools are used in creating some basic models and effects.

What you can model using Blender is only limited by your imagination and your knowledge of what tools are available and where to find them.

11.1 Creating a Landscape – Proportional Vertex Editing

Proportional Vertex Editing can be employed to create a landscape or ground as a background for a Scene. Simply select Vertices on a subdivided Plane and move them up or down the Z Axis. Vertices moved down forming depressions can be turned into lakes or rivers by positioning a second Plane below the original and giving it a different color (Chapter 4 - 4.18). When the landscape is formed in Edit Mode, Tab to Object Mode, select the ground and select **Shading Smooth** in the **Object Context Menu** (RMB click in the Editor).

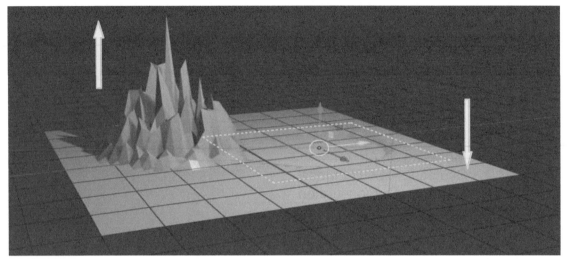

Figure 11.1

Cook Book Instructions

Delete the Cube from the default 3D View Editor.
Add a Plane Object and scale up four times.
Tab to Edit Mode.
Subdivide the Plane.
In the Last Operator Panel increase the Number of Cuts to 10.
Subdivide again. Increase the Number of Cuts to 3 (10 + 3 = 13).
Deselect the Vertices and select a single Vertex.
Enable Proportional Editing and select Random Falloff.
Press G Key plus Z Key and drag the Mouse Cursor up.
Deselect the Vertex and select a second Vertex. Repeat the process for another mountain or with Spherical Fall off drag down creating a depression for a lake.
Add a second Plane to the Scene just below the first scaled to sit in the depression.
Give the new Plane a geen-blue color.

> **Note:** There is an Add-on for Blender which automates landscape generation. There are also external programs

Note: When following these instructions, at this point, you will not see the view of the Scene in the 3D View Editor exactly as shown in the diagram. What is seen in the Editor is dependent on how Material (Color) is applied (Chapter 16), what lighting (Lamps) have been been introduced (Chapter 15) and the Viewport Shading that is implemented (Chapter 14).

11.2 Dupliverts

Dupliverts means **Duplicating at Vertices**, which means creating an Array of Objects by duplication. Each duplicated Object is positioned at the location of a Vertices of a secondary Object. To demonstrate, a **UV Sphere** Object will be duplicated at the position of each Vertex of a **Plane** that has been Subdivided.

Delete the default **Cube** Object in the default Blender Scene. In the **3D View Editor** add a **Plane** Object. Scale the Plane up four times (S Key + 4, LMB click) then **Tab** to **Edit Mode** and **Subdivide.**

To replicate the Subdivision in the diagrams, in 3D View Editor Header, RMB click in the Editor and select Subdivide in the Object Context menu. In the Subdivide Last Operator Panel increase the Number of Cuts to 10. RMB click again, Subdivide a second time. In the Last Operator Panel the Number of Cuts resets to 1. Increase to 2. If you like to examine the subdivision in detail you will find you have 1156 Vertices.

How many times you Subdivide is arbitrary but having a decent number of Vertices produces a good effect.

Figure 11.2

Tab to **Object mode** deselect the Plane.

Add a **UV Sphere** object to the Scene, scale it down (Figure 11.2). In the Resize Last Operator Panel make the Vector values = 0.158.

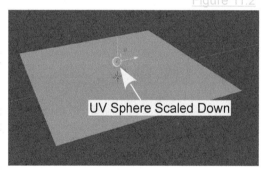

With the Sphere selected (in Object Mode), **Shift** select the **Plane**. Press **CTRL + P key** and select **Set Parent to Object** to parent the Sphere to the Plane (Figure 11.3).

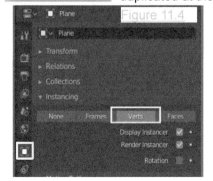

Deselect the Sphere and the Plane. Select the Plane only.

Figure 11.3

With the Plane selected go to the **Properties Editor, Object buttons (NOT Object Data), Instancing Tab** and select **Verts** (Figure 11.4). The Sphere is duplicated at the location of each Vertex on the Plane (Figure 11.5).

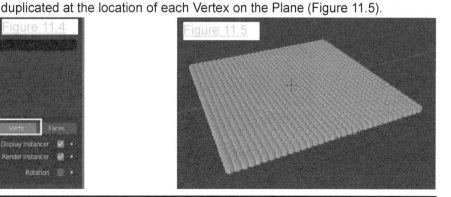

Deselect the Plane.

Figure 11.6

Scale the **Sphere** to adjust its size and create some separation between the duplicates. Since the Sphere is at the center of the Plane it is more than likely hidden among the duplications and difficult (impossible) to select.

To select the Sphere, go to the **Outliner Editor** and locate the Sphere in the File tree (Figure 11.6). Select the Sphere in the **Outliner Editor** (Click LMB) then in the **3D View Editor** Scale the Sphere down to make gaps between the duplicates (Figure 11.7).

Figure 11.7

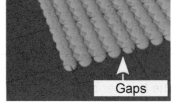

Gaps

With Sphere selected, in Object mode, Move up on the Z Axis (Figure 11.8). Deselect the Sphere.

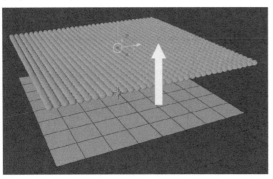

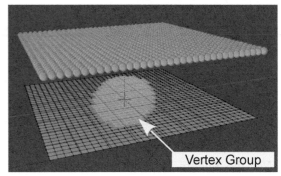

Vertex Group

Figure 11.8   Figure 11.9

Select the **Plane,** then in **Edit Mode** a group of Vertices may be selected (Figure 11.9) and with **Proportional Editing** turned on, translated deforming the Array of Spheres (Figure 11.10).

Figure 11.10

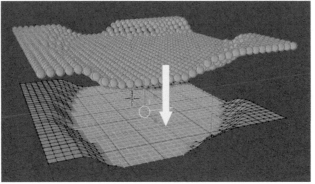

160

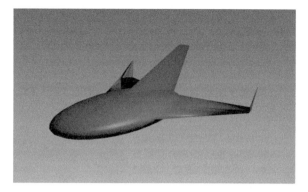

Figure 11.11

To model the aircraft shown in Figure 11.11 open a new Blender Scene. Delete the default Cube and add a **UV Sphere**. Zoom in (scroll MMB or press Num Pad +). Scale down on the Z Axis (S Key + 0.5 + Z Key). Scale the Sphere times 2 on the Y Axis (press S key + Y Key + 2 and LMB click) (Figure 11.12).

Figure 11.12

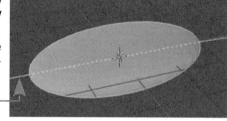

Y Axis (Green Line)

You will be modeling the reshaped Sphere and want it to be identical either side of the Y Axis (the green line). That is to say you want it to be mirrored **on the X Axis** (along the red line).

In Top Orthographic view, place the UV Sphere in **Edit Mode** and delete all the vertices on the LHS of the Y Axis (press the B key for Box select, place the Cursor as shown by the white cross, click and hold drag a rectangle around the LHS Vertices). **Don't forget, turn Limit Selection to Visible off**. With the Vertices selected press the **X Key** and select **Delete Vertices** .

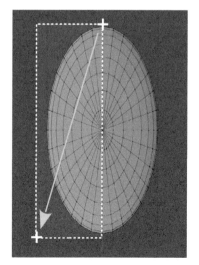
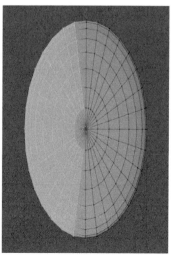
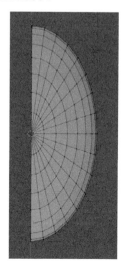

Place the UV Sphere in **Object Mode** (press Tab). Add a **Mirror Modifier** (Ref: Chapter 8 - 8.8) which by default is set to mirror on the X Axis. Change to **Right Orthographic** view (press the Num Pad 3 Key)

Figure 11.14

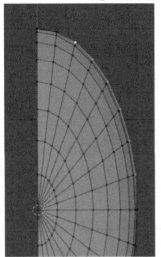

Tab to Edit Mode and select the Vertices as shown in Figure 11.14 (hold Shift and RMB click on each Vertex).

Change back to **Top Orthographic** view. Press the E Key (Extrude) and use the **Widget** to move the Vertices to the right (Figure 11.15).

With the **Vertex Group** still selected press the **S Key** (Scale) and Scale the group in.

Figure 11.15

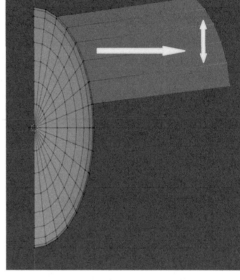

Use the **Widget** to move the group towards the back of the aircraft forming a wing (Figure 11.16).

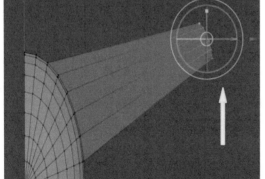

Figure 11.16

Rotate to align with the fuselage (Figure 11.16).

Extrude up, Scale the group in and move back forming the wing stabiliser (Figure 11.17)

Figure 11.17

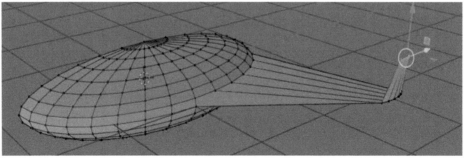

Select vertices at the rear of the fuselage on the centerline, Move up and repeat the procedure for the wing stabiliser forming a tail (Figure 11.18)

Figure 11.18

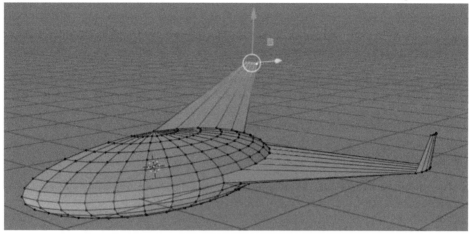

Go into **Object Mode**, apply a **Mirror Modifier**, add a **Material**. In the **3D View Editor Header** click on **Object** and select **Shade Smooth**. Rotate the 3D View Editor to see your super duper aircraft.

Figure 11.19

11.4 Sculpting

Sculpting, in Blender, allows you to add detail to the surface of a model by manipulating the Mesh Vertices. The process produces results similar to kneading a piece of clay. Vertices are pulled or pushed or added to using a variety of Tools which deform the mesh surface.

Sculpting is performed after you have created a model. To demonstrate the basics of the process a UV Sphere will be employed. The UV Sphere has a reasonable number of Vertices forming its surface but for Sculpting to be effective a high vertex count is required. Replace the default Cube Object with a UV Sphere in the 3D View Editor. In the demonstration the whole surface of the Sphere will be used but in reality you would Subdivide the surface of a model in the area where you wanted to add detail.

With the UV Sphere selected in Object Mode, Tab to Edit Mode and with all Vertices selected, Subdivide with Number of Cuts 10 (Chapter 5 – 5.5) (Figure 11.20).

Figure 11.20

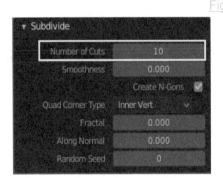

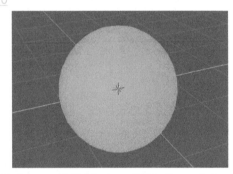

Last Operator Panel

UV Sphere – Edit Mode – All Vertices Selected

With the UV Sphere Subdivided change to Sculpt Mode.

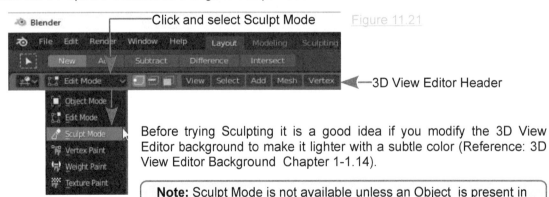

Click and select Sculpt Mode

Figure 11.21

—3D View Editor Header

Before trying Sculpting it is a good idea if you modify the 3D View Editor background to make it lighter with a subtle color (Reference: 3D View Editor Background Chapter 1-1.14).

Note: Sculpt Mode is not available unless an Object is present in the 3D View Editor.

The first thing you will notice when changing to Sculpt Mode is the change in the 3D View Editor Header and the arrangement of Tools down the LHS of the Screen. The second observation is, the subdivided UV Sphere is displayed as it would be in Object Mode with with Flat Shading. Change back to Object Mode and set the Shading to Smooth (Chapter 4 – 4.21).

A third significant change is, the 3D View Editor Cursor has a red circle attached. The circle is called the **Brush** (Figure 11.22).

Note: The color of the Brush Circle changes depending on the Tool selected.

Figure 11.22

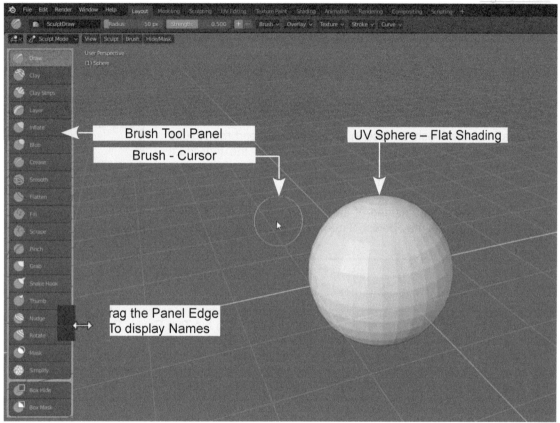

Brush Tool Panel

Brush - Cursor

UV Sphere – Flat Shading

rag the Panel Edge
To display Names

Sculpt Mode Tools

The **Brush** (Cursor) performs different functions depending on which Sculpt Mode Tool is selected. By default the Draw Tool is active as indicated by the blue highlight in the Tool Selection Panel.

In general, sculpting is performed by positioning the Brush on the Mesh Surface, clicking LMB, holding and dragging the Brush over the surface. The surface will be pulled out or pushed in depending on the Brush settings.

How the surface is deformed depends on which Tool is selected and the Tool Settings.

You can alter the size of the Brush (Diameter of the Circle) with the Radius Slider in the Tool Header. The Strength of the Brush (also in the Header) affects how much push or pull is applied.

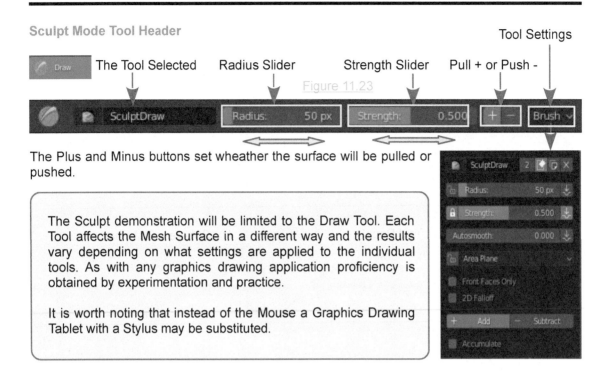

Tool Settings

The Tool Selected Radius Slider Strength Slider Pull + or Push -

Figure 11.23

The Plus and Minus buttons set wheather the surface will be pulled or pushed.

The Sculpt demonstration will be limited to the Draw Tool. Each Tool affects the Mesh Surface in a different way and the results vary depending on what settings are applied to the individual tools. As with any graphics drawing application proficiency is obtained by experimentation and practice.

It is worth noting that instead of the Mouse a Graphics Drawing Tablet with a Stylus may be substituted.

11.5 Sculpting Demonstration (Basic)

To see how the Draw Tools operates, select the Draw tool in the Tool Panel. The buttons in the Tool Header will control the properties of the Draw Tool. Set the **Radius** slider to approximately 30 px (pixels) and have the plus + setting for Pull engaged. Change the Strength value to 1.000 (drag the slider). The effect of the Tool will have a more pronounced effect with a higher value.

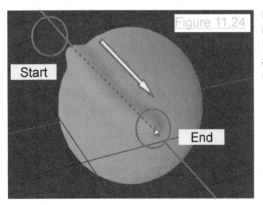

Figure 11.24

Start

End

Position the Brush in the 3D View Editor as shown in Figure 11.24, click and hold LMB and drag the Brush over the surface of the UV Sphere (generally along the red X Axis). At the end of the stroke release the mouse button.

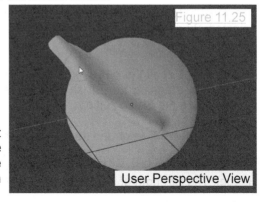

Figure 11.25

User Perspective View

As the Brush moves over the surface a welt appears as the Vertices are pulled away from the surface. Repeatedly dragging the Brush over the top of the welt further increases the deformation (Figure 11.25).

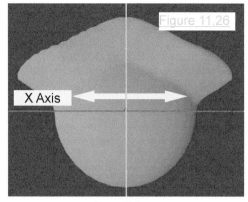

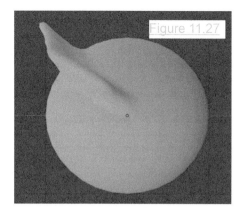

X Axis

Front View

Side View

Mirror Stroke Figure 11.28

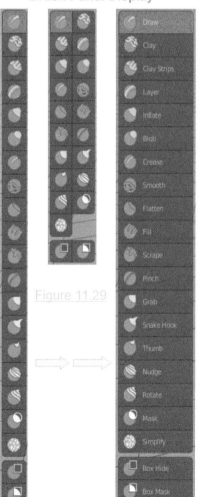

Figure 11.29

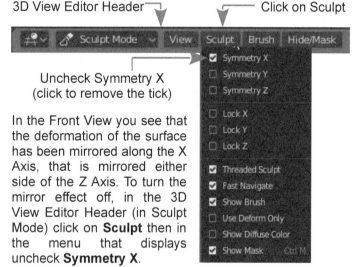

3D View Editor Header ⌐   ⌐ Click on Sculpt

Uncheck Symmetry X
(click to remove the tick)

In the Front View you see that the deformation of the surface has been mirrored along the X Axis, that is mirrored either side of the Z Axis. To turn the mirror effect off, in the 3D View Editor Header (in Sculpt Mode) click on **Sculpt** then in the menu that displays uncheck **Symmetry X**.

With Symmetry unchecked you can stroke over the surface in any direction modeling freehand.

The Brush Selection Panel at the LH side of the 3D View Editor displays as a single column by default.

Mouse over on the edge of the panel, click, hold and drag the double headed arrow to consolidate the panel into two columns or continue dragging to maintain the single column with Brush names shown.

At this stage some clarification in respect to the relationship between the options available in the different Headers may be required. In changing from Object Mode to Sculpt Mode, the area on the Screen between the Screen Header and the 3D View Editor Header is occupied by buttons relating to the individual Brushes and is, therefore, referred to as the **Brush Header**.

Figure 11.30 shows some of the options available in the different Headers.

Screen Header   Brush Header   3D View Editor Header

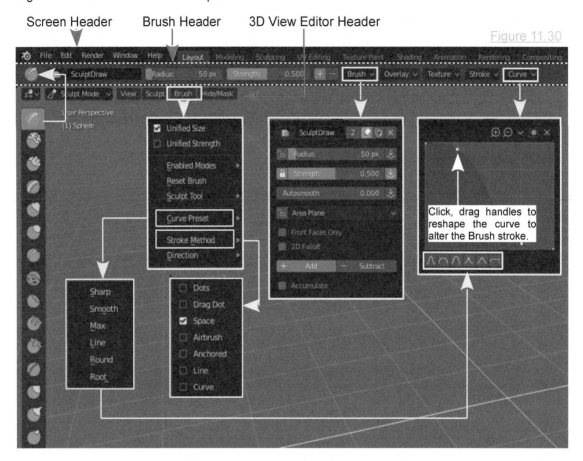

Figure 11.30

Click, drag handles to reshape the curve to alter the Brush stroke.

The uppermost Header, the **Screen Header**, houses the controls for the Blender Screen.

The **Brush Header** provides controls for the particular Brush selected from the Brush Panel. In the diagram the Draw Brush is selected (highlighted blue). You see the icon representing Draw at the LHS of the Brush Header. Selecting **Brush** in the **Brush Header** opens the menu for setting the Radius, Strength and Pull /Push settings. These controls have a quick access in the Header itself. The menu also contains additional settings.

The **3D View Editor Header** houses controls for the 3D View Editor.

The Headers provide a variety of options for selecting how the Brush affects the mesh surface. Many of the selection options are duplicated.

For example; selecting **Brush** in the **3D View Editor Header**, then selecting **Stroke Method**, is duplicated by selecting **Stroke** in the **Tool Header** then clicking on **Stroke Method** (Figure 11.31 over).

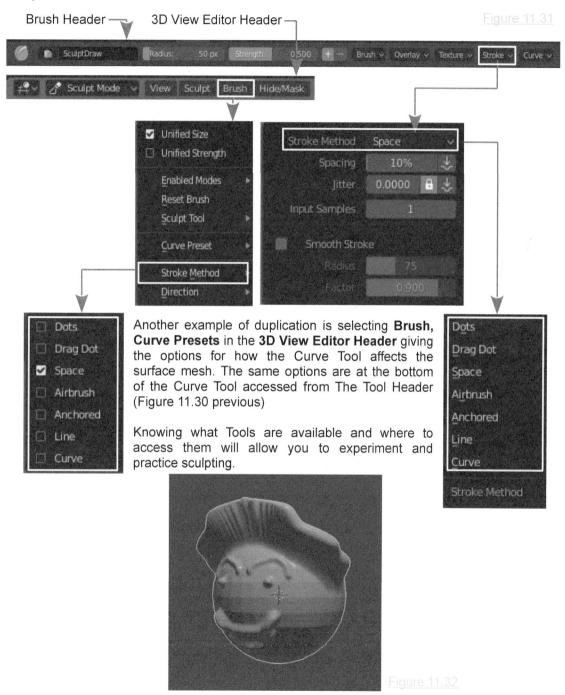

Brush Header

3D View Editor Header

Figure 11.31

Another example of duplication is selecting **Brush, Curve Presets** in the **3D View Editor Header** giving the options for how the Curve Tool affects the surface mesh. The same options are at the bottom of the Curve Tool accessed from The Tool Header (Figure 11.30 previous)

Knowing what Tools are available and where to access them will allow you to experiment and practice sculpting.

Figure 11.32

11.6 Creating a Humanoid Figure

At some stage you will want to make a character figure for animation. As with the Aircraft Modeling Exercise this starts with one of Blender's primitives (a Cube) and by a process of selecting Vertices, Extrusion, Scaling, Manipulation and the application of Modifiers a simple figure may be generated. The following is intended to demonstrate the process only and not to produce a refined result. Modeling requires time and patience and plenty of practice. Place the Cube in **Edit Mode – Front Orthographic View.**

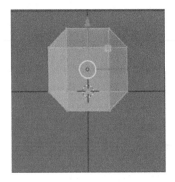

Cube with Bevel Modifier applied. Width = 0.401

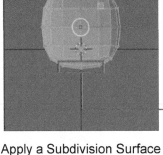

Apply a Subdivision Surface Modifier to add Vertices.

Figure 11.33

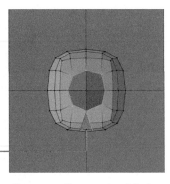

Remove the center Vertex and reshape perimeter of the hole on the base.

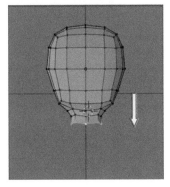

Select perimeter Vertices and Extrude down to form the neck.

Continue extrusions and Scale out forming the body.

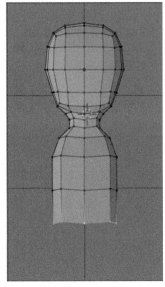

With the body formed select one half of the Vertices and delete.

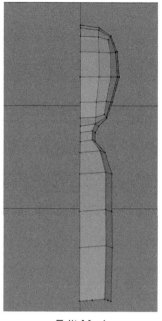

Edit Mode

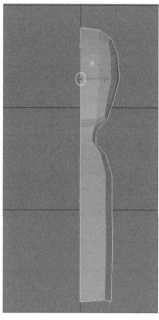

Object Mode

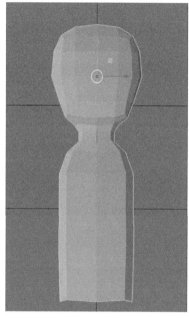

Add a Mirror Modifier in Object Mode (Do **NOT** Apply).

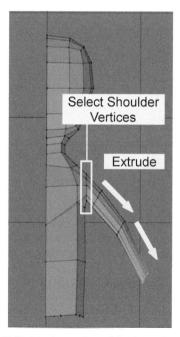

Select Shoulder Vertices

Extrude

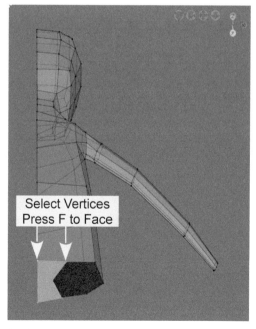

Select Vertices Press F to Face

In Edit Mode, select Vertices in the shoulder. Delete one Vertex to create a hole. Extrude and Scale the arm.

At the base, Subdivide to create Vertices and Face the center portion leaving a hole for the leg.

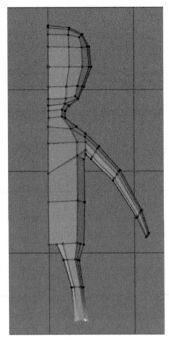

Extrude, Scale and position Vertices
forming a leg and foot (not shown).

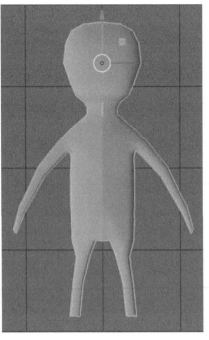

In Object Mode set Shading to Smooth
and Apply the Mirror Modifier.

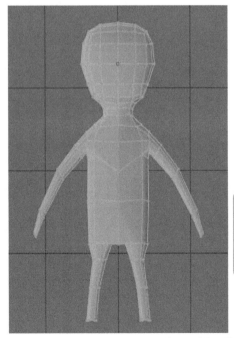

Note: This is a very rough
crude model shown for
modeling technique only.

See CH20-20.19

Edit Mode showing Vertices when the Mirror Modifier is Applied

12

The Outliner and Collections

The Outliner Window

The **Outliner Editor** provides a visual display in the form of a **File Tree** showing everything in the Scene in the **3D View Editor**. Each Object is listed showing its relationship to other Objects such as whether it is joined to another Object or has a Child Parent Relationship or whether it has Material or Texture applied. This information is the Object's Data which can be displayed in different configurations depending on the function being performed.

Collections

The File Tree in the **Outliner Editor** may be customised allowing Objects in the 3D View Editor to be arranged in groups called **Collections**. Collections may be added and named and arranged in a hierarchy much the same as the folders on an operating system. Objects in the 3D View Editor may be selected and deselected in the Outliner Editor or hidden from view in the 3D View Editor by turning a Collection's visibility off. This assists when working on Objects in a complicated Scene.

12.1 Collections in The Outliner Editor

Outliner Editor (default display)

The **Outliner Editor** (upper RHS of the Screen) provides a visual display, in the form of a file tree, of everything in your Scene and shows how the different items are related (Figure 12.1).

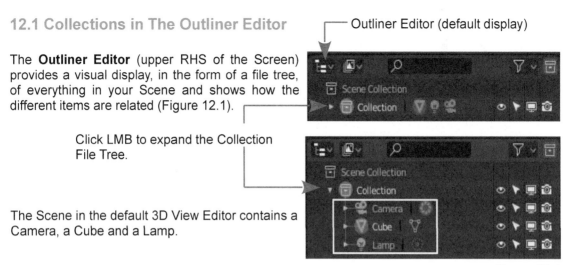

Click LMB to expand the Collection File Tree.

The Scene in the default 3D View Editor contains a Camera, a Cube and a Lamp.

Figure 12.1

To understand how Collections operate work through the following procedure.

Start with the default Blender Screen showing the four default Editors. The **Outliner Editor** is displayed in the upper right hand corner of the Screen (Figure 12.1).

The **Outliner Editor** contains information about the current Scene in the default 3D View Editor. Under **Scene Collection** is the single entry **Collection**. Click on the **expansion icon** preceding Collection to expand the File Tree showing a list of Objects in the current Scene in the 3D View Editor.

Expansion Icon ▶

The 3D View Editor contains three Objects: a Cube, a Camera and a Lamp. The three Objects are grouped together and placed in the Collection named **Collection**.

Click on the expansion icon at the begining of the line where you see **Collection** to show the Camera, Cube and Lamp listed. Note that in front of each Object there is also an expansion icon. You click on each icon to display data beloning to the Objects.

Clicking the icon in front of Cube reveals; **Cube** (the data creating the display of the Cube in the 3D View Editor), **Material** (the data producing the gray color of the Cube). Each line represents a **Datablock** (block of data) producing the display in the 3D View Editor.

Data Displaying the Cube ——————

Data Displaying the Material (color) ——————

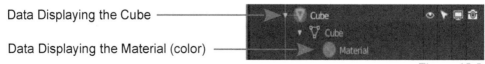

Figure 12.2

Adding Objects

Clicking LMB on the Collection name selects the Collection (highlighted light gray or blue).

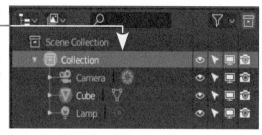

When you add a new Object to the Scene in the 3D View Editor it is automatically added to the Collection that is selected, in this case **Collection**.

Add a UV Sphere Object to the Scene followed by an Icosphere Object.

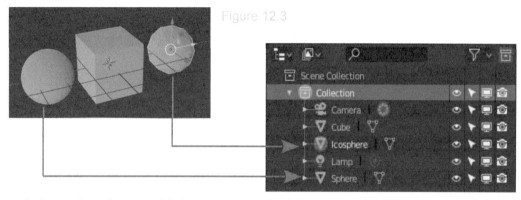

Figure 12.3

You immediatly see Icosphere and Sphere added to **Collection**. Note that they are placed in the list alphabetically.

Adding Collections

As the Scene is developed, with Objects being added, it can be advantageous to create new Collections, grouping Objects together. You add (create) new Collections by clicking the Add Collection button in the Outliner Editor Header.

The Add Collection Button

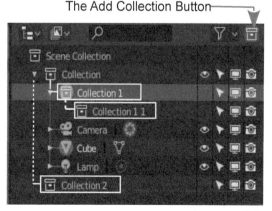

Where Collections are added depends on the location you select before adding. If you select **Collection** in the Outliner Editor a new Collection will be added as a sub entry in Collection . The sub entry will be named Collection 1. If you select **Scene Collection** before adding the new Collection it will be added as a sub Collection named Collection 2. Selecting **Collection 1** and adding a new Collection produces **Collection 1.1**

Note the Collection Names: New Collection 2 under Scene Collection and new Collection 1.1 under Collection 1.

Figure 12.4

You may rename Collection to something meaningful by double clicking on the Collection Name.

Deleting Collections

In the Outliner Editor you select the Collection name (highlights gray or blue) and press delete to remove the Collection.

Be aware that in deleting a Collection in the Outliner Editor does not delete Objects in the Collection displayed in the 3D View Editor. When you delete a Collection, Objects in the Collection are automacially transfered to the preceding Collection in the heirachy.

Deleting Objects

You may select Objects in the Outliner Editor then RMB click and select delete in the menu to remove the Object from the 3D View Editor. Deleting a Collection in the Outliner Editor transfers all Ojects in the Collection to the preceding Collection in the hierarchy.

Hiding and Restricting Object Display and Selection

Objects in the 3D View Editor can be controlled in the Outliner Editor.

Prevents Rendering ───────────────
Restricts Visibility ──────────────
Prevents Selection ───────────

UV Sphere Object selected in   Hide the Object from View───
the Outliner Editor (or in the 3D
View Editor)

The control options are applicable to individual Objects and Collections.   Figure 12.5

Moving Objects to Different Collections

Objects listed under a Collection in the Outliner Editor may be moved to a different Collection by simply clicking on the Object name (LMB), holding, dragging and releasing the mouse button with the Mouse Cursor positioned over the new Collection name. Alternativly press the **M Key** to display the **Move menu**.

Click LMB on Sphere.001 hold, drag to Collection 2, release.

UV Sphere.001 added under Scene Collection

176

Collections may be repositioned in a similar manner.

12.2 View Options in the Outliner Editor

Click to display Options

View Layer is the default display in the Outliner Editor which includes Collections.

 Figure 12.6

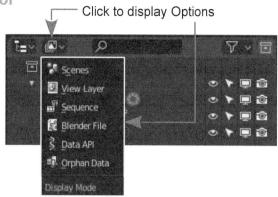

Alternative options are accessed in the Editor Header. The alternatives display information about the Scene in the 3D View Editor and the current Blender File.

Scenes

Sequence

Blender File

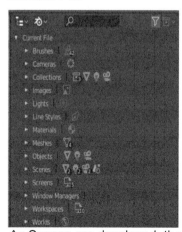

Data API   Figure 12.7

Orphan Data

As Scenes are developed the data contained in a Blender file increases accordingly. The display options in the Outliner Editor provide a record of the data and allow it to be organised.

13

3D Text

Introduction to 3D Text

3D text can be a very important element to add to a Scene. Think of all the television advertisements that contain text and how it is animated. There are two ways of adding text to a Scene in Blender. One way is to use the built-in text generator and the other is to use an external program.

Text made in Blender can be easily edited in the **Properties Editor**. Text made in an external program like **Elefont** or one of the on-line 3D text generating programs may give you additional options and different fonts.

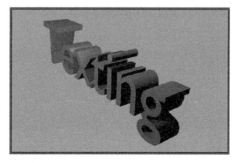

179

13.1 Creating 3D Text in Blender

To create text in Blender, place the Scene in top view with **Orthographic Projection** (Num Pad 7). Delete the Cube Object. Select the Cursor Tool in the Tool Panel and locate the Editor Cursor at the point in the Scene where you want your text to go. Press **Shift + A key** and select **Add - Text** (Figure 13.1). The word **Text** displays in the 3D View Editor in Object mode.

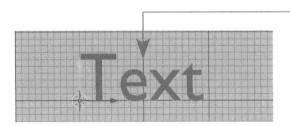

Figure 13.1

Tab into Edit mode—the word **Text** now has a Typing cursor at the end. (Figure 13.2).

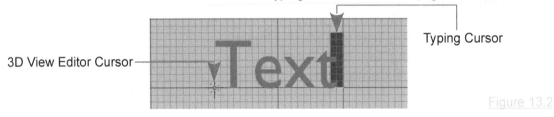

Typing Cursor

3D View Editor Cursor

Figure 13.2

Backspace to delete letters and type in your own words just like in a text editor. Don't worry about the font style or size at this stage. When you have typed in the words, tab back into Object Mode; to shape and color the text (Figure 13.3).

Edit Mode: The word Text has been modified by retyping

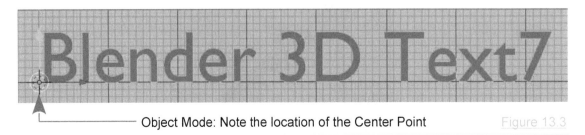

Object Mode: Note the location of the Center Point

Figure 13.3

180

Properties Editor

Typing Text in Blender is a little different to typing in a text editor program. When you Add Text in the 3D View Editor in Object Mode the default word Text is an Object (a shape) similar to adding one of the Blender Primitives (Objects) such as a Cube, UV Sphere or Cone. When you entered Edit Mode, backspace and retyped a different word you modified the default Text Object. Besides modifying the letters in the the text (the two dimensional shape of the characters) you can extrude thickness, bevel and round the shape. You can also add Material color, Texture and other effects. Modifying the text is done in the **Properties Editor**. Select the text in the 3D View Editor, then go to the **Properties Editor, Data buttons**. Note: For Text the **Data button** is denoted by an **a**.

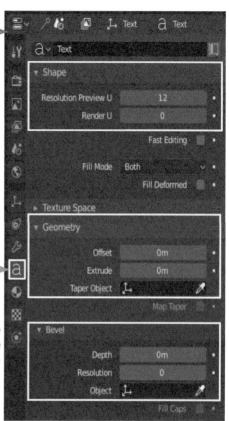

Figure 13.4

13.2 The Object Data Button "a"

The Geometry Tab has settings for shaping the text into a three dimensional Object. To see the effect of the different settings rotate the text about the X Axis of the Scene then rotate the 3D View Editor as shown below.

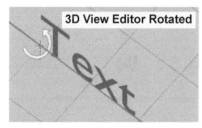

3D View Editor Rotated

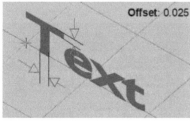

Offset: 0.025

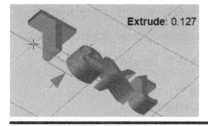

Extrude: 0.127

Bevel

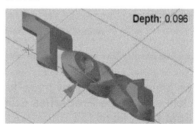

Depth: 0.096

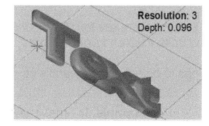

Resolution: 3
Depth: 0.096

13.3 Fonts

The default **Font Style** is entered as **Bfont** as seen in the **Properties Editor, Data button, Font Tab**. **Bfont** is a **Vector Font for Text Objects** which is compiled into the Blender program and as such is not a standard font used in Windows or other operating systems.

You can change the style to whatever font you have on your system.

If you are using a Windows operating system, font styles can be found in C:/Windows/Fonts.

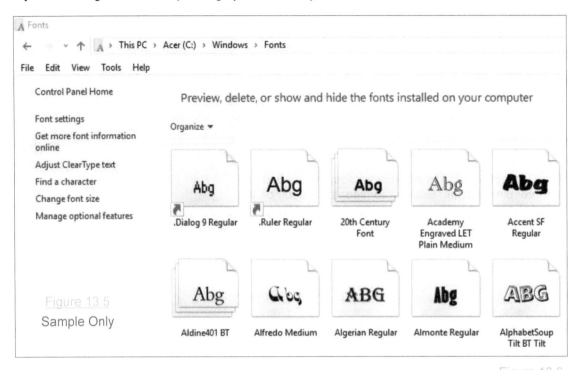

Figure 13.5
Sample Only

Figure 13.6

To use Windows fonts in Blender they have to be entered in the font slots in the **Properties Editor, Data button, Font tab** (Figure 13.6).

Note: In the Font tab there are four Font Style slots; Regular, Bold, Italic and Bold & Italic.

A Font Style has to be entered for each slot.

For Example: If Times New Roman Font Style is to be used;

Regular: times.ttf   **Bold**: timesbd.ttf
Italic: timesbi.ttf   **Bold & Italic**: timesi.ttf

To enter a Font Style click on the **Folder icon** (Figure 13.7).

Clicking the Folder icon opens **Blender's File Browser** where you navigate and locate the Font style (Figure 13.8). On a Windows system go to: C:\Windows\Fonts\

Click to see Fonts as Thumbnail Images

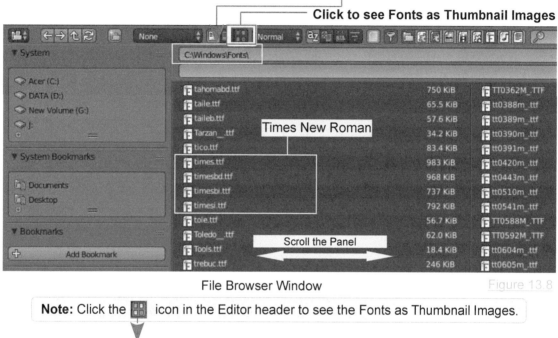

File Browser Window

Figure 13.8

Note: Click the ▦ icon in the Editor header to see the Fonts as Thumbnail Images.

Figure 13.9

Blender will accept any of the Windows fonts, but some may be distorted when they are extruded into 3D shapes.

Having selected a font click on the **Open Font button** in the upper RH corner of the screen. Do this for each font slot.

Note: you can mix and match different font styles and options. For instance you can have one font for regular text and a different font for bold or italic.

> **Note:** Entering Fonts in the Properties Editor, Fonts buttons, Font tab modifies the data for the particular Text Object you are working on in the 3D View Editor (the object you have selected). It does not set the Font type for every time you add Text into the 3D View Editor. When you add a new Text Object it will be the default Blender Bfont.

By default typing will enter text in the 3D View Editor in **Regular** text. To enter text in one of the alternative options (Bold, Italic, Underline, Small Caps) click one of the option **buttons** in the **Font Tab** (Figure 13.10).

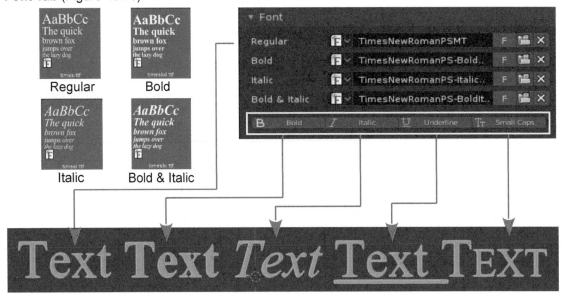

Figure 13.10

To change text that has already been entered, locate the **Text Cursor** (in Edit mode) using the arrow keys on the keyboard, press and hold shift while using the arrow keys to highlight text, delete the text then check one of the **Character buttons** to change the text option. Retype the text with the new option. Pressing **Ctrl + L or R** arrow keys moves the text cursor to the end of the word.

In the **Font tab**, the underline position and thickness values only operate when **Underline** is ticked under the **Character** heading. Underlining occurs as you type your text in Edit mode.

Also in the **Font Tab,** adjusting the Size and Shear value sliders increases the size of the selected Text object and shears the Text (similar to Italic – Figure 13.11).

Figure 13.11

 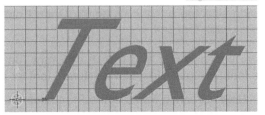

13.4 Creating Text on a Curve

Text in Blender can be made to follow the shape of a Curved Path. Add text to your Scene as previously described then in Edit mode type something to extend the text (Figure 13.12).

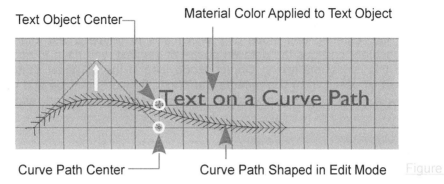

Text Object Center —

Material Color Applied to Text Object

Curve Path Center ——

Curve Path Shaped in Edit Mode

Figure 13.12

Add a **Curve - Path** to the Scene (**Shift + A key – Curve – Path**). Note by default the path is named **NurbsPath**.

The Curve Path is added to the Scene in Object mode and appears as a straight line. Scale the Path to make it longer and reposition it in Object mode.

- In Edit Mode Extrude or shape the Curve (Figure 13.12). With the Curve shaped tab back to Object mode and deselect it.

Figure 13.13

Select the Text Object then in the **Properties Editor, Data button, Font Tab**, find the **Text on Curve panel**. Click on the little cube icon and in the drop down menu that displays select **NurbsPath** (Figure 13.13).

The text is shaped to follow the profile of the curve (Figure 13.14).

Tip: After entering Nurbs Path in the Text on Curve panel, click on Size increment to activate the Text Curving.

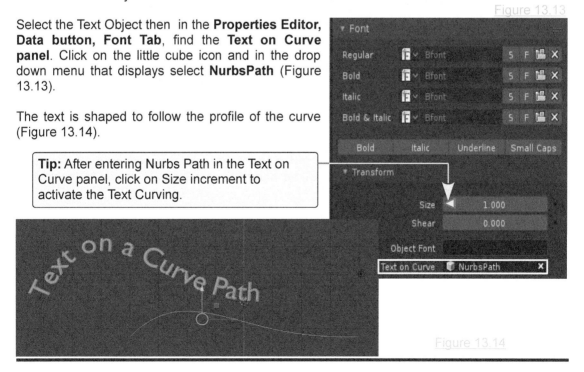

Figure 13.14

185

13.5 Converting Text to a Mesh Object

There is only limited functionality in the text **Object Data button, Geometry tab** for modifying the text shape (see 13.1 Figure 13.4).

When you add Text to a Scene it remains a 2D Plane Object unless you have extruded the text in the Geometry tab. Entering Edit mode only allows you to retype a text change. To perform editing, which actually changes the detailed shape of the Text, you have to convert to a **Mesh Object**. To do this, select the text in **Object Mode** then in the **3D View Editor Header** click **Object**, **Convert to**, **Mesh from Curve/Meta/Surf/Text** . Tab to Edit mode and you will see that the text is now a Mesh Object with vertices that can be moved, rotated, and scaled (Figure 13.15).

Figure 13.15

Object Mode with Text Extruded

Edit Mode after Conversion to Mesh

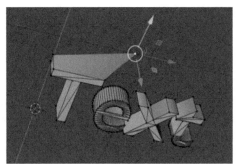

Vertices Selected and Moved

13.6 Converting Text to a Curve

If you would like to perform some fancy editing of a single letter, you can convert the letter into a Curve. The outline of the letter becomes a Curve with handles, which allows you to manipulate the shape into anything you wish.

Add **Text**, then in **Edit Mode** backspace until you are left with the single letter T . Scale, rotate, and move it where you like then tab to **Object Mode**. In the **3D View Editor Header** click **Object- Convert to - Curve from Mesh/Text**. In **Edit mode** you will see the outline of your letter as a curve with manipulating handles (Figure 13.17).

Figure 13.16

 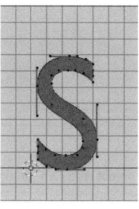 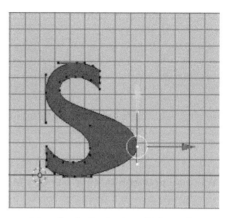

Object Mode – Convert Curve From Mesh Text	Edit Mode Control Handles	Handle Selected and Moved

Figure 13.17

13.7 Entering External Font

Text created in a Text Editor such as Word Pad or any editor that saves a file in .txt format may be entered into Blender.

For example a **Text File** named **Test_Text.txt** created in **Word Pad**, using **Font Style: Courier New size 36** saved in **MyDocuments** folder. The file contains the single word **Texting**.

To enter this in Blender, click **Add - Text** in the **3D window header** (alternatively press **Shift + A key** and select **Text** from the menu.

Remember have the **3D window in Top Orthographic** View.

Tab to **Edit mode** and backspace deleting the default word **Text**.

In the **3D View Editor Header** click on Edit and select **Past File** from the menu. The File Browser window opens where you navigate and find the saved .txt file (Figure 13.18).

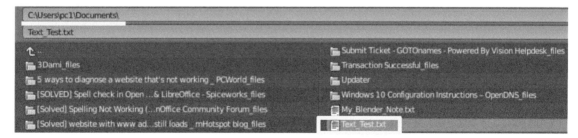

File Browser Window

Figure 13.18

Click on the file name to highlight then click on **Paste File** in the upper RH corner of the window.

The text **Testing** is entered into the 3D View Editor in Edit mode (Figure 13.19).

Figure 13.19

You may now convert the text to a **Mesh object** (see 13.4) or to a **Curve** (see 13.5).

14

Viewport Shading

Viewport Shading

Definitions: **Viewport:** The View in an Editor. **Shading:** How the View in an Editor is displayed.

Blender provides a variety of shading options which allows a Scene to be previewed during construction. Previewing in turn allows editing to be performed as the Scene is developed.

As Scenes are created, with Objects being added and Materials (colors) applied and lighting effects and textures introduced, it can be difficult to isolate a particular Object or even a component of an Object. By shading the **Viewport**, making the Objects display in a simplified way, allows a selection to be Edited.

Rendered Viewport Shading

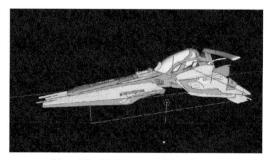

Simplified Viewport Shading

14.1 Viewport Shading Options

Options for **Viewport Shading** (displaying the 3D View Editor) are found in the upper RH corner of the **3D View Editor Header** (Figure 14.1).

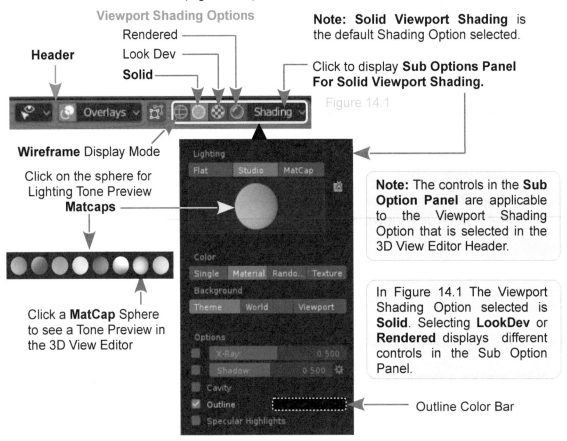

Viewport Shading Options

Rendered

Header

Look Dev

Solid

Note: Solid Viewport Shading is the default Shading Option selected.

Click to display **Sub Options Panel For Solid Viewport Shading.**

Figure 14.1

Wireframe Display Mode

Click on the sphere for Lighting Tone Preview
Matcaps

Note: The controls in the **Sub Option Panel** are applicable to the Viewport Shading Option that is selected in the 3D View Editor Header.

Click a **MatCap** Sphere to see a Tone Preview in the 3D View Editor

In Figure 14.1 The Viewport Shading Option selected is **Solid**. Selecting **LookDev** or **Rendered** displays different controls in the Sub Option Panel.

Outline Color Bar

Lighting
Flat   Studio   MatCap

Color
Single   Material   Rando..   Texture
Background
Theme   World   Viewport

Options
X-Ray   0.500
Shadow   0.500
Cavity
Outline
Specular Highlights

Solid Viewport Shading: The default display mode which has generally been used to produce figures for demonstration and is the basic construction mode.

LookDev Viewport Shading: Provides a quick method of previewing **Scene Lighting Modes**.

Rendered Viewport Shading: Places the Viewport in Render Mode allowing you to see what you get when an image is rendered (produced).

The **Solid** and **LookDev** Viewport Shading options have a **Sub Option Panel**. **Solid** is the default Shading and has by far the most comprehensive choice of Sub Options. As noted above the display in the Sub Options Panels is different, depending on the Shading Mode selected.

MatCap (Material Capture) shaders are complete materials, including lighting and reflections. They let you view an Object in the way in which you want the surface to appear.

14.2 Solid Viewport Shading Sub Options

The Sub Options for **Solid Viewport Shading** are categorised into four sections; Lighting, Color, Background and Options (sub, sub options).

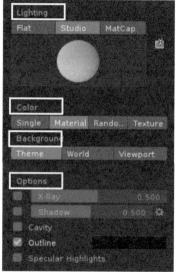

Figure 14.2

14.2.1 Lighting

A Scene is illuminated by placing Lamps (Lights) at strategic positions or having Emitter Objects (Objects that emit light) located thorough the Scene (Chapter 15). In the course of construction complicated Scene Lighting can be a hindrance, therefore, a simplified Viewport display is preferable.

Solid Viewport Shading provides three lighting methods; Flat, Studio and MatCap. These lighting methods are all independent of any Lamps placed in the 3D View Editor. While in Solid Viewport Shading Mode Lamps in the 3D View Editor have no effect. **Studio Lighting** is the default method.

Studio Lighting is an arbitrary lighting arrangement which is independent of the Lamps in the Scene. When the Viewport is rotated mesh faces are shaded for visualisation but the shading is not influenced by light sources such as the Lamps in the Scene. Rendering the Scene produces a different shading based on the lighting generated by the Lamps.

To examine and understand the relationship of Object illumination shadows can be used. To see the effect of shadows there has to be something on which the shadows will be cast. In the default Scene add a Plane Object. The Plane is positioned on the Mid Plane Grid and scaled up. Position the Cube Object just above the Plane (Figure 14.3). With Solid Viewport Shading active, in the **Sub Options Panel**, **Options** (at the bottom of the panel) **check Shadow**.

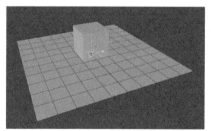
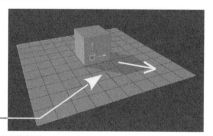

Shadow Cast ———

With the Scene rotated the shadow is cast relative to the Cube demonstrating that the light source is fixed relative to the Scene

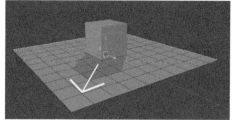

Figure 14.3

191

In the Figure 14.3 the Cube and the Plane do NOT have any Material (color) applied. To continue with the demonstration add color (Reference Chapter 4 - 4.18). Figure 14.4 shows Studio Lighting with color added.

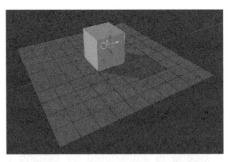

By clicking on the sphere below Studio, MatCap Lighting Tones display. Clicking either of these alters the lighting tone in the 3D View Editor.

Click the sphere

Figure 14.4

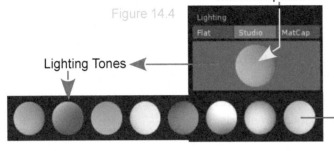

Lighting Tones

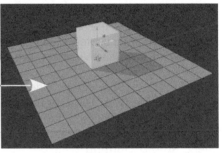

Click LMB on the sphere to preview **Lighting Tones**.

Matcap Lighting stands for **material capture** – it is a complete material including lighting and reflections. A Matcap is added for quick feedback, to see how an Object's shape is changing under different lighting conditions. This is a preview only, not a permanent lighting set-up.

Figure 14.5

With Matcap selected Clicking on the Sphere in the Sub Options Panel displays a selection of MatCap shading options which when pressed show you how Objects will display under different shading effects.

Click LMB to display MatCap options

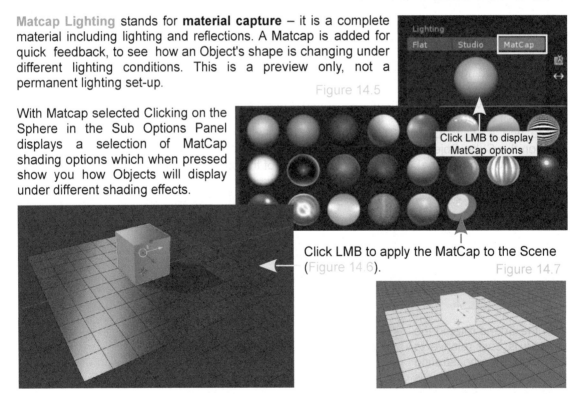

Click LMB to apply the MatCap to the Scene (Figure 14.6).

Figure 14.7

Flat Lighting applies the Material (color) set in the Properties Editor, Material buttons as a plain flat color (Figure 14.7).

Note: In the diagram, the Objects in the Scene have a Material (color) applied. The MatCap generates a lighting effect which affects the colors of the Objects giving an indication of how the Scene will appear. This effect does not render in an image.

14.2.2 Color Display Options (Figure 14.7)

With either **Studio Lighting** or **Flat Lighting** there are four **Color Type** settings in the **Sub Options Panel.** The default is **Material,** which means Objects in the Scene (Viewport) are displayed with the Material color that has been assigned to the Object in the **Properties Editor, Material buttons** when Nodes are deactivated.

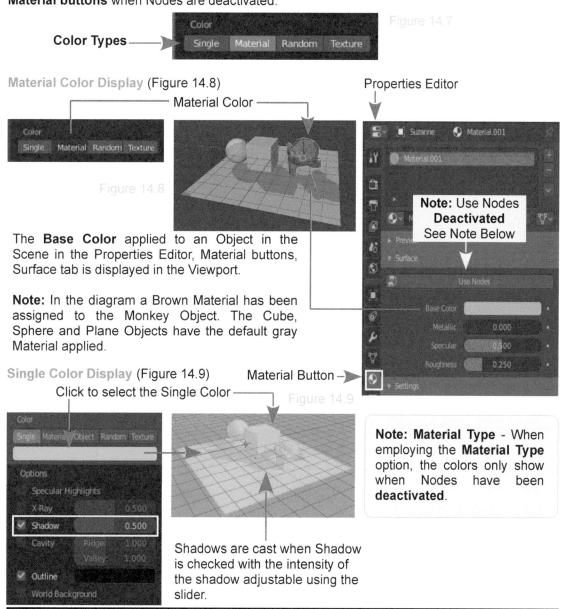

Color Types

Figure 14.7

Material Color Display (Figure 14.8)

Material Color

Properties Editor

The **Base Color** applied to an Object in the Scene in the Properties Editor, Material buttons, Surface tab is displayed in the Viewport.

Note: In the diagram a Brown Material has been assigned to the Monkey Object. The Cube, Sphere and Plane Objects have the default gray Material applied.

Note: Use Nodes **Deactivated** See Note Below

Figure 14.8

Single Color Display (Figure 14.9)

Click to select the Single Color

Material Button

Figure 14.9

Note: Material Type - When employing the **Material Type** option, the colors only show when Nodes have been **deactivated**.

Shadows are cast when Shadow is checked with the intensity of the shadow adjustable using the slider.

Random Color Display (Figure 14.10)

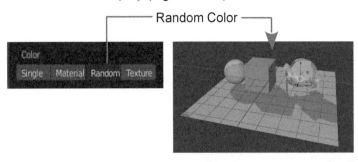

Random Color

Random Color displays each Object in the Scene with a different color. The color assignment is automatic.

Figure 14.10

Texture Color Display (Figure 14.11)

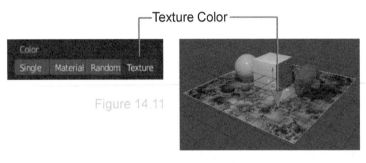

Texture Color

Figure 14.11

Textures are effects which give the surface of an Object characteristics. Texture Color displays Objects with a Texture that has been previously set as the Base Color in the Properties Editor, Material buttons (Reference Chapter 16).

Background Display

In **Solid Viewport Shading Mode** there are three **Background** display options.

Figure 14.12

Theme

Background option **Theme** displays the Viewport with the Theme that has been set in the **User Preferences Editor** (Reference Chapter 1 - 1.14 Figure 1.21).

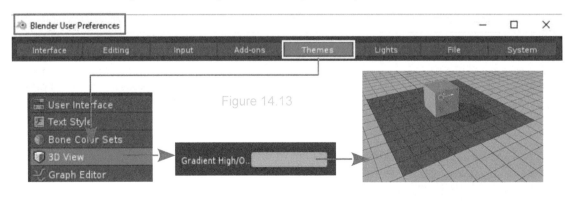

Figure 14.13

World

Background option **World** displays the Viewport with the Background that has been set in the **Properties Editor, World buttons, Surface tab**.

Properties Editor ——————►

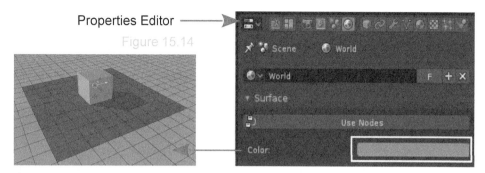

Figure 15.14

Viewport

A preview of the Scene Background may be set in the Shading Sub Options Panel.

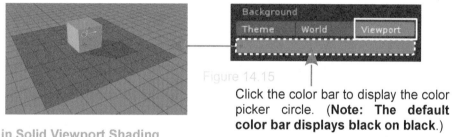

Figure 14.15

Click the color bar to display the color picker circle. (**Note: The default color bar displays black on black**.)

More Options in Solid Viewport Shading

X-Ray:

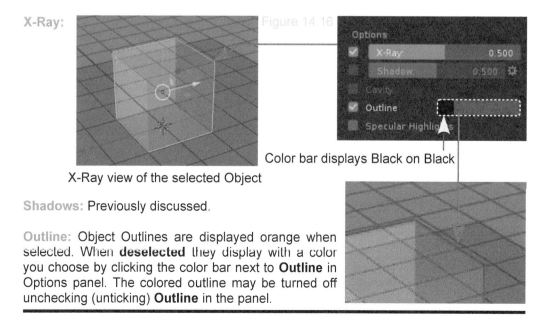

Figure 14.16

X-Ray view of the selected Object

Color bar displays Black on Black

Shadows: Previously discussed.

Outline: Object Outlines are displayed orange when selected. When **deselected** they display with a color you choose by clicking the color bar next to **Outline** in Options panel. The colored outline may be turned off unchecking (unticking) **Outline** in the panel.

14.3 Rendered Viewport Shading

Rendered Viewport Shading gives a quick access to a preview showing exactly what you will see in a Rendered view. Unlike Solid and LocDev Viewport Shading Modes it has no sub options. Clicking Rendered Viewport Shading displays the 3D View Editor as a Rendered view and as such, the Lighting in the view is influenced by the Lamps and lighting arrangement set in the Scene.

Note: Textures used to color objects will NOT display in a Rendered view unless the Material **Node System** has been employed.

Figure 14.17

Figure 14.18

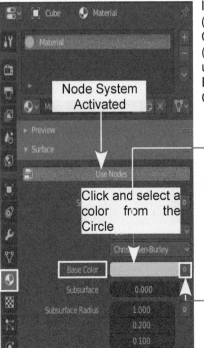

In Figures 14.17 and 14.18 the Objects have Materials (colors) applied using the Material Node System (Reference: Chapter 16) in the Properties Editor, Materials buttons (Figure 14.19). The Materials Shader Editor has NOT been used, instead, with Use Nodes active in the Properties Editor Base Colors have been selected by clicking on the Base Color bar.

Node System Activated

Click and select a color from the Circle

Figure 14.19

Click and select Image Texture

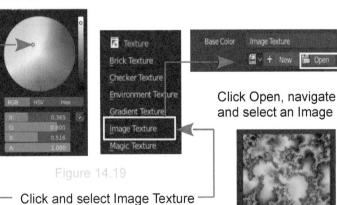

Click Open, navigate and select an Image

In the case of the Plane Object an Image Texture has been used for the color.

14.4 LookDev Viewport Shading

When creating or modifying a Scene using Solid Viewport Shading you may wish to quickly view the Scene as it appears with illumination provided by the Lamps instead of the illumination from the Solid Shading Mode. At times illumination is provided by special HDRI images used as a background to the Scene (Reference Chapter 15 – 15.8). If an HDRI image has been installed and you are in Solid Viewport Shading Mode LocDev provides a quick preview.

Figure 14.20

Figure 14.20 shows the Scene in the 3D View Editor in Solid Viewport Shading Mode with the Monkey Object selected in Edit Mode. If this were a complicated Scene where the Monkey was obscured by shadow you could clearly see the Monkey and manipulate Vertices.

The Scene is viewed under Studio Lighting.

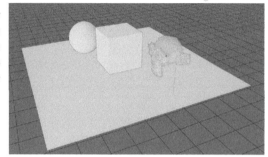

Figure 14.21

To quickly see how the Scene looks with the edits to the Monkey select **LookDev Viewport Shading** (Figure 14.21).

In the Sub Options select **Scene Lighting** to view the Scene using the lighting effects in the Scene (Lamps)

You may use the **Matcap** to preview how adjustments to Lamp setting would affect the display.

Figure 14.22

If an image has been used to illuminate the Scene select **Scene World** instead of Scene Lights to preview the Scene (Figure 14.22)

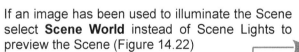

HDRI Image used as Scene background (Reference Chapter 15 – 15.8).

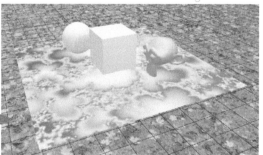

14.5 World Settings

Figure 14.23

World background color settings in the Properties Editor, World buttons also influence the display in the 3D View Editor (Figure 14.23).

Note: The background color set in the World buttons can only be seen in the 3D View Editor in LocDev with Scene World checked and Renderer Viewport Shading Modes.

15

Scene Lighting and Cameras

Introduction

Scene lighting (illumination) plays a very important part in determining what you see in the 3D View Editor and what will be captured by the Camera and Render as a final image.

How the Scene is viewed is dependent on the Lighting (arrangement of Lamps) and how the Camera or Cameras are positioned and configured.

Think of the Scene in the 3D View Editor as if it were a set on a theatre stage or a set for a movie. The theatre audience sees the illuminated stage, the movie goer sees what has been captured by the camera. Neither see the conglomeration of paraphernalia in the background.

A Scene in Blender has this same arrangement of equipment producing a final rendered image.

Where the Camera is positioned determines what is captured as an image and how the Scene is illuminated determines what the image looks like.

To start with, there is a single Point Lamp in the default Blender Scene but, be aware that the Scene is NOT illuminated by this Lamp rather by Viewport Shading (Chapter 14). The conundrum is, to understand Viewport Shading you have to understand Scene Lighting.

15.1 Scene Lighting

The default Scene in the 3D View Editor is illuminated by Studio Lighting in Solid Viewport Shading Mode (Reference Chapter 14 - 14.1). This Shading Mode is independent of Lamps, therefore, the default Point Lamp in the default Blender Scene has no effect. To discuss Blender Lamps change the Viewport Shading to **LookDev Viewport Shading** and activate **Scene Lights and Scene World**.

Viewport Shading Options are located in the **3D View Editor Header** at the RH side of the Editor.

Figure 15.1

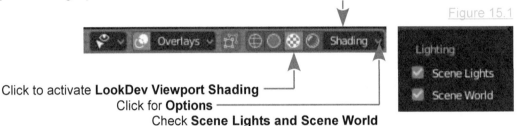

Click to activate **LookDev Viewport Shading**
Click for **Options**
Check **Scene Lights and Scene World**

15.2 Lamps

Properties Editor

The default Blender Scene contains a single **Point Lamp.**

Figure 15.2

With the Lamp selected, go to the **Properties Editor, Object Data buttons** to display the setting options (Figure 15.2). You may change the Lamp by selecting one of the types in the **Light tab**.

The Properties Editor display will vary depending on the Lamp Type selected.

The color of light may be selected by clicking the color bar to display a color picker circle.

Object Data Button ———→

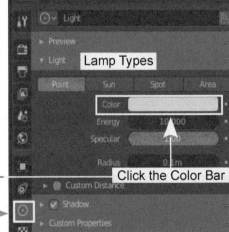

Lamp Types

Click the Color Bar

Adding Lamps

To add additional Lamps to the Scene, position the cursor in the 3D View Editor, press **Shift + A Key** and select **Light** from the menu that displays. You can choose **Point, Sun, Spot, Hemi, or Are**a.

The diagrammatic representation of the Lamp in the 3D View Editor varies depending on the type (Figure 15.3).

Note: The **Object Data** button icon for the Lamp in the Properties Editor Header changes to represent the **Lamp Type**.

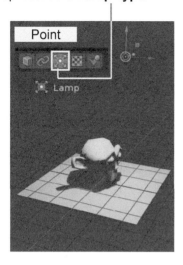

Point

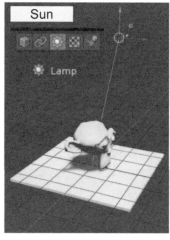

Sun

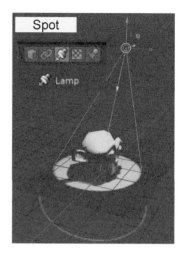

Spot

Figure 15.3

To see the effect of the different Lamp Types and settings create a Scene as shown in Figure 15.4.

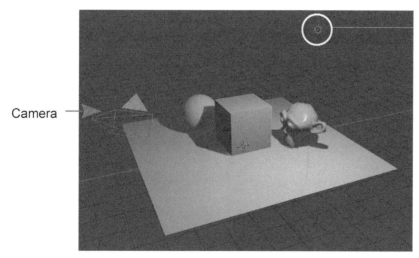

Point Lamp

Camera

Figure 15.4

In the Scene a Plane has been added and scaled up five times. The Plane has been Translated (Moved) up just above the Midplane Grid. A UV Sphere and a Monkey have been added and positioned each side of the default Cube. The Cube, UV Sphere and Monkey have been Translated up to sit just above the Plane. Colors have been added with the Node System deactivated (Reference: Chapter 4 – 4.18).

The Camera and the default Point Lamp are in their default positions.

The 3D View Editor is in LookDev Viewport Shading Mode (Chapter 14 – 14.4).

Make note of the different effect when you change the Lamp Type in the Properties Editor, Data buttons, Light tab (with the Lamp selected).

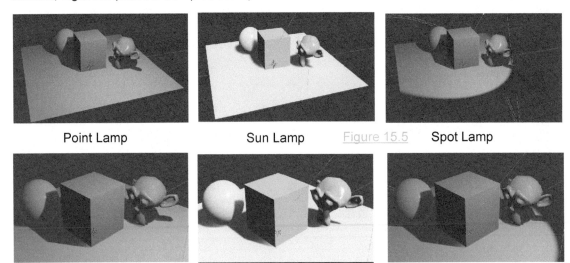

Point Lamp   Sun Lamp   Figure 15.5   Spot Lamp

The upper row of images shows part of the 3D View Editor. The lower row shows Camera View.

By leaving the default Point Lamp in position, then adding an additional Spot Lamp and directing it towards the left hand face of the Cube you remove the shadow on the Cube and the Monkey (Figure 15.6).

Figure 15.6

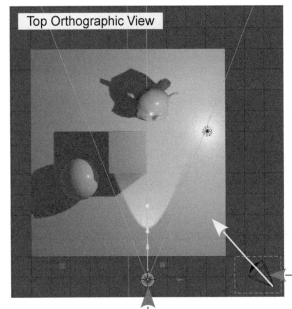

Camera View

The Camera in its default position.

Additional Spot Lamp pointing towards the Cube and the Monkey.

15.3 Cameras

By default the Scene has one Camera which is positioned to capture an image of the Cube Object. What the Camera sees and what is captured as an image is called **Camera View**. You can see Camera View in the 3D View Editor by pressing Num Pad 0 on the Keyboard. To return to User Perspective View, press Num Pad 5 (User Orthographic View) then Num Pad 5 again for User Perspective View. **You have to rotate the View to reinstate the default Scene**.

In a complex Scene you may wish to add more Cameras to capture shots from different angles. You add Cameras by pressing **Shift + A key** and selecting **Camera** from the menu or click Add in the Header and select Camera. The new Camera will be located where the 3D Cursor is positioned. If you add a Camera in the default Scene with the 3D Cursor at the center of the Scene it will coincide with the default Cube Object. Click the Move Tool in the Tool Panel and move the Camera to one side. You have to rotate the new Camera to capture the part of the Scene you require.

Depending on the Scene arrangement the Cameras may or may not be visible in the 3D View. Camera View depends on which camera is selected. If the camera is visible RMB click to select. If it is not visible you can select it in the Outliner Editor by clicking LMB on the name. The original Camera is named Camera the new Camera is named Camera.001. You may rename these to something meaningful if you wish.

> **Note:** If you select Camera.001 and press Num Pad 0 you will get a Camera View taken by the original Camera. To get Camera View from Camera.001, have Camera.001 selected then press **Ctrl + Num Pad 0**. Similarly if you have been using Camera.001 for Camera View and you select the original Camera and press Num Pad 0 you get a Camera View from Camera.001.
>
> The Camera View is taken from the last Camera used.

Outliner Editor

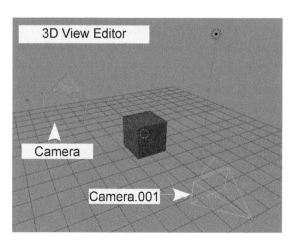

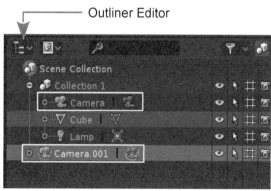

Select a Camera press Ctrl + Num Pad 0 For Camera View.

Figure 15.7

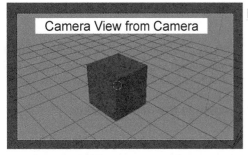

Camera View from Camera

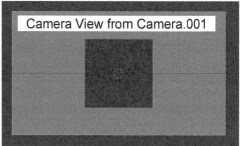

Camera View from Camera.001

Figure 15.8

15.4 Camera Settings

Properties Editor

Figure 15.9

Settings are found in the **Properties Editor, Data buttons** (Figure 15.9).

Lens Tab: (Figure 15.10)

Perspective, Orthographic or Panoramic: Used to change the camera from showing a true-life perspective view to an orthographic view.

Figure 15.10

Focal Length: Sets up a lens length much like a real camera; 35mm is a good safe setting but wide and tight angle settings work for different needs.

Data button→

Shift: Pushes the camera's view in a direction, without changing perspective.

Clip Start: How close an object can be to the camera and still be seen (Figure15.11).

Clip End: How far away objects can be seen by the Camera; in very large Scenes, this needs to be set higher or objects disappear from view (Figure 15.11).

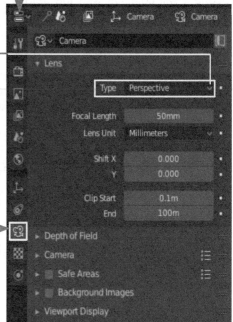

To view Limits, check **Limits** in the Viewport Display Tab (Figure 15.15)

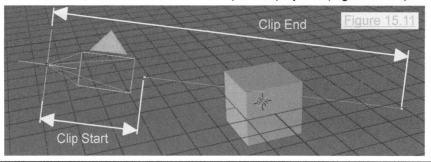

Clip End   Figure 15.11

Clip Start

Camera Tab: (Figure 15.12)

Figure 15.12

Camera Presets: Allows matching the virtual Camera in the Blender Scene with a real camera used to record video. This produces a more realistic effect when Camera Tracking (see Camera Tracking 15.6).

Depth of Field Tab: (Figure 15.13)

Used with **Nodes** to blur foreground and background objects (Nodes are discussed in Chapter 16). Figure 15.13

Aperture Tab: (Figure 15.14)

Mimics f-stop settings on a real camera which controle the amount of light entering the camera.

Figure 15.14

Viewport Display Tab: (Figure 15.15)

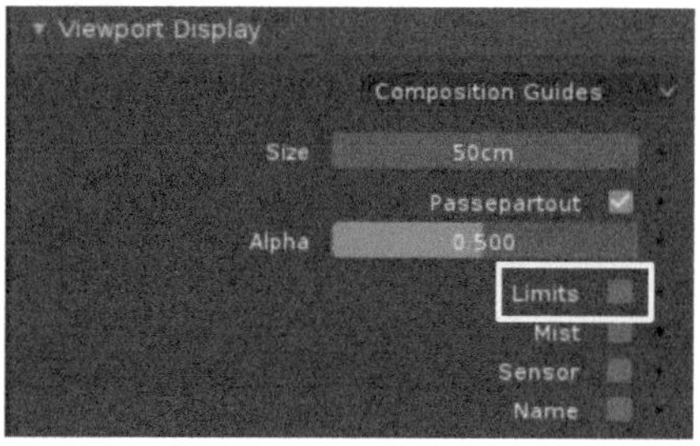

Composition Guides: Check options to display guidelines in Camera View (see Figure 15.18).

Size: How big to draw the Camera on the Screen; you can also control the size with scale.

Figure 15.15

Passepartout: Is also in the Display Tab and when checked Shades the area on the Screen outside of the Camera View (Figure 15.18).

Alpha: Controls the darkness of the shaded area with the slider.

Limits: Draws a line in the scene to help you visualise the Camera's range (Figure 15.17)

Mist: Gives you a visual display of how far the Camera sees if you are adding a mist effect.

Figure 15.16

Sensor: Shows the sensor size (Film Gate) in Camera View (Figure 15.18).

Name: Displays the name of the active Camera in Camera View (Num Pad 0) (Figure 15.18).

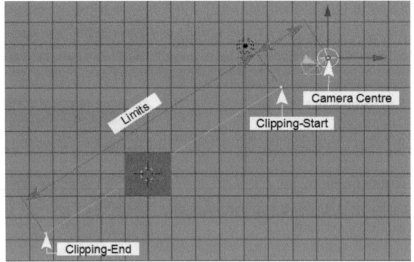

Figure 15.17

Objects in front of the **Clipping Start** point or beyond the **Clipping End** point will not be seen in Camera View.

Figure 15.18

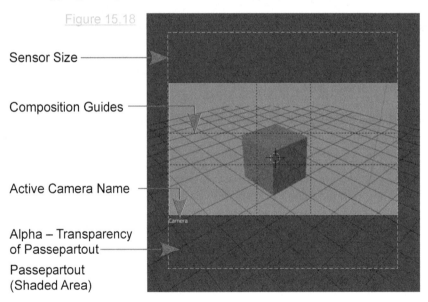

Sensor Size

Composition Guides

Active Camera Name

Alpha – Transparency of Passepartout

Passepartout (Shaded Area)

15.5 Camera Switching

In **Cameras 14.3** it was shown that you may have more than one Camera in a Scene and you can switch between Cameras by selecting one, then pressing **Ctrl + Num pad 0**. This makes the selected Camera active and opens **Camera View** showing what is seen by that Camera. Manual selection is fine for rendering single images of an object from different viewing perspectives but you may want to animate the switching so that when rendering an animation you switch between Cameras as the animation plays.

Animation is discussed in Chapter 18 but the inclusion of a prelude in the following demonstration will be beneficial.

Set up a Scene similar to that shown in Figure 14.19, with three **Cameras** pointed at **Suzanne** (Monkey) from different locations. You can use the default Camera and add two others.

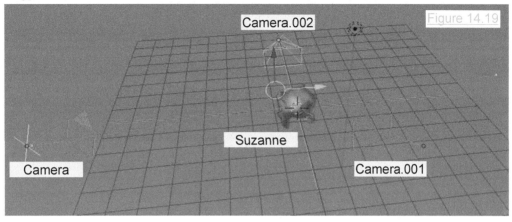

Figure 14.19

In the 3D View Editor select the default Camera named **Camera**. In the **Timeline Editor** with the vertical blue cursor line at Frame 1 and the **Mouse cursor in the Timeline Editor** press the **M Key** to place a **Marker** at frame 1. **Note:** You can only place the marker when the **Mouse cursor** is positioned in the Timeline (Figure 14.20).

Timeline Editor

Marker only at Frame 70

Timeline Editor Cursor

Figure 14.20

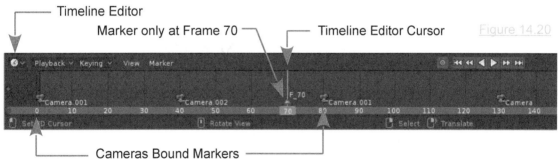

Cameras Bound Markers

The selected **Camera** has to be **Parented** to the **Marker**. Click on **Marker** in the **Timeline Editor Header** and select **Bind Camera to Markers**.

Select one of the other Cameras. In the Timeline Editor move the blue cursor line to another Frame. With the **Mouse Cursor** in the Timeline Editor press the **Ctrl + B Key** to place a second marker and bind the Camera to the Marker.

> **Note:** You can place a Marker without a Camera being selected by pressing the **M Key** with the Timeline Cursor positioned at a Frame.

Repeat the process for the 3rd Camera. Remember, select a different frame in the **Timeline** and when you place a marker have your **Mouse cursor** in the **Timeline window**. Select Camera (the original) and press **Ctrl + Num Pad 0** for Camera View. When you press **Play in the Timeline Header** an animation will play switching from one Camera View to the other.

The Animation plays from Frame 1 to Frame 250 then repeats. Figure 14.21

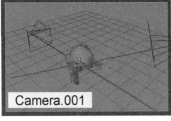
Camera.001

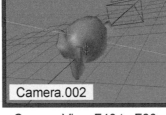
Camera.002

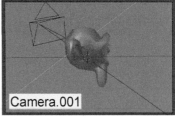
Camera.001

Camera View F1 to F40   Camera View F40 to F80   Camera View F80 to F130

15.6 Camera Tracking

Camera Tracking is a technique that imitates the real Camera motion which occurs when recording a video. This motion is applied to a 3D Camera in a Blender Scene providing a realistic effect when a 3D model is superimposed over a video background (Figure 15.22). Without this effect the Blender 3D Camera would track to a stable imaginary point or to a predetermined curve track in the Scene. This would be fine for the superimposed 3D Object but the actual video used as a background would move differently and produce an unrealistic effect.

The essence of the technique is to plot the movement of multiple points in the video Scene and feed that information to the motion of the Blender 3D Camera.

At this point the technique is mentioned to make you aware of its existence and the following video tutorial is suggested: https:www.youtube.com/watch?v=O3fGc_QM3yI//w

Figure 15.22

15.7 Basic Scene Lighting

To demonstrate **Basic Scene Lighting,** create a Scene as shown in Figure 15.23 including a Cube, a UV Sphere, a Plane and a Monkey Object. **Note**: The Plane has been Translated up slightly on the Z Axis. When the Plane is added to the Scene with the 3D View Editor Cursor located at the center of the Scene, the grid lines show in the surface of the Plane. Translating up, puts the Plane above the Grid. The Cube, UV Sphere and Monkey are all Translated and positioned above the Plane.

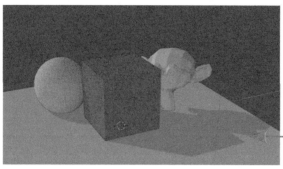

Figure 15.23

Note: Direction of shadows due to the Studio Lighting

You may create the Scene with the 3D View Editor in **Solid Viewport Shading Mode** (Chapter 14). The default settings in the Sub Options Panel can be left as they are, with the one exception, **check Shadows**.

Note; the default color setting is **Material,** meaning the Material (color) added to the Objects will be displayed.

Add a basic Material (color) to all Objects (Chapter 4 - 4.18).

Figure 15.24 is a screen capture of part of the view in the 3D View Editor approximating Camera View (what the Camera sees).

With the Scene created, change to **LookDev Viewport Shading Mode** (Chapter 14) and check **Scene Lighting** in the Sub Options panel. You will immediately see a difference in the view since the effect of the single default Point Lamp is displayed.

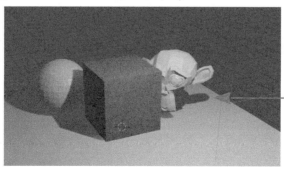

Colors brighter and the direction of shadows changed due to the single Point Lamp in the Scene

Figure 15.24

Make note that the Light emitted by the Lamp, by default, is white (RGB 1.000).

In the **Outliner Editor** click on **Lamp** to select the Point Lamp in Collection 1. Selecting in the Outliner Editor selects the Lamp in the 3D View Editor.

In the Properties Editor, Data buttons the settings will be applicable to the Lamp in the 3D View Editor (the selected Object). Change the Lamp setting Point to **Area**. Again you see a change to the lighting in the 3D View Editor demonstrating the effect of Lamp settings (Figure 15.25).

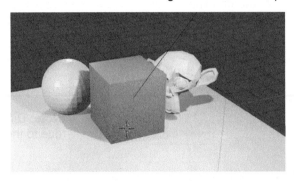

Figure 15.25

In the 3D View Editor add two more <u>Point Lamps</u> and position as shown in Figure 15.26.

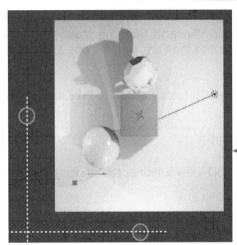

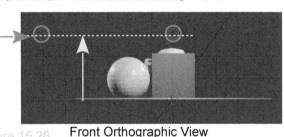

Figure 15.26   Front Orthographic View

Top Orthographic View
Orange circles showing the approximate location of the additional (two) Lamps.

With the 3D View Editor in **User Perspective View** go to the **Outliner Editor** and toggle hide and display of the new Lamps to see the different Lighting effects.

Note: The new Lamps listed in the Outliner Editor are named **Point** and **Point.001**   Figure 15.27

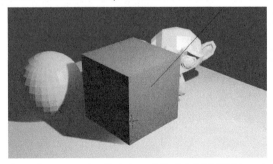

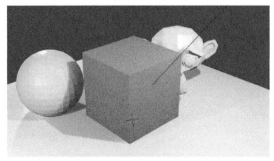

Area Lamp only, Point and Point.001 Hidden (off)   Area Lamp + Two Point Lamps

15.8 Background Scene Lighting

Beside the effect of Lamps in the Scene you should be aware that the Scene Background plays a part in determining how Materials display. As in the real world the ambient light surrounding Objects determines how they are seen. In Blender, the World Background light has a similar effect.

Background Color Lighting

To demonstrate this phenomena replace the Cube Object in the default Scene with a UV Sphere and set the Sphere's surface to Shade Smooth (Chapter 4 - 4.21).

Have the 3D View Editor in **Rendered Viewport Shading Mode** (Chapter 14).

With the UV Sphere selected, In the Properties Editor, Material buttons, click **New** to add a Material. Since this is a new Object in the Scene, **Use Nodes** will be activated.

Use Nodes, means that the **Blender Node System** for applying Materials is being used. An explanation describing what Nodes are and how to use them is given in Chapter 16.

For the moment, with **Nodes active**, click on the **Base Color** bar to display the Color Picker Circle and give the UV Sphere a yellow color by setting the RGB color values (R: 0.753, G: 0.531, B: 0.002). Have the intensity slider cranked all the way to the top (very bright).

Remaining in the Properties Editor, click on the **World button** and in click **Use Nodes**. By default **Surface** is set as **Background**. Click on the Color bar (the default color is gray) and change to a blue color (R: 0.011, G: 0.789, B: 0.900). Move the Intensity Slider up to about half way.

Result: Blue Background causing the Yellow Sphere to appear Green.

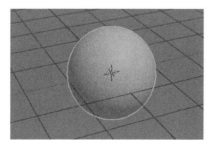 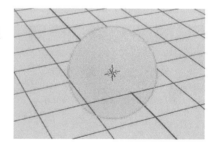

Figure 15.28

Images as a Background

Colored Scene backgrounds are suitable in many cases but an image used as a background can significantly add atmosphere. Special images called **HDRI Maps** are particularly spectacular in giving a three dimensional effect when the Scene is rotated. This type of image adds lighting to the Scene thus affecting how Objects are seen.

One source of HDRI images is: https://hdrihaven.com

To demonstrate the use of HDRIs use the Scene arrangement in Figure 15.23. Deselect all the Objects in the Scene and have an **HDRI image** saved on your computer.

 World Button

In the **Properties Editor, World buttons** click on **Use Nodes**. In the Surface tab you will see that Surface is set to **Background**.

Figure 15.29

Click on the dot at the end of the **Color Bar** and select **Environmental Texture** in the menu that displays. Click on Open and navigate to your HDRI file.

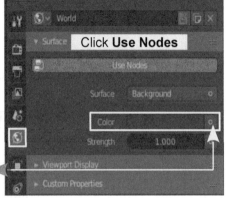

Figure 15.30

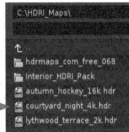

Have the 3D View Editor with **Look/Dev Viewport Shading** and with **Scene World checked** in the Shading options. The HDRI image will display as the Background to your Scene.

Figure 15.31

Image courtyard_night_4K.hdr

At this point you manipulate the view in the 3D View Editor and move the Objects to position in the Scene as shown in Figure 15.32 over.

In Figure 15.32 the Objects have been positioned to appear as if they are sitting on the floor just outside the open door. All the Lamps in the Scene have been deleted showing that the Light from the image affects the Objects.

Figure 15.32

15.9 Volumetric Lighting

Using HDRI Maps as a background can give you a quick way to illuminate a Scene and combine a background but you are limited to what you can source in an image. You may want something completely unique and maybe not as complicated. Volumetric Lighting may be the answer.

Volumetric Lighting uses the light provided by Blenders Lamps and scatters or diffuses the light in the Scene. A simple demonstration is to place a light source in a Scene behind an Object such that the diffuse light shines through the Object, casting shadows towards the Camera.

Figure 15.33

To produce a Volumetric Lighting effect as shown in Figure 15.33 Blender's Node System is used. How to use Nodes is explained in Chapter 16 – 16.23 with a full description of creating this simple effect.

Nodes - Materials and Textures

In **Blender,** consider **Nodes** as **a** graphical displays representing **computer code** for producing effects such as the application of **Materials** and **Textures** to the surface of Objects. They may also be used for creating Scene backgrounds and in the enhancement of **Images** or **Video**. In fact there are many uses.

The discourse in this chapter will be an **introduction only** into the use of Nodes. The subject is extensive and requires a dedicated publication. To begin with, the application of Materials and Textures using Nodes, will be discussed followed by a brief look at other uses. The examples provided will act as a starting point and assist in understanding detailed tutorials for advanced applications. Proficiency in the use of Nodes will only come with practice and experience and the accumulation of a library of Node Arrangements.

The discussion will be limited to the use of Nodes with the **Eevee Render** system active. Although the principles of operation apply to both Eevee and Cycles the latter has a more extensive Node system.

Material Nodes in their basic application allow you to add color to the surface of an Object. In Chapter 4 - 4.18 instruction is provided describing how to color an Object **with the Node System disabled**. When the Properties Editor, Material buttons are opened the default controls are for the **Application of Materials (colors) using the Node System** (Use Nodes, highlighted blue).

Some **Material Nodes** are called **Shaders**. Material Nodes are accessed in the **Shader Editor,** but before opening the Editor run through some preliminaries so you know what to expect.

For the purpose of the discussion consider a Node as a point in a pipeline of information which contributes to a result. In the case of Material Nodes the result is the appearance of the surface of an Object in the 3D View Editor. There are usually numerous Nodes connected together producing the result, each of which may be disconnected, rearranged or replaced to vary the final display.

The **Node** is graphical representation of computer data or instruction which is arranged in a pipeline. Think about mixing colors. The primary colors are Red, Green and Blue, which when mixed in equal proportions produce White (Figure 16.1).

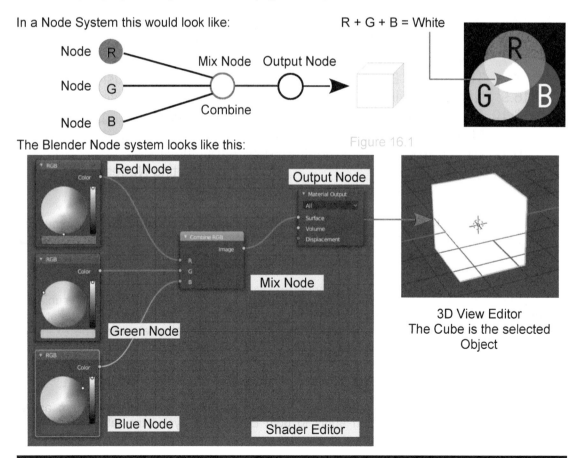

In a Node System this would look like:

R + G + B = White

The Blender Node system looks like this:

Figure 16.1

3D View Editor
The Cube is the selected Object

Figure 16.1 shows a simple Node arrangement.

```
Computer Code                           Text Editor
shader simple_material(
    color Diffuse_Color = color(0.6, 0.8, 0.6),
    float Noise_Factor = 0.5,
    output closure color BSDF = diffuse(N))
{
    color material_color = Diffuse_Color * mix(1.0, noise(P * 10.0), Noise_Factor);
    BSDF = material_color * diffuse(N);
}
```

Computer Code written in **Python**, is represented by the **Diffuse BSDF Node**, which outputs data to the **Material Output Node.** This in turn applies Material (color) to the surface of the **Cube** Object in the 3D View Editor.

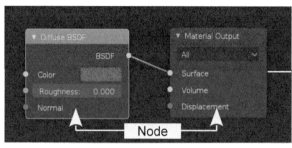

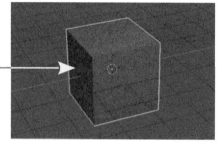

Shader Editor   Figure 16.2   3D View Editor

Figure 16.2 shows two Nodes in a very simple Node arrangement (pipeline). The **Diffuse BSDF Node** represents computer code written in Python which generates a red Material (Color). This Node is linked to a **Material Output Node** which applies the Material to the Cube Object in the 3D View Editor (the Cube is the selected Object).

Properties Editor

16.2 Materials – Using Nodes   Figure 16.3

In Chapter 4 - 4.18 **Material** was applied to Objects in the 3D View Editor with the Blender Node System disabled. **In the default Blender Scene** the default Cube in the 3D View Editor is selected and displays with a gray Material (color). In the Properties Editor, Material buttons **Use Nodes** is highlighted red indicating that the **Node System is engaged** (Figure 16.3). Click on the Base Color bar and you will see in the color picker circle that the R, G and B values are all 0.800 which are the values producing the default gray Material (R,G,B all 1.000 = White. R,G,B all 0.000 = Black).

Note: Surface – Principled BSDF.

Principled BSDF is the name of the Node being used.

Use Nodes Highlighted
Node System Engaged

Material Button

RGB: 0.800

16.3 Displaying Materials

When Nodes are cancelled, by clicking the **Use Nodes** button, a basic Material application is used (Reference: Chapter 4.18). The Material selected as the Base Color for the Object's surface will display in all three **Viewport Shading Modes**. The Material Base Color selected **with Use Nodes active** only displays when the Viewport Shading is in LookDev Mode or in Rendered Mode (see Chapter 14).

The term **Material** is used to distinguish between simple Color and how the surface of an Object is seen under certain lighting conditions. Material includes color, reflection, transparency, shadows etc., in fact the inclusive reflective characteristics of the surface. Materials do not include visible characteristics such as how lumpy or bumpy a surface is. These visible characteristics are called Textures.

16.4 Creating Materials

A Material is created when you modify the data producing the default gray color on the surface of the selected Object and apply the data (apply the Material Color) to the Object. The modified data (Material Datablock) is stored in a **Cache** making it available for application to other Objects in the Scene in the particular Blender file being worked.

To understand the process, open a new Blender file with the default Scene containing the Cube Object. The Cube is selected and the 3D View Editor is in **Solid Viewport Shading Mode** (Chapter 14). In the **Properties Editor** select the **Material button**.

The Cube displays with the default Gray Material which is named **Material**. The data (datablock) producing this gray color is stored in the **Material Cache**. In the default Scene, the Material named **Material** has been automatically selected from the **Cache**. With the Cube selected the Material named **Material** is entered into the **Material Slot** which is then applied to the Cube Object. The default gray **Material** is used to display all new Objects entered into a Scene.

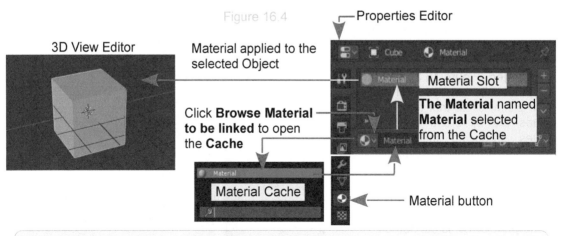

Figure 16.4

3D View Editor

Material applied to the selected Object

Properties Editor

Material Slot

The **Material** named **Material** selected from the Cache

Click **Browse Material to be linked** to open the **Cache**

Material Cache

Material button

Note: The only time the controls for the Material buttons automatically display is when you click the Material button for the default Cube Object in the default Blender Scene.

To demonstrate, delete the Cube. On deleting the Cube the Material button in the Properties Editor disappears. The World button becomes active, therefore, the Use Nodes button in the Properties Editor will activate the Node System applicable to the World settings NOT for Materials.

Add a new Cube to the Scene in the 3D View Editor. The Material buttons are reinstated but are empty except for the **New** button. Click **New** then click **Use Nodes** to cancel the Node System.

You will see a new Material named **Material.001** in the Material Slot.

Figure 16.5

Click the **Browse Material to be linked** button to open the Cache and you will see two Materials, one named **Material** (the default) and the other named **Material.001.**

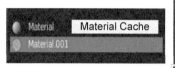

 ◀— Material button

Entering the new Cube has created the new Material which by default is identical to the original, the default Gray.

With Material.001 in the Material Slot, selecting a Base Color in the Color Picker modifies Material.001 to display the chosen color. The color displays on the surface of the Cube.

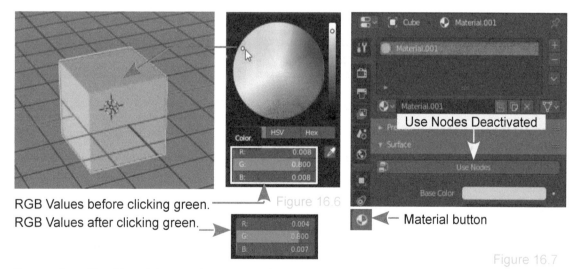

RGB Values before clicking green.
RGB Values after clicking green.

Figure 16.6

Use Nodes Deactivated

◀— Material button

Figure 16.7

Remember: The Material Node System is **NOT** being used.

The entries in the Material Cache indicate the material color.

Be Aware: The controls displayed in the Properties Editor, Material buttons are only applicable to **the selected Object** in the 3D View Editor. To reinforce this concept, deselect the Cube and add a UV Sphere to the Scene. The UV Sphere displays gray.

With the UV Sphere selected the Properties Editor, Material buttons, are empty except for the **New** button.

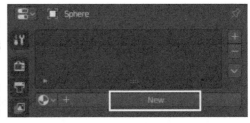

Figure 16.8

Click the **New** button to add to add a new Material. The Material buttons will display with **Nodes** active as indicated by the **Use Nodes** bar highlighted. Click **Use Nodes** to cancel the Node System. With the UV Sphere selected click the Base Color bar and in the Color Picker, note the RGB values 0.800 (the default grey) (Figure 16.6). In the top panel of the Material buttons (Material Slot) you will see a new material named **Material.002** which has been selected from the Material Cache, entered in the Material Slot and applied to the UV Sphere in the 3D View Editor. Material.002 is gray (the default color). If you open the Cache you will see three Materials. Material (gray), Material.001(green) and Material.002 (gray). With the UV Sphere selected click on the Base Color bar and select a color from the Color Picker Circle. This changes Material.002 from the default gray to the color you choose (brown) and applies it to the UV Sphere.

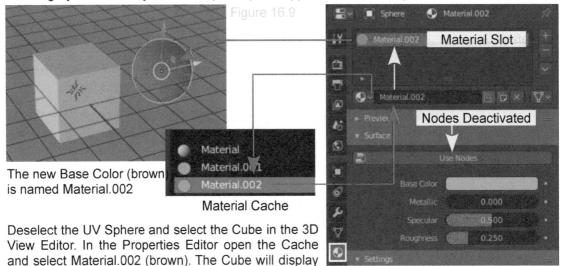

Figure 16.9

The new Base Color (brown) is named Material.002

Material Cache

Deselect the UV Sphere and select the Cube in the 3D View Editor. In the Properties Editor open the Cache and select Material.002 (brown). The Cube will display brown (Figure 16.10).

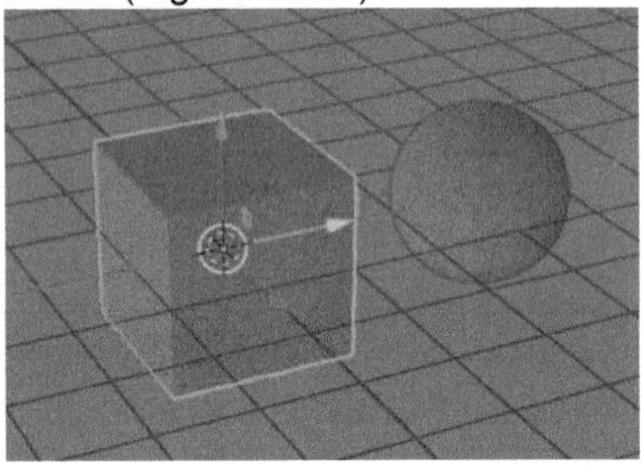

Figure 16.10

Note: The demonstration has been performed **without using the Material Nodes (Nodes Deactivated).** The colors display in all Viewport Shading Modes (Chapter 14). With the Node System active the Material colors only display in LookDev and Rendered Viewport Shading Mode. You may Render by pressing F12 (press **Esc** to cancel).

Solid Viewport Shading Mode is there to provide a simplified environment for modeling and compiling a Scene. You can Render the Scene and generate an image but for more sophisticated Material and Lighting effects the Node System is employed.

Figure 16.11

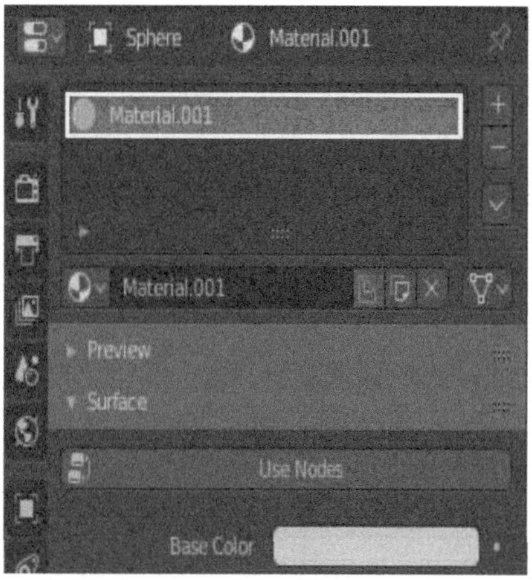

Before considering Material Nodes you should look at **Multiple Material Slots**. Start a new Blender file and replace the default Cube with a UV Sphere.

There are occasions when you require more than one Material color to be applied to an Object.

In the Properties Editor, Material buttons, click on New to add a Material. **Cancel the Node System**. The material will be entered in the Material Slot as Material.001 (Figure 16.11) and will be the default gray. You may click in the Base Color bar and change Material.001 from gray if you wish.The Cache contains Material and Material.001

Figure 16.12

Click on the **plus button** adjacent to the Material slot to add a second Slot (Figure 16.12). You may open the Cache and select a Material to enter in the new Slot or alternatively, click the New button, cancel the Node System and select a new Base Color to create a new Material. The new Material is entered in the new Material Slot and is named Material.002.

The UV Sphere does not change color since Material.001 is being applied from the original Slot.

Figure 16.13

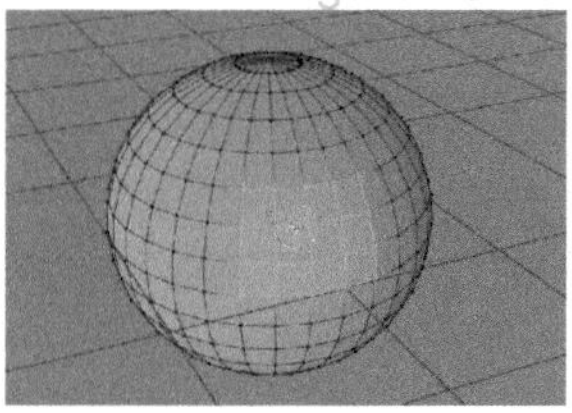

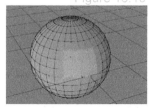

One way to use a second Material Slot is to apply it to a **Vertex Group**.

Figure 16.14

With the UV Sphere selected, Tab to Edit Mode, deselect the Vertices then select a group of vertices (Figure 16.13). In the **Properties Editor, Data buttons** create a Vertex Group (Chapter 5 – 5.9) (Figure 16.14).

Figure 16.15

In the Properties Editor, Material buttons with the second slot selected (highlighted) containing Material.002, click the Assign Button (Figure 16.14). Material.002 is displayed on the Vertex Group in the 3D View Editor (Figure 16.15).

Note: The Assign button only displays with the selected Object in **Edit Mode**.

16.6 Materials Nodes

Start over with a new Blender file. Delete the default Cube and replace it with a UV Sphere. Scale the UV Sphere down in the Z Axis forming a flatx disk and set Shading Smooth (3D View Editor Header in Object Mode – Click Object – Click Shade Smooth in the menu).

You may use any Object you like. A flat smooth disk is a nice shape.

To work with Nodes divide the 3D View Editor in two horizontally and make the lower half the **Shader Editor** (Figure 16.16). Having both Editors displayed allows you to see changes to Objects in the Scene as adjustments are made via the Nodes.

Figure 16.16

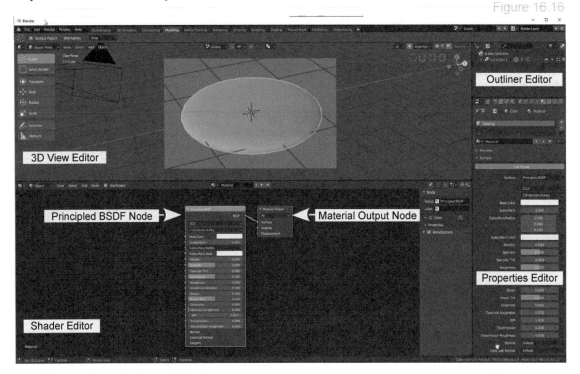

In the new Scene with the flat disk selected go to the Material buttons in the Properties Editor and click **New**. Before clicking New the Shader Editor will be empty.

The Material buttons display, **Use Nodes** is highlighted blue indicating that the Node System is active. In the **Shader Editor** two rectangles are displayed, one labelled **Principled BSDF** and the other **Material Output**. The rectangles are the Nodes. (zoom in – scroll MMB or press plus + or minus – on the Keyboard. You may also click MMB, hold and drag the Mouse to pan the view.)

Note: The **Principled BSDF Node** is not typical of all Nodes. This Node is what you might call a Super Node when you compare it with the **Diffuse BSDF Node** shown in Figure 16.2. It is shown here since it is displayed when Nodes are activated by clicking **Use Notes** in the **Properties Editor**.

Compare the Principled BSDF Node to the content of the Properties Editor, Material buttons. You will see that the controls are identical.

Nodes in the Shader Editor

Figure 16.17

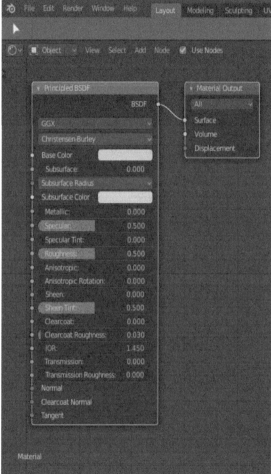

Material

Properties Editor Material Buttons

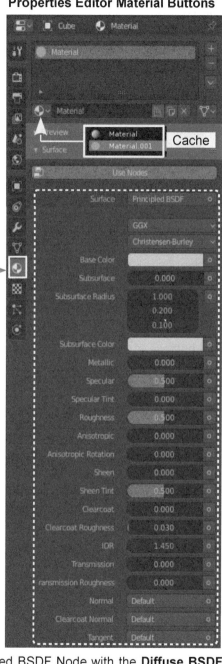

Note: The Material Button is in the vertical column at the side of the Properties Editor. In some diagrams the original horizontal configuration has been employed.

To simplify the introduction to Nodes replace the Principled BSDF Node with the **Diffuse BSDF Node**. With the Mouse Cursor in the **Shader Editor**, press Alt ⊦ A Key on the Keyboard to deselect both Nodes.LMB click on a blank part of the Principled BSDF Node. The outline of the Node will display white. Press the **X Key** on the Keyboard to delete. Only the Material Output Node remains.

In the **Shader Editor Header** click **Add**, then navigate the menu that displays and click on **Diffuse BSDF**. **Note:** You may alternatively press **Shift + A Key**

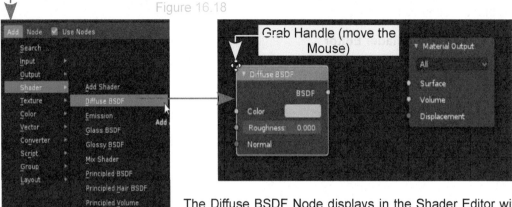

Figure 16.18

Grab Handle (move the Mouse)

The Diffuse BSDF Node displays in the Shader Editor with a **Grab Handle** attached which follows Mouse movement allowing you to position the Node in the Editor. LMB click to set in position. The handle is cancelled.

To adjust the position LMB click and hold on the Node (Grab Handle reappears) hold and drag the Mouse. Release.

The purpose of the Diffuse BSDF Node is to add a Diffuse Material (color) to the surface of the Object selected in the 3D View Editor. To achieve this it has to be connected to the Material Output Node. At this point the Diffuse BSDF Node is not connected (Figure 16.18). To connect, click LMB on the green dot at the RHS of the Node, hold the Mouse button down and drag over to the green dot next to Surface at the LHS of the Material Output Node. Release the Mouse button to connect the Nodes (Figure 16.19 - 20). The connecting line is called a **Noodle**. The green dots are called **Sockets**.

Figure 16.19

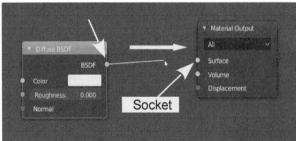

Socket

Figure 16.20

Noodle

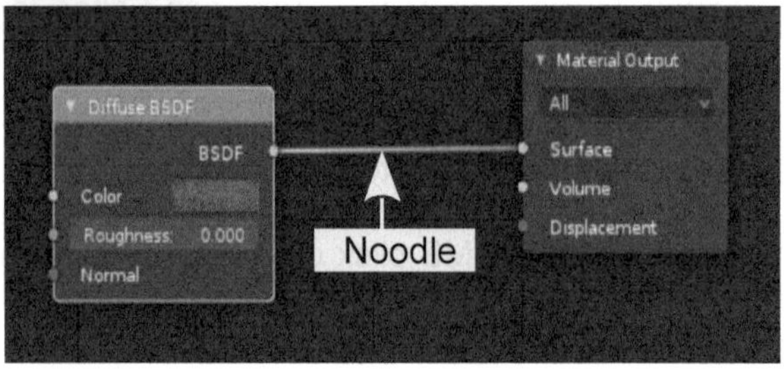

With the Nodes connected click on the color bar in the Diffuse BSDF Node and select a color from the color picker.

Nodes in the Shader Editor Figure 16.21 **Properties Editor Material Buttons**

Click the Color Bar

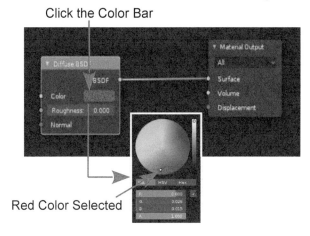

Red Color Selected

With a color selected and the Nodes connected you may be disappointed to find that the Cube in the **3D View Editor** is still gray. The color bar in the Node shows the color selected as does the color bar in the **Properties Editor, Material buttons, Surface tab**.

Remember Viewport Shading!

The default **Viewport Shading** is **Solid** which provides a simplified Viewport for Modeling. This Viewport Mode **does not** display Materials when Nodes or Textures are used. To see the Material applied by the Diffuse BSDF Node change the Viewport Shading to **LookDev Mode** with Scene Lights checked in the options or to **Rendered Viewport Shading Mode**.

Solid Mode ⌐ Figure 16.22 LookDev Mode ⌐

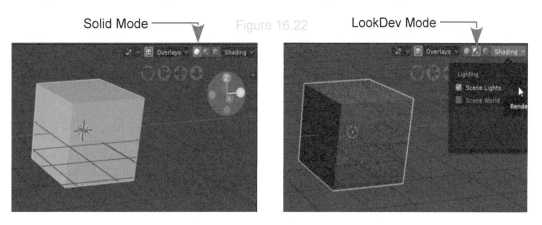

With the correct Viewport Shading Mode set in the 3D View Editor you will be able to see the effects generated by Nodes in the Shader Editor.

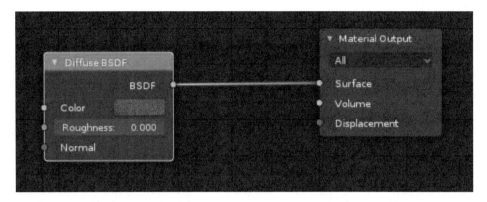

The Node arrangement in Figure 16.23 shows a **Diffuse BSDF Node** connected to a **Material Output Node**. The information from the Diffuse BSDF Node is conveyed to the Material Output Node which transfers the data to the Object selected in the 3D View Editor.

In a Node arrangement data transfer is generally from left to right in the Shader Editor although in complicated arrangements this may appear not to be the case.

Nodes have Input Sockets on the LHS and Output Sockets on the RHS. These are the colored dots at the sides of the Node. Output Sockets connect to Input Sockets as previously described.

To disconnect, click LMB on an Input Socket, hold and drag away from the socket. The Noodle disappears. Alternatively, with the Mouse Cursor in the Editor, press the T Key to display the Tool Panel, select the **Links Cut Tool.** Click LMB in the Editor. The Cursor becomes a Knife Tool. Hold LMB and drag the Knife across the Noodle then release.

Figure 16.24

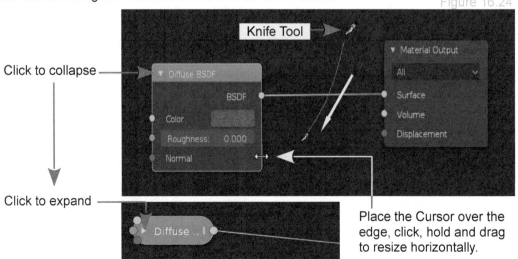

Sockets generally connect by color, green to green, yellow to yellow, blue to blue. **There are exceptions.** Nodes may be resized and or collapsed.

16.8 The Shader Editor

Examine the content of the **Shader Editor Header**. The buttons generally display selection menus which, by and large, are self explanatory. One button of note is the **View button** with the **Toggle Sidebar (N)** and **Toggle Tool Shelf (T)** entries in the menu.

The **Sidebar** is the panel at the RHS of the Editor which displays information about the Node that is selected in the Editor.

The Tool Shelf contains: The **Tool Shelf** displays at the LHS of the Editor and contains three Tools; click to select (highlight blue).

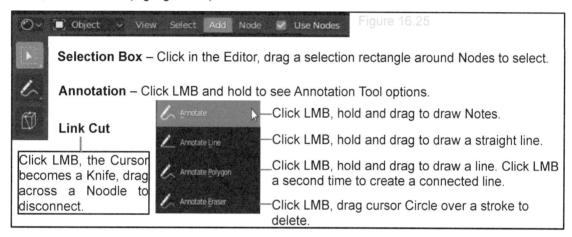

Figure 16.25

Selection Box – Click in the Editor, drag a selection rectangle around Nodes to select.

Annotation – Click LMB and hold to see Annotation Tool options.

Annotate ———Click LMB, hold and drag to draw Notes.

Link Cut

Annotate Line ———Click LMB, hold and drag to draw a straight line.

Click LMB, the Cursor becomes a Knife, drag across a Noodle to disconnect.

Annotate Polygon ———Click LMB, hold and drag to draw a line. Click LMB a second time to create a connected line.

Annotate Eraser ———Click LMB, drag cursor Circle over a stroke to delete.

Adding Nodes

Figure 16.18 introduced the procedure for adding Nodes into the Editor by demonstrating entering a Diffuse BSDF Node. Clicking the Add button in the Shader Editor Header opens a category list where you select a category to display the relevant Nodes. The categories assist when you are conversant with the function of each Node and how to arrange them to produce an effect. Knowing which Node to select and how to connect comes from experience which in the beginning is gained by following tutorials and copying and experimenting. In practical terms the Add button in the Shader Editor Header is the gateway to the maze of Nodes. When following tutorials you find a particular Node by either entering the name of the Node in the search panel at the top of the Category list or by navigating through the different categories.

Figure 16.26 on the following page displays the different categories which will assist in your search.

Becoming proficient in the use of Nodes comes with a certain amount of experimentation and organisation. When you have created a Node arrangement which produces a result, save it in a Blender file for future use. You may wish to use it again in another project or use it as a starting point for further development.

Node Selection Menu

To add a Node click the **Add** button.

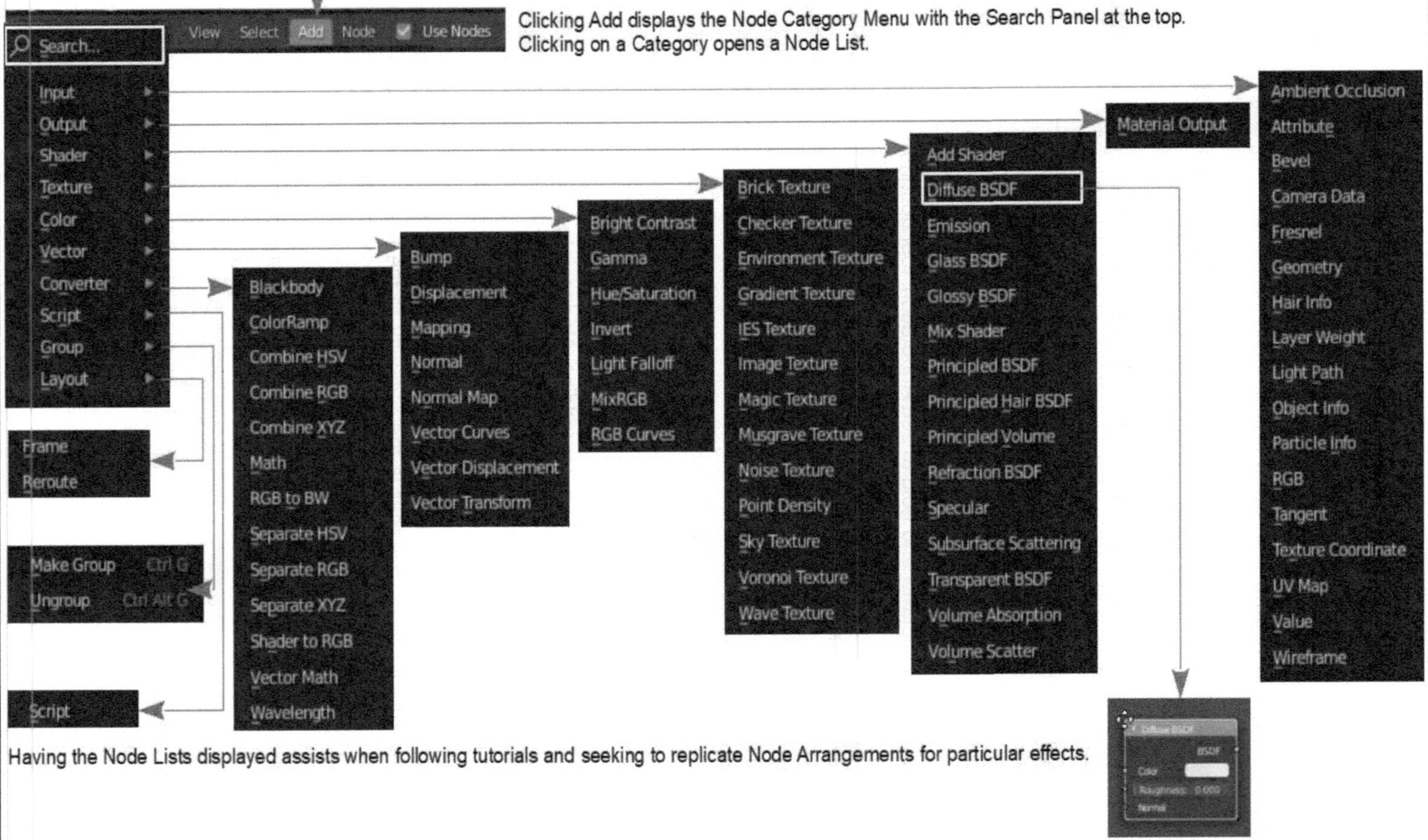

Clicking Add displays the Node Category Menu with the Search Panel at the top.

Clicking on a Category opens a Node List.

Figure 16.26

Having the Node Lists displayed assists when following tutorials and seeking to replicate Node Arrangements for particular effects.

To Add a Node into the Editor click on the Node Name. Clicking On **Diffuse BSDF** in Shader Category enters the Node into the Shader Editor. While the Node is selected you position it to suit the Node Arrangement.

16.9 Noodle Curving

Note: The Shader Editor is sometimes called the Node Editor

The default Noodle is drawn as a curved line connecting Sockets. You may adjust the curve between 1 (straight line) or 10 in the **Preferences Editor.** Go to **Themes - Node Editor** and scroll down to **Noodle curving.**

Figure 16.27

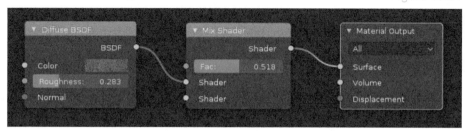

When Noodles are drawn they have a nice curve leading out and into the Sockets. This is purely a matter of preference and how much curve is up to you.

16.10 Scene Arrangements

Before trying examples of Node Arrangements set up a Scene with a smooth UV Sphere scaled down on the Z Axis forming a flat disc. Have the disc sitting above a Plane and place Lamps similar to those in Chapter 15 – 15.7 (Basic Scene Lighting). Have the 3D View Editor in Camera View with LookDev Viewport Shading and Scene Lights checked in the Options. Alternatively be in Rendered Viewport Shading Mode.

16.11 Mixing Material Example

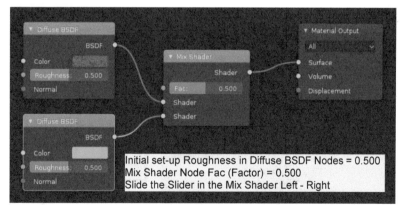

Initial set-up Roughness in Diffuse BSDF Nodes = 0.500
Mix Shader Node Fac (Factor) = 0.500
Slide the Slider in the Mix Shader Left - Right

Figure 16.28

Mix Shader Fac: 0.000

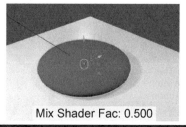

Mix Shader Fac: 0.500

Mix Shader Fac: 1.000

16.12 Simple Node Arrangement

Figure 16.29

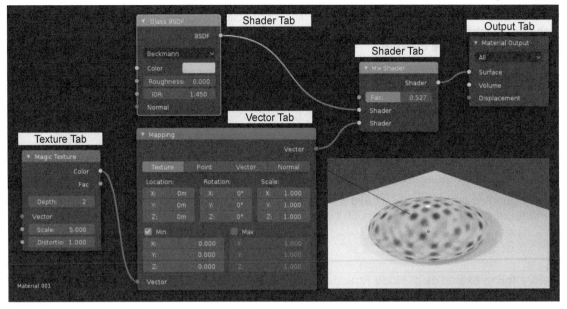

With the Node arrangement shown in Figure 16.29 the disk takes on a **Magic Texture** which is one of Blenders in built **Textures** and at the same time is given the look of glass by the Glass BSDF Node. The Nodes shown are accessed from the Shader Editor Tool Panel **Tabs**

By deselecting the Disk (UV Sphere flattened) and selecting the Plane, then applying the following Nodes to the Plane, the disk sits above a Textured surface.

Image Texture Node
Click Open and navigate to an image stored on your computer

Figure 16.30

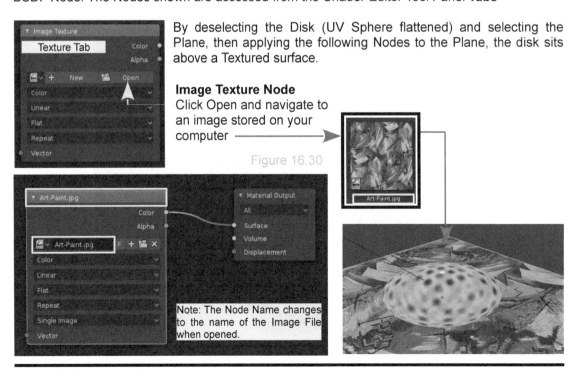

Note: The Node Name changes to the name of the Image File when opened.

16.13 Texture Nodes

In the Simple Node Arrangement (Figures 16.29, 16.30) a Magic Texture and an Image Texture were introduced. The use of Nodes prior to this was introduced with reference to the application of Materials (color). Nodes are also used to apply **Texture** to the surface of an Object which defines surface characteristics such as how lumpy or bumpy the surface appears or whether the surface is wood, gravel, bricks or glass etc.

Texture Nodes are similar to Material Nodes in that they represent code that produces the effect on the surface of an Object. Texture code is also created and stored in a Cache similar to Materials.

The major difference between Textures and Materials is, to make a Texture appear realistic on the surface, the surface has to be **Unwrapped** and the Texture has to be Mapped to the surface. Think of a Texture which represents the surface of the Earth being applied to a UV Sphere. The surface of the UV Sphere is Unwrapped (laid out flat as if you carefully pealed an orange and laid the skin flat) then the Texture is mapped to (overlaid in the flat surface) such that when the peel is put back on the orange it looks like the Earth as viewed from Space.

Note: In Figure 16.20 no action was performed to Unwrap the surface but, in fact, Blender automatically performed the operation.

16.14 Unwrapping a Surface

To demonstrate Unwrapping use the default Cube Object in the 3D View Editor in two and make one half the UV Editor (Figure 16.31).

Figure 16.31

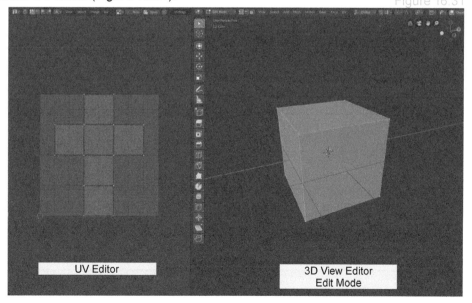

UV Editor

3D View Editor
Edit Mode

With the 3D View Editor **in Edit Mode** the Cube is shown with its Faces laid flat in the UV Editor.

With the 3D View Editor in Object Mode with the Cube selected and the UV Editor is empty (Figure 16.32).

Figure 16.32

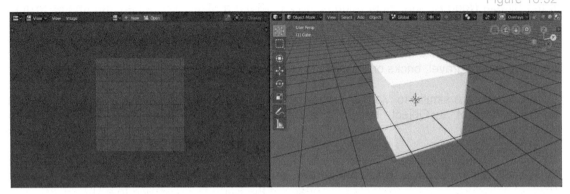

In Edit Mode the Cube is automatically **Unwrapped**. The Unwrapped profile has Vertices, Edges and Faces which may be selected and deselected, Translated, Rotated and Scaled as you would in the 3D View Editor in Edit Mode. You will see selection Mode buttons in the UV Editor Header (Figure 16.33).

Figure 16.33

Vertex, Edge, Face, Island

Figure 16.34 shows the Unwrapped Cube selected (press the A Key) and Rotated (R Key).

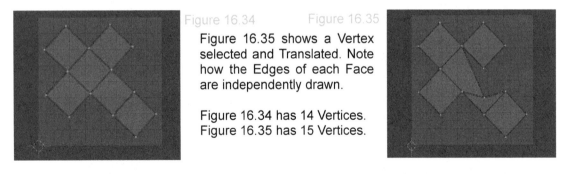

Figure 16.34   Figure 16.35

Figure 16.35 shows a Vertex selected and Translated. Note how the Edges of each Face are independently drawn.

Figure 16.34 has 14 Vertices.
Figure 16.35 has 15 Vertices.

The automatic Unwrapping may be considered as Simple Unwrapping which is one of several methods. Alternative methods are found in the 3D View Editor Header (in Edit Mode) **UV button**.

Which Projection method is used depends on how you want a Texture to be displayed.

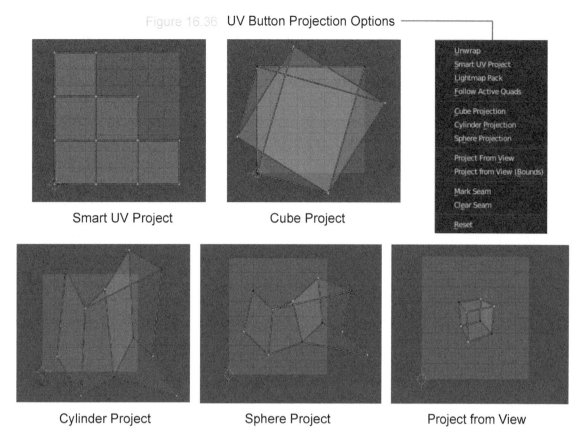

Figure 16.36 UV Button Projection Options

Smart UV Project Cube Project

Unwrap
Smart UV Project
Lightmap Pack
Follow Active Quads

Cube Projection
Cylinder Projection
Sphere Projection

Project From View
Project from View (Bounds)

Mark Seam
Clear Seam

Reset

Cylinder Project Sphere Project Project from View

16.15 Unwrapping with Seams

Mesh Objects may also be Unwrapped by selecting Edges and marking as Seams.

Figure 16.37

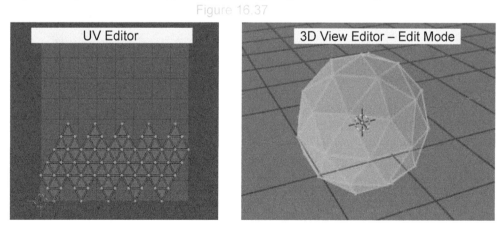

UV Editor 3D View Editor – Edit Mode

Figure16.37 shows an Ico Sphere selected and automatically Unwrapped.

To Mark Seams, have the Ico Sphere in the 3D View Editor in Edit Mode with **Edge Select** active. Deselect all Edges, then shift select individual Edges while rotating the View, dividing the surface into three sections. With the Edges selected click **Mark Seams** from the menu that displays when you click the UV button in Header. The selected Edges change color indicating that they are now **Seams**. Press the **A Key to select all the Edges**. From the UV button in the Header menu click **Unwrap**. The Unwrapped sections are displayed in the UV Editor.

Figure 16.38

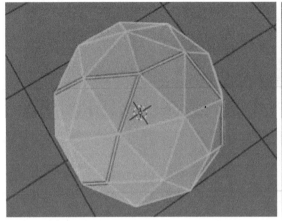

Seams Marked – All Edges Selected

Sections Unwrapped in the UV Editor

16.16 Applying a Texture

Figure 16.39

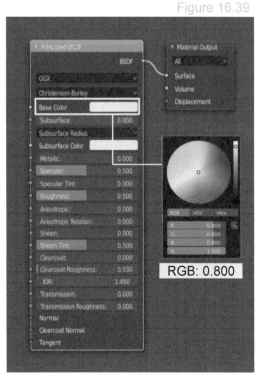

RGB: 0.800

In the previous examples of Simple Node Arrangements, Textures were shown applied to the surface of an Object. The fact that the Textures were able to be applied was due to the Automatic Unwrapping of the Object's surface. To apply a Texture there are two prerequisites; the surface must be Unwrapped and a Material has to be applied.

To demonstrate, continue with the Unwrapped Icosphere.

The Ico Sphere was a new Object added to the Scene, therefore, it has no Material applied. In the Properties Editor, Material buttons click New to add a Material. By default the material is the default Gray color.

In the Shader Editor you will see the Principled BSDF Node connected to a Material Output Node. The Base Color in the Principled BSDF Node is the default Gray, RGB values all 0.800 (Figure 16.39).

In Figure 16.17 the similarities between the Principled BSDF Node and the Materials button with Use Nodes active were pointed out. Herein lies two methods of introducing a Texture.

Method 1: In the Shader Editor select a Texture from the Add Menu. In the demonstration an Image Texture will be used.

Method 2: In the Properties Editor, Material buttons, with Use Nodes active, click on the button at the end of the Base Color bar and select Image Texture from the menu.

Material Buttons

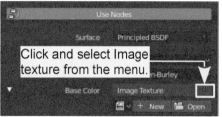

Figure 16.40

In using Method 2, the Image Texture Node is automatically entered in the Shader Editor and connected to the Principled BSDF Node. With Method 1 you have to position the Node and manually connect.

Figure 16.41

With an Image Texture Node you have to open an image saved on your computer to be used as the Texture. Click Open in the Node (or in the Materials Buttons) navigate in the File Browser and select an image. Click Open in the Upper RH corner of the File Browser.

See Chapter 03-3.6 Navigation

Selected Image File

Figure 16.42

Important: To see the image Mapped to the Icosphere make sure the 3D View Editor is in **LocDev** or **Rendered Viewport Shading** Mode.

To position the Texture on the Object's surface (The Ico Sphere) open the same Image File in the UV Editor by clicking Open in the Header and navigating to the file.

16.17 Mapping to a Surface

In the UV Editor you may select part of the Unwrapping and position it in the image to have that part displayed on the corresponding Faces in the 3D View Editor. Click UV in the Header and select– Show/Hide Faces to display the unwrapped surface.

Figure 16.43

Part of Unwrapping Selected in UV Editor

Part Translated positioning over the dark center of the sunflower.

Figure 16 44

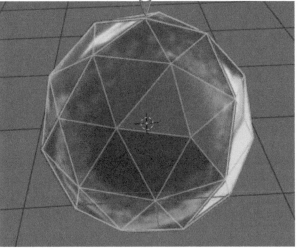

Rotating the view in the 3D View Editor shows the dark center of the sunflower inside the Unwrapped selection.

16.18 Texture Painting

Texture Painting allows you to paint or draw, modifying a Texture that has been Mapped to the surface of an Object. The following procedure will provide a basic introduction showing controls.

Have the default Cube Object in the 3D View Editor with the sunflower Image Texture mapped to the surface. You could modify the Screen arrangement by changing the UV Editor from View Mode to Paint Mode and pressing the T Key to toggle the Tool Panel open but for convenience select the **Texture Paint Workspace** from Header at the top of the Screen.

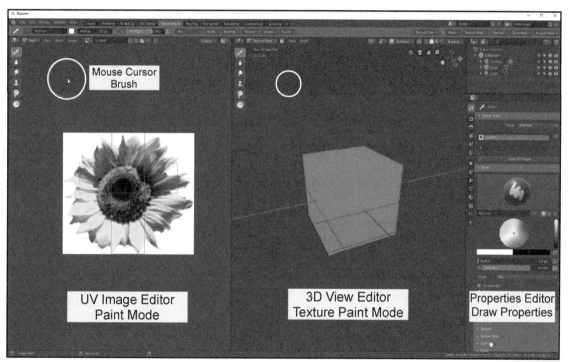

UV Image Editor
Paint Mode

3D View Editor
Texture Paint Mode

Properties Editor
Draw Properties

The **Texture Paint Workspace** displays with the UV Editor in **Paint Mode** and the 3D View Editor in **Texture Paint Mode**. The Mouse Cursor in both Editors displays as a white circle (Brush). In the Properties Editor, with the **Active Tools** button selected, Draw Properties display.

By default the Brush Radius is 50 px and the Strength value is 0.700 as displayed in the Header.

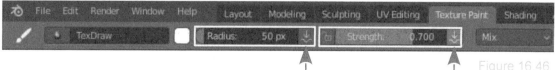

Both values allow Tablet Pressure Sensitivity

Change the 3D View Editor to Object Mode (in LocDev Viewport Shading Mode) to show the Cube with the sunflower Texture Mapped to its surface unencumbered by Edge lines. Changing to Object Mode also removes the Unwrapping from the image in the UV Image Editor.

As a quick demonstration, reduce the Brush Radius to 6 px. Click on the **Draw Tool** in the Tool Panel in the Image Editor or the 3D View Editor. Click in the color button in the Header to select a Brush Color and Paint (click, hold and drag) the Mouse Cursor Circle over the image in the UV Image Editor. **Note:** You may also adjust the Brush Radius in the slider just below the color picker circle in the Properties Editor.

Figure 16.47

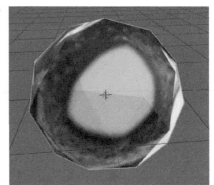

Paint applied in the UV Image Editor

Paint applied in the 3D View Editor
View rotated to display the center of
the sunflower.

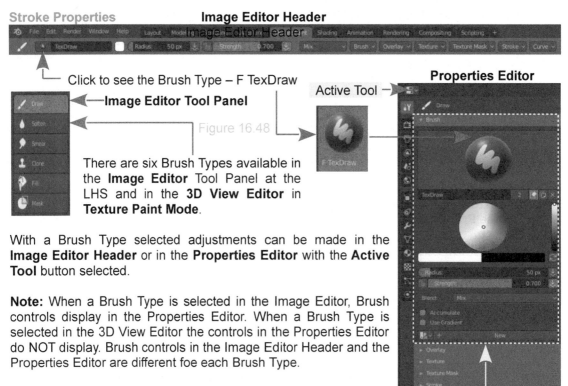

Stroke Properties **Image Editor Header**

Image Editor Header

Click to see the Brush Type – F TexDraw

Properties Editor

Active Tool →

◀——**Image Editor Tool Panel**

Figure 16.48

There are six Brush Types available in the **Image Editor** Tool Panel at the LHS and in the **3D View Editor** in **Texture Paint Mode**.

With a Brush Type selected adjustments can be made in the **Image Editor Header** or in the **Properties Editor** with the **Active Tool** button selected.

Note: When a Brush Type is selected in the Image Editor, Brush controls display in the Properties Editor. When a Brush Type is selected in the 3D View Editor the controls in the Properties Editor do NOT display. Brush controls in the Image Editor Header and the Properties Editor are different foe each Brush Type.

To fully understand all the controls available for Texture Painting you will have to refer to on line documentation.

Brush Controls

In the Properties Editor, Texture buttons you can select a Procedural Texture (Blender Inbuilt Texture) and paint it to the image Mapped to the Object in the 3D View Editor. The first step in this procedure is to enter the texture in the Cache.

Properties Editor (Figure 16.49)

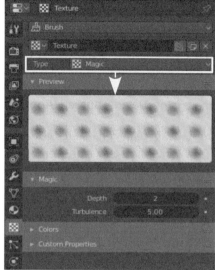

In the Properties Editor, Texture buttons, click New to open the Texture Tabs. Change Type: Image or Movie to Magic (or any of the types in the menu). Make note that in the Texture Cache the Texture named Texture displays as Type Magic.

Drawing on the image in the UV Editor paints the Magic Texture (Figure 16.50) which displays in the 3D View Editor when in Object Mode (Figure 16.51).

Magic Texture Painted in the UV Image Editor

Display in the 3D View Editor

Rember: While discussing **Texture Paint** the **Image Texture Node** has been residing in the Shader Editor connected to the **Principled BSDF Node**.

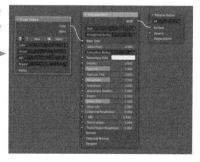

At this point the **Principled BSDF Node** has been briefly mentioned in relation to 16.6 Material Nodes and 16.13 Applying Textures. As previously stated you could consider this Node as a Super Node since it has in-built properties which can be employed and connection sockets for other Nodes.

16.19 Vertex Paint

Vertex Paint tool allows you to manually paint a Material onto the surface of an Object. The tool is accessed in the 3D View Editor Header by changing to **Vertex Paint Mode** (Figure 16.52).

In **Vertex Paint Mode** you will be able to paint a selected Object immediately, but before you can render an image with the paint showing, you must have a Material added and configure Nodes in the Shader Editor. Have the 3D View Editor in LocDev Viewport Shading Mode.

Remember: A new Object added to the 3D View Editor displays with the default gray color, but there is no Material applied. **Apply a Material**.

As **Vertex Paint** suggests, the process involves painting vertices. The default Cube in the 3D View Editor has only eight vertices, therefore, it doesn't provide much scope for a demonstration. Delete the Cube and add a **UV Sphere**. The default UV Sphere has 32 segments and 16 rings, which provides a vertex at each intersection point of the mesh. In **Edit mode** subdivide to add more vertices or alternatively, add and apply a **Subdivision Surface Modifier** to the UV Sphere.

Vertex Paint Mode

Change the 3D View Editor to Vertex Paint Mode.

Figure 16.53

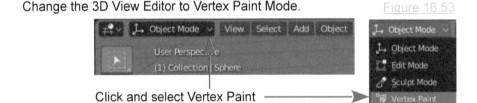

Click and select Vertex Paint

In the 3D View Editor, in Vertex Paint Mode the Cursor has a circle attached (Figure 16.55). The circle is called the **Brush**.

By default Vertex Paint is in **Draw Mode** as seen by the **Draw Tool** highlighted in the Tool Panel at the LH side of the Editor and the notation in the **Tool Panel Information Header**.

Brush Controls

The **Bush Properties** are controlled in the **Tool Panel Information Header** (Figure 16.55).

Figure 16.54

Clicking on the icon next to **Draw** displays options for a selection of **Brush Types**. These same options are duplicated in the **Properties Editor, Active Tool and Workspace Button** (Figure 16.54).

The Brush properties may also be controlled by clicking the Brush button in the Header.

Click on the preview to display the options (Figure 16.55).

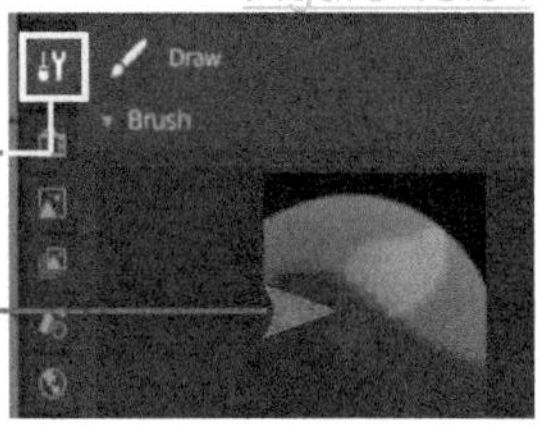

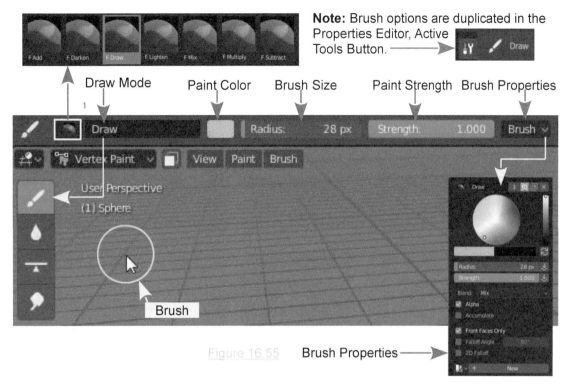

Note: Brush options are duplicated in the Properties Editor, Active Tools Button. ──────►

Draw Mode   Paint Color   Brush Size   Paint Strength   Brush Properties

Figure 16.55   Brush Properties ──────►

Drawing Strokes

To Draw a Stroke (Paint) on the surface of the Object simply click, hold and drag the Brush (circle) over the surface. You will be drawing on the Vertices that are in the visible surface. Rotate the Object or the Viewport to draw on the reverse side surface.

Be aware that, with the surface painted, when you revert to Object Mode or attempt to render an image you will NOT see what has been drawn.

At this point you have to configure the Material Nodes producing the color.

Node Configuration

If you forgot to add a Material to the Object, add one now.

Open the Shader Editor (drag the upper edge of the Timeline Editor up and change it to the Shader Editor).

By default adding a Material activates the Material Node system. In the Properties Editor, Material buttons you see **Use Nodes** highlighted red.

In the Shader Editor you will have the **Principled BSDF** Node connected to a **Material Output** Node.

In the Properties Editor, open the Object Data buttons and expand the Vertex Colors Tab.

Figure 16.56

Note: The data block named **Col**.

In the Shader Editor add an **Input** - **Attribute Node**. Enter the name of the Vertex Colors Data Block (Col) in the Attribute Node Name panel and connect the Node to the Base Color input Socket of the Principled BSDF Node.

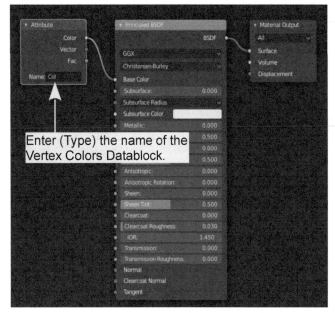

Enter (Type) the name of the Vertex Colors Datablock.

Figure 16.57

Color Datablock

Object Data

Note: You may rename the Datablock.

With the Nodes configured as shown Vertex Color Paint will be visible in Object Mode and in Loc Dev and Renderd Viewport Shading Modes (Figure 16.58)

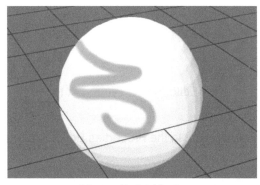

Vertex Paint Mode

Figure 16.58

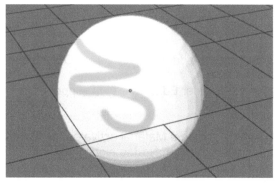

Object Mode

16.20 The Principled BSDF Node

When discussing **Material Nodes 16.6** the comparison was made between the **Principled BSDF Node** which displays in the Shader Editor and the controls in the Properties Editor, Materials buttons (Figure 16.17). In effect the controls are identical in both cases.

Figure 16.59 shows the **Principled BSDF Node** in the **Shader Editor** listing some of the functions contained in the Node.

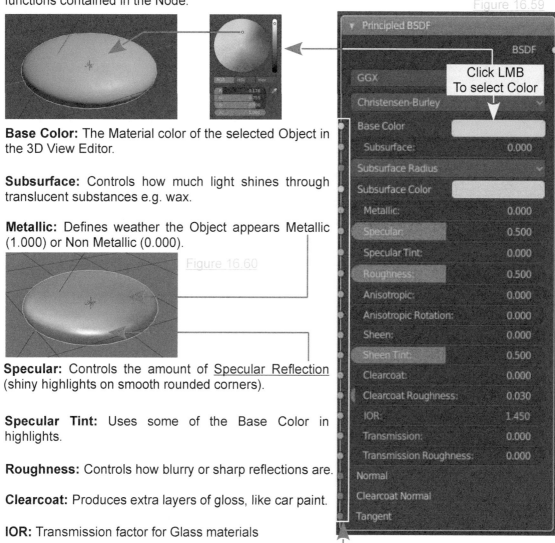

Figure 16.59

Base Color: The Material color of the selected Object in the 3D View Editor.

Subsurface: Controls how much light shines through translucent substances e.g. wax.

Metallic: Defines weather the Object appears Metallic (1.000) or Non Metallic (0.000).

Figure 16.60

Specular: Controls the amount of <u>Specular Reflection</u> (shiny highlights on smooth rounded corners).

Specular Tint: Uses some of the Base Color in highlights.

Roughness: Controls how blurry or sharp reflections are.

Clearcoat: Produces extra layers of gloss, like car paint.

IOR: Transmission factor for Glass materials

Node Connection Sockets

With the Principled BSDF Node connected to the Material Output Node in the Shader Editor, adjusting controls (sliders) in the Node, axffects the surface appearance of the selected Object in the 3D View Editor.

The controls for the **Principled BSDF Node** are replicated in the **Properties Editor, Materials buttons**. ➤

Additional Nodes may be selected and automatically connected to the Principled BSDF Node in the **Properties Editor.**

Figure 16.61

For example; Clicking LMB on the button at the RH end of the Base Color bar displays a Node selection menu.

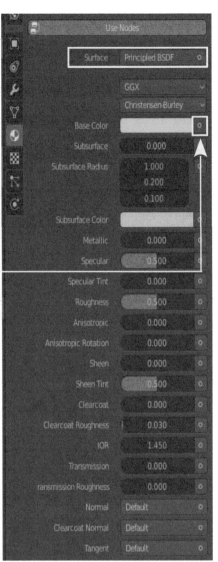

Figure 16.63

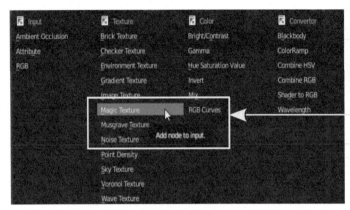

Selecting **Magic Texture** in the menu automatically connects the **Magic Texture Node** to the **Base Color** input socket of the Principled BSDF Node (Figure 16.62).

Figure 16.62

The selected Object in the 3D View Editor displays with the Magic Texture applied.

Principled BSDF Nodes for two Monkeys and a Plane.

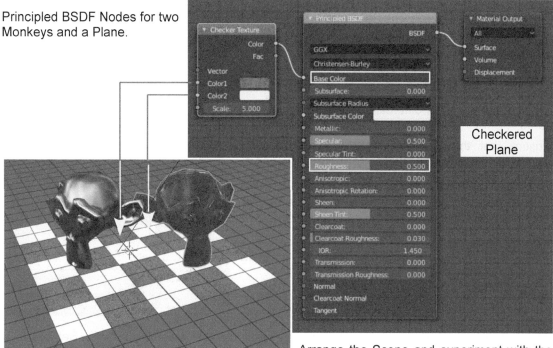

Arrange the Scene and experiment with the controls in the Nodes for each Object

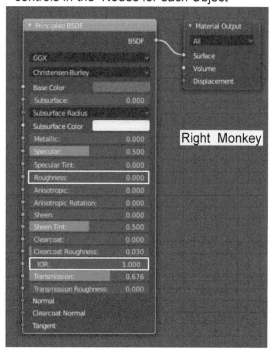

16.22 Transparency Using Nodes

To demonstrate Transparency a Plane Object will be turned into a pane of glass. Add a Plane to the default Blender Scene. Stand the Plane on edge and position in front of the default Cube. Give the Cube a Material (Figure 16.65).

Figure 16.65

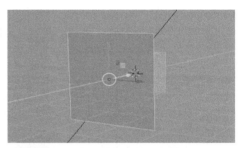

Change the default Point Lamp to an Area or Sun Lamp.

Ensure that the **3D View Editor** is in **LocDev Viewport Display Mode** or **Rendered Viewport Display Mode.**

Figure 16.66

In the **Properties Editor, World buttons, Surface Tab** set the Background as shown in Figure 16.65.

Select the Plane Object, add a Material, then in The Shader Editor create the Node arrangement in Figure 16.67. Pay attention to the settings.

Figure 16.67

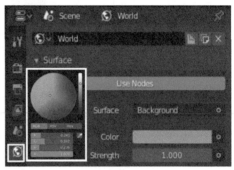

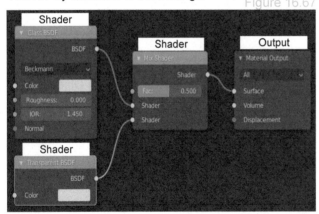

In the Material buttons, Settings Tab change the Blend Mode to **Additive.**

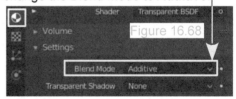

Figure 16.68

In the Scene buttons, check **Screen Space Reflections** and **Refraction.**

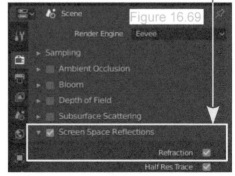

Figure 16.69

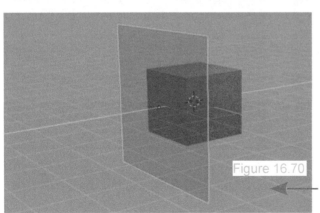

Figure 16.70

3D View Editor showing the Plane as Transparent Glass with a slight blue tint.

With the identical Node arrangement but with an HDRI image (Ref Chapter 15 – 15.8) used in the World Background fantastic results can be generated.

Figure 16.70 shows the pane of glass partially in front of the Cube. With the view rotated the glass reflects light cast by the background.

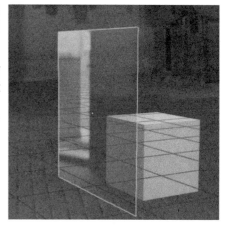

Figure 16.71

16.23 Other Node Uses

Scene Illumination - Volumetric Lighting

Using HDRI Maps as a background can give you a quick way to illuminate a Scene and create a background but, you are limited to what you can source in an image. You may want something completely unique and maybe not as complicated. Volumetric Lighting may be the answer.

Volumetric Lighting uses the light provided by Blender's Lamps and scatters or diffuses the light in the Scene. A simple demonstration is to place a light source in a Scene behind an Object such that the diffuse light shines through the Object, casting shadows towards the Camera.

Scene Arrangement

Figure 16.72

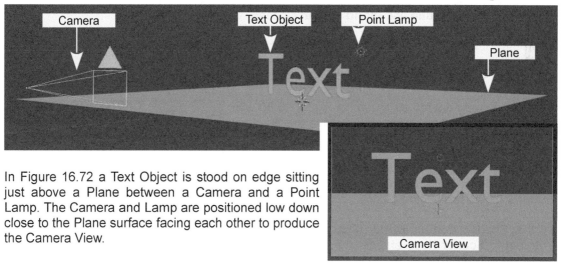

In Figure 16.72 a Text Object is stood on edge sitting just above a Plane between a Camera and a Point Lamp. The Camera and Lamp are positioned low down close to the Plane surface facing each other to produce the Camera View.

Volumetric Lighting is concerned with the background to the Scene which is part of the 3D World and has its own set of Nodes.

World Nodes

The use of Nodes, so far, has been concerned with the application of Materials and Textures to Objects and, therefore, has been confined to the use of **Object Nodes**. In the **Shader Editor Header** you see the **Object button** with a cube icon which when clicked opens a selection menu. To access **World Nodes** click on **World** in the menu. In the **Properties Editor, World buttons**, click on **Use Nodes**.

Shader Editor   Figure 16.73   Properties Editor, World buttons

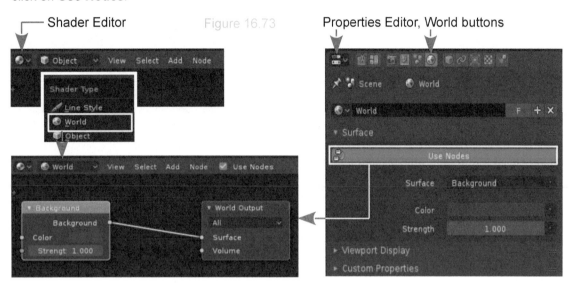

Activating **Use Nodes** in the **Properties Editor** and **Shader Type**, **World** in the **Shader Editor**, displays the **Background** and **World Output** Nodes.

Volumetric Light   Figure 16.74   Properties Editor

To create a Volumetric Light effect perform the following:

Have the Screen divided as shown in Figure 16.30 with Scene arrangement in Figure 16.71. Have the 3D View Editor in **Camera View**.

With the Point Lamp selected in the 3D View Editor check **Shadows** in the **Properties Editor, Object Data buttons, Light Tab** (Figure 16.74).

In the **Shader Editor, World type**, add a Shader, **Volumetric Scatter** Node and set the **Density** value in the Node to 0.100 (Figure 16.75). Connect the Nodes as shown.

Object Data ———▶

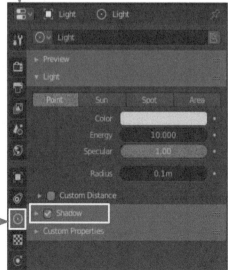

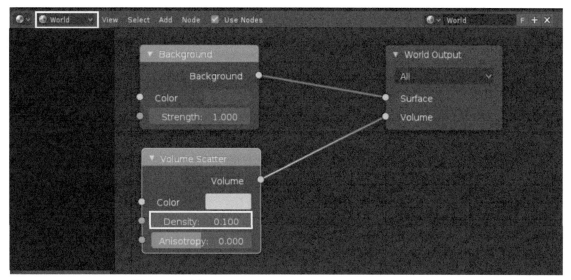

Figure 16.75

In the **Properties Editor, Render buttons** check **Ambiant Occlusion**. Also check **Volumetric** with **Volumetric Lighting** and **Volumetric Shadows**.

Properties Editor, Render Buttons

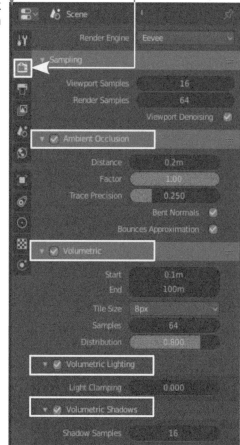

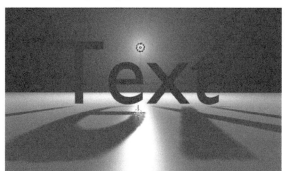

Camera View – Default Lighting Color

Camera View – Lamp Color Changed
Lamp Hidden Behind Text

Figure 16.76

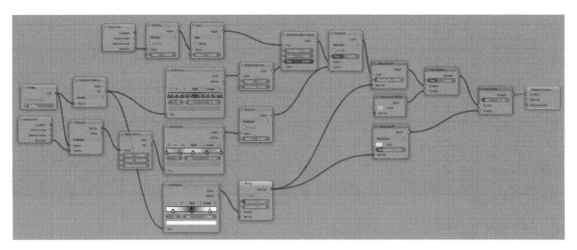

Figure 16.77 shows a reasonably complex Node arrangement and they can become even more complex. Creating such an arrangement involves a considerable amount of work and possibly a good deal of experimentation in achieving the result. This being the case you may wish to save the arrangement for future use. To do this you create a Node Group.

To simplify the explanation of how to achieve the above a simple Node arrangement similar to that previously used in demonstrating Mixing Materials 16.11 will be employed (Figure 16.78)

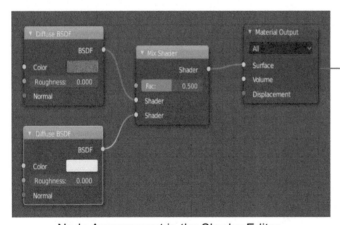

Node Arrangement in the Shader Editor

Figure 16.78

UV Sphere Scaled and Smoothed In the 3D View Editor in LocDev Viewport Shading Mode.

A Node Group will be created for the two Diffuse BSDF Nodes and the Mix Shader Node. This Node combination is producing the Material applied to the modified UV Sphere which is selected in the 3D View Editor.

It is assumed you wish to save this arrangement to reproduce the Material in the future.

In the **Shader Editor,** select the three nodes to be Grouped and press **Ctrl + G Key**. Alternatively click **Node – Make Group** in the Header.

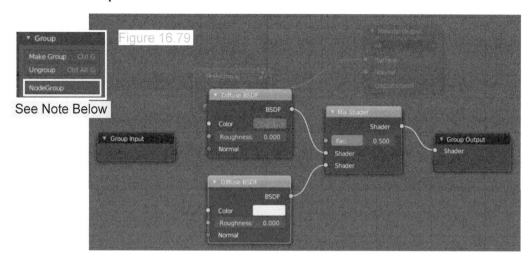

Figure 16.79

See Note Below

The Shader Editor display changes showing the three grouped Nodes in the configuration shown in Figure 16.79. You will see Node Group and the Material Output Node ghosted in the background.

Press **Tab** to consolidate the Group (Figure 16.80).

Note: When the Group is consolidated a **Node Group** button is entered in the Tool Panel. Clicking this button enters an instance of the Node Group into the Shader Editor.

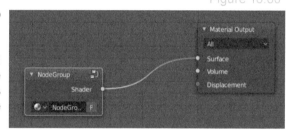

Figure 16.80

When a new Object is added to the Scene in the 3D View Editor, connecting the instance of the Node Group to the Material Output Node, produces a copy of the Material.

With the instance of the Node Group or the original selected in the Shader Editor, pressing the Tab Key expands the Group allowing the Mix Shader Slider value to be adjusted altering the Material. Note the Group is associated with both Objects in the 3D View Editor, therefore, both have their material altered. You may **Tab** to consolidate then click the **Ungroup** button in the Tool Panel. This will allow individual Object Material modification.

As well as using the Node Group in the current Blender file the Group may be appended to a new file (providing the current file has been saved).

Click to display Options

When a Node Group is created it becomes part of the data for the Blender File. This is found in the **Outliner Editor** under **Data API** (Figure 16.81).

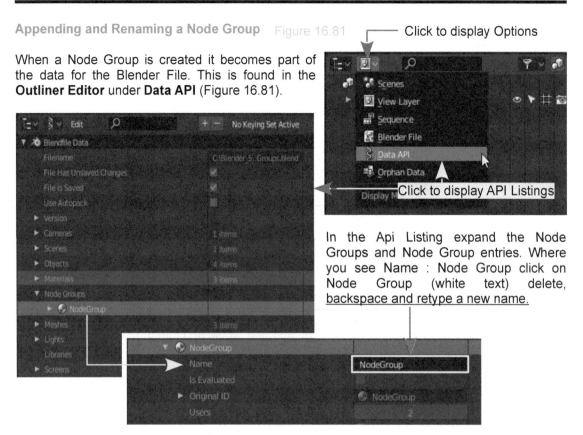

Click to display API Listings

In the Api Listing expand the Node Groups and Node Group entries. Where you see Name : Node Group click on Node Group (white text) delete, backspace and retype a new name.

In a new Blender file you may Append the Node Group Data from this location.

16.25 Compositing Nodes

Compositing Nodes (or composite, for short) allow you to create and enhance image files and video files. The contents of the Blender Scene can be the basis for the image or you may use an image already saved on your computer. A pre-saved image can be combined with other images or the Blender Scene to create a new image. Unlike Material and Texture Nodes, it is not necessary to have an Object selected in the 3D View Editor or to have a Material applied to an Object. Of course, by default, any Object added to a Scene has the default material added to it even though this does not display in the **Properties Editor** until the **New** button is pressed.

To demonstrate the **Compositing Node Editor**, change the Screen arrangement as shown in Figure 16.78. To create this arrangement, start by changing the default **Layout Workspace** to the **Compositing Workspace.**

The **Timeline Editor** at the bottom of the Screen will not be required in the demonstration since only still images will be used. Change the Timeline to the Composite Editor, change the existing Compositing Editor to the 3D View Editor, divide in two and make one half the UV Editor.

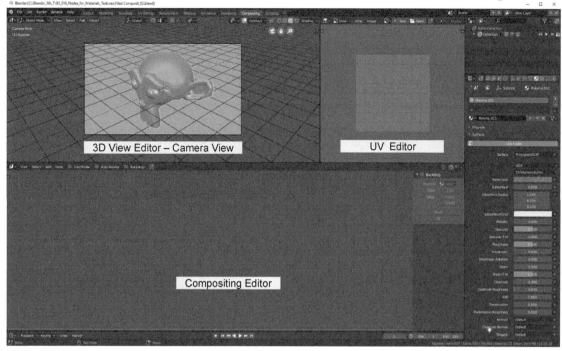

Figure 16.82

3D View Editor – Camera View

UV Editor

Compositing Editor

In this demonstration an image rendered from the Scene in the 3D View editor will be combined (composited) with an image file downloaded from the internet.

In the 3D View Editor, delete the default Cube and add a **Monkey Object.** Give it a nice bright Material (color). Change the **Viewport Shading to LocDev Mode to see the Material**. Go into Camera View, Scale Monkey up to fill the view then deselect it in the 3D View Editor (Figure 16.83).

Render a view of Camera View. In the Screen Header click Render and select Render Image. The image is Rendered and displayed in a full Screen version of the UV Editor. Cancel this Editor (click the X- upper RH of Screen).

In the **UV Editor** click on the **Browse Image to be linked** button in the Header and select **Render Result** to display the rendered image of the Monkey (scroll out).

Browse Image to be linked

Figure 16.83

To combine the Rendered Image with another file click Use Nodes and Auto Render in the Compositing Editor Header. With the Mouse Cursor in the Compositing Editor press the T Key to display the Tool Panel at the LH side of the Editor.

Figure 16.84

Clicking Use Nodes displays the Render Layers Node connected to the Composite Node. A view of the Rendered Monkey shows in the Render Layer Node (Figure16.84).

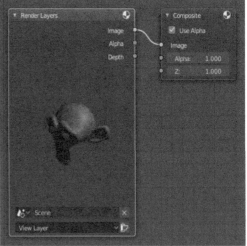

In the Header click Add and enter an Image Node and a Color Mix Node.

Figure 16.85

Arrange and connect the Nodes as shown in Figure 16.86.

In the Image Node click on Open, navigate in the File Browser that opens and select the downloaded image.

Figure 16.86

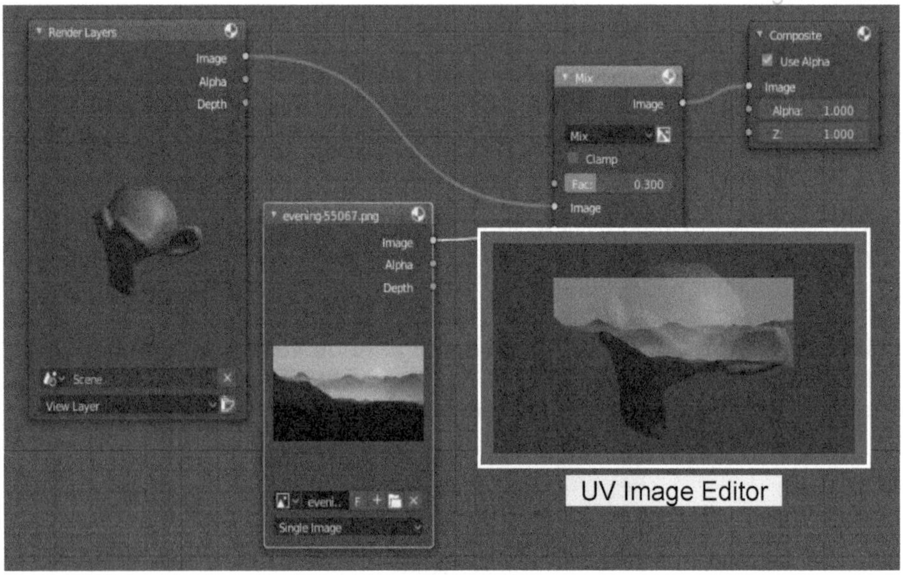

The selected image displays in the Image Node. In the Mix Node set the slider Fac: to approximately 0.300 and the Monkey Image in the Render layer is combined with the downloaded image and displayed in the UV Editor.

17

Rendering

Rendering is the process of converting the Blender file information into an image file or a movie file. In practice this entails taking the data producing what you see in **Camera View** in Blender and converting it into image or movie **file format**. The conversion may then be viewed as a digital still image or in the case of a video file, played on a variety of media devices depending on the format chosen. Controls and settings for Rendering are located in the **Properties Editor**

Note: There are three separate rendering systems in Blender. One is the Blender **Eevee** system, the second is the **Cycles** system and the third is **Workbench**.

This chapter explains the basic   render procedure using the default **Eevee** system limiting the discussion to producing a still image file or video file.

Eevee is a fully-featured PBR (physically based-rendering) engine for real-time visualization. with advanced features such as volumetrics, screen-space reflections and refractions, subsurface scattering, soft and contact shadows, post-processing effects such as ambient occlusion, depth of field, camera motion blur and bloom, to name a few (definition from the Blender Wiki).

As you work with Eevee engaged, what you see in Camera View with Rendered Viewport Shading Mode active, is what you get when the Blender file is converted to an image file.

17.1 Rendering

Rendering in the practical sense converts the data producing what is seen in **Camera View** in the 3D View Editor into a still image or in the case of an animation into a video clip.

To Render a still image press the **F12** button on the Keyboard. An image is Rendered and displayed in a full Screen version of the **Image Editor**. Press **Esc** to cancel.

To Render an animation press **Ctrl + F12.**

These Render options are also located in the Render button in the Screen Header.

With the Eevee Render Engine active (default) it is not necessary to Render to see what you get in an image . With Eevee engaged and the 3D View Editor in **Rendered Viewport Shading Mode** you see the equivalent of a Render in the 3D View Editor. However, at some stage, you will Render a Scene and save it as a still image or Render an animation to a video sequence and then produce a Video Clip.

Properties Editor, Render buttons

Note: Rendering a still image does not save a file to the computer. With the default settings in the Properties Editor, Render buttons Rendering a still image merely displays the Render in the Image Editor. Rendering an animation, however, saves an image for each Frame in the animation and by default, saves to the /tmp\ directory as seen in the Render buttons, Output Tab. On a Windows 10 Computer this means the files are saved in Local Disk (C:)\tmp.

17.2 The Properties Editor Render Buttons
Figure 17.1

The detailed output from the Render process is controlled in the **Properties Editor, Render buttons**.

The Render controls are shown here to make you aware of their existence. As you see there are numerous categories arranged in Tabs. Opening a Tab displays the controls for that particular subject which in some cases requires activation by checking the button preceding the subject name.

Click to open a Tab ————

Check (tick) to activate ————

When Rendering, the computer is converting the data producing the Screen display into a format for an Image display. In doing this it processes in a series of passes which in each pass improves on the quality of the previous pass. How many passes performed is referred to as the number of **Samples**. As you see in Figure 17.1 the default number of Samples is; Viewport 16 (what you see in the Viewport) and Render 64 (what you see when you press F12).

17.3 The Properties Editor Output Buttons

In accepting the default number of Render Samples and Render Settings, to produce an image or video, all you have to do in practice is specify the Resolution and where you want the file saved. This is done in the **Properties Editor, Output buttons** (Figure 17.2)

Figure 17.2

In the Output buttons the **Dimensions Tab**, and **Output Tab** are expanded.

You may consider the expanded tabs as the basic controls for setting the rendering process.

17.4 The Dimensions Tab

The **Dimensions Tab** (Figure 17.2) is where you tell Blender how big to make your image, the shape of the image, the quality of the image (Resolution) the shape of the pixels (Aspect Ratio) and in the case of an animation where to start and stop rendering and how fast you want it to play back when finished (Frame Rate).

Properties Editor, Output buttons

Render Quality %

Resolution

X : The number of pixels wide in the display. **Y:** The number of pixels high in the display.

Pixels are the tiny little rectangles which display on the computer or television screen.

> **Note:** The default **Resolution** 1920 x 1080 equates to the HDTV 1080p **Preset.**

The percentage slider sets the quality of the render. The default is 100% which scales the resolution. If the value were 50% although the resolution is set at 1920 x 1080 the render would be a preview at 960 x 540. Since rendering takes time this is a way of seeing your image or movie as a preview prior to a final render and therefore saving time. For the final render you set the slider to 100%.

Aspect (Aspect Ratio)

The aspect ratio refers to the shape of the pixels. The default ratio X:1.000, Y:1.000 (1:1) is for computer monitors which have square pixels. TV screens have rectangular pixels so you have to set a ratio for the appropriate format i.e. HDV NTSC 1080p for America the ratio is 4:3 and HDV PAL 1080p for Europe is also 4:3 but TV PAL 16.9 the ratio is 16:11.

Aspect ratios are very confusing. Figures 17.3 and 17.4 on the following page are offered as a guide.

This is fairly self explanatory and shows the start frame (Frame Start) and end frame of the animation and the **Steps** which means which frames to render. **Frame Steps: 1** means render every frame, **Frame Steps: 2** would mean render every other frame **Frame Steps: 3** would mean render every third frame etc.

> **Note:** Pressing **F12** with an animation paused renders an image of the single frame in the animation where it paused.

Frame Size	Aspect Ratio	Description (note these are only the most common formats)
		Figure 17.3
1920x1080	16x9	1080p/i
1440x1080	16x9	1080i **(Most HDV use this format)**
1280x720	16x9	720p
852x480	16x9	480p
720x480	4:3	DV NTSC (when the pixels are square it is actually 3:2)
720x480	16:9*	DV NTSC / Anamorphic* / Wide Screen (non square pixles)
720x576	5:4	DV PAL
640x480	4:3	a ration suitable for square size pixle multimeida video.
640x360	16:9	a ration suitable for square size pixle multimeida thats widescreen.
480x360	4:3	Multimedia large (480x360 : 75%(640x480))
480x270	16:9	Multimedia Large (similar to Apple's large move trailer standard 480x272) (480x270 : 75%(640x360))
320x240	4:3	Multimedia Large
320x180	16:9	Multimedia Large / Wide Screen
240x180	4:3	Multimedia Small
160x120	4:3	Thumbnail
1600x1200	4:3	Computer Display
1280x1024	4:3	Computer Display
1152x870	4:3	Computer Display
1024x768	4:3	Computer Display
800x600	4:3	Computer Display

Aspect Ratio

Figure 17.4

The ratio between the length and width of video images. **NTSC, PAL,** and **Secam** formats use a **4:3** aspect ratio. Newer, more advanced formations such as **HDTV** (High Definition Television) use a much wider aspect ratio of **16:9**.

- Television is 4:3
- Widescreen TV 16:9
- 35mm Film 1.85:1
- 70mm Film 2.0:1

Frame Rate The playback speed of the animation expressed in Frames per second. The selection menu provides options for a variety of formats. 24 Frames per second is the default setting (25 FPS for PAL TV European format and 30 FPS for NTSC TV US format – These frame rates are approximate and vary with the actual **Render Preset** selected).

Border

Check (Tick) Border. In Camera View, press Shift + B Key, drag the mouse to define a portion of the view to render instead of the whole Camera View.

Crop

Enabling **Crop** will crop the rendered image instead of rendering a black region around it.

17.5 The Output Tab

In the **Output tab** (Figure 17.5) you set options to tell Blender where to save your render and the file format you require.

By default Blender will save your render to the **temporary** folder on your hard drive as seen by the **/tmp** notation in the output file address bar. On this computer this is C:\tmp\. You can choose a different location by clicking on the folder icon at the end of the bar and navigating in the file browser that opens.

Figure 17.5

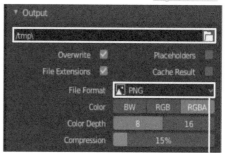

Figure 17.6

Blender will save your render in a variety of file formats. The default format is **PNG** (Portable Network Graphics). Where you see this in the Output Tab is a selection menu for choosing alternative formats (Figure 17.6). In the menu you will see that the options are in two categories: **Image** and **Movie**. Image types such as PNG or JPEG produce a render of a still image in that particular file type. Selecting one of the Movie options produces a render of an animation in a compressed movie file such as AVI Raw or FFmpeg.

Note: With an Image file selected a render of an animation will consist of a series of images of each frame of the animation. Although this takes up a lot of room in a folder it is an acceptable method of producing a video file.

Note: The default **Image** type PNG with the RGB color scheme and **Compression** ratio of 15%. Some formats can compress images to use less disk space, for instance; Lossless PNG or JPEG.

17.6 Rendering a JPEG Image

1. When you have created a scene in the 3D View Editor and decide that you wish to save an image of what you see in the **Camera View** go to the **Properties Editor, Render buttons**. For the time being leave all the default settings just as they are except in the **Output tab** click on the selection menu where you see **PNG** and change to **JPEG**.

With your mouse cursor back in the 3D View Editor, press F12 on the keyboard to render the camera view. The image displays in the Image Editor. In the Header click Image and select Save As (Shift + S Key) to save the Rendered image. If you have opened a previously saved image you will press Save (Alt + S Key). The File Browser displays (Figure 17.7) which allows you to name your image file and navigate to a folder on your hard drive where you wish to save the JPEG image.

Figure 17.7

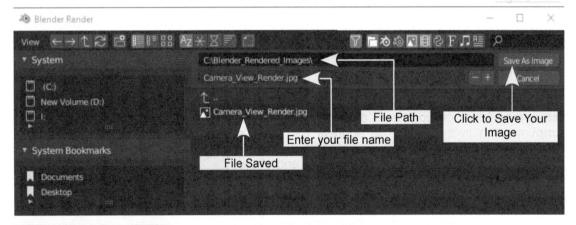

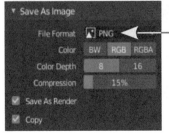

Note: If you have forgotten to change the file format from PNG to JPEG when you saved you can change it in the Tool Panel at the lower LH side of the File Browser window.

In Figure 17.7 the image file has been named **Camera_View_Rendre.png** which is a folder on the hard drive. With this information entered as shown, click **Save As Image** in the upper RH corner of the Editor. **Note:** If you have an animation sequence paused you can render and save an image of the animation frame.

17.7 Rendering a Movie File

The title, **Rendering a Movie File** should possibly be named, **Rendering a Video Clip**. Movies are made by combining a series of video clips (short sections of video). Video clips are made from animation frames compiled into a sequence. Before you can render a video file you must have an animation sequence.

To demonstrate the process an animation will be created and rendered to video . Animation is covered in the next chapter so assuming you are working your way through the book chapter by chapter you will not have covered the topic at this stage. To create an animation work through the following instructions.

In the **3D View Editor** go into **Camera View** (Num Pad 0) and Translate the default Cube back along the X Axis outside the Camera View (Figure 17.8). Press the **I Key** and in the drop down menu, select **Location**. In the **Timeline Editor** at the bottom of the screen click RMB on the vertical blue line, hold and drag the line to frame 10. In the 3D View Editor, Translate the Cube along the X Axis to outside Camera View on the opposite side. Press **I Key** again and select **Location**.

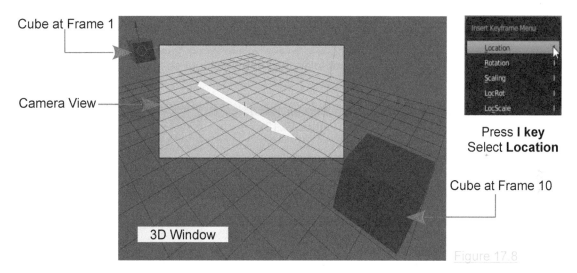

Cube at Frame 1

Camera View

Insert Keyframe Menu
Location
Rotation
Scaling
LocRot
LocScale

Press **I key**
Select **Location**

Cube at Frame 10

3D Window

Figure 17.8

In the **Timeline Editor** Header change the **End: 250** value to **End: 10** (Figure 17.9).

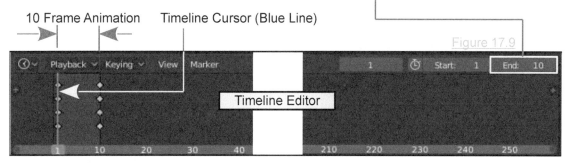

10 Frame Animation   Timeline Cursor (Blue Line)

Figure 17.9

Playback   Keying   View   Marker

Start: 1   End: 10

Timeline Editor

1   10   20   30   40   210   220   230   240   250

You have made an animation consisting of 10 frames. In the Timeline Editor click on the reverse arrows to set the animation at frame 1 (Figure 17.10) . Click the start button to play the animation in the 3D View Editor. The Cube zips across the Camera View and repeats the 10 frame animation over and over. Press **Esc** to quit.

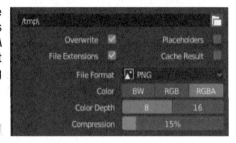

Figure 17.10

OK! Now for the render.   Reverse Arrows - Go to Start Frame (1) ——⌐   Start Play

In this demonstration use the default settings in the **Properties Editor, Render buttons.** The **Output Tab** is set to render a **PNG** file format and save it to the **/tmp** folder on the hard drive (Figure 17.11). If you haven't been messing with your hard drive and repartitioning the /tmp\ folder should be in **C:\tmp**.

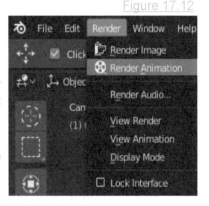

Figure 17.11

> **tmp** stands for temporary. Programs use this location for storing information while they work therefore there could be files in the folder.

Before you do any rendering to the **/tmp** folder give it a clean out so you have a clean slate for this demo.

Figure 17.12

To Render the animation **Render** in the **Screen Header** and select **Render Animation (Ctrl _ F12)** (Figure 17.12).

Blender will start making an image for each frame of the animation and save it to the **/tmp** folder. The reason for Rendering an image for each frame is that the default output file type is **PNG** which is an image file. The same thing would happen if you had JPEG selected. The Render is performed in the Image Editor where progress displays at the top of the Screen. When the render is finished Close the Image Editor. If you look in the /tmp\ folder when the render is finished you will see 10 image files (Figure 17.13).

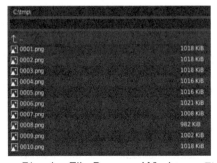

Blender File Browser Window   Figure 17.13   Windows 10 File Explorer

17.8 Video Playback

To playback your rendered animation from within Blender you go to the **Screen Header** and click on **Render** and select **View Animation**.

Playing the animation at this stage is simply cycling through the sequence of image files that has been created. Ten simple image files constitute a very very basic animation. Animations can run to thousands of image files which would accumulate and create a massive storage problem on your hard drive. To save space you render the animation sequence to a **Movie File**.

As an example take the same 10 Frame animation previously created and in the **Properties Editor, Render buttons, Output tab**, change the default **PNG** to one of the other **Movie** options, for example **AVI Raw**, which is a video file format (Figure 17.141). Video file formats compress the data from the rendered animation into a single file instead of the series of image files.

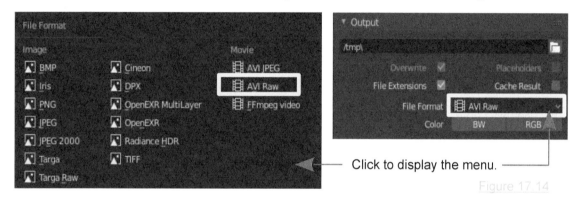

Click to display the menu.

Figure 17.14

Before you Render with the video file format clean out the **tmp** folder again.

OK! With a clean slate go ahead and select **Render Animation** to start Rendering. When Blender is finished Rendering press **Esc** to exit the Image Editor.

Go look in your **tmp** folder and you will find a single video file (Figure 17.15). Press the **Play** button to replay the rendered animation in the inbuilt player. Since this is a video file you could also play it in some external application such as **VLC Media Player**. If you try this with the 10 frame animation pay attention since 10 frames plays pretty quickly. An external player only plays the file once and at 24 frames per second this is less than half a second of video.

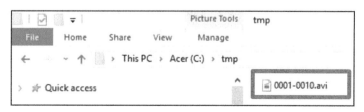

Windows 10 File Explorer   Figure 17.15

17.9 Video Codecs

In the preceding example, changing the default **PNG** file format to **AVI Raw**, elected to use the **AVI Raw Video Codec** which tells the computer how you want your animation data encoded. There are many many video codecs to chose from and simply selecting a codec type in Blender doesn't necessarily mean that you will get the result that you want. You must have the **Codec** installed on your computer.

A Codec is a little routine that compresses the video so that it will fit on a DVD, or be able to be streamed over the internet, or over cable, or just be a reasonable file size.

Simply put, using a codec, you encode the Blender animation data to a video file which suits a particular output media such as PAL TV or NTSC TV. When you have used the encoded data to create a video CD or DVD, the CD or DVD is played in a device (CD / DVD Player) which decodes the data for display i.e. Television Screen.

As previously stated you must have the codec installed on your computer.

Codec Packs are available for download from the internet.

Two examples area:

> K-Lite Codec Pack 12.4.7
>
> media.player.codec.pack.v4.4.2.setup.exe

17.10 Making a Movie

In the preceding information the procedure for rendering an image or a animation sequence has been briefly explained. In rendering the animation you first created a series of image files and then repeated the process creating a video file. The video file does not constitute a movie. In this case the video was a mere 10 frames but even if it were a thousand frames it would not be a movie. It is merely a render of one animation sequence from one Scene into a video file. Movies are made by combining many video files and then rendering the combination to a movie file. At the same time as this combination is compiled sound effects are added and synchronized with the video.

This combining, synchronizing and editing takes place in a **Video Sequence Editor** (VSE). Blender has its own VSE which is discussed in Chapter 27.

A video clip (movie file) will take some time to compile depending on the length of the animation. Each Frame of the animation has to be rendered and saved. Depending on the complexity of the Scene, a Frame can take from a few seconds to several minutes to render. To begin, it is best to keep everything very basic and simple. If you get to the stage where you have created a wonderful movie, you can send the animation files to a **Render Farm** on the Internet to have them rendered—it saves you time but it costs you money.

18

Animation

Animation is the illusion of motion, of making objects depicted in a still image appear to move. In its simplest form stick figures drawn on separate pages appear to move when the pages are viewed in quick succession. Animation has advanced from that simple technique to sophisticated full length feature films with sound and voice which are experienced today. In the past Movies were produced by laboriously drawing many images, posing figures, each slightly different to the next which were photographed and transcribed to film. Each image was then said to be a Frame in an animation sequence. Today the process is accomplished by Computer Graphics which essentially mimics that same process.

In Blender animation is accomplished by creating data which displays on the computer Screen. The display is programmed to change over a period of time (**The Timeline**) and then captured by a camera at intervals producing **Frames** of the animation. Each Frame is **Rendered**, which means the Blender data is correlated and turned into a series of digital images. The images are compiled into a video clip or sequence depicting an action. Finally a series of video clips are assembled, edited, combined with effects such as audio and converted to a movie file.

This chapter will explore some of the techniques used for creating animation effects.

18.1 The Animation Screen

Animation may be performed in the default Blender Screen, in the **3D View Editor**, in conjunction with the **Timeline Editor.** Alternatively Blender has a dedicated **Animation Workspace** (Screen Arrangement)(Figure 18.1).

The **Workspace** is accessed in the Blender <u>Screen Header</u>.

3D Animation Workspace

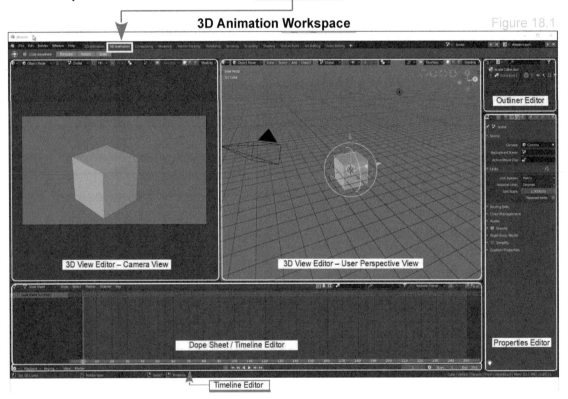

Figure 18.1

3D View Editor – Camera View

3D View Editor – User Perspective View

Outliner Editor

Properties Editor

Dope Sheet / Timeline Editor

Timeline Editor

The **3D Animation Workspace** comprises a **3D View Editor** in Camera View (upper LHS), a second **3D View Editor** in User Perspective View (center), the **Outliner Editor** and **Properties Editor** at the RH side of the Screen and the **Dope Sheet and Timeline Editors** across the bottom. To see the Timeline Editor drag the border up.

To demonstrate the very basics of the animation process the default Cube Object will be animated to move in the Scene, and change shape at the same time. Simple motion and deformation of an Object are only two of many features which may be animated.

The objective in creating an animation is to capture what you see on the Screen in the **Camera View**. This will be what is included in the final render. You may set up an animations sequence in the Blender Scene then position the Camera or position multiple Cameras to capture parts of the sequence. What is captured will be rendered to a series of still images (Frames) producing a video clip. The clip will be finally compiled (spliced together) with other clips to make a movie file.

18.2 Movement in the 3D View Editor

Moving or Translating Objects in the 3D View Editor may be performed by selecting the Object, pressing the **G Key** and moving the Mouse or by using the **Manipulation Widget**. The two methods move the Object in the Scene in different ways.

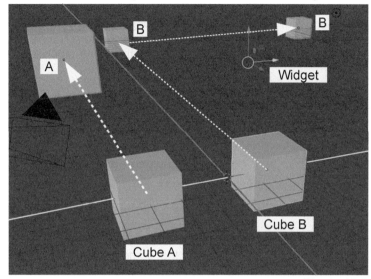

What you see in the 3D View Editor when you move Objects depends on the method of Translation. In Figure 18.2 **Cube A** is Translated by pressing the G Key (Grab) and moved up and to the left. **Cube B** is translated using the **Move Tool** which activates the Manipulation **Widget**.

Note: The Widget in the diagram is positioned at the center of geometry of the three B Cube Objects . This is for diagram construction only.

Figure 18.2

When **Cube A** is Translated by using the **G Key** the movement is confined to the plane of the computer Screen.

When **Cube B** is Translated by using the Move Tool Widget the movement is confined to either the X, Y or Z Axis of the 3D World (the Scene).

Cube B has been moved back along the X Axis then to the right along the Y Axis. In **User Perspective View** you see its size diminish as it recedes into the distance. In fact all views of the Cube have the same physical size as seen in Top Orthographic View (Figure 18.3).

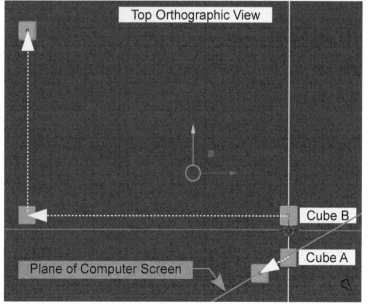

Figure 18.3

Understanding this concept of Translation on the Computer Screen and in the 3D World will assist when animating Objects to move.

18.3 Planning the Animation

Planing the animation is an important part of the process. Without having even a rudimentary idea of what you want to achieve can lead to disaster when the Scene becomes a little complicated.

In demonstrating the concept of animation, with a view to illustration, begin with a very simple sequence. The default Cube Object in the default 3D View Editor will be relocated (Translated) then animated to move forward along the X Axis of the 3D World and at the same time Scaled along the Y Axis.

Figure 18.4

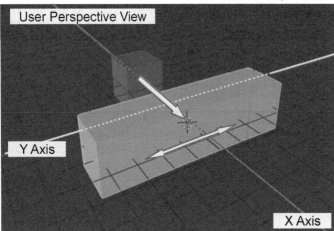

Figures 18.4 and 18.5 show the default Cube Object positioned approximatly three Blender units on the X Axis towards the back of the Scene in the 3D View Editor (minus 3 Units).

The Cube will be animated to move forward along the X Axis.

At the same time the Cube will be Scaled on the Y Axis.

Figure 18.5

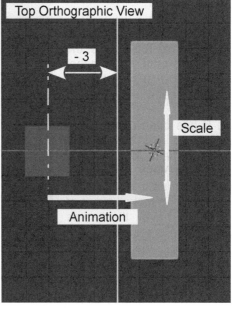

Note: In following the demonstration the position and the scale of the Cube are arbitrary but to explain features to follow it will help if they are copied (approximately).

Translating and Scaling will generate Curves in the Graph Editor which may be edited to affect the animation.

The first step in an animation is to decide what you want your actor to do in a given time. In this demonstration, the actor will be the Cube Object. How long it takes the actor to do something will depend on how many Frames per second the animation is run and this is determined by which format your final render will be.

The **Render Format** determines how many Frames per second the animation should run (For example when playing in a television format, **NTSC** for the US at 30 fps, **PAL** for Australia at 25 fps). When considering the animation, make the motion occur in an appropriate time. Look at the frames per second and relate it to time. If you want a movement to take 3 seconds and you are running at 25 frames per second, then the animation has to occur in 75 Frames (3 x 25 = 75).

In Blender you do not have to create every single Frame of the animation. You set up single Frames (**Keyframes**) at specific points and the program works out all the intermediate Frames.

Think of a 10-second animation that, when running at 25 Frames per second, would consist of 250 Frames. If you want your actor to go from point A to point B and then to point C in the Scene within the 250-Frame animation, you first insert a **Keyframe** at Frame 1 with the actor at position A. This is giving Blender data that says, at the Frame 1, locate the actor at location A. Then at another Frame, mid way in the animation, insert a second **Keyframe** with the actor at location B. Finally insert a third **Keyframe** at frame 250 with the actor at location C. These are the **Keyframes** for the animation. Blender will work out all the in-between Frames. The Keyframes can also include the data for other features such as scale, rotation and color.

Determining the in-between data is called **Interpolation.** There are different methods of interpolation. By default, Blender uses **Bezier Interpolation**, which for motion gives a nice acceleration and deceleration between **Keyframes**. When an object moves from point A to point B in a given time, it is said to move at a certain velocity (speed). In theory, the speed could be represented as a straight line graph, but in practice an Object at rest (motionless) has to go from being motionless to moving at a certain velocity. The rate at which it attains the velocity is called acceleration. Blender's **Bezier Interpolation** draws curves at the beginning and end of the straight line graph (acceleration and deceleration). You have the options to choose **Constant** or **Linear** type interpolation if appropriate. Selection of interpolation types will be discussed later in the chapter.

Using the term **Bezier** to describe interpolation is in fact an anomaly. Bezier actually describes a type of line (the line on a graph described in the previous paragraph). A Bezier line or curve in Blender is a line that has control points that allow the shape of the line to be altered or edited (see Editing Using Curves Chapter 10). In Blender, the control points are located at the position of the **Keyframes**. Interpolation is performed according to a mathematical formula that determines the shape of the line. When the data for the Frames in the animation is drawn as a line on a graph, the line conforms to that mathematical formula.

For the moment, accept the default Bezier-Type interpolation to demonstrate the insertion of Keyframes and the creation of a simple animation.

18.5 Animation Speed and Length

Set the animation to run at 24 frames per second, which would be suitable for PAL format. Go to the **Properties Editor, Output button, Dimensions tab – Frame Rate** (Figure 18.6).

Figure 18.6

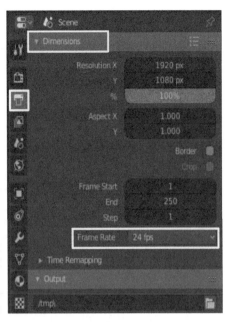

Note that in the **Timeline Editor** the Frame range settings are, **Start: 1** and **End: 250** (Figure 18.7); this says the animation will begin at Frame 1 and end at Frame 250. Running at the rate of 24 Frames per second will give an animation time of approximately 10 seconds. If you think about it, 10 seconds is quite a long time for a single action to take place in a video clip. Also in the Timeline Editor, make note of the lighter grayed area beginning at Frame 1 and ending at Frame 250. Changing the **Start Frame** and **End Frame** values in the header panel will move the end positions of the lighter grayed area. Note the vertical blue line at Frame 1. This is the **Timeline Cursor**.

Cursor (Blue Line) ⌐   **Dope Sheet Editor** (Truncated)   Figure 18.7

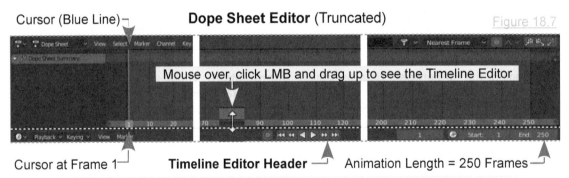

Cursor at Frame 1 ⌐   **Timeline Editor Header** ⌐   Animation Length = 250 Frames ⌐

Note: The the Scale and Cursor are replicated in the Dope Sheet and Timeline.

To make the process relatively simple and suitable for a demonstration, the actor (the Cube) will be made to move in a straight line along the X Axis and at the same time increase in size on the Y Axis. Make sure the Cube is selected in the 3D View Editor. Initially only two Keyframes will be inserted.

In the default Scene, the actor (the selected object – the Cube) is located at Frame 1 in the animation. In the upper LH corner of the 3D Editor, you will see **(1) Cube** in white lettering. This indicates that you have the Cube selected. If you had ten objects in the Scene, all of which were actors with perhaps some hidden, it's nice to know which one is selected.

Observe the **Timeline Editor** at the bottom of the Screen. The buttons labelled **Start: 1, End: 250**, and **1** show the start Frame and end Frame that was set by default for the animation and the current Frame of the animation (Frame 1).

Along the bottom of the Editor is a scale showing the Frame numbers of the animation and in the Editor itself you see the number of Frames set for the animation represented by the light gray area. The default is 250 Frames. Drag the upper edge of the Timeline Editor up to see the scale.

Click LMB on the scale, hold and drag the mouse to repositions the scale. With the mouse cursor in the **Timeline Editor** pressing **Num Pad + or –** zooms the scale. Scrolling the Mouse Wheel zooms the scale.

At Frame 1 is the **Timeline Cursor** (vertical blue) line . Click on the cursor with the RMB, hold and drag it across to Frame 25 (Figure 18.8). Note the number change at the bottom of the Cursor and next to **Cube** at the upper LH side of the 3D View Editor and in the Header bar of the **Timeline Editor**. You may also click RMB in the Timeline and Dope Sheet Editors to relocate the Cursor. Other ways to change the Frame are to click on the little arrows on either end of the **Frame Number** in the Timeline Editor Header, or click LMB on the button, hold and drag to change the Frame number or click on the **button**, hit delete, and retype the required frame number. *There is always more than one way to skin a cat.*

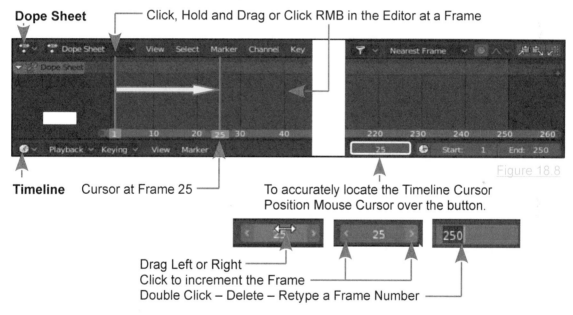

Dope Sheet   Click, Hold and Drag or Click RMB in the Editor at a Frame

Timeline   Cursor at Frame 25 ——

Figure 18.8

To accurately locate the Timeline Cursor Position Mouse Cursor over the button.

Drag Left or Right ——
Click to increment the Frame ——
Double Click – Delete – Retype a Frame Number ——

18.6 Inserting Keyframes

Keyframes are inserted in the animation at specific Frames. For example, with the Cube Object located at minus three (-3) units on the X Axis, position the **Timeline Cursor** at Frame 25.

Place the **Mouse Cursor** in the **3D View Editor** and press the **I key** to insert a **Keyframe**. In the selection list that displays, select (click) **LocRotScale**, which covers moving, rotating and changing the size of the Object (Figure 18.9). You will see orange diamonds appear at Frame 25, in the Timeline Editor and Dope Sheet Editor.

Figure 18.9

Keyframe inserted in the animation at Frame 25.

Figure 18.10

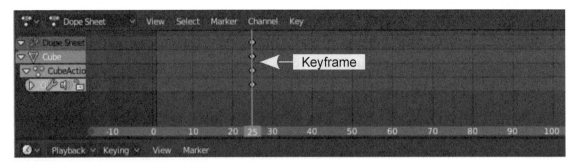

At this point, only one Keyframe has been inserted and the Cube remains stationary at minus three units on the X Axis of the Scene.

If you click RMB on the **Dope Sheet Editor Cursor** (blue line) ,hold and drag the mouse from Frame 1 along the timeline the Cube (actor) remains stationary. Clicking RMB and dragging the blue line in the Editor is called **scrubbing the animation**, which is actually manually playing the animation. You can play the animation by clicking the **Play button** in the **Timeline Editor Header**.

Figure 18.11

Since you haven't told the actor (the Cube) to do anything, nothing happens.

Each orange diamond is located on a colored strip representing an animation channel. Click on the **Object Transformation Channel** to see the full display.

Figure 18.12

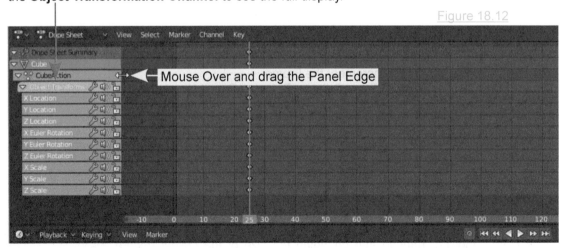

The animation channels give a visual reference to the **Keyframes**.

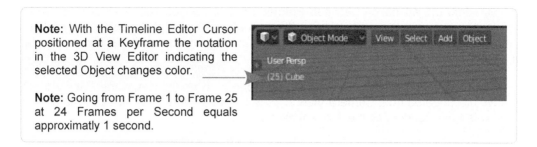

Note: With the Timeline Editor Cursor positioned at a Keyframe the notation in the 3D View Editor indicating the selected Object changes color.

Note: Going from Frame 1 to Frame 25 at 24 Frames per Second equals approximatly 1 second.

Continue creating the animation by moving the Cursor to Frame 75 (drag the blue line or click on Frame 75).

In the 3D View Editor, grab and move the Cube to plus 6 Blender units on the X Axis and scale it up four (4) times on the Y Axis (Figure 18.13). With the Mouse Cursor in the 3D View Editor, press the **I key** and select **LocRotScale** to insert a second Keyframe. You will see another set of orange diamonds in the Timeleine at Frame 75 (Figure 18.15).

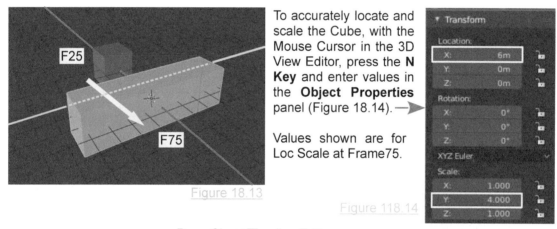

To accurately locate and scale the Cube, with the Mouse Cursor in the 3D View Editor, press the **N Key** and enter values in the **Object Properties** panel (Figure 18.14).——▶

Values shown are for Loc Scale at Frame75.

Figure 18.13

Figure 118.14

Figure 18.15

Dope Sheet/Timeline Editor

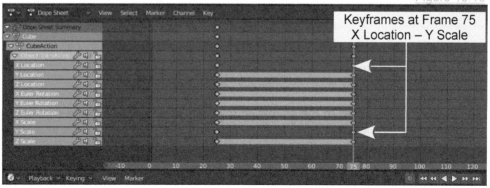

Keyframes at Frame 75
X Location – Y Scale

Note: Only **X Location** and **Y Scale** Channels have data recorded. The orange Channels indicate that there is no change in state between the Keyframes.

When you scrub the animation between Frames 25 and 75, you will see the Cube move and change in size—you are manually playing the animation. Note that the action only takes place between frames 25 and 75, which is the location of the Keyframes; no action takes place on either side of the Keyframes.

> **Note:** In moving the Cube from minus three to plus six on the X Axis the Cube will have disappeared from Camera View. This will require addressing since Camera View is what Renders as the final animation.

18.7 Playing the Animation

To actually play a preview of the animation, move the Cursor in the Timeline to frame 1 then press the **Spacebar** with the Cursor in the 3D View Editor. Say "one thousand" to yourself slowly (counting one second, while the Cursor in the **Timeline** moves across to frame 25). You will see the Cube remain stationary until the Cursor reaches frame 25 then the Cube will move and increase in size. At frame 75, it stops moving and changing size. The Cursor in the Timeline continues on to frame 250 then jumps back to frame 1 and the preview of the animation plays again. Press **Esc** to stop playing.

Another way to play the animation is to press the **Play** button in the **Timeline Editor Header** (Figure 18.16). This button is much like the play button on any video or audio player.

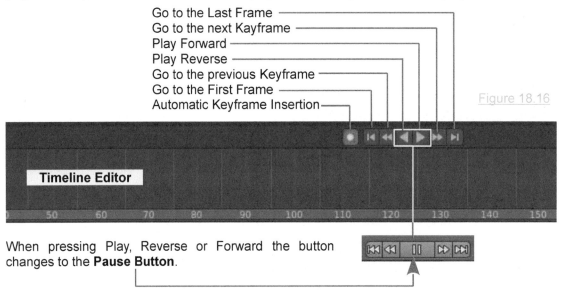

Go to the Last Frame
Go to the next Kayframe
Play Forward
Play Reverse
Go to the previous Keyframe
Go to the First Frame
Automatic Keyframe Insertion

Figure 18.16

Timeline Editor

50   60   70   80   90   100   110   120   130   140   150

When pressing Play, Reverse or Forward the button changes to the **Pause Button**.

More Keyframes may be added to the animation to move, scale and rotate the actor around the Scene. For the most part, location and size keys work flawlessly but care needs to be taken with rotation keys . If you try to rotate an Object too far in one set of keys, the Object may not rotate in the direction you want it to and it may rotate oddly. Try small angular movements between keys while rotating. There are better ways to control this and tools to simplify the process, (see 18.14). Be aware that the movement of the actor may not be exactly as planned. Blender automatically defaults to trying to create a smooth flow through the animation.

18.8 Automatic Keyframing

Keyframes have been inserted in the animation by placing the Mouse Cursor in the 3D View Editor, moving to a Frame in the Timeline, changing the status of the Object and then pressing the **I Key** and selecting one of the Keyframe options.

Blender has an **Automatic Keyframe** insertion function which is activated by pressing the white button in the **Timeline Editor Header** (highlights red when active)(Figure 11.17).

Figure 18.17

With auto on, whenever you Move, Scale, or Rotate the actor Object in the 3D View Editor, a Keyframe will be inserted at whatever Frame has been selected in the Timeline.

For example; With the Cube Object in the default Scene in the 3D View Editor it is located at the intersection of the X Axis and Y Axis. The Cursor in the Timeline Editor is located at Frame 1. With Auto on, Translating the Cube along the X Axis inserts a Keyframe at Frame 1 recording that this is the state of the Cube at Frame 1.

If the Timeline Cursor had been positioned at Frame 25 then the Cube Translated, a Keyframe will have been inserted at Frame 25. This will be the First frame in the animation. If the Timeline Cursor is moved back to Frame 1 the Cube remains in its position for frame 25.

The procedure for Automatic Keyframing is, position the Timeline Cursor, Translate, Rotate or Scale the selected Object to insert Keyframes.

Remember to turn this off after you're finished using it (press the button a second time).

18.9 Controlling the Animations

When an animation has been created it may be controlled (modified) in the **Dope Sheet/Timeline Editor** and by using the **Graph Editor**. Modifying the animation means adjusting how motion is performed, such as the speed and when the motion occurs in the animation. Adjustment also entails what type of motion is performed, when movement takes place and how fast the motion is may be adjusted by repositioning Keyframes in the Dope Sheet/Timeline Editor. Different types of motion adhere to mathematical formula and, therefore, are represented by graphs. The shape of the graph line represents the motion, therefore, altering the shape of the graph line changes the motion.

To modify and control the animation, in the **3D Animation Workspace**, change the 3D View Editor with Camera View to the **Graph Editor** and align the **Dope Sheet Timeline** (Frames) (Figure 18.18 over)

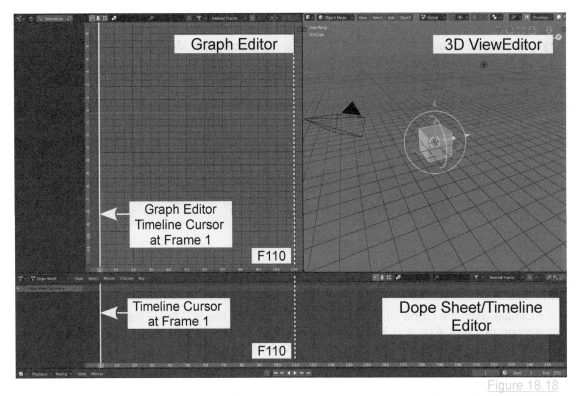

Graph Editor

3D ViewEditor

Graph Editor
Timeline Cursor
at Frame 1

F110

Timeline Cursor
at Frame 1

F110

Dope Sheet/Timeline
Editor

Figure 18.18

To align the **Timelines** click and drag the **Frame Scale** and **Pan the Graph Editor panel**.

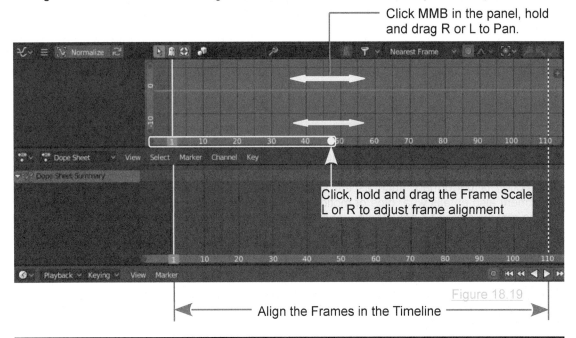

Click MMB in the panel, hold
and drag R or L to Pan.

Click, hold and drag the Frame Scale
L or R to adjust frame alignment

Figure 18.19

◄──────── Align the Frames in the Timeline ────────►

18.10 The Graph Editor

The **Graph Editor** shows a graphical display of the animation. The graphs can be edited to refine and control the animation actions. When using the 3D Animation Workspace Screen arrangement change the 3D View Editor in Camera View to the Graph Editor. By adjusting the position and scaling panels you can align the Graph Editor with the Dope Sheet/Timeline Editor (Figure 18.20).

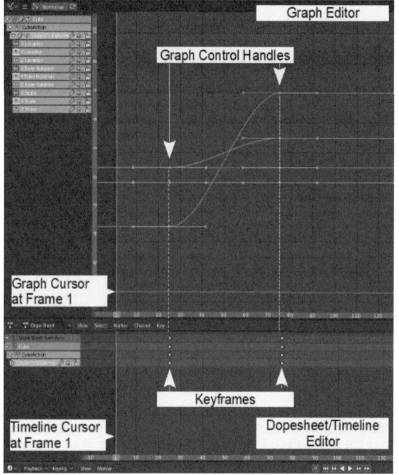

Figure 18.20

Zoom the horizontal and vertical scales by placing the Mouse Cursor on a scale bar and rotating the Mouse Wheel or dragging the ends of the scale bar.

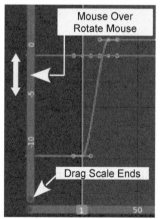

In Figure 18.20 the Keyframes in the Dope Sheet/Timeline Editor have been aligned (approximately) with the Graph Control Handles in the Graph Editor to demonstrate the correlation between the two Editors.

The graph lines in the diagram represent the Keyframes which were inserted when Translating and Scaling the Cube Object (Figure 18.4)

Examine the Graph Editor in more detail (Figure 18.21 over).

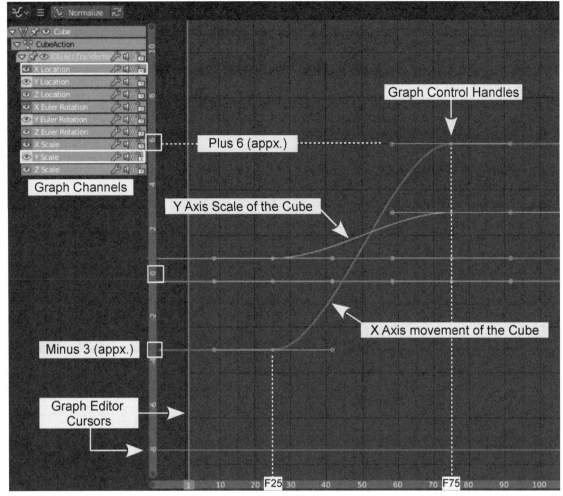

Graph Control Handles

Plus 6 (appx.)

Y Axis Scale of the Cube

X Axis movement of the Cube

Graph Channels

Minus 3 (appx.)

Graph Editor
Cursors

F25 F75

Figure 18.21

In the Graph Editor the red line represents the movement of the Cube Object on the X Axis of the 3D World. The movements initial position of minus three units changes to plus six units between Frame 25 and 75 (the position of the Keyframes). The green line represents the change in scale of the Cube on the Y Axis (Scale = 3X along the Y Axis). The two horizontal lines represent the change in other Location, Rotation and Scale (LocRotScale Keyframes) values in the animation (no change) and coincide in the graph. You see Frame numbers in the scale at the bottom of the Editor and Blender units in the vertical scale. Note: The vertical alignment of graph lines with the scale is approximate.

The Graph Channels in the panel at the LH side of the Editor list the actions that have been entered in the animation by inserting Keyframes. When entering Keyframes type **LocRotScale** was selected, therefore, the Graph Channels list Location, Rotation and Scale actions. In the Cube animation in the demonstration only the X Location and Y Scale Channels are of significance. The remaining Channels are shown since LocRotScale type was selected.

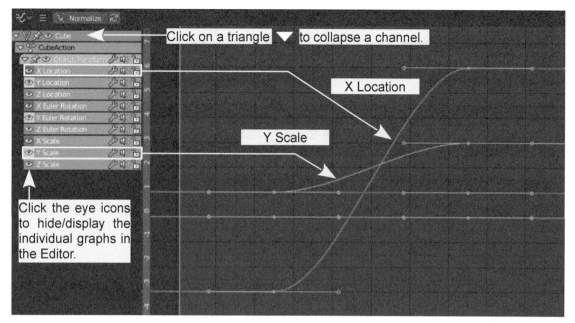

Click on a triangle ▼ to collapse a channel.

X Location

Y Scale

Click the eye icons to hide/display the individual graphs in the Editor.

Figure 18.22

Graph Editor Cursors are the Vertical and Horizontal blue lines – RMB click, hold and drag to position. The Cursors provide an alignment reference.

Scaling the Graph Editor may be done by clicking on the Scale Bar, holding and dragging the Mouse. Click and hold a dot at either end of a scale to shrink or extend the scale.

Scaling the Frame Bar may be done in a similar manner.

The Dope Sheet Channels, Cube, CubeAction and Object Transforms may be expanded or collapsed by clicking the white triangle preceding each name. (Figure 18.22).

Hiding Graphs: Clicking the eye icons preceding each Graph Channel toggles hide and display of the graph lines in the Editor.

Collapsing Channels in the Dope Sheet and hiding graph lines in the Editor can be very useful in a complicated animation. In the demonstration only the X Axis Translation and Y Axis Scale have been animated. There are many more features of the Cube alone which may be animated, therefore, you can imagine the Graph Editor could become congested with information.

Positioning the Graphs relative to the Timeline in the Graph Editor may be accomplished by selecting Control Handles on a Graph Line, clicking and holding LMB (in the Graph Editor) and dragging the Mouse. This action Pans the selection, moving the Graph Line. The movement is relative to the Timeline. Graph Lines that are not selected remain stationary, therefore, the movement of the selected line alters the action of the Object in the 3D View Editor relative to other actions.

18.11 Editing the Graph

Editing (changing the shape of the curve) in the Graph Editor will affect the animation that takes place in the 3D View Editor. The curves (graph lines) are Bezier Curves as described in Chapter 10.

To understand how the animation is edited in the Graph Editor arrange the **3D Animation Workspace** as shown in Figure 18.23 aligning the display in the Graph Editor with the Dope Sheet/Timeline Editor at the bottom of the Screen. Change the 3D View Editor, Camera View to User Perspective View by pressing Num Pad 5 twice with the Mouse Cursor in the 3D View Editor panel. This will allow you to see the movement of the Cube without it disappearing from the Viewport. Cancel the display of all but the X Axis Location Curve.

Figure 18.23

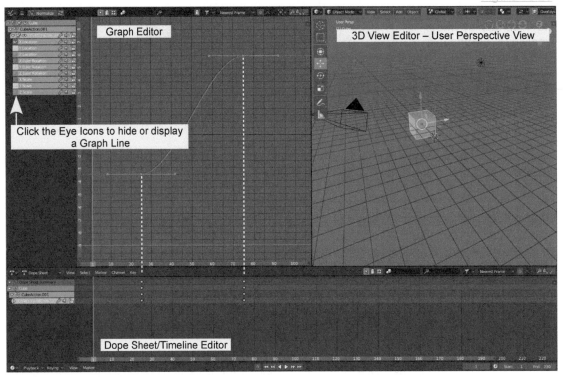

Note: The Curve Control Handles in the Graph Editor are aligned with the Keyframes in the Timeline. The Timeline Cursors are also aligned.

To recap on the animation, press the Play button in the Timeline Editor. The blue line Cursors in the Timeline and in the Graph Editor move. Initially the Cube in the 3D View Editor remains stationary. When the Cursors reach Frame 25 (position of the first Keyframe) the Cube begins to move along the X Axis of the Scene. The movement of the Cube continues until it reaches Frame 75 (position of the last Keyframe). As the Cube moves between Frame 25 and 75 it scales on the Y Axis. At Frame 75 the Cube ceases to move and change shape.

The X Location Curve in the Graph Editor is a Bezier Curve representing the X Axis movement of the Cube, therefore, the Control Handles can be selected and manipulated. The following commands execute selection procedures when the Mouse Cursor is in the Graph Editor panel:

Press **Alt + A Key** deselects the Control Handles. Press the **A Key** reselects the Control Handles.

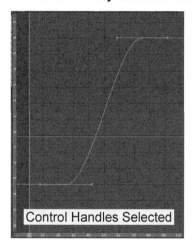
Control Handles Selected

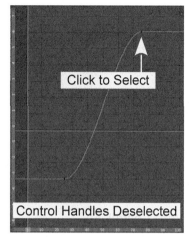
Click to Select
Control Handles Deselected

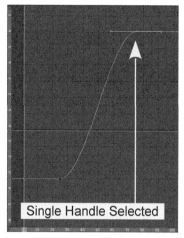
Single Handle Selected

Figure 18.24

With Control Handles deselected click RMB on a Control Handle (black dot) to select.
With a Control Handle selected it may be Translated, Rotated and Scaled by:
      G Key (Grab), move the Mouse, LMB click to locate.
      R Key (Rotate) move the Mouse, LMB click to set.
      S Key (Scale) move the Mouse, LMB click to set.

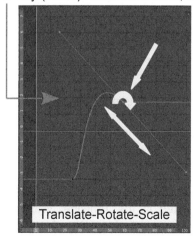
Translate-Rotate-Scale

Figure 18.25

Uneditable Dotted Line

Each of the above actions reshapes the Curve affecting the X Axis movement of the Cube in the animation. With all Control handles selected or deselected, pressing the Tab Key leaves the Curve displayed but makes it uneditable. The Curve displays as a dotted line.

To edit the X Axis movement of the Cube, select the top Control Handle, press the G Key and move the handle down approximately three units and left towards the Cursor aligning with Frame 50. Click LMB to set in position (Figure 18.26).

Note: When the Control Handle is moved you will see a set of Keyframes move to the Frame where you position the handle (Frame 50). This set of Keyframes is for the X Axis movement of the Cube. The Keyframes remaining at Frame 75 are for the Y Axis scale of the Cube.

Playing the animation at this point will see the Cube start to move on the X Axis at Frame 25 then stop at Frame 50. The Cube will scale on the Y Axis between Frame 25 and frame 75. Before frame 25 and after frame 75 no change in state occurs.

By scaling and rotating the top Control Handle you further edit the Curve (Figure 18.27.

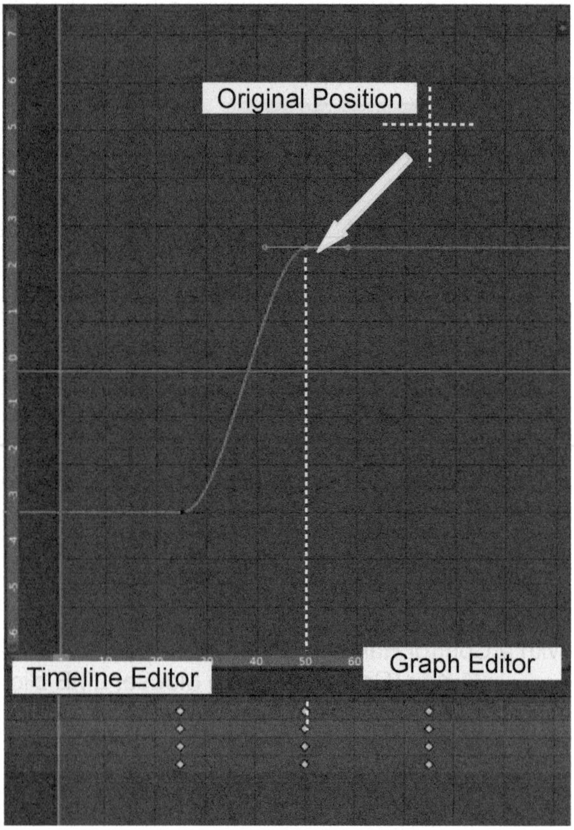

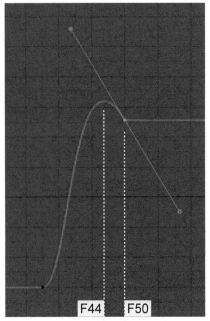

F44   F50

Figure 18.27

Original Position

Timeline Editor   Graph Editor

Figure 18.26

With the handle shaping the Curve as shown in Figure 18.27, when the animation is played the Cube moves forward on the X Axis between Frame 25 and Frame 44 then reverses direction until frame 50. **Note:** With this method no additional Keyframes are added to the Timeline.

Alternatively, instead of rotating the top Control handle, deselect all handles then press **Ctrl** and **LMB Click on the Curve** to add a new Control Handle (Figure 18.28). New Keyframes are inserted in the Timeline. With the handle selected press G Key and Translate it up and Scale approximating the Curve previously created.

Using this alternative method gives more control in editing since it provides an additional Control Handle and Keyframes.

Figure 18.28

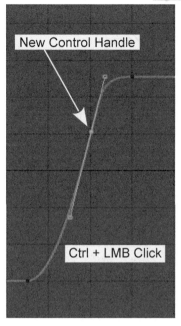

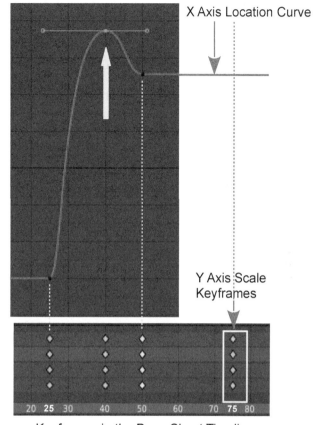

New Control Handle

Ctrl + LMB Click

X Axis Location Curve

Y Axis Scale Keyframes

Note: The Keyframes in the Timeline.

Yellow Keyframes are selected.

White Keyframes are deselected.

Keyframes in the Dope Sheet Timeline

Editing the Curve in the Dope Sheet Timeline

Curves and, therefore, the animation may be edited, by repositioning Keyframes in the Timeline of the Dope Sheet Editor. The first operation is to select individual Keyframes.

Figure 18.29

Click **RMB** on either of the first four channels to select Keyframes

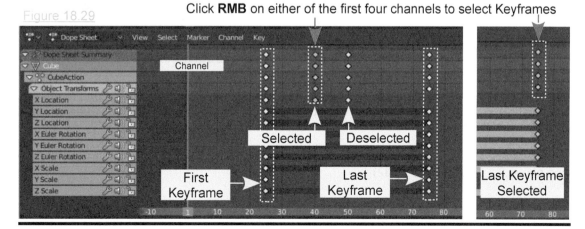

Channel

Selected

Deselected

First Keyframe

Last Keyframe

Last Keyframe Selected

Selecting Keyframes in the Dope Sheet Editor follows the basic rules for all Editors. **RMB** Click to select. Press **Alt + A Key** to deselect. Press **A Key** to select all.

With a Keyframe selected press **Delete** or the **X Key** to delete the Keyframe.

With a Keyframe selected press the **G Key**, hold **LMB** and drag to reposition the Keyframe.

With the Object Transforms Channel Expanded (click the white triangle) displaying the Location, Euler Rotation and Scale Channels, click **RMB** on an individual Keyframe to select it. Press **G Key**, hold **LMB** and reposition.

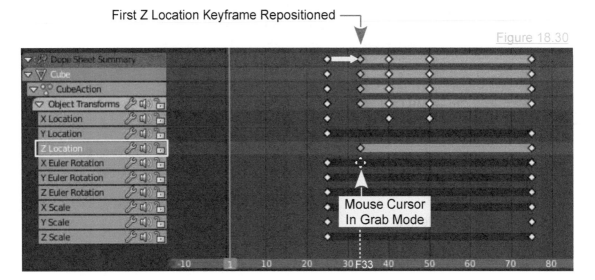

First Z Location Keyframe Repositioned —

Figure 18.30

Mouse Cursor In Grab Mode

Note: Repositioning the Z Location Keyframe as shown has no effect on the Cube in the 3D View Editor. When inserting the LocRotScale Keyframe no change was made to the Z Location in the 3D View Editor, therefore, the Z Location Graph is a horizontal straight line.

Control Handle

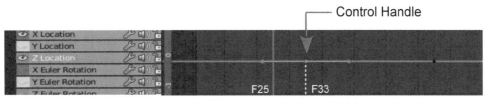

Figure 18.31

Repositioning the Keyframe in the Dope Sheet has repositioned the Control handle in the Graph Editor which, if there were a change in elevation on the Z Axis in the scene for the Cube, it would commence at this point.

To understand the correlation between the Graph Editor and the Dope Sheet align the two Editors one above the other (Figure 18.32).

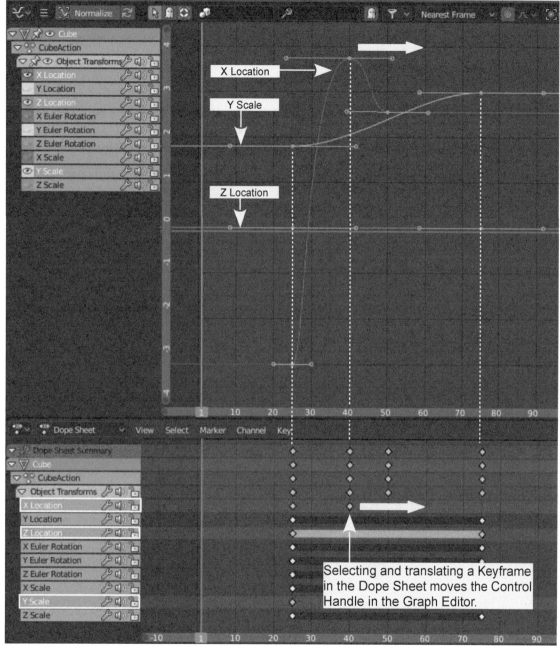

Figure 18.32

Translating a Keyframe in the Dope Sheet moves the Control Handle in the Graph Editor. Where the Keyframe/Control Handle is positioned determines where the action in the animation occurs. In Figure XXX the apex of the X Location Curve is the point where the forward movement of the Cube in the 3D View Editor is reversed.

Besides moving Keyframes adjustment to when an action takes place in the animation may also be adjusted by Scaling on the Timeline in the Dope Sheet.

Note: Scaling is relative to the Dope Sheet Editor Cursor.

To demonstrate consider the movement of the Cube on the X Axis between the apex of the Curve in the Graph Editor (Frame 40) and the final position (Frame 50).

Figure 18.33

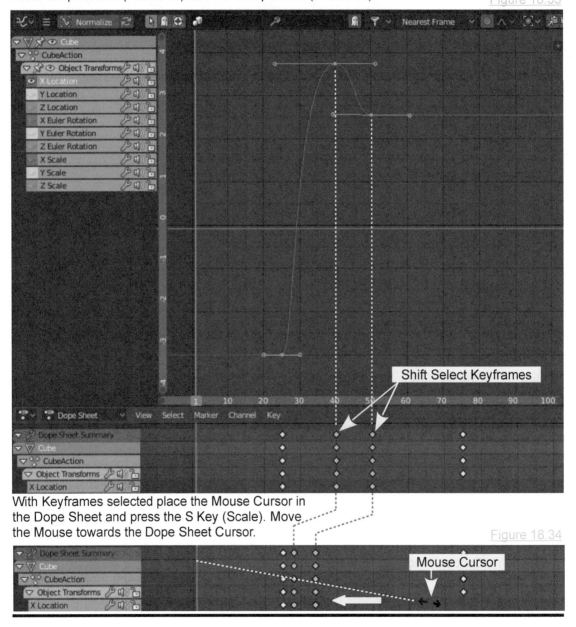

Shift Select Keyframes

With Keyframes selected place the Mouse Cursor in the Dope Sheet and press the S Key (Scale). Move the Mouse towards the Dope Sheet Cursor.

Figure 18.34

Mouse Cursor

The selected Keyframes are Scaled relative to the Dope Sheet Cursor (blue line). You will see the shape of the Curve in the Graph Editor modified accordingly.

Repeat the procedure, this time, positioning the Dope Sheet Cursor between the selected Keyframes. The Scaling is relative to the Cursor.

Figure 18.35

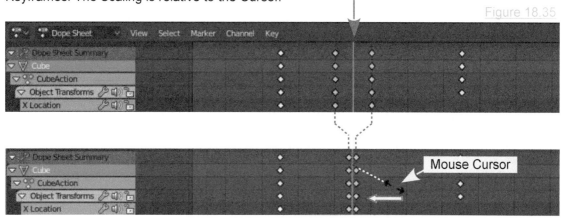

Moving Keyframes and manipulating Control Handles edits the animation Curve. The Curve has been a Bezier Type but there are alternative types to be considered which means alternative types of Interpolation between Keyframes resulting in different types of motion for the selected Object.

18.12 Other Types of Curves

By default, Blender displays **Bezier Type Curves** in the Graph Editor which means that **Bezier Type Interpolation** is used between **Keyframes**.

When considering Bezier Type Interpolation (the Curve shape) the curves at either end of the graph line represent the acceleration of the Object.

Other Types of Interpolation (Curves) are accessed in the Graph Editor or the Dope Sheet Editor. In the Dope Sheet Header click **Key** and select **Interpolation Mode** or with the Mouse Cursor in either Editor press the T Key. Either method opens the Set Keyframe Interpolation menu.

At this point only be concerned with the Constant, Linear and Bezier options.

Figure 18.36

With a Curve selected in the Graph Editor (the default is Type bezier) select Constant or Linear.

Figure 18.37

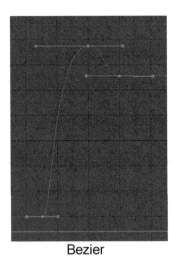  

| Bezier | Constant | Linear |

Each Type of Interpolation (Curve) produces a different motion in the animation. **Constant Interpolation** results in a dramatic quick change from one state to the other at a given Frame while **Linear Interpolation** produces a change following a straight line graph between points . The choice of these types of graphs and motions depends on how you want your actor to behave in the animation. Both of the alternatives to Bezier give the option to grab and move points and to add additional points on the graph, but Bezier is by far the most flexible of the three.

Extrapolation

Blender interpolates to add frames between the Keyframes according to which of the previous Curve options were selected. Blender can also figure out what to do with the frames of the animation before the first Keyframe and after the last Keyframe, which is called **Extrapolation**.

With the Mouse Cursor in the Graph Editor press **Shift + E Key** to display the **Set Keyframe Extrapolation** menu.

Set Keyframe Extrapolation
Constant Extrapolation   Shift E
Linear Extrapolation   Shift E
Make Cyclic (F-Modifier)   Shift E
Clear Cyclic (F-Modifier)   Shift E

Figure 18.38

Constant Extrapolation: Blender has inserted frames that comply with a Bezier curve. On either side of the Keyframes, you can see horizontal lines that indicate there is no further change in status. This is constant extrapolation.

Linear Extrapolation: Blender plots a straight line curve leaving and entering the curve. The action of the actor before and after first and last Keyframes follows these straight line curves.

Cyclic Extrapolation: Blender copies the graph between the first and the last Keyframes and duplicates it to infinity on either side of the graph. You **Make** the Extrapolation Cyclic or you **Clear** the Cyclic Extrapolation.

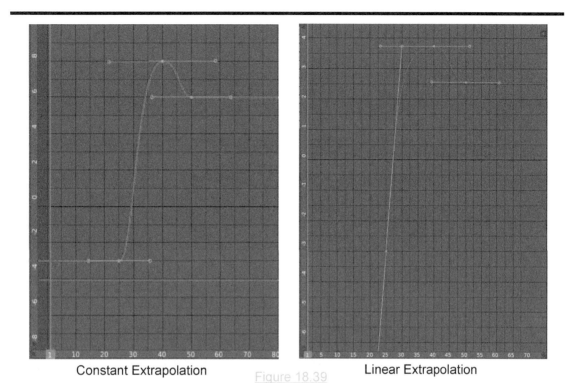

Constant Extrapolation   Figure 18.39   Linear Extrapolation

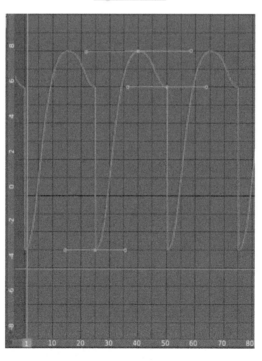

Cyclic Extrapolation

18.13 The Curve Properties Panel

The **Curve Properties panel** (Figures 18.40, 18.41) provides data and gives control to certain functions in the Graph panel. With the **Mouse Cursor** in the **Graph Editor**, press the **N key** to display the **Curve Properties panel** at the RHS of the Editor. The panel is divided into three Tabs; **F-Curve**, **Modifiers** and **View** Properties.

Figure 18.40

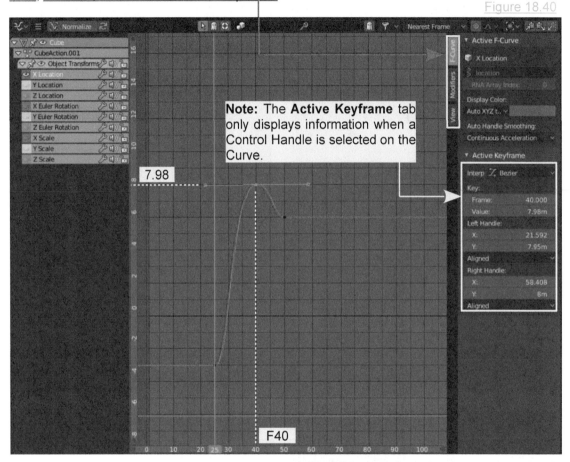

Note: The **Active Keyframe** tab only displays information when a Control Handle is selected on the Curve.

This introduction to the Curve Properties panel is presented to make you aware of its existence. Experiment with the values, especially the **Modifiers.** For example: With only the X Location Curve displayed in the Graph Editor click on the **Modifiers Tab** and then click Add Modifier. Select the **Noise Modifier** which adds a jittered effect to the Curve. Playing the animation sees the Cube shake as it moves in the 3D View Editor. For a more dramatic shake increase the **Amplitude** of the **Noise.**

Figure 18.41

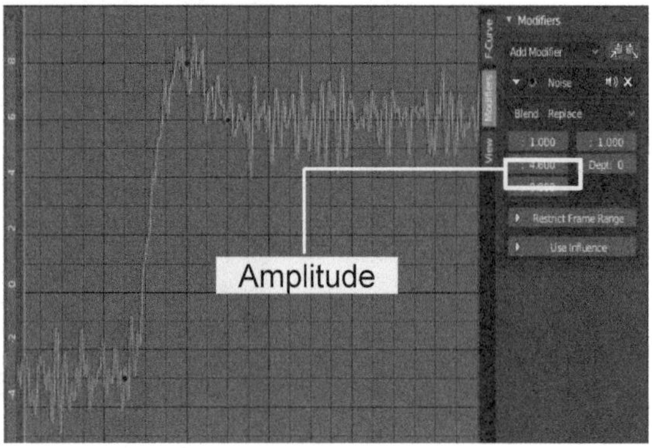

18.14 Animating Rotation

Figure 18.42

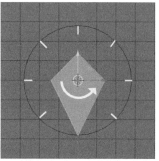

Animating Rotation deserves special consideration when attempting to create a continuous smooth Rotation. As an example use the default Cube Object in **Top Orthographic View** with one corner move to form a pointer (Figure 18.42).

Have the 3D Animation Workspace arranged as shown in Figure 18.23 and **turn on Automatic Keyframing**.

Figure 18.43

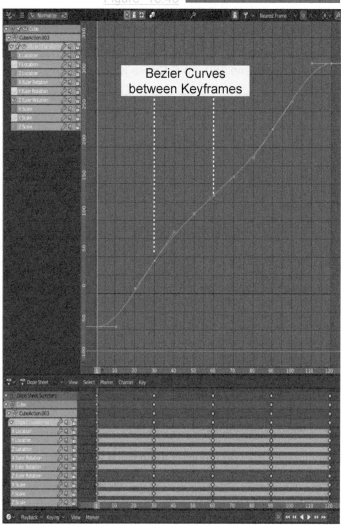

Bezier Curves between Keyframes

With the Cube selected in the 3D View Editor, and the Timeline Cursor in the Dope Sheet Editor at Frame 1, Rotate the Cube slightly using the Mouse, and before releasing the Mouse button return it to the start position. This creates Keyframes at Frame 1. Move the Dope Sheet Timeline Cursor to Frame 30 and Rotate the Cube 45° (Approx.). Move the Timeline Cursor to Frame 60. Rotate the Cube 45°. Repeat for Frames 90 and 120 for one complete revolution.

Observe the Graph Editor and Dope Sheet Timeline Editor. The rotation has been about the Z Axis, therefore, the Curve in the Graph Editor is in the Z Euler Ruler Rotation Channel.

The Curve drawn in the Graph is a Bezier Curve with Control Handles at the Keyframes. When playing the animation you will observe the rotation hesitates at each Keyframe, as the motion decelerates and accelerates. To correct, press **Shift + E Key** and select **Linear Extrapolation**. This produces a straight line Curve in the Graph Editor resulting in a smooth rotation, however the rotation is not constant since it takes place between Frame 1 and Frame 120. The rotation stops after one revolution at Frame 120 while the animation plays on to the default 250 Frames. To correct, change the **End Frame** value in the Timeline Editor Header to 120.

291

18.15 Rotation Using F-Curves

The Blender Manual states, "After animating some property in Blender using Keyframes you can edit their corresponding curves. When something is "animated", it changes over time. This curve is shown as something called an **F-Curve**. Basically what an F-Curve does is an interpolation between two animated properties. In Blender, animating an object means changing one of its properties, such as the object's location, or its scale.

As demonstrated, when an Object is animated a Curve is created in the graph Editor. It, therefore, follows that this is an **F-Curve**. When considering the default Cube Object in the 3D View Editor, before it is animated there is no Curve in the Graph Editor. The Cube may be made to Rotate by animating to create a **Location Curve** then editing the Curve using Modifiers.

Animate the Cube to move from minus 5 units on the X Axis to plus 5 units on the X Axis between Frame 1 and frame 180. An **F-Curve** is drawn in the Graph Editor.

Figure 18.44

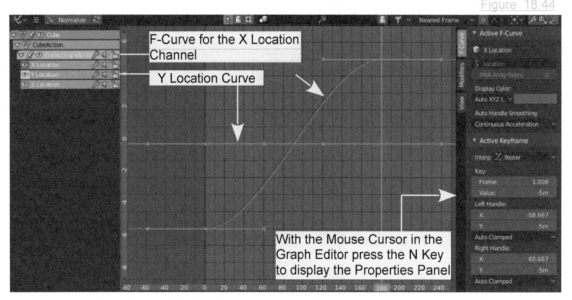

F-Curve for the X Location Channel

Y Location Curve

With the Mouse Cursor in the Graph Editor press the N Key to display the Properties Panel

With the Curve drawn, playing the animation shows the Cube move from minus 5 to plus 5 along the X Axis in the 3D View Editor. As well as the X Location Curve a Y Location Curve has also been created (straight line).

Both Curves may be modified to produce a Rotation of the Cube.

In the Properties Panel click on the Modifiers Tab, click Add Modifier and select Built in Function (Figure 18.45). The default Built in Function is Sine which immediately changes the Bezier Curve in the Graph Editor to a Sine Curve or rather a Sinusoidal Curve since it repeats to infinity (Figure 18.46 over).

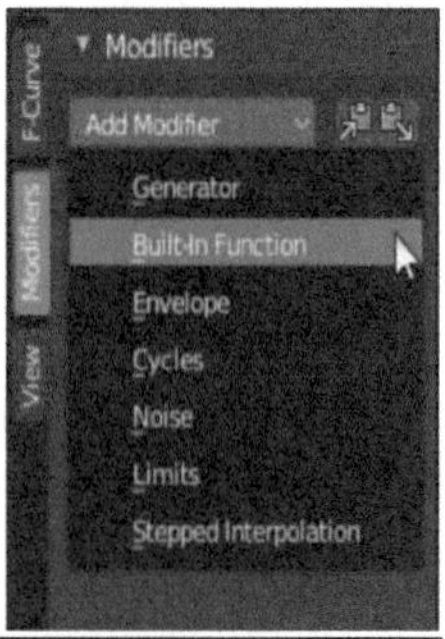

Figure 18.45

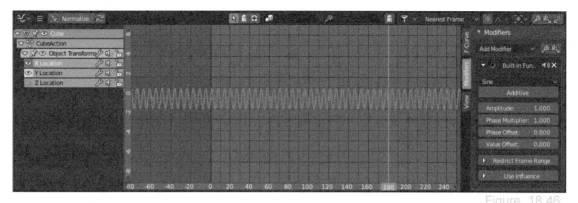

Figure 18.46

Playing the animation shows the Cube in the 3D View Editor oscillate on the X Axis. The degree of oscillation is governed by the Amplitude value in the Modifier. The movement of the Cube is best seen in Top Orthographic View.

In the Modifier panel, increase the Amplitude to 2.000 and reduce the Phase Modifier to 0.100. This reduces the oscillation of the Cube to a nice smooth motion

Figure 18.47

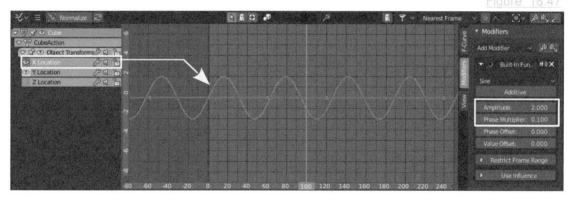

The Curve under consideration at this point has been the Curve representing the **X Axis** motion of the Cube (see the **X Location Channel** in the Graph Editor). As previously stated a **Y Axis** motion Curve is also drawn (straight line) as seen by selecting the **Y Location Channel**. By applying a Built in Function Modifier and making it **Type Cosine** with Amplitude 2.00 and Phase Multiplier 0.100, the Cube rotates around the center of the Scene.

Figure 18.48

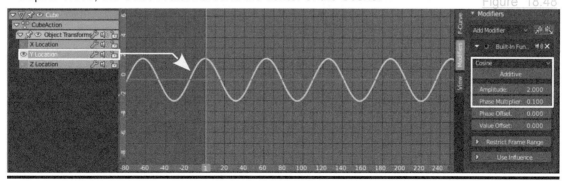

18.16 Animating Other Features

There are many features in Blender which may be animated. For example:

Material (color) Animation

Figure 18.49

As an example of animating color change perform the following using the 3D Animation Workspace;

Add a UV Sphere in the 3D View Editor and set the surface to Smooth Shading. In the Properties Editor, Material buttons, add a Material and leave Use Nodes active.

Change the 3D View Editor to rendered Viewport Shading.

In the Material buttons, click on the base Color bar and select a color. **RMB click the color bar** and select **Insert Keyframe** from the menu. Figure 18.50

This enters a Keyframe in the Dope Sheet Timeline at the location of the Cursor (the default is frame 1).

Relocate the Timeline Cursor to another Frame (Frame 50). Select a different color. RMB click the color bar and select Insert Keyframe. A Keyframe is entered at frame 50.

Repeat for Frame 100 then play the animation to see the color change in the 3D View Editor.

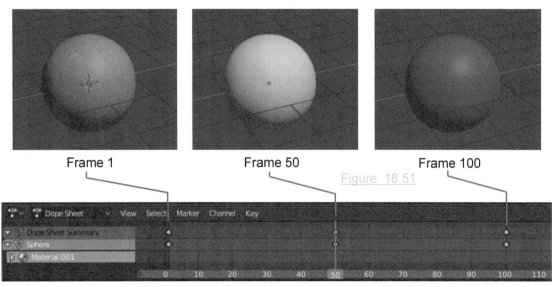

Timeline Cursor at Frame 50 (blue line)

Spotlight Size Animation

Properties Editor ——▶

The size of a Spotlight beam may be animated to change.

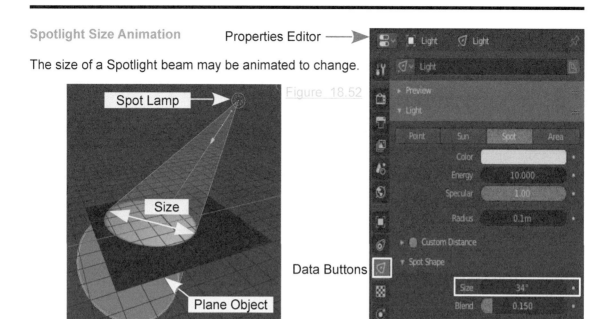

Using the 3D Animation Workspace be at Frame 1 in the Timeline . With the Spot Lamp selected in the 3D View Editor, in the Properties Editor, Data buttons, Spot Shape tab, **RMB click** on Size and select **Insert Keyframe**. Change to Frame 50. Change the Size and insert a second Keyframe. Repeat at frame 100 and play the animation.

18.17 Keying Sets

You may add multiple properties to a group called a **Keying Set**, which allows you to animate a series of actions at one time. You do this by first defining a Keying Set.

For the demonstration be in the 3D Animation Workspace.

Consider the default Cube in the default Blender 3D View Editor. It is assumed you want the Cube to move along the X-Axis and change color in the same given time. Not too difficult ? merely add a bunch of Keyframes. Consider if you had many property changes in the same time. Adding all those Keyframes one by one would be tedious. It would be nice if you could do the property changes then hit a button to add all the Keyframes in one go.

With the Cube selected in the 3D View Editor, Translate the Cube back along the X Axis minus 10.118. Go to the **Properties window, Object buttons, Transform tab** and note the **Location buttons** (Figure 18.53).

You will see the values X: -10.118m, Y: 0m, and Z: 0m. This shows that the Cube is located at minus 10.118 meters on the X Axis (the position set) in the 3D View Editor.

At this point you are concerned with the movement on the X-Axis.

In the Transform Tab RMB click on the **Location X** and in the panel that displays, click **Add Single to Keying Set** (Figure 18.53).

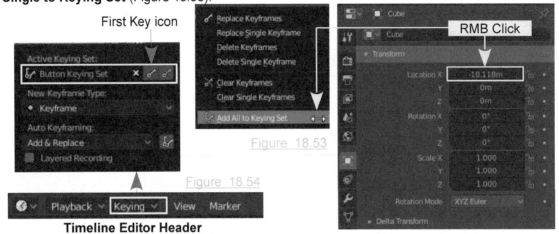

Timeline Editor Header

Figure 18.53

Figure 18.54

In the **Timeline Editor Header** (Figure 18.54) (**NOT the Dope Sheet**), click the button labelled **Keying.** In the menu that displays is an entry labelled: **Button Keying Set** with two **Key icons**. One Key icon has a red line across it. **Note:** In the **Dope Sheet Timeline**, you are at Frame 1. Click on the first **Key icon** to enter the Cube Location information into the **Keying Set.**

Consider the color part of the exercise.

Change the 3D View Editor to Rendered Viewport Shading.

In the **Properties Editor, Material buttons with Use Nodes active,** select a Base Color for the Cube at Frame 1. RMB click on the Base Color bar, and select, **Add to Keying Set**. The information for the color at Frame 1 has been added to the Keying Set.

At this point you may add additional data to the Keying Set for other features you wish to animate.

In the **Timeline Editor Header**, click the Keying button then click on the first of the little Key icons (Figure 18.54). This enters a **Keyframe** at Frame 1 for the location and color of the Cube. You see this in the **Dope Sheet Editor Timeline**.

Move the Timeline Cursor (blue line) to the next animation Frame (say Frame 80). Change the value for the **Transform – Location – X axis** in the **Properties Editor, Object buttons, Transform tab**.

Note: The X axis Location value is highlighted yellow indicating that a Keyframe has been added.

Right click the new value you have entered and click **Add Single to Keying Set**.

Do the same thing for the **Material – Base color** value (select a new color from the color picker circle). RMB click on on the Base Color bar and **Add to Keying Set**.

Now click on the first of the Key icons again to add the new **Keyframe** at frame 80. Scrub the **Timeline** or play the animation to see the Cube move and change color.

By following this procedure you may add multiple animated features to the Keying Set thus saving time when inserting a Keyframe in the Timeline.

Other features of Keying Sets are found in the Timeline Editor Header (Figure18.55).

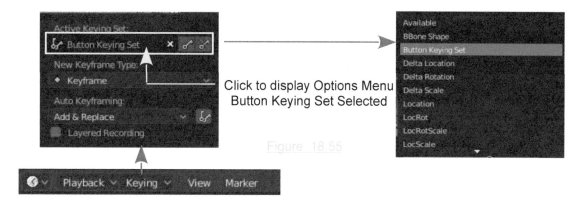

Click to display Options Menu
Button Keying Set Selected

Figure 18.55

18.18 Animation Follow Path

As demonstrated, animating an Object to move is achieved by entering Keyframes in the Timeline with the Object located at positions in the 3D View Editor. With the animation created it may be edited by modifying the Curve in the Graph Editor or relocating Keyframes in the Dope Sheet Editor Timeline.

On occasion you may wish to animate an Object to follow a pre constructed Path. Once the Object is made to follow the Path, reshape the Path to alter the movement.

To demonstrate the procedure for animation following a Path open the 3D Animation Workspace and change the 3D View Editor Camera View to the Graph Editor. Have the other 3D View Editor in top Orthographic View with default Cube Object at the center of the Scene.

Deselect the Cube and add a Curve Type Bezier to the Scene. You may use any Curve Type but the Bezier Curve has a nice profile when entered. Scale the bezier Curve up six times (Figure 18.56).

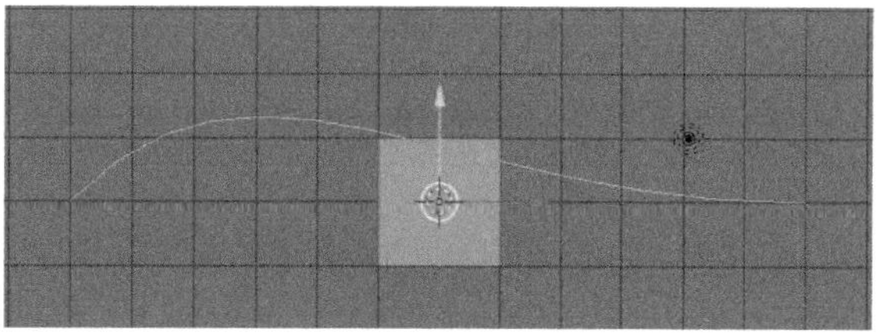

Figure 18.56

Deselect the Curve and select the Cube.

Properties Editor

In the **Properties Editor, Constraints buttons**, click Add Object Constraint and select **Follow Path** in the Relationship category. The **Follow Path Tab** displays

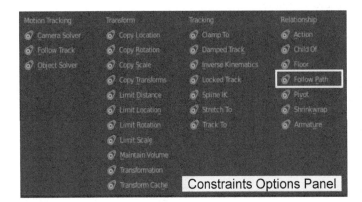

Constraints Options Panel

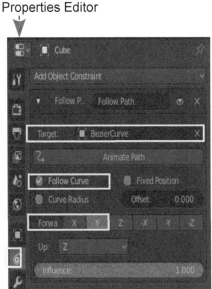

Figure 18.57

In the Follow Path Tab click in the bar where you see the **Target** cube icon and select **Bezier Curve** from the panel that displays. Also in the Tab check (tick) **Follow Curve**. **Note: Forward Y** is selected (the direction of movement, L to R on the Y Axis).

Entering the Target locates the Cube in the 3D View Editor at the LH end of the Curve Path. Checking Follow Curve aligns the Cube to the Path (Figure 18.58).

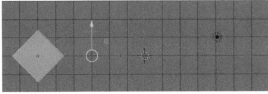

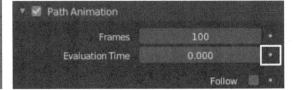

Figure 18.58   Figure 18.59

With the Cube aligned deselect the Cube and select the Path.

Go to the Properties Editor, Data buttons and see the Path Animation Tab at the bottom of the panel. Ensure that Path Animation is checked (Figure 18.59).

To animate the Cube, following the Path, Keyframes have to be entered in the Dope Sheet Editor Timeleine.

With the Cube at the LH end of the Path and the Timeline Cursor at Frame 1, LMB click on the button (white dot) at the end of the **Evaluation Time bar** in the **Properties Editor**.

Clicking the button animates the Evaluation Time value. The bar turns yellow and a Keyframe is entered in the Dope Sheet Editor. ⌐

Figure 18.60

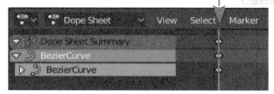
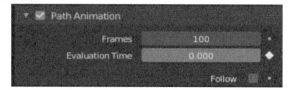

Move the Timeline Cursor to Frame 100. In the Path Animation Tab the default number of Frames for the animation of the Cube is 100. Note: This is different to the number of Frames for the total animation which is End Frame 250, set in the Timeline Editor Header. Placing the Timeline Cursor at Frame 100 means you are accepting the default Value.

In the Path Animation Tab change the Evaluation Time value to 100 which is saying, at Frame 100 the Cube is to be at the RH end of the Path in the 3D View Editor. The Cube will have traversed 100% of the Path Length. You may choose any number of Frames but to have the animated Object reach the end of the Path, set the Evaluation Time equal to the number of Frames.

Having set the Evaluation Time LMB click the button at the end of the Evaluation Time bar which at this point is a white diamond. A Keyframe is added in the Timeline at Frame 100.

Play the animation to see the Cube move along the Path in 100 frames.

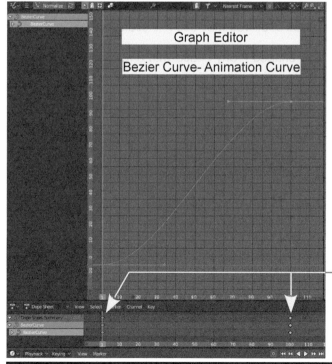

At this point there are two Keyframes in the Dope Sheet Editor Timeline and a Bezier Curve has been drawn in the Graph Editor representing the animation. The Bezier Curve in the Graph Editor is completely different to the Bezier Curve Path in the 3D View Editor.

3D View Editor

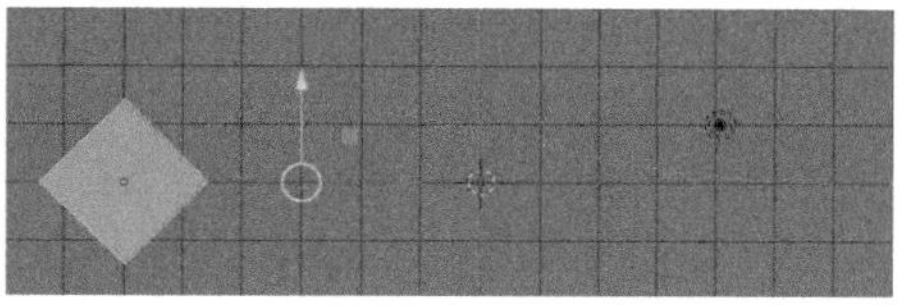

Bezier Curve – Animation Path

Keyframes in the Dope Sheet Timeline

Figure 18.61

When playing the animation the Cube accelerates at the beginning of the Path and decelerates at the end as it conforms to the Curve in the Graph Editor. The movement of the Cube may be adjusted by modifying the Curve in the Graph Editor or by inserting and positioning Keyframes in the Dope Sheet Timeline.

For example: Position the Timeline Cursor at Frame 50. In the Properties Editor, Path Animation Tab set the Evaluation Time to 25.142 and LMB click the white diamond button. This enters a Keyframe at Frame 50 in the Timeline and a Control handle is inserted on the Curve in the Graph Editor. Entering 25.142 as the Evaluation Time at Frame 50 is saying; move the Cube 25% of the way along the Path between Frame 1 and frame 50 (move ¼ of the Path length in ½ of the animation).

Further adjustments to the movement may be made by moving, scaling and rotating the Control handle in the Graph Editor or by scaling and repositioning the Keyframes in the Dope Sheet Editor Timeline.

18.19 Displacement Sound Animations

A sound file (Music) can be used to affect the movement of vertices producing an interesting display effect.

For a demonstration have an image file (texture) such as that shown in Figure 18.62 and a sound file (music) saved on your hard drive. The Image Texture used in this demonstration is named Art-Fibers.jpg while the sound file is named Flex_Vector_-_Born_Ready.mp3.

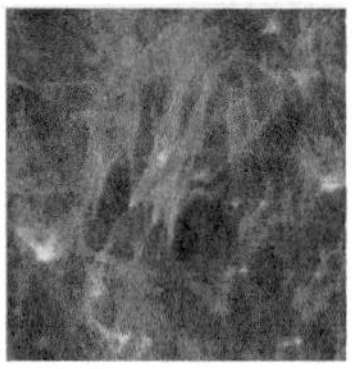

Figure 18.62

Flex_Vector is a Hip Hop file with a distinct base beat. You may use any sound file (MP3).

To demonstrate, set up a Sphere object (egg shaped – any shape with a reasonable number of Vertices) (Figure 18.63).

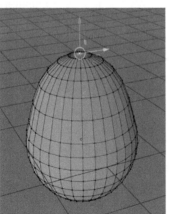

Figure 18.63

3D View Editor Header

Proportional Editing ——————┐ Spherical Falloff

UV Sphere with a single Vertex selected and translated up on the Z Axis. **Proportional Editing** has been activated with **Spherical Falloff**.

With the Egg selected in the 3D View Editor, in **Object Mode** go to the **Properties Editor, Material buttons** and **Add a Material. Have Use Nodes active**.

Click the button at the RHS of the Base Color bar and select Image Texture. Navigate to the Texture Image file and click Open Image.

Figure 18.64

Change the 3D View Editor to Rendered Viewport Shading to see the Image applied as a Material to the Egg.

With the Egg selected in the 3D View Editor go to the Properties Editor, Texture buttons and Add a Texture, selecting the same Image as before.

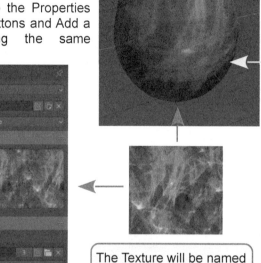

Click to select Image Texture File.

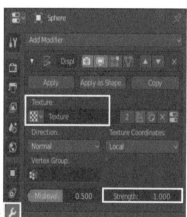

The Texture will be named **Texture**.

In the Properties Editor, Modifier buttons Add a **Displace** Modifier to the Egg selecting the Texture named **Texture**.

Modifier Buttons

With the Strength value in the Modifier: 1.000 the Egg in the 3D View Editor is deformed by the Texture. Set the Strength value to 0.000.

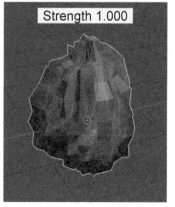

Strength 1.000

Figure 18.65

Strength 0.000

Divide the 3D View Editor horizontally and make the lower part the Timeline Editor. Divide the upper part vertically and make the LH part the Video Sequence Editor.

With the Egg selected and the Timeline Editor Cursor at Frame 1 in the Timeline, in the Displace Modifier panel RMB click on the Strength value and select Insert Keyframe.

The Strength value slider turns yellow and a Keyframe is entered in the Timeline at frame 1.

In the Video sequence Editor Header click Add – Sound and navigate to the sound file then click Add Sound at the upper RHS, The file is entered in Channel 1 in the Video Sequence Editor.

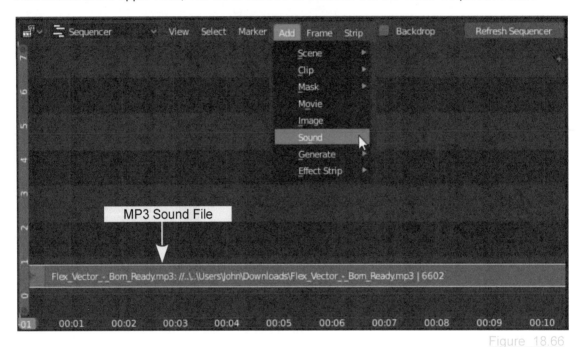

Figure 18.66

Change the Video Sequence Editor to the Graph Editor and in the Header click Key and select Bake Sound to F-Curve. Navigate to and select the Sound File then click Bake Sound to F-Curve in upper RHS of the panel. **Note:** A Keyframe must be entered before this instruction.

Figure 18.67

A Sound Curve is drawn in the Graph Editor.

Figure 18.68

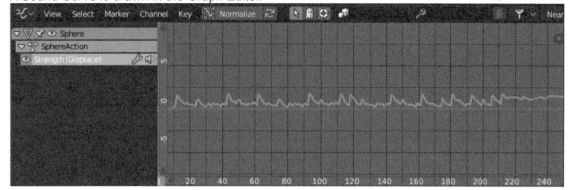

Playing the animation sees the Egg pulsate in the 3D View Editor to the beat of the Sound (have the speakers turned on).

This result may be what is required but if not you can modify the Curve in the Graph Editor. With the Mouse Cursor in the Graph Editor press the N Key to display a Properties Panel and select the Modifiers tab.

Click Add Modifier and select Envelope. Click Add Point to add control points. Adjusting the Control Point values alters the Sound Curve in the Graph Editor which alters the the way in which the sound affects the animation.

Figure 18.69

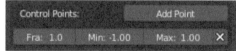

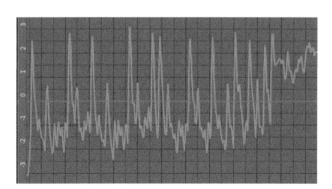

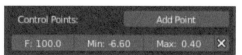

303

18.20 Sound Effect and Cast Modifier

Displacement Sound Animation in the previous section used a sound file to affect the **Strength value** of a **Displacement modifier.** A sound file was then **Baked** to an **F-Curve** and modified. This was to control the displacement of the Object's surface.

You may combine a sound file **F-Curve** and a **Cast modifier** with an **Empty** control object to influence an animation of the Object's surface deformation.

To demonstrate set up a Plane object with a **Cast Modifier** and an **Empty** object (Figure 18.70).

Set up the 3D View Editor

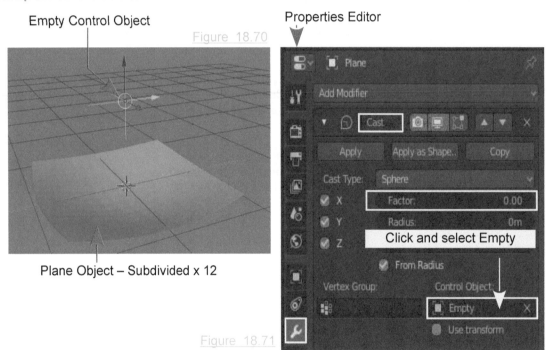

Empty Control Object

Properties Editor

Figure 18.70

Plane Object – Subdivided x 12

Click and select Empty

Figure 18.71

Add a Sound File to the **Video Sequence Editor**.

Create an F-Curve for the **Factor value** of the Cast modifier by selecting the Plane, then setting the **Factor value** in the **Cast modifier to 0.000.** In the **Timeline Editor** position the cursor at Frame 1. Right click on the **Factor value slider** in the Cast Modifier and select **Insert Keyframe**.

Declare the sound file to affect the Factor value by dividing the 3D View Editor in two and changing one half to the **Graph Editor.** In the Header click on **Key** and select **Bake Sound to F Curves**. Navigate to the sound file, select the file and click Bake Sound to F-Curves in upper RH corner of the Editor. The bake can take a while.

The sound file **F-Curve** is inserted in the **Graph Editor.**

Automatically Insert Keyframes by turning on **Auto Keyframing** in the **Timeline Editor Header**. With the **Empty Object** selected in the 3D View Editor play the animation and at the same time press **G Key** in the **3D View Editor** and move the Empty object about. Keyframes are added to the Timeline. Stop the animation, reinstate the sound file in the Video Sequence Editor and replay to see the effect.

Figure 18.72

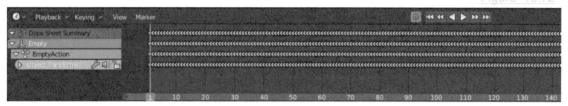

Keyframes added to the Timeline Editor

Figure 18.73

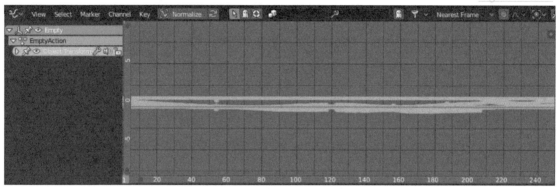

F-Curves in the Graph Editor Window with the Empty Selected

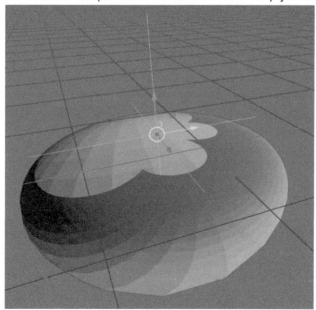

Figure 18.74

When the Animation is played the Mesh Deforms to the beat in the 3D View Editor

19

Constraints

Constraints control an Object's properties such as its Location, Rotation and Scale by Targeting the Object to a secondary Object or connecting Objects in a Scene together, such that they act as a single entity while maintaining individual characteristics. Another way to define Constraints is to say they define relationships between Objects.

For example, the **Track To Constraint** applied to a **Camera** Object, with a **Target** set as another Object in the Scene, causes the Camera to always point to the second Object no matter where it moves.

Another example is a **Child Of Constraint** which when applied to one Object (the child) with a **Target** set as a second Object (the parent) causes the child to follow the parent. Using a Child Of Constraint creates what is termed a **Child / Parent Relationship.** This has a particular application in animating characters.

Constraints are applied to Objects in the **Properties Editor, Constraints buttons**, clicking on **Add Object Constraint** then selecting a Constraint from the menu that displays.

Constraints in Blender are listed in four categories as shown in Figure 19.2 on the following page.

In this chapter, Constraints are briefly defined and several examples provided which will allow you to understand their application.

19.1 Introduction to Constraints

Constraints are are accessed in the **Properties Editor, Constraints buttons** (Figure 19.1).

Clicking **Add Object Constraint** displays the Constraint selection menu listing Constraints in four categories (Figure 19.2).

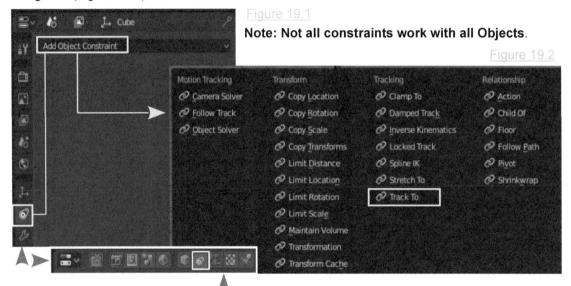

Figure 19.1

Note: Not all constraints work with all Objects.

Figure 19.2

19.2 Track to Constraint

Note: Horizontal buttons arrangement in Figures

The Track To Constraint provides an introduction demonstrating what a Constraint is, in practical terms and how Constraints are used.

In the default Blender Scene a Camera Object is directed towards the Cube Object such that it captures the Cube in Camera View (Num Pad 0). When the Cube is animated to move across the Screen the Cube can move in and out of Camera View. If you want the Cube to remain in view no matter where the Cube is in the Scene, you track the Camera to the Cube by employing the **Track To Constraint** (add the Constraint to the Camera).

Note: The default camera has been rotated and locked in position to point towards the center of the Scene (default position of the Cube). The rotation of the default Camera has to be unlocked to use the Track To Constraint. This only applies to the default Camera. A new camera entered in the Scene is not locked.

To unlock the default Camera have it selected then press **Alt + R Key**. The rotation is cleared and the Camera points down in the Scene. **Note:** The **Clear Rotation Panel** displays in the lower LH corner of the Editor.

If **Delta Transform Rotation** values have been entered in the **Properties Editor Delta Transform Tab**, check **Clear Delta** in the Clear Rotation Panel.

With the Camera selected click **Add Object Constraint** (Figure 19.1) and select **Track To** in the menu (Figure 19.2).

Figure 19.3

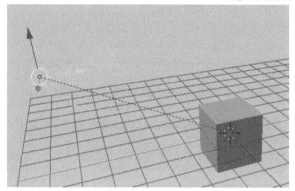

Figure 19.4

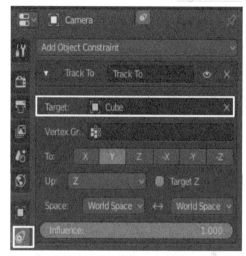

In the Track To Constraint panel click on Target and select the **Target Object** (Cube) in the menu (Figure 19.4).

Note: On entering the Target (Cube) the Camera swings around pointing away from the Cube. There is a broken line connecting the Camera to the Cube indicating that a Constraint is applied, but you have to adjust **To** and **Up** directions in the Constraint Panel. Set **To** as **-Z** and **Up** as **Y**. With the Cube animated to move in the Scene the Camera always points to the Cube.

Constraints are associated with an object by selecting the Object in the 3D View Editor then clicking on **Add Object Constraint** in the **Properties Editor, Object Constraints buttons and** selecting the Constraint from the menu that displays (Figure 19.2).

19.3 Constraint Stack

Figure 19.5

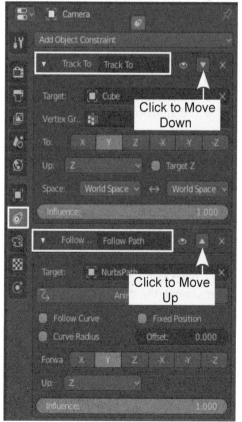

It should be noted that, in some cases, it is appropriate to apply more than one Constraint to an Object. When this is done, the Constraints are placed in a stack in order of priority. The priority can be changed by moving a constraint up or down in the stack (Figure 19.5).

In Figure 19.5 a Follow Path and a Track To Constraint are applied to the same Object. The **Track To** takes precedence over the **Follow Path**. To reverse the precedence click either of the up or down arrows.

When using Constraints, in many cases, there are control values to be inserted in the Constraint Panel to regulate the functions. The following pages in this chapter contain a brief description of Constraint functions. Most Constraints are self explanatory, therefore a detailed explanation will only be given for a few common Constraints, or where it is not self evident.

19.4 Transform Constraints List

- **Copy Location.** Forces the Object with the constraint added to take up the location of the Target Object.
- **Copy Rotation.** Forces the Object with the constraint added to copy the rotation of the Target Object. When the target rotates, the Object rotates.
- **Copy Scale.** Forces the Object with the constraint added to copy the scale of the Target Object
- **Copy Transforms.** Similar to the copy location constraint.
- **Limit Distance.** Constrains the Object to remain within a set distance from the Target Object. The distance is a spherical field surrounding the target and the Object is constrained within or outside the spherical field.
- **Limit Location.** Constrains the Object's location between a minimum and maximum distance on a specific axis. The distance is relative to either the world center or a parented Object.
- **Limit Rotation.** Constrains an Object's rotation about a specific axis between limits.
- **Limit Scale.** Constrains the scale of an Object between limits on a specified axis.
- **Maintain Volume.** Constrains the dimensions of a side on a specified axis.
- **Transformation.** See Section 19.5.
- **Transform Cache.**

19.5 The Transformation Constraint

The Transformation Constraint allows you to control the Location, Rotation or Scale of one Object or part of an Object by adjusting the Location, Rotation, or Scale of another Object. The location, rotation or scale values in either case can be set to operate within a specific range.

The Object to be controlled is termed the **Source** and has the Constraint applied to it, while the other Object (the controlling Object) is termed the **Target object**.

To demonstrate have a Cube Object and a UV Sphere in the 3D View Editor in Top Orthographic View (Figure 19.6)

To apply the **Constraint**, click **Add Object Constraint** in the **Properties Editor, Constraints buttons** and select **Transformation** under the **Transform** heading.

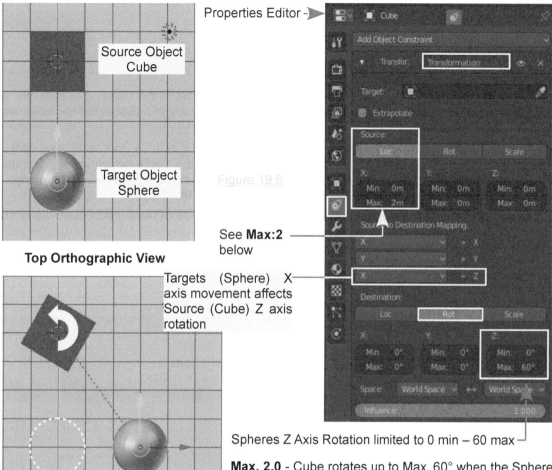

Properties Editor →

Source Object Cube

Target Object Sphere

Figure 19.6

Top Orthographic View

See **Max:2** below

Targets (Sphere) X axis movement affects Source (Cube) Z axis rotation

Spheres Z Axis Rotation limited to 0 min – 60 max

Max. 2.0 - Cube rotates up to Max. 60° when the Sphere moves 2 Units on the X Axis. No further rotation takes place when the Sphere is Translated more than 2 Units.

19.6 Tracking Constraints

- **Clamp To:** Clamps or locks the position of the Object to a target curve
- **Damped Track:** Constrains one local axis of the Object to always point towards the target   Object .
- **Locked Track:** Similar to a Damped Track Constraint with more axis control.
- **Inverse Kinematics:** Can only be applied to Bones (see Chapter 20 Armatures).
- **Spline IK:** Can only be applied to Bones (see Chapter 20 Armatures).
- **Stretch To:** Stretches the Object towards the Target Object or compresses the Object away from the Target Object.
- **Track To:** As seen in the introduction to Constraints the Track To Constraint causes the Object to always point towards the Target Object no matter where either the Object or the Target is positioned (Figure 19.5).

19.7 Relationship Constraints

- **Action:** See Section 19.8.
- **Child Of:** Chapter 20 – 20.3.
- **Floor:** Allows the Target Object to obstruct the movement of the Object. For example, a Sphere animated to descend in a Scene will not pass through a Plane that has been set as a Target Object.
- **Follow Path:** Causes the Object to be animated to follow a Curve Path nominated as the Target. This Constraint also has the feature to follow the Curve, which means that the Object will rotate and bank as it follows the Curve. This constraint can also be employed to duplicate Objects along a Curve Path. (See Chapter 18 – 18.18).
- **Pivot:** Causes the Object to leapfrog to the opposite side of the Target Object along an axis between the Object and the Target Center. The location can be offset on either side of the axis by inserting offset values.
- **Shrinkwrap:** Locks an Object to the surface of another mesh Object that is set as the Target.

19.8 The Action Constraint

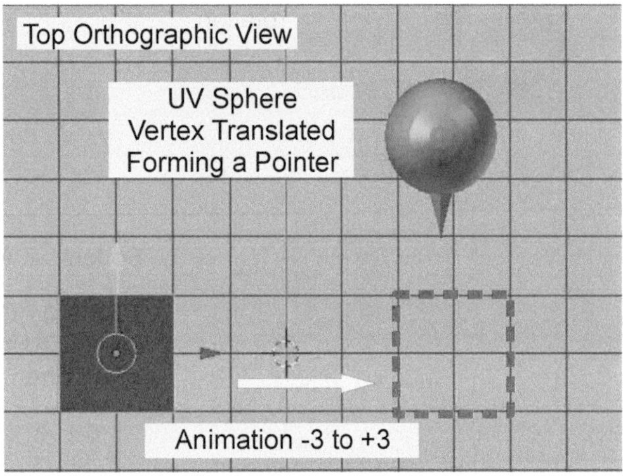

The **Action Constraint** allows you to control the action of one Object by manipulating the action of another. For the purpose of this explanation, consider an action to mean a Translation, Rotation, or Scale of an Object. To demonstrate, the rotation of a Sphere Object will control the translation of a Cube.

The location of the UV Sphere in the Scene is not important.

Animate the Cube to move from minus three Blender units to plus three units on the X Axis in 100 Frames (see Chapter 18 for Animation). Place the animation at Frame 1.

Figure 19.7

Top Orthographic View

UV Sphere
Vertex Translated
Forming a Pointer

Animation -3 to +3

Select the **Cube** then in the **Properties Editor, Constraints buttons, Add Object Constraint** type **Action**. In the Constraint panel set the values as shown in Figure 19.8.

Note: The **Cube Action** value under **To Action** does not exist until the Cube is animated to move.

The Z Rotation of the Target (UV Sphere) controls the Action of the Cube within the Animation (CubeAction).

The Z Rotation (Target Range) is limited to: 0 to 90°.

The Action Range is between Frame 1 and frame 100 of the animation. Note: When the Action Constraint is applied the Cube Animation changes to minus 6 to 0 in the 3D window?

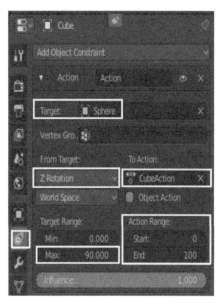
Figure 19.8

Figure 19.9

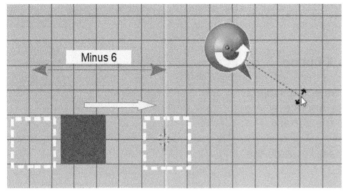

You may set an Animation to rotate the UV Sphere in which case when the Cube is Translated (Moved) the Sphere Rotates.

19.9 The Shrinkwrap Constraint

Figure 19.10

The **Shrinkwrap Constraint** could be more aptly named the **Mesh Surface Lock** since the constraint locks an Object to the surface of another mesh Object that's set as the Target. Do not confuse this constraint with the **Shrinkwrap Modifier**. To demonstrate how the constraint operates, follow this procedure:

In the default Blender Scene in Top Orthographic view, add a **UV Sphere.** Scale the **Cube** up, and arrange the objects as shown in Figure 19.10. Select the Sphere and in the **Properties Editor, Constraints buttons**, add a **Shrinkwrap Constraint** (Figure 19.11).

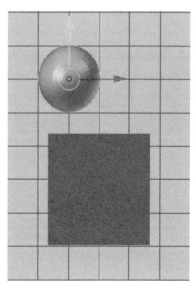

In the **Shrinkwrap Constraint panel**, click in the **Target selection bar** and select **Cube** as the Target (Figure 19.11).

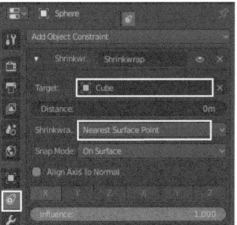
Figure 19.11

313

Besides projecting to Nearest Surface or Nearest Vertex you may also use the Local Axis of an Object to project to a surface.

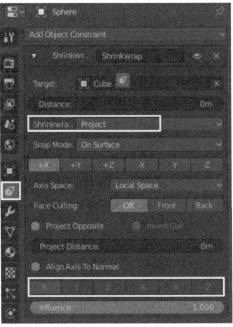

Figure 19.13

Note: The Manipulation Widget arrows represent direction.

With Shrinkwrap Type: Project selected, **Axis X, Axis Y, and Axis Z** buttons are present in the **Constraints panel** (Figure 19.13 - Note there are positive and negative values).

Check (highlight blue) the positive **Axis X button**.

This instructs Blender to project the selected Object which has the Constraint applied, to the surface of the Target Object when the X Axis points to the surface.

In order to project the X Axis of the Sphere towards the surface of the Cube, Rotate the Sphere.

Rotate the Sphere (slowly) until the X Axis points at the Cube. That is, rotate about the Z Axis. (Figure 19.14). As soon as the Axis points to the surface on the Cube, the Sphere is located on the surface. By slowly rotating the Sphere you will see it move along the surface as the direction of the Axis changes. In the **Object Constraints** panel, the **Distance** and **Influence** sliders affect how far the Sphere is located between its original position and the surface of the Cube. By checking **Axis X** and **Axis Y**, the projection line is at 45 degrees between the Axes.

Figure 19.14

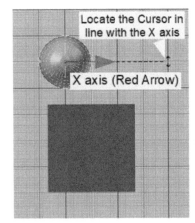
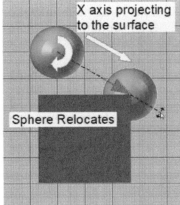
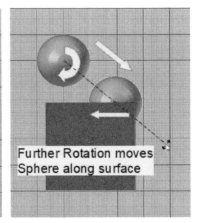

x

19.10 The Follow Path Constraint

The **Follow Path Constraint** causes an Object which has been animated to follow a **Path** set as the Target. The constraint has **Follow Curve** settings which make the Object rotate and bank as it follows the Path. This has been demonstrated in Chapter 18-18.18

The **Follow Path Constraint may** also be used to **Extrude** shapes.

To demonstrate the different applications set up a Scene containing the default Cube Object and a **Bezier Curve Path** as shown in Figure 19.15. The Bezier Curve has been Scaled up eight times and the Cube Object scaled down (S Key + 0.300 , Enter). You may alter the shape of the curve in Edit Mode to anything you wish but for simplicity the shape has been left as the default.

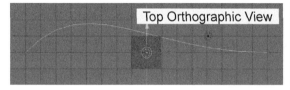

Default Bezier Curve Scaled
Up Eight Times

Figure 19.15

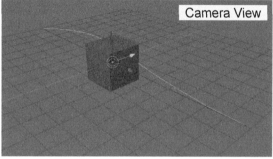

Figure 19.16

Simple Animation

Animation following a Curve Path was explained in detail in Chapter 18 – 18.18. There is, however, a quick simple method which may be appropriate.

Select the Cube Object and add a Follow Path Constraint. In the Constraint Panel enter **BezierCurve** as the **Target** (Figure 19.17).

The Cube locates at the start of the BezierCurve.

With the BezierCurve in Edit Mode you will see chevrons spaced along the length of the Curve indicating the direction of travel when an Object is animated to follow the Curve.

With the Cube Object selected, in the Properties Editor Follow Path Constraint panel check **Follow Curve** to align the Cube with the Curve. This is not essential but if you were animating a model to follow the Curve you would want it pointing in the right direction.

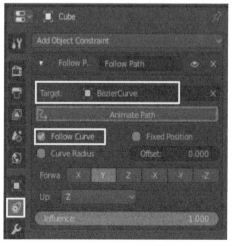

Figure 19.17

If you press Play in the Timeline Editor nothing happens!

In the Object Constraint panel click on Animate Path.

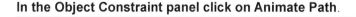

Pressing Play again shows the Cube moving along the Curve in 100 Frames. You will see the number of Frames set for the animation in the **Properties Editor, Object Data buttons, Path Animation Tab** when the BezierCurve is selected in the 3D View Editor (Figure 19.18).

Figure 19.18

Extruding Shapes

A shape (cross section profile) can be extruded along a Curve Path to produce a solid object. As an example, start with the default Blender Scene and delete the Cube object.

Add a **Bezier Curve** and scale it up as you did in the previous example (eight times). For simplicity, put the **3D window** into **Top Orthographic View**.

The **Bezier Curve** may be scaled and shaped in **Edit mode** to produce a shape for your extrusion to follow. For simplicity the default curve shape will be used.

Deselect the curve and add a **Curve Circle** or **Nurbs Circle.** Either circle may be shaped in Edit mode to produce a cross section shape for your extrusion.

With the 3D View Editor in Top Orthographic View Curve Circles are entered in the Scene flat on the XY plane. Rotate the Circle 90° on the Y Axis to stand it on edge (Figure 19.19)

Scale the Circle down approximately one third size (you may also scale after extruding).

Deselect the **Circle** and select the **Bezier Curve**.

Figure 19.19

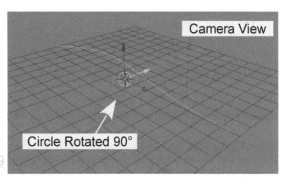

Camera View

Circle Rotated 90°

In the **Properties Editor, Data buttons, Geometry, Bevel Tab**, enter **Bezier** or **Nurbes** Circle in the **Bevel Object data panel** (Figure 19.20).

Figure 19.20

Figure 19.21

Circle Extruded Along the Curve Path

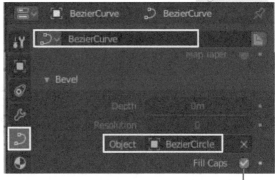

Note: Fill Caps, fills in the end of the extrusion.

316

20

Armatures & Character Rigging

Armatures are used to control the movement of Objects or components of an Object in animation. In intricate assemblies, components are linked or associated with Armatures, such that, when the Armature moves the components move. Armatures themselves are made up from components called **Bones** and may consist of a single Bone or multiple Bones linked in **Child Parent Relationships**. This means that when one Bone moves other Bones move according to the hierarchy in the relationship. Armatures do not Render, therefore, Bones can be animated controlling the animation of the components of an assembly.

A particular application for Armatures is the control and animation of Character Models. Figure 20.1 shows an **Armature** (blue bones) inside a character model. Each bone is linked to part of the surface mesh. The bones are animated to move which causes the surface mesh to move, posing the character.

The complete assembly of model, mesh, armature and controls is called a **Rig**.

Figure 20.1

317

20.1 Single Bone Armature Figure 20.2

Armatures can, and usually do, comprise multiple Bones, but for an understanding of **Bone** manipulation start with the default single **Bone Armature** (Figure 20.2) which is displayed in type **Octahedral** (due to the object having eight surfaces): The Bone appears as two four-sided pyramids conjoined at the base with spheres at the apexes. For the purpose of the demonstration, the parts of the Armature will be named **Tip, Body**, and **Base**. **Note:** The red and blue arrows are the Manipulation Widget.

Although the armature is an Object in Blender, it is not a Mesh Object. Its shape cannot be edited other than scaling it larger or smaller. It can be rotated and translated. It has a center like any other Object, which by default is located at the apex of the lower (smaller) pyramid.

20.2 Adding Armatures Figure 20.3

An Armature is added to the Scene from the Add Menu in the 3D View Editor Header or by pressing **Shift + A Key.** It is located wherever you positioned the Editor Cursor, just like any other Object. You will see **Armature** listed in the **Outliner Editor**.

If you relocate the Cursor and repeat the process you add a second **Single Bone Armature**. Note: The new name, **Armature.001** in the **Outliner Editor** and the sub entries, **Armature.001** and **Pose** (the same entries as the original Armature – Figure 20.3). If you select either Armature in the 3D View Editor and press **Shift + D key** (Duplicate) and Translate (drag the mouse) you create a third single Bone Armature. The name in the **Outliner Editor** for this third Armature is **Armature.002**.

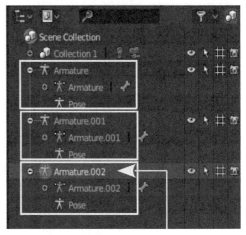

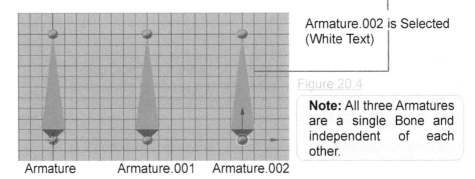

Armature.002 is Selected (White Text)

Figure 20.4

Note: All three Armatures are a single Bone and independent of each other.

Armature   Armature.001   Armature.002

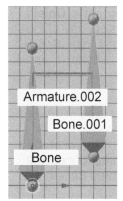

Armature.002

Bone.001

Bone

Select one of the three Armatures, say **Armature.002** and **Tab into Edit mode**. In Edit Mode only the Tip of the Armature is selected. Press **A Key** or **RMB click** on the body of the Armature to select the whole Armature.

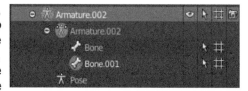

Figure 20.5

Figure 20.6

Note: You are in Edit Mode. Press **Shift + D key** (Duplicate) and drag the Mouse to reveal a new Bone. The point here is, **it is a new Bone which is part of Armature.002** , not a new Armature. If you select the original Armature **Bone** and **Tab to Object Mode** both Bones will be selected (Figure 20.6). Translating the original will cause the new Bone to follow. There is no link shown between the two but they are connected. In the **Outliner Editor** you will see **Bone.001** entered under **Armature.002** (Figure 20.5).

In **Edit mode** (Armature.002 selected), press **Alt + A Key** to deselect then **RMB click** on the Tip to select the Tip of Bone.001. Press **E key** (Extrude) and drag the mouse to extrude a new Bone from the tip of Bone.001. This is a new bone which again is part of the armature, not a new armature.

Note the entries in the **Outliner Editor**. You now have sub entry Bone.002 under Bone.001.

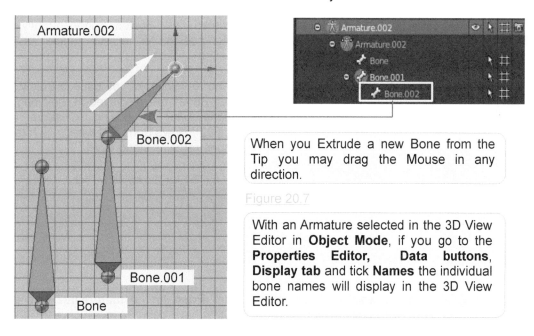

When you Extrude a new Bone from the Tip you may drag the Mouse in any direction.

Figure 20.7

With an Armature selected in the 3D View Editor in **Object Mode**, if you go to the **Properties Editor, Data buttons, Display tab** and tick **Names** the individual bone names will display in the 3D View Editor.

Remember: You are still in Edit Mode with Armature.002 selected.

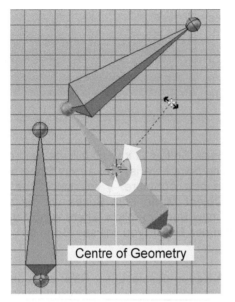

Centre of Geometry

If you press the **Tab Key** and enter **Object Mode** you can deselect and select any of the three Armatures. Armature has one Bone, Armature.001 has one Bone and Armature.002 has three Bones.

Figure 20.8

Have Armature.002 selected. In **Object Mode** RMB clicking on any of its three Bones will select the entire Armature (all three Bones).

In Edit Mode you can select the individual Bones of the Armature and Translate, Rotate and Scale. The Rotation and Scale takes place about the center of geometry of the Bone selected (Figure 20.8).

In the 3D View Editor Header select **Pose Mode** .

The selected Bone will have a blue outline.

Any Bone may be selected then Rotated, Translated or Scaled independently to enable posing for a still image or for animating.

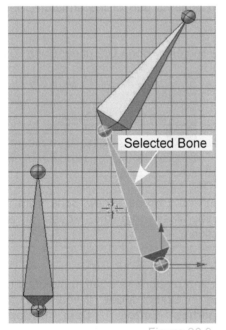

Selected Bone

The Tab Key will take you back to Edit Mode and all Bones are displayed in their original positions prior to posing. Observe that Bone.002 follows Bone.001 when it is rotated but Bone remains stationary.

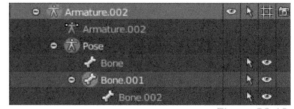

Figure 20.9

Figure 20.10

In the **Outliner Editor,** while in **Pose Mode** under **Pose** for **Armature.002** (the selected Armature) you see a hierarchical listing of the Bones that have been Posed (Figure 20.10).

Adding, Editing and Posing Armatures at this stage may be somewhat confusing but with practice it will begin to make sense. Working through examples will be invaluable. Before continuing just a few more facts to explain.

20.3 Child/Parent Relationship

The Bones in an Armature are connected in a **Child/Parent Relationship**. When a second Bone (Bone 2) is extruded from the tip of an Armature (Bone 1) it automatically becomes the Child of the first Bone. Extruding a third Bone (Bone 3) from the tip of the second Bone makes the third Bone the Child of the second Bone. Being a Child means that the Bone follows its parent.

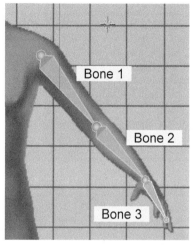

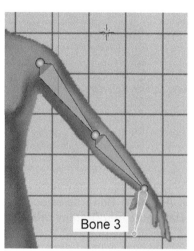

Figure 20.11
Pose Mode

Bone 2 Extruded from Tip of Bone 1.
Bone 3 Extruded from Tip of Bone 2.

Bone 3 Rotates independently
but is fixed to Bone 2.

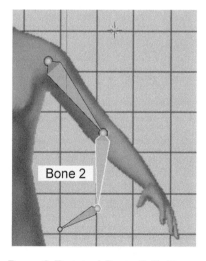

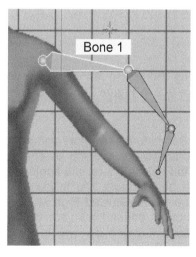

Bone 2 Rotated Bone 3 Follows.
Bone 3 is the Child of Bone 2.

Bone 1 Rotated Bones 2 and 3 Follow.
Bone 2 is the Child of Bone 1.

Note: With the Bones linked to the mesh forming the arm, the Mesh will follow the Bones.

20.4 Armature Display Types

The default Armature display type is **Octahedral.** There are four alternative display types (Figure 20.12).

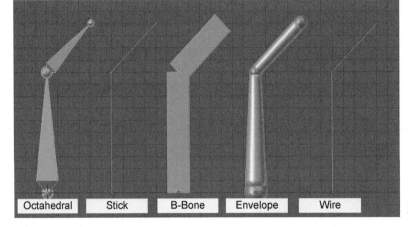

| Octahedral | Stick | B-Bone | Envelope | Wire |

Figure 20.12

With the Armature Bone selected, see the **Properties Editor, Data buttons, Display tab** (Figure 20.13).

Which display type is used depends on what you will do with the Armature. The different uses will not be explained at this time but since the basic function of an Armature is to deform a mesh Object, you need to understand how this occurs.

Figure 20.13

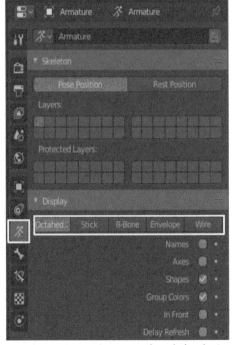

20.5 Multi-Bone Armatures

In adding Bones to an Armature, as you did with Armature.002 in Figure 20.7, you have created a Multi-Bone Armature.

Adding Bones to an Armature and creating an Armature Rig is primarily for posing or animating a Character Model. In Figure 20.1 (at the beginning of this chapter) you see an Armature Rig inside a Character Model. There are pre-assembled Rigs which may be used but you should understand how they are created. Understanding will allow you to create Rigs for any application. Rigs are employed for many characters such as strange creatures and weird robots, not only human figures. They are also used when animating machine parts.

A **Character Rig** or **Armature** is constructed using the Extrusion method (see Chapter 6 - 6.4). A Rig is constructed to fit a particular model and there are pre assembled Rigs which can be modified to fit models.

You may construct your own model, create and import models from external applications or download and use pre-assembled models. The process for constructing an Armature Rig to fit any model is the same.

In Chapter 8–8.12 **Skin Modifier** instruction is provided showing how to extrude a model. The **Skin Modifier** has a function which automatically creates an Armature for the model.

In this demonstration showing how to create a Multi-bone Armature, a model of a human figure has been generated in the **Make Human** program.

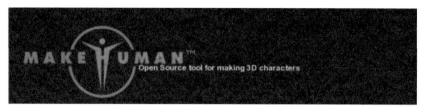

http://www.makehuman.org/index.php   Figure 20.14

Make Human is a **free Open Source** human character modeling program. You can import a model from the program into a Blender file. Importing Objects is discussed in Chapter 3-3.12.

Figure 20.15 shows the imported model with the Multi-Bone Armature fully constructed. The Armature is shown here so you can see what you are aiming for in the exercise. Figure 20.16 shows the Armature moved to one side as a reference for construction.

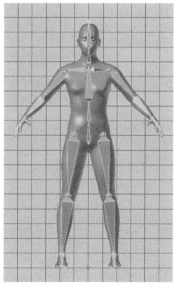

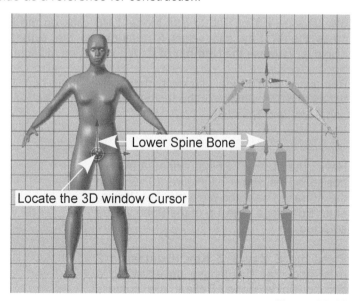

Lower Spine Bone

Locate the 3D window Cursor

Figure 20.15   Figure 20.16

When constructing the Armature think of it as a human skeleton.

To start the construction the first Bone to be placed is the **Lower Spine Bone**. Locate the 3D View Editor Cursor where you want to place the Base of the Bone. Press **Shift + A key** and select **Add – Armature – Single Bone**.

The single Bone Armature is entered in the Scene but it may be way too big or too small for the model. Scale to fit.

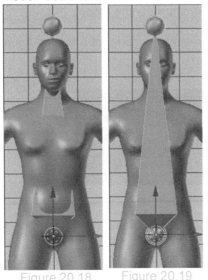

Figure 20.17

Note: When the Armature is scaled, depending on its location, it may disappear inside the model (Figure 20.18).

To see the Bone inside, check **In Front** in the **Display tab** in the **Properties Editor, Data buttons** (Figure 20.17). The bone must be selected in the 3D View Editor.

With **In Front** checked you will see the Bone (Figure 20.19).

Figure 20.18   Figure 20.19

Figure 20.20

20.6 Multi-bone by Subdivision

To create a **Multi-bone Armature** from a single Bone, have the bone selected in the 3D View Editor. Tab to Edit Mode. LMB click on the Body of the Bone then press the **W Key** and select **Subdivide**. In the **Subdivide Multi** panel that displays, increase the **Number of Cuts** to produce multiple Bones (Figure 20.20).

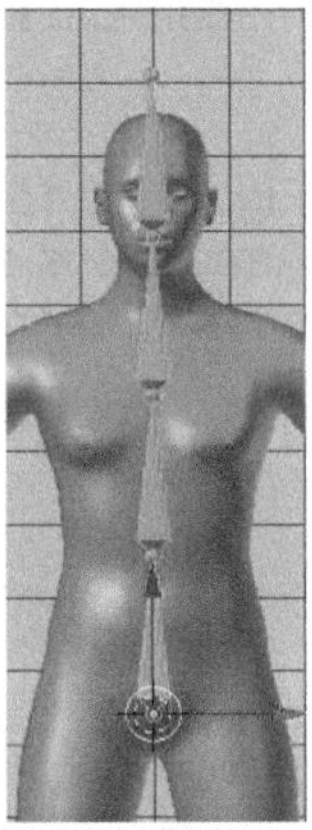

Remain in Edit Mode, deselect, then select individual Tips and Bases of the bones and Translate to fit the model. You may also select individual Bone bodies and Scale and Translate.

20.7 Multi-bone by Extrusion

Have the Lower Spine bone Armature positioned as shown in Figure 20.16. With the Armature selected press the **Tab Key** to enter Edit Mode. The Tip of the Bone will be selected.

Figure 20.21

Press the **E Key + Z Key** (Extrude on Z axis) and drag the mouse up extruding a second Spine Bone. Repeat the process extruding a chest Bone, a neck Bone and a head Bone (Figure 20.21).

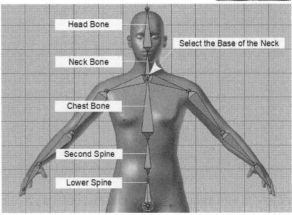

An alternative to pressing the E Key to Extrude a Bone is to click the Extrude Tool in the Tool Panel. There are three options; Roll,Size and Extrude. Size and Extrude have sub options.

Note: When an Armature has been added to the Scene and selected in the 3D View Editor, the Edit Mode Tool Panel is an abbreviated version which has three Armature Tools.

Figure 20.22

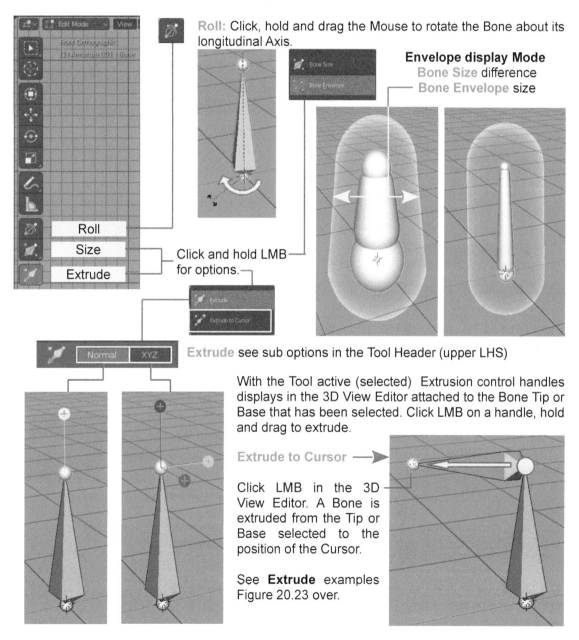

Roll: Click, hold and drag the Mouse to rotate the Bone about its longitudinal Axis.

Envelope display Mode
Bone Size difference
Bone Envelope size

Roll
Size
Extrude

Click and hold LMB for options.

Extrude see sub options in the Tool Header (upper LHS)

With the Tool active (selected) Extrusion control handles displays in the 3D View Editor attached to the Bone Tip or Base that has been selected. Click LMB on a handle, hold and drag to extrude.

Extrude to Cursor ───►

Click LMB in the 3D View Editor. A Bone is extruded from the Tip or Base selected to the position of the Cursor.

See **Extrude** examples Figure 20.23 over.

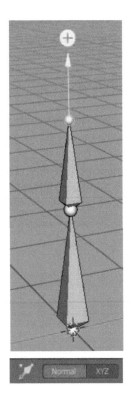
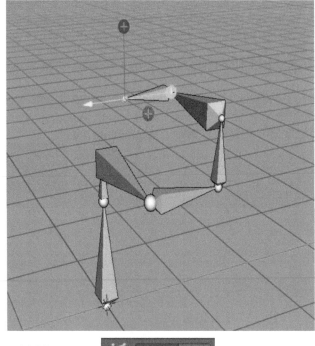

Figure 20.23

20.8 Axis Mirror Extrusion

For Extruding Bones simultaneously either side of an axis to produce arm or leg Bones the procedure is as follows:

Have the Bone Chain in Front Orthographic View. In Edit Mode, select the Base or Tip of intermediate Bones in a chain. Press the E Key (Extrude), click LMB, hold and drag the Mouse to Extrude a Bone (one side only).

Figure 20.24

In the upper RH corner of the Screen click **Armature Options** and check **X-Axis Mirror** in the panel that displays (Figure 20.24).

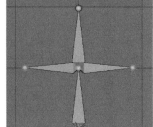

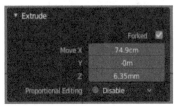

Figure 20.25

In the Extrude panel (lower Left of Screen) that displays when the single intermediate Bone is Extruded check **Forked** (Figure 20.25). The Extruded Bone is Mirrored (Figure 20.26).

The Mouse remains in Extrude Mode allowing multiple X Axis Mirror extrusions to be performed.

Figure 20.26

20.9 Extruding Shoulder and Arms

With the Base of the Neck selected and X-Axis Mirror checked, press **Shift + E key** and drag the mouse to Extrude Shoulder Bones on both sides of the model. The Tip of the Bone will be selected. Press Shift + E key again and extrude Arm Bones and finally a Hand Bone.

Continue the X-Axis Extrusion for the lower limbs starting by selecting the Base of the Lower Spine Bone.

Creating the Multi-Bone Armature this way in Front Orthographic View is fine for the front view but in Right or Left Orthographic Views you will find the Bones are way out of position. You now have to select individual Bone Tips/Bases and manoeuvre them into their correct locations (Figure 20.27).

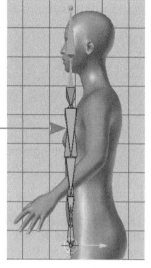

Right Orthographic View – Bones way out of position.

Figure 20.27

Head and Neck Bone correctly positioned

20.10 Naming Bones

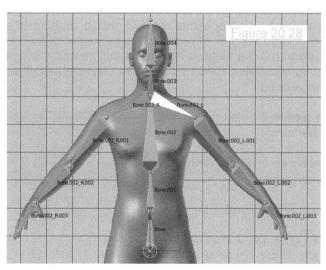

Figure 20.28

For a human figure there are many Bones included in an Armature. In Figure 20.21 a few of the Bones were labelled for the demonstration but Blender has an automatic Bone naming system for dealing with complex Armatures.

With an Armature selected in the 3D window in Object mode go to the **Properties Editor, Data buttons** and in the **Display tab** check (tick) **Names**. Names are displayed in the 3D View Editor (Figure 20.28).

You will also see the names displayed in the Outliner Editor (Figure 20.29 opposite).

You may change the names to something meaningful for your application by double clicking on the name in the Outliner Editor, deleting and retyping a new name. The new name is automatically updated in the 3D View Editor.

20.11 Deforming a Mesh

Figure 20.29

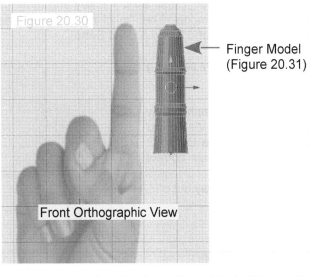

Figure 20.30

Front Orthographic View

Finger Model
(Figure 20.31)

The basic procedure for deforming a Mesh Object with an Armature is to link or associate vertices on the mesh surface to Bones in the Armature. When the Bones are moved the Vertices in the mesh move.

Make Human models come with a considerable number of Vertices in the surface mesh. That's why they look so good. When deforming a mesh using an Armature you should consider the number of vertices that will be manipulated. A large number of vertices means the computer has to perform a large number of calculations when moving vertices about and that can slow things down considerably. That being the case, in demonstrating mesh deformation, a simple model will be used that has a minimal number of mesh vertices.

In Figure 20.30 a simple finger has been modeled by extruding a Circle. The finger is shown in Edit Mode displaying its Vertices.

Figure 20.31

Arrange the finger model so that it is pointing up in **Front Orthographic** view with its center of rotation on the center of the Scene.

Construct a three Bone Armature as shown in Figure 20.31.

Place the Armature inside the model. With the Armature in place you associate parts of the mesh with the Bones. There are several ways of doing this.

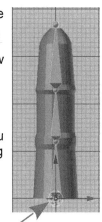

Center of Rotation

20.12 Assigning Vertices - Modifier

In Object Mode select the Model then in the **Properties Editor, Modifier buttons**, add an **Armature Modifier** (Figure 20.32).

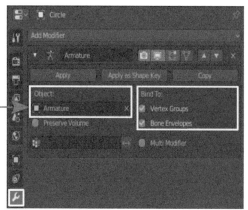

In the Modifier panel set **Object** as **Armature.**

In the modifier panel check **Vertex Groups** and **Bone Envelope** under the **Bind To** heading. This is telling Blender to associate the Armature Bones with Vertices that are enclosed by the Bone Envelopes (Field of Influence Figure 20.32).

Figure 20.32

To see what this means have the Armature selected in the 3D View Editor then in the **Properties Editor, Data buttons, Display tab** change **Octahedral** display to **Envelope** display (Figure 20.33).

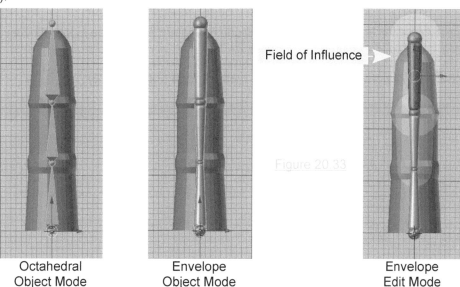

Field of Influence

Figure 20.33

| Octahedral | Envelope | Envelope |
| Object Mode | Object Mode | Edit Mode |

Have the **Armature selected** in **Edit Mode**. In the diagram you see the upper finger Bone selected in Edit mode and with Envelope Display Mode you see the Field of Influence. This field indicates which part of the Mesh will be influenced when the Armature is moved.

As you can see, the top of the Finger is fully encapsulated by the Field but at the upper finger joint it is questionable.

To ensure the Mesh is fully within the Field of Influence increase the **Envelope Distance** value in the **Properties Editor, Bone buttons, Deform Tab** (ensure that **Deform** is checked).

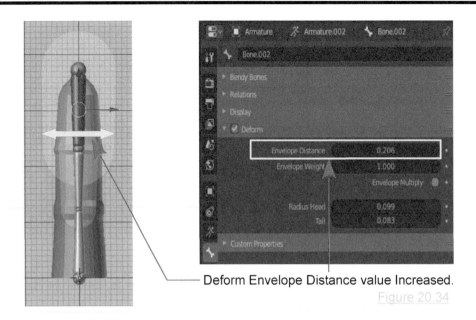

Deform Envelope Distance value Increased.

Figure 20.34

With the upper Armature Bone selected in Edit Mode change to Pose Mode in the 3D View Editor Header. The Bone displays colored   (Figure 20.35).

Rotate the Bone (R key drag mouse) to see the mesh deform (Figure 20.36).

Figure 20.35

Figure 20.36

20.13 Assigning Vertices – Vertex Groups

In the previous examples **Mesh Vertices** were located within the **Field of Influence** of the Armature. An alternative to this, is to manually nominate which vertices will be affected by the Armature.

Employ the same Finger – Armature arrangement previously described. Select the **Armature** then in the **Properties Editor, Data buttons, Display Tab**, tick **Names** to show the Bones named **Bone** and **Bone.001** and **Bone.002**. Deselect the Armature.

Select the **Finger** (Mesh), and in **Edit Mode** press **Alt + A key** to deselect the Vertices. In the **Properties Editor, Data buttons**, **Vertex Groups Tab**, click the **Plus** sign to add a **Vertex Group**; a Vertex Group is added and named **Group**. By renaming **Group** to **Bone.002** (Figure 20.37), the **Vertex Group** will automatically be controlled by the Bone named **Bone.002**. Groups and Bones may be renamed to whatever you want, but for a Group to be controlled by a Bone, the names must be identical.

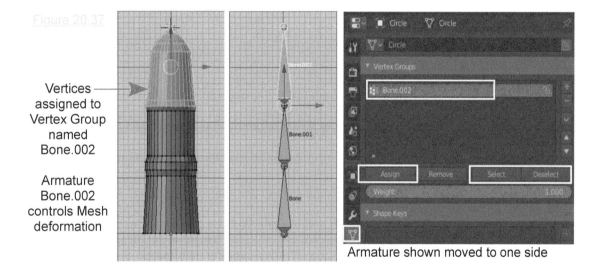

Figure 20.37

Vertices assigned to Vertex Group named Bone.002

Armature Bone.002 controls Mesh deformation

Armature shown moved to one side

In the 3D View Editor, select the Vertices in the upper part of the finger (press the B key – drag a rectangle). Make sure you have the **Select Only Visible button turned off** in the 3D View Editor Header or you will only be selecting the front Vertices of the finger.

In the **Vertex Groups** tab, click **Assign** to assign the selected Vertices to the Group. Check out the assignment by alternately clicking on **Deselect** and **Select** (Figure 20.35).

Tab into **Object mode** and deselect the finger with **Alt + A key**. Select the **Armature** and change to **Pose Mode**. Select **Bone.002** and press the **R Key** to rotate. Nothing happens because you haven't applied an **Armature Modifier** to the finger.

Go back and select the finger and in the **Properties Editor, Modifier buttons**, click **Add Modifier** and select **Armature**. In the **Armature Object** panel, click and select **Armature**.

Deselect the finger and select the **Armature** in **Pose Mode**. Select **Bone.002** and rotate it—the upper part of the finger will now deform as the Bone is rotated (Figure 20.38).

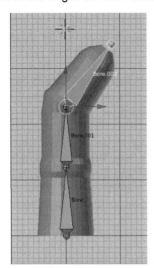

Figure 20.38

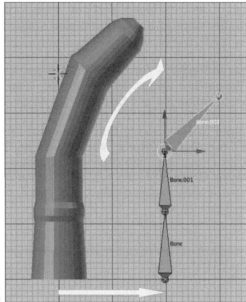

Figure 20.39

The armature may be located well away from the finger and still deform the Mesh. The Field of Influence of the Armature described in the previous exercise is not enforced, but with the Armature displaced away from the Mesh, the Mesh deformation is exaggerated (Figure 20.39).

Select Vertices, assign them to Vertex Groups named identical to the Armature Bones.

20.14 Assigning Vertices – Weight Paint

Blender has a painting method that selects and assigns Vertices to a group, automatically linking to an armature Bone. The Paint method allows a graduated weight to be given to vertices that dictate how much influence the armature Bone will have over the deformation of the Mesh.

Set up a new Scene as you did for the previous examples. Select the **Finger** in **Object Mode** and add an **Armature Modifier** in the Properties Editor. Don't forget to enter **Armature** in the **Object panel**. Select the Armature and enter **Pose Mode**. In the **Properties Editor, Data buttons**, **Display Tab**, tick **Names** to display the Bone names in the 3D View Editor; the names should be **Bone, Bone.001** and **Bone.002** as before.

When ticking **Names** make sure you are in the **Data buttons** not the **Object buttons**. If you are in the Object buttons only the name Armature will display.

With the Armature as the selected Object in the 3D View Editor, in Pose Mode, select **Bone.001** (the middle Bone) then change to Object Mode and right click the Finger to select it. With the finger selected, go to the 3D View Editor Header and change from Object Mode to **Weight Paint Mode**. The Finger displays blue, indicating that no Vertices are selected (Figure 20.40 over).

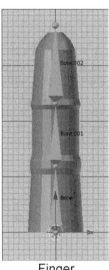

The Finger displays in blue, which indicates that no Vertices are selected.

Figure 20.40

Figure 20.41

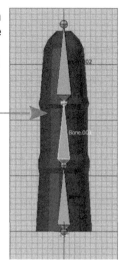

| Armature
Pose Mode | Finger
Object Mode | 3DView Editor Header
Click to select Editor Modes | Finger
Weight Paint |

In the **Tool Panel** at the left-hand side of the 3D View Editor have the **Draw Tool** selected. Make sure the **Weight** and **Strength** sliders are set to 1.000 in the Header (Figure 20.42). You are about to paint over the finger mesh to select Vertices, and by setting the strength to a high value you are telling Blender that the selected Vertices are to be rigorously controlled by Bone.001. In Weight Paint Mode, the cursor in the 3D View Editor is a circle(Figure 20.42). The Radius control for the circle is in the Header. You want the middle part of the finger to be transformed by Bone.001 therefore click, hold, and drag the Cursor circle over

the middle part of the Finger. As with selecting vertices make sure **Show whole Screen Transparent** is turned on in the Header. The part of the Finger painted turns red, which indicates a rigorous control (Figure 20.43). Altering the **Strength** value changes the control strength and will display a different color.

Turn the mesh around and make sure the Vertices on the back side of the finger are painted (pan the 3D View around).

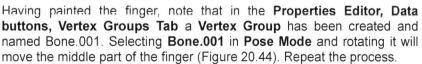

Having painted the finger, note that in the **Properties Editor, Data buttons, Vertex Groups Tab** a **Vertex Group** has been created and named Bone.001. Selecting **Bone.001** in **Pose Mode** and rotating it will move the middle part of the finger (Figure 20.44). Repeat the process.

20.15 Vertex Groups vs Field of Influence

Having described the deformation of a mesh by employing Vertex Groups and field of influence, the question arises as to which is being employed when the armature is located inside the mesh. If you follow the preceding examples by either selecting Vertices or weight painting, you assign Vertices to a Vertex Group. It is unclear whether the Vertex Group or the field of influence is controlling the deformation of the mesh. If the armature is moved away from the mesh posing, the Bone will still cause a deformation; therefore, the Vertex Group is in control. But when the armature is inside the mesh, is it the field of influence or the Vertex Group?

Follow this example to clarify this question.

Create the same Scene as before and select only the Vertices at the tip of the finger. Assign them to a Vertex Group. Name the group Bone.002. Make sure you have added an Armature Modifier to the finger and have assigned Armature in the Object panel. Rotate Bone.002 in Pose Mode and only the Tip of the finger deforms.

Place the Armature in Object mode and move it away from the finger. Rotate the Bone a second time and again only the tip of the finger deforms—this only proves that the Vertex Group is active.

Place the Armature back inside the finger.

Select the finger and take a look at the Armature Modifier. Under the heading **Bind To** there are the two boxes labelled **Vertex Group** and **Bone Envelopes**. Untick **Vertex Group** and tick **Bone Envelope**; rotating the Bone now deforms the whole upper part of the finger. Obviously you have turned the **Vertex Group** off and activated the **Field of Influence**, so herein lies the control for selecting either the Field of Influence or the Vertex Group.

Another way of negating the Field of Influence is to set the **Distance** and **Weight** values to 0.000 in the **Properties Editor, Bone buttons, Deform tab**.

20.16 Inverse Kinematics Constraint

Inverse Kinematics (IK) Constraint is a method of controlling the posing and animation of a chain of Bones. This is a wonderful tool for animators. The activation of the tool is found in the Properties Editor, Bone Constraints buttons which are only displayed when an Armature has been added in the 3D View Editor.

With IK, dragging the end Bone of the chain will result in the chain following the selected Bone.

IK (Inverse Kinematics) is the opposite of FK (Forward Kinematics). With FK, you have to rotate the chain of Bones one by one to pose for animation; this is a tedious process but gives you full control.

> Do not confuse **IK (Inverse Kinematics)** with the **Spline IK** .

An example of **Inverse Kinematics** would be to create a chain of Bones (Figure 20.45). An **Armature – Single Bone** has been added to the 3D View Editor then Extruded up from the Tip creating six Bones. The Bones are automatically connected forming a single Armature.

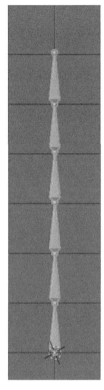

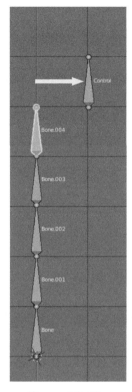

In Figure 20.46 the top Bone has been selected in Edit Mode and disconnected from the Armature by pressing **Alt + P Key** and selecting **Clear Parent** in the menu that displays. In Edit Mode **Control** (the top Bone) has been moved aside.

With the Armature selected in Object or Edit Mode, Bone names are displayed in the 3D View Editor by checking **Names** in the Properties Editor, Armature buttons, Display Tab (Figure 30.47).

Figure 20.45   Figure 20.46

Figure 20.47

The disconnected top Bone has been renamed **Control** in the **Outliner Editor**. The Bones forming the Armature are listed in the Outliner Editor in the order of connection (Figure 20.48).

Note: The Bone named **Control** is shown separate to the list. This Bone will be, as the name suggests, a Control Bone for manipulating the Armature.

The Bones in the Armature are connected but at this stage, selecting an individual Bone in Pose Mode will only see it Rotate about its Base. Bones above in the chain will also Rotate but that is the limit of the Posing.

Figure 20.48

For the Armature to follow the Control Bone an **Inverse Kinematic (IK) Constraint** is required.

An IK Constraint is applied to one of the Bones in the Armature with the Constraint instructed to use the Armature Control Bone.

> **Note:** Bone Constraint buttons only display with an Armature selected in the 3D View Editor. Without an Armature only Object Constraints display.

Figure 20.49

To demonstrate the IK Constraint select Bone.004 in the Armature in **Pose Mode**. In the Properties Editor click the **Bone Constraints** button and click **Add Bone Constraint**. Select **Inverse Kinematics** in the menu that displays.

In the IK Bone Constraint Panel (Figure 20.50) set **Target** as **Armature** and **Bone** as **Control**.

Remember: This is setting controls for Bone.004 in the Armature. When the Control Bone is selected in Pose Mode and Translated in the 3D View Editor Bone.004 follows. Having the IK Constraint in place means the remainder of the Bones in the Armature Chain follow.

Figure 20.50

Make particular note of the **Chain Length** setting in the IK Constraint Panel. Chain Length: 0 means all the Bones in the Armature Chain are affected (Figures 20.51, 20.52, 20.53).

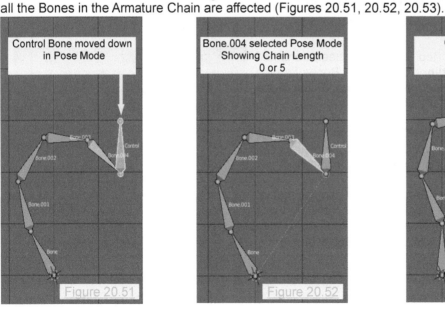

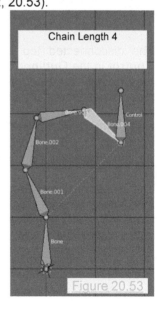

20.17 Spline IK Constraint

The **Spline IK Constraint** forces a multi Bone **Armature** to follow the shape of a Curve. With the Armature constrained to the Curve, the Curve is then manipulated to adjust the shape of the Armature and in turn any mesh assigned to the Armature.

To demonstrate, in the default 3D View Editor, delete the **Cube** and add a **Bezier Curve**. Scale the Curve up twice. Create a multi Bone **Armature** (add Armature, scale x 2, subdivide). (Figure 20.54).

Leave the 3D window in **User Perspective View**.

Both the origin of the Armature and the center of the Bezier Curve are located at the center of the Scene.

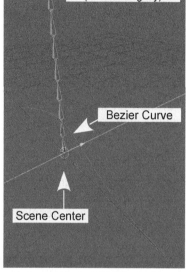

Figure 20.54

User Perspective View (Rotated Slightly)

Bezier Curve

Scene Center

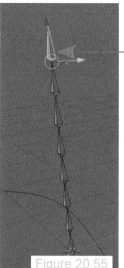

With the Armature selected, go into **Pose Mode**. **When selected,** the outline of the Armature will be displayed in blue.

Deselect the Armature then select the top Bone in the Armature (Figure 20.55).

In the **Properties window, Bone Constraints buttons** add a **Spline IK Constraint** (Figure 20.56).

In the **Constraint panel** change the **Spline Fittings: Chain Length** value to 8 (the number of Bones in the armature).

In the **Target** panel select **Bezier Curve**.

Figure 20.55

Figure 20.56

Figure 20.57

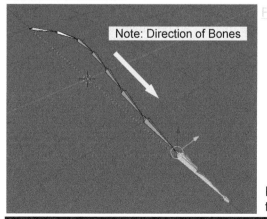

Note: Direction of Bones

In selecting the target the Armature is relocated in the 3D View Editor and shaped to the Curve.

337

The Armature Bones are arranged with the direction of the curve. If the Curve were being used as an Animation Path, the movement along the path would be in the direction of the chevrons spaced along the Curve (Figure 20.58).

The direction may be reversed **in Edit Mode** by clicking RMB to display the **Curve Context Menu** and selecting **Switch Direction**. In doing this the chevrons are reversed and so are the Bones in the Armature.

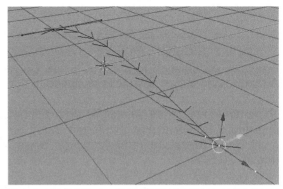

Figure 20.58

With the Armature constrained to the curve the **Armature** may be posed by selecting the **Control Handles** on the **Bezier Curve**. The Curve may be subdivided in Edit Mode to add additional control handles and give more control over the posing. Remember the practical use of the Armature is to control the shape and movement of a mesh Object which is assigned to the Armature.

Hooks may be assigned to the control handles of the Curve giving a non renderable Object with which to translate and pose the Armature. To add a **Hook** place the Curve in **Edit Mode** and ensure everything is **deselected**. Select a Control Handle then press **Ctrl + H key** and select **Hook to New Object** in the menu that displays. A **Hook** is displayed in the form of a **3D Cross**. To display the **Hook** in a different format go to the **Outliner Editor,** RMB click on **Empty - Select** . In the **Properties Editor, Object Data buttons** the **Empty tab** will show with a **Display As** selection menu. You select a different display format from this menu .

Anther method of introducing an non renderable Objects to allow Curve manipulation, when you have an Armature constrained to the Curve, is to add single Bones. You then parent the Bone to the Hook.

20.18 Forward

With knowledge of Armatures and how they are constructed, manipulated and used to deform Mesh Objects you are placed to learn the intricacies of Character Rigging. This is the process of constructing an Armature to fit a Character model. The model can be anything your imagination allows but for demonstration purposes, the subject will be devoted to Character Rigging a Humanoid Figure.

There are pre-assembled Rigs you may download from the internet which are free to use, but using a ready made Rig for your particular application may require you to modify the download. It is therefore advisable to understand how a Rig is constructed.

20.19 Character Rigging

Character Rigging is the process of creating an Armature to suit a Model of a Character then associating the Bones in the Armature with parts of the Model. The Bones are Posed and animated and the parts of the Model follow suit. To facilitate Posing, special Control Bones are incorporated in the Armature to manipulate the Bones.

Before constructing an Armature and Rigging you require a Mesh Model of a Character.

Free to use models may be downloaded from the internet or you may construct your own model in Blender or use an external application such as the Make Human program.

Constructing a crude humanoid figure by extrusion in Blender was discussed in Chapter 11–11.6.

Constructing a model of a human figure can be a lengthy process depending on the detail employed. There are several websites where you can download pre-built models, some of which are pre-rigged. To understand the rigging process you should begin with a simple **Low Poly Mesh** model. **Low Poly** means a mesh model with a minimum number of Vertices, Edges and Faces.

Figure 20.59

Figure 20.60

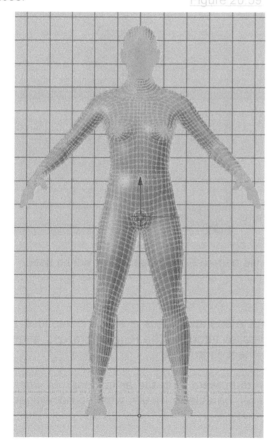
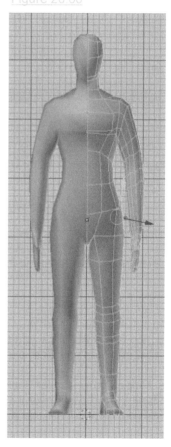

Figure 20.59 shows a model created using the **Make Human** program. As you see there is a vast difference in the number of vertices in the **Low Poly** model in Figure 20.60.

The **Low Poly** Model of a human is shown in Figure 20.60, supplied by **tweediez** released under the Creative Commons Attribution 3.0.

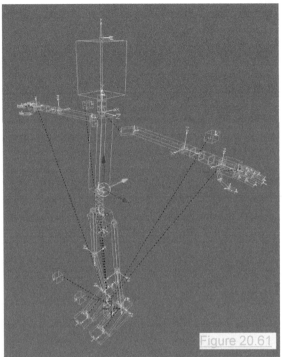

Figure 20.61

Rigged Armature – B-Bone Display Type

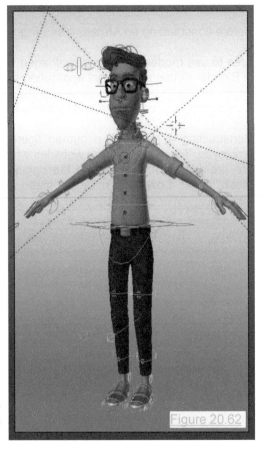

Figure 20.62

Figures 20.61 and 20.62 show examples of pre-rigged character models which demonstrate where you will be heading in the following exercise.

In the exercise a model created in Blender in the file named **ChibiBase.blend** will be used.

Proviso

Rigging a Character Model is a reasonably intricate operation. This exercise is intended as an introduction which will allow you to understand detailed tutorials. The Rigging process, even at a basic level, requires patience, perseverance and attention to detail.

It is to enticing to reach for a pre-rigged model and create fantastic animations but when you understand the process involved in Rigging you will be able to modify what you download and generate your own unique characters.

The Character Model to be used is named **Chibi**. To get this model go to the **Blend Swap** Website;

http://www.blendswap.com/

To download a model you have to register as a member. This means entering an email address and creating a user password and agreeing to the terms of use. If you don't do this you won't be able to download any of the fantastic **free models** available on the site.

Assuming that you have signed up, log in, then click on **Search** in the header at the top of the website home page. Select **Search** in **Blends** and enter **Chibi** in the Search Keywords bar. Click on **Search**.

The Model you are looking for is titled **CHIBI MODEL BASE**.

When you are logged in there will be a download link. The download is a ZIP file which you have to decompress to get the Blender file containing the model. Remember where you download to, and where you unzip to on your computer.

At this point it is assumed you have the file downloaded and unzipped.

Chibi is a humanoid character (Figure 20.63). Use your imagination to decide whether Chibi is a child or an alien or a little bow legged guy with a big head. Chibi can be whatever you decide.

The first thing you want to do is save the **ChibiBase.blend** file as a new Blender file with a new name. This gives you a new file to work with and leaves ChibiBase.blend for a future work.

Here, it is assumed you have the new Blender file opened.

Click RMB on **Chibi** to select the model. It is not selected when you first open the file. The 3D View Editor is in **Front Orthographic View.**

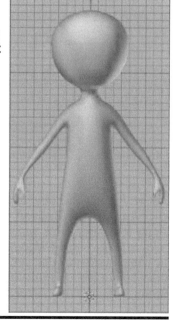

> **Note:** In the **ChibiBase.blend** file all you have is a Mesh Character Model. There is no Camera or Lamp in the Scene. You may see a slight resemblance to the model created in Chapter 11–11.6. Chibi is a much nicer model.
>
> **Chibe** has been created by **Magiclass** and released under the **CC Zero License**.

Figure 20.63

When you download a model or append from another Blender file, you should examine it before using. In examining **ChibiBase.blend** you will see, in the **User Preferences Editor, Object data buttons, Vertex Groups tab**, that **Vertex Groups** have been generated. These are probably left over from a previous Blender operation. To begin with a clean slate, click on the minus button at the side of the list until all groups have been deleted. You may also find the 3D View Editor Header at the bottom of the Editor.

Take a closer look at Chibi. **Tab** into **Edit Mode**. You see that the model only has Vertices on the right hand side (your right, Chibie's left) (Figure 20.64). In the **Properties Editor, Modifier buttons** you will see that a **Mirror Modifier** and a **Subserf** (Subdivision Surface) **Modifier** have been used when creating the model. The Mirror Modifier allows Vertex creation and manipulation on one side to be mirrored on the other side. Subserf makes the surface of the model appear smooth without increasing the Vertex count.

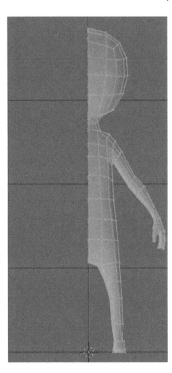

Figure 21.64

Actually, it will be better to have a few more Vertices when posing the figure so go ahead and click **Apply** in the **Subserf Modifier** panel (in Object Mode). You have to be in Object Mode to Apply a Modifier. Note that in the Modifier panel, under **Subdivisions**, the **View value is 1**. This means that when the Modifier is applied, the mesh surface of the model will be subdivided once. In other words the Vertices will be doubled. In Edit Mode you will see there are more Vertices than before. You also want the model to have Vertices on both sides, so go back into **Object Mode** and apply the **Mirror Modifier** (click the Apply button).

Figure 20.65 shows Chibi with the Subserf Modifier and the Mirror Modifier applied.

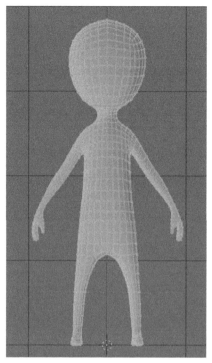

Figure 20.65

Some Definitions: This chapter has been titled Character Rigging, therefore, what does Character Rigging mean?

A Character refers to a Model, specifically a model of a Human Character. The model is a Mesh Model in that it is made up of a surface mesh constituting Vertices connected by Edges. There is nothing inside the mesh to begin with.

An Armature is constructed inside the mesh, specifically a Multi-bone Armature (single individual Bones connected together). The Armature may be considered as a skeleton for the Human Character.

Areas of the surface mesh are assigned (associated with or connected) to single Bones of the Armature or to multiple Bones.

Following the construction of the Armature the bones are translated or rotated (moved) to set the mesh in various poses or animated to move. When the bones move the surface mesh associated with the bones follow, therefore, the Character Model is set into a Pose or animated to move.

20.20 Creating the Armature (Root Bone)

The Armature **Root Bone** is the starting point for creating the Armature and acts as the primary Control Bone for moving and manipulating the Model in the Scene.

With Chibi displayed as shown in Figure 20.65, **Tab to Object Mode** in **Front Orthographic View**. This presents the figure face on with the Object's center located on the center of the Scene mid way between the feet. The center of the Scene on the XZ Axis is located between the feet.

Make sure you have the 3D View Editor Cursor located at the center of the Scene. Be in Object Mode with everything deselected. Press Shift + S Key to display the **Snap** Pie Menu and select **Cursor to World Origin** .

> **Tip:** In following this demonstration save the Blender file repeatedly at each stage of the exercise. If you get off track it will be frustrating to have to repeat the entire procedure. If you have to repeat, the consolation is that repeating consolidates the learning process. I do it often.

With Chibi deselected add an Amature-Single Bone. The Bone is entered at the location of the 3D View Editor Cursor at the center of the Scene (Center of World Origin).

With the Root Bone bone selected **Tab to Edit mode**. The Tip of the Bone will be selected as shown by the orange outline.

The Bone is orientated vertically with its Tip at the top and with the Base of the Bone accurately located at the center of the Scene. Lay the Bone flat along the ground plane of the Scene on the Y Axis (Figure 20.66).

In the Properties Editor, Armature buttons, Display Tab check **In Front**.

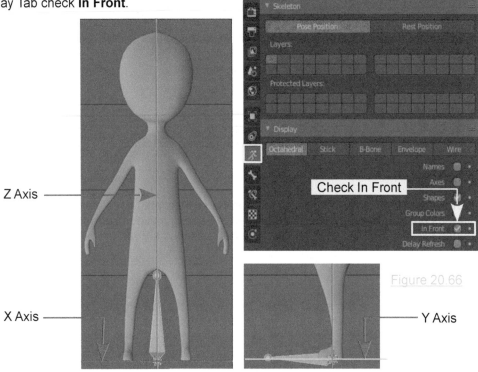

Figure 20.66

Z Axis

X Axis

Y Axis

Front Orthographic View   Right Orthographic View

To lay the bone flat and accurately, position it on the Y Axis and use **Increment Snapping**. Press **Ctrl + Shift + Tab** and select Snap Type – **Increment**, from the menu that displays.

With the Bone Tip selected in Edit Mode press **G key (Grab) and hold Ctrl** and drag the mouse pulling the Tip down flat along the ground plane (Y Axis). As you drag, the bone tip will jump from one grid intersection to the next and finally locate precisely on the mid plane **Y axis** (Green Line). Release Ctrl then LMB click to release Grab.

20.21 Adding More Bones

A second Bone will be added to the Rig. Select the **Body** of the **Armature_Root bone** in **Edit mode** then press **Shift + D key (Duplicate)**. Drag the mouse and move the duplicated bone up to the pelvic area of the figure, rotate and position as shown in Figure 20.67 by selecting the Body of the Bone, or by selecting the Tip or the Base.

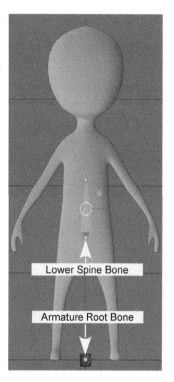

Figure 20.67

Remember: In the Properties Editor, Data buttons, Display tab (with the Bone selected) have **In Front** checked (ticked) so you can see the Bone inside the model.

The Base should be positioned approximately where the pelvis would be. Switch between Front Orthographic and Right Orthographic views to orientate the Bone.

Consider this Bone to be the Lower Spine Bone.

The Armature_Root bone was Duplicated in Edit Mode to produce the Lower Spine because this second Bone has to be linked to the Armature_Root Bone and to be part of the Rig. Duplicating in Object Mode would cause the new Bone to be an independent Armature not connected to the Rig.

Lower Spine Bone

Armature Root Bone

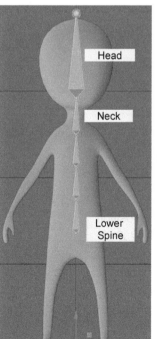

Figure 20.68

Head

Neck

Lower Spine

When selecting either Armature_Root or Lower Spine in Object Mode both Bones will be selected. In Object Mode you are selecting the entire Rig not individual Bones. To select individually you have to be in Edit Mode.

With the Lower Spine Bone selected in Edit mode move the Base down to where the belly button would be then extrude Bones to form the remainder of spine (Figure 20.68). In Edit mode select the Tip of Lower Spine, press E key then Z and drag the mouse to extrude a new Bone (E key – extrude, Z key confines the extrusion to the Z axis.).

Repeat the process for each new Bone in the spine. Right Orthographic view allows you to position Bones to shape the spine. In Front Orthographic view the Bones follow the centerline of the figure. For the Head Bone restrain the extrusion to the Z axis by pressing E key + Z key.

Note: In positioning the Bones in Right Orthographic View it is not intended to replicate a human spine. Bones are placed to associate with parts of the Mesh model i.e. the Neck Bone will be linked to the Neck mesh.

Obviously there are many more Bones in a human skeleton than shown in the diagrams. In creating an Armature for animation it is good practice to minimise the number of Bones since this saves computer power in the animation process and simplifies the naming. The more Bones you have in a **Rig** the more flexible posing will be, therefore, you have to compromise.

20.22 Creating Arm Bones

Note: In creating Bones for the arms Blender has the ability to mirror Bones to the opposite side of the model.

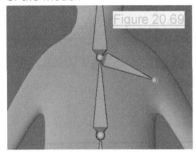

Figure 20.69

In **Edit Mode** select the base of the Neck Bone in Front Orthographic view and extrude a Shoulder Bone (Figure 20.29). In the upper RH corner of the Screen click on Armature Options and check X-Axis Mirror in the panel that displays (Figure 20.70).

Armature Options

X-Axis Mirror   Figure 20.70

Note: There is no effect in the 3D View Editor.

When extruding a Bone the Extrude Panel displays in the lower RHS of the Screen. With X-Axis Mirror checked in Armature Options, check **Forked** in the Extrude Panel (Figure 20.71) to duplicate the Bone on the opposite side of the Armature.

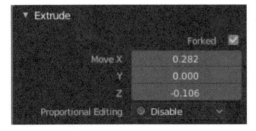

Extrude

Forked ☑

Move X   0.282

Y   0.000

Z   -0.106

Proportional Editing   Disable

Figure 20.71

Shoulder Bone
Duplicated

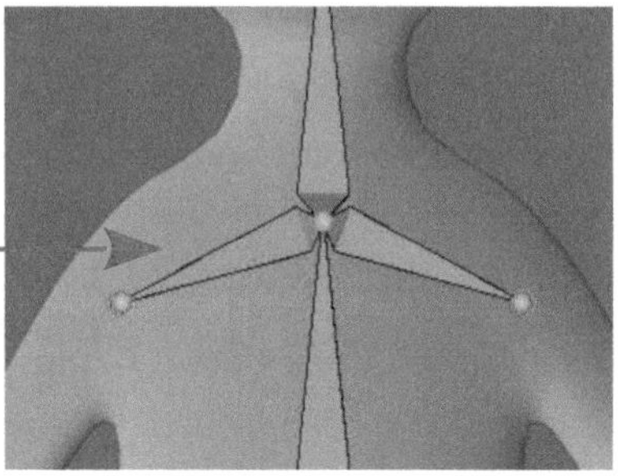

Figure 20.72

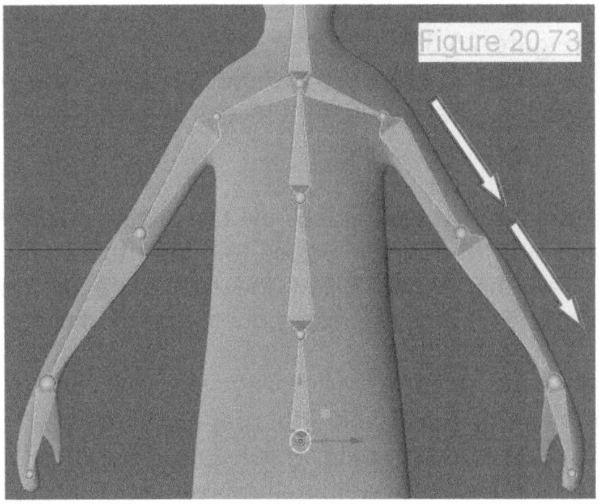

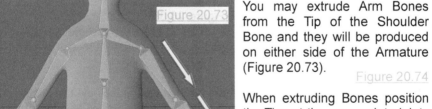

Figure 20.73

You may extrude Arm Bones from the Tip of the Shoulder Bone and they will be produced on either side of the Armature (Figure 20.73).

Figure 20.74

When extruding Bones position the Tips at the appropriate joints in the Character Model, shoulder, elbow, wrist.

In Right Orthographic View select the Bone Tips and align the Bones with the Model.

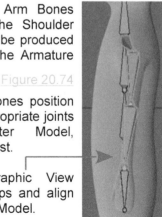

20.23 Creating Leg Bones

Figure 20.75

To add leg Bones for the figure repeat the process used for the arms, this time extruding from the Base of the Lower Spine Bone (Figure 20.75).

When you come to the Ankle go to Right Orthographic View and extrude a Foot Bone and a Heel Bone (Figure 20.76).

Figure 20.76

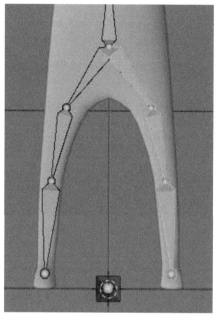

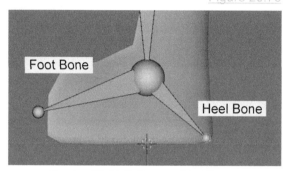

Foot Bone

Heel Bone

Foot – Right Orthographic View

Legs - Front Orthographic View

20.24 Bone Naming

Figure 20.77

At this point you have created a significant number of Bones even in this relatively simple Armature. The individual Bones have been referred to as Armature Root, Lower Spine, Neck, Head etc. but there is nothing in the View to specifically indicate which Bone is which. Naming Bones and importantly giving the Bones meaningful names is very important, especially in a complicated Rig.

Blender automatically names Bones as they are extruded but the naming system provides names such as Bone, Bone.001, Bone.002 etc. and when Mirroring is involved, Bone.002_R and Bone.002_L.

Bone Names may be displayed in the 3D View Editor by checking Names in the Properties Editor, Data buttons for the Armature in the Display Tab (Figure 20.77).

The default names are displayed adjacent to each Bone in the Armature in the 3D View Editor and a hierarchy listing is shown in the Outliner Editor (Figures 20.78 and 20.79 over).

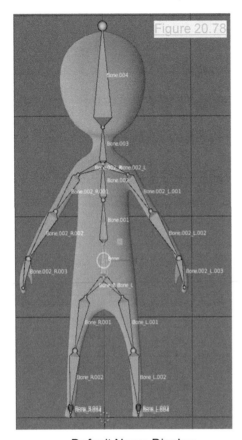

Default Name Display

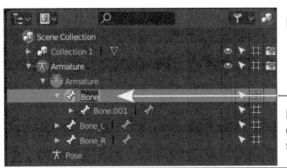

Outliner Editor Name Display

Individual Bones can be renamed by selecting a Bone in Edit Mode then editing the Bone name in the Properties Editor, Bone buttons (Figure 20.80).

Alternatively click on the name in the Outliner Editor (Figure 20.80) to select the Bone. Double click to edit.

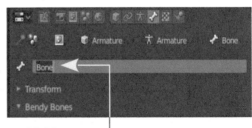

Figure 20.80

Double click, backspace or delete and retype the name.

In either case the edited name will be displayed in the 3D View Editor adjacent to the selected Bone.

20.25 Assigning the Mesh

At this point, although the **Armature Rig** is incomplete, you may assign it to the **Mesh Figure**.

This is the process of linking Vertex Groups (groups of vertices) on the figure's mesh surface to individual Bones. Blender has an automated process for doing this. The Bones will then control the posing or posturing of the mesh.

At this point it is worth reviewing the complete Armature assembly by comparing the Rig in the **3D View Editor** with the name displaying the hierarchy of Bones in the **Outliner Editor** (Figure 20.81).

Figure 20.81

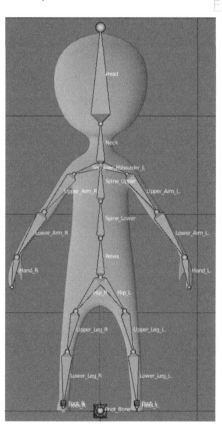
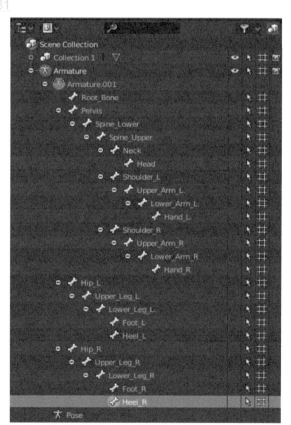

In Figure 20.41 the 3D View Editor is shown in Object Mode. To see the full list of all the Bones in the Outliner Editor expand each entry.

Before engaging the automated mesh assigning process you need to exclude the **Root_Bone** This bone is a **Control Bone** for moving the figure around in the Scene and is not a **Posing Bone**. Posing is the process of posturing the figure.

In the 3D View Editor in **Edit Mode** select **Root_Bone**. In the **Properties Editor, Bone buttons, Deform tab** click on the **Deform button** to remove the tick. This tells Blender that you do not want **Root_Bone** to be part of the deforming Rig.

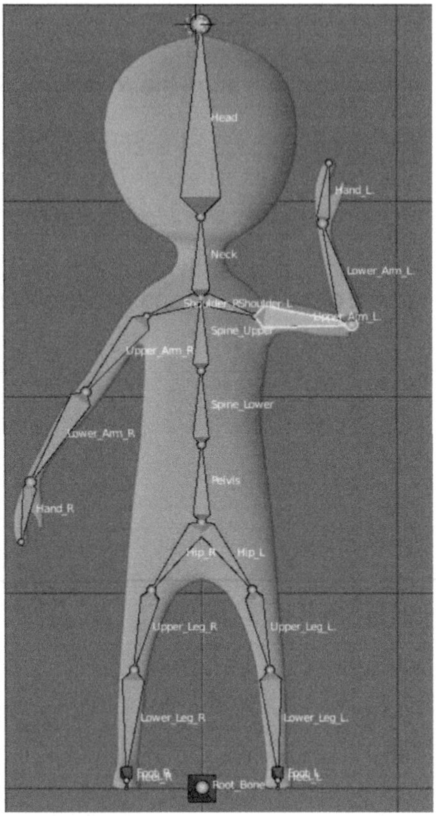

Figure 20.82

In the **3D View Editor** deselect the bone and change to **Object Mode**. Press the **Alt + A key** to deselect the Armature Rig.

Select the **Mesh figure (Chibi)** then **Shift** select the **Armature Rig** (RMB click the Figure, hold Shift, RMB click on the Armature protruding from the Head). With the mouse cursor in the 3D View Editor press **Ctrl + P key** to display the **Set Parent To** menu and select the **With Automatic Weights** option.

Go into **Pose mode** and select and rotate individual Bones to pose the figure (Figure 20.42 - Bones **Lower_Arm_L** and **Upper_Arm_L** are rotated).

20.26 Vertex Groups

When you employ the automatic Mesh Assignment two things happen:

An Armature Modifier is added to the Mesh (Figure 20.83).

Figure 20.83

Vertex Groups are created in the Mesh and assigned to each Bone in the Armature.

With the mesh selected in **Object Mode** go to the **Properties Editor, Data buttons, Vertex Groups tab** and you will see the **Vertex Groups** (Figure 20.84 - There is a scroll bar at the RHS of the Vertex Group panel or expand the panel).

The Vertex Groups may be used for correcting incorrect Mesh Deformation. This is accomplished by selecting a **Vertex Group** and employing the **Weight Paint Tool** to clean up the connections between the Mesh and the Vertex Groups (refer to the section on Weight Painting).

> **Note:** After posing in **Pose mode,** Bones will be returned to their original positions (Reset), individually by selecting each bone or collectivly by selecting all Bones and pressing **Alt + R key** (Reset rotation) and **Alt + G key** (Reset Location - Resets Grab).

In a complicated Rig, as well as incorrect Mesh assignment, there may be Parenting issues which require addressing. Detailed tutorials provide instruction for correcting such issues but at this stage just be aware that automatic processes do not always provide perfect results.

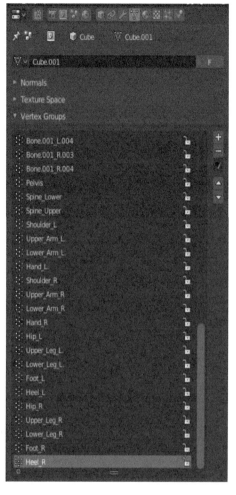

Figure 20.84

20.27 Posing the Character Model

Posing a Model may be simply to give a character attitude when creating a still image but is mainly employed to create Keyframes in an animation sequence (see Chapter 18-18.6).

Even with a relatively simple Character Rig, posing individual Bones to create **Keyframes** can be a tedious process. There are semi automated procedures which can be set up such as using an **Inverse Kinematics Constraint** (see 20.10) with a Hand or Foot such that when either is moved the Arms or Legs follow.

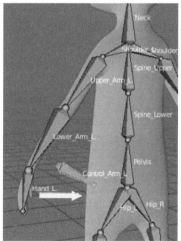

Figure 20.85

In Figure 20.85 a Control Bone has been extruded from the Tip of Lower_Arm_L. The Parenting has been cleared and the Control Bone moved aside in Edit Mode.

Figures 20.86 and 20.87 (over) show an Inverse Kinematic Constraint applied to Lower_Arm_L. The Target in the Constraint is set as Armature with Bone set to Control_Arm_L.

Control_Arm_L has been renamed in the Outliner Editor.

The Chain Length in the Constraint is 2 making the Constraint effective only to Lower_Arm_L and Upper_Arm_l

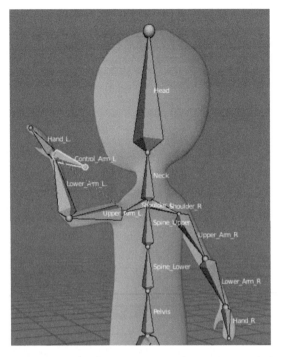

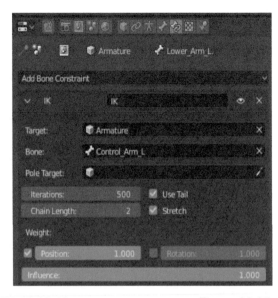

Figure 20.86　　　　　　　　Figure 20.87

Lowe_Arm_L displays olive green indicating that a constraint has been applied.

Selecting the Control Bone, Control_Arm_L in Pose Mode and Translating allows the left arm to be Posed. Control Bones would be generated for the right arm and the legs in the same maner and in fact for any portion of the Armature you wish to Pose.

Figure 20.88

Plane

Control Bones may be displayed as different individual shapes to distinguish from the Bones in the Armature. In the 3D View Editor, create a shape from one of Blenders Primitives. Figure 20.88 shows a Plane Object reshaped. Park the Object to one side in the Scene.

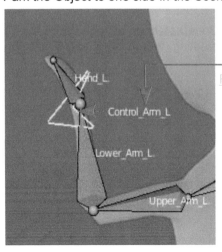

Figure 20.89

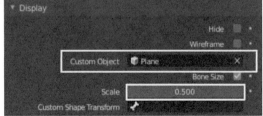

Select the Control Bone in Pose Mode and in the Properties Editor, Display Tab enter the name of the new Object in the Custom Object panel. Adjust the Scale.

At the beginning of the chapter it was emphasised that the instructions were to be an introduction to Character Rigging only. The forgoing is intended to get you started and encourage you to research detailed tutorials. The following images depict how a Character Rig may be developed to provide detailed control of Posing.

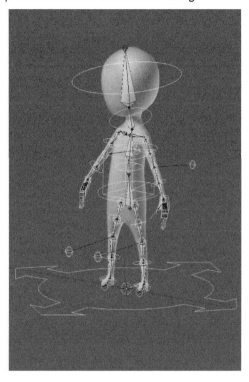

Figure 20.50 shows Chibi with a myriad of Control Bones which are more precisely named Control Handles. Each handle allows Posing of separate parts of the Character Mesh.

The large Control Handle at the Base of the Character is developed from the Root_Bone and is used for moving the entire Rig in the Scene.

Using Control Handles the Character Figure is Posed at Frames in an animation creating Keyframes. This produces a Walk Cycle.

Figure 20.90

Walk Cycle

Animating the Base Control Handle to follow a Path creates the illusion of the Character walking in the Scene.

Armatures may be generated to include intricate detail such as Chibi's hands. Again, Control Handles can be created to manipulate fingers and thumbs.

Figure 20.91

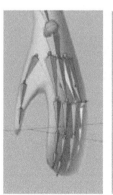 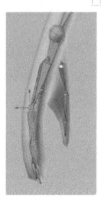

Hand Bones inside the Mesh

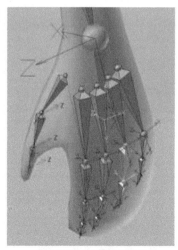

Bone Axis Displayed

20.28 Pre_Assembled Armatures

To save you time Blender has several pre-assembled armatures hidden in the Preferences Editor in the Add-ons Tab named **Rigging; Rigify**.

Figure 20.92

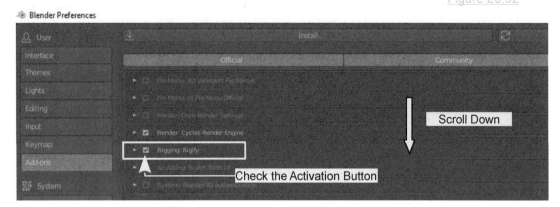

With the **Rigging: Rigify** Add-on activated, with the 3D View Cursor in the 3D View Editor, Press Shift + A Key and select **Armature** in the Add Menu.

In the Sub Menu select Animals to display a selection menu.

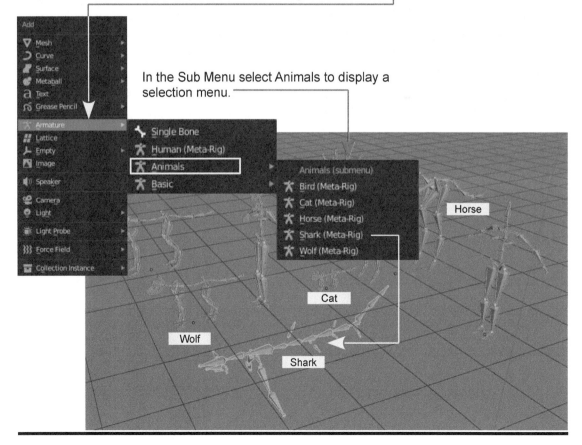

Shape Keys & Action Editors

The **Shape Key** and **Action Editors** provide a method of quickly controlling the shape of an Object or the pose of a character when setting the Keyframes in an Animation Timeline. Armature Control Handles allow the posing of the character as a whole but when detail is animated, such as facial expression or finger movement, a more refined control is desirable.

If you think about an Object or a character model and all the Vertices contained in its mesh surface you will realise the impossibility of individually manipulating Vertices between the Frames of an Animation.

The **Shape Key** and **Action Editor** allow you to create **Slider Controls** for manipulating shapes or poses and setting **Animation Keyframes.**

The **Shape Key Editor** controls the manipulation of Vertices or groups of Vertices, while the **Action Editor** allows you to set up an animation of an Object's movement and scale.

21.1 Shape Key Editor

The **Shape Key Editor** allows you to control the manipulation of Vertices or groups of Vertices.

The Shapes Key Editor is located in the **Dope Sheet Editor**.

To demonstrate, start with the default Blender Scene, delete the Cube, and add a simple Plane Object which contains four Vertices. Place the Scene in **Top Orthographic View** and zoom in.

Below the 3D View Editor is the **Timeline Editor**. Change the Timeline to the **Dope Sheet Editor**.

In the Dope Sheet Editor, click on the drop down in the Header where you see **Dope Sheet** and select **Shape Key Editor**.

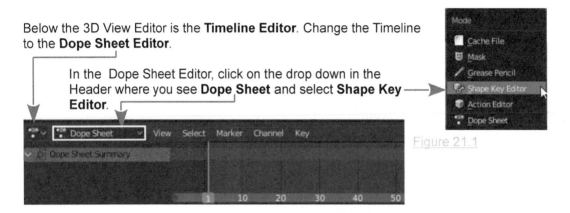

Figure 21.1

With the **Shapes Key Editor** selected, the Editor has become a simple Animation Timeline (Figure 21.2) with **Frame** numbers in the horizontal bar at the bottom of the Editor. There is also a vertical blue (green) line in the Editor which is the **Timeline Cursor**.

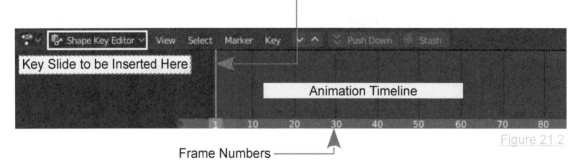

Figure 21.2

Key Sliders will be added in the Shape Key Editor which will allow you to control the shape of an Object in the 3D View Editor. The movement of the Object's Vertices will be set within minimum and maximum limits. By moving the Vertices, via the Key Sliders, to different positions within the limits, at different Frames of the Animation Timeline you create an animation of the change in shape of the Object.

21.2 Add a Key Slider

Select the Plane in the 3D View Editor. In the **Properties Editor, Data buttons, Shape Keys Tab** click on the **Plus sign** (Figure 21.3).

Properties Editor

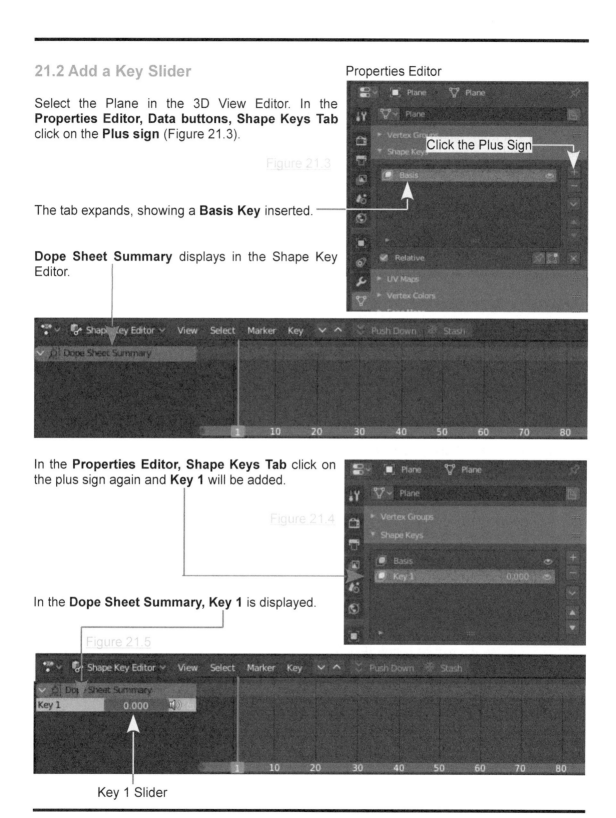

Click the Plus Sign

The tab expands, showing a **Basis Key** inserted.

Dope Sheet Summary displays in the Shape Key Editor.

In the **Properties Editor, Shape Keys Tab** click on the plus sign again and **Key 1** will be added.

In the **Dope Sheet Summary, Key 1** is displayed.

Key 1 Slider

21.3 Set Limits of Movement Figure 21.6

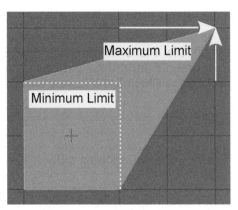

With the Mouse Cursor in the 3D View Editor, in Top Orthographic View, **Tab to Edit Mode**. Deselect the Plane (Alt + A Key). Select a Vertex and drag it (press the G Key and drag the Mouse) to where you want it to move to (maximum movement Limit - Figure 21.6). Tab back to **Object Mode.** The Vertex reverts to its original position. Moving the vertex in Edit Mode has **set the limits** for the movement.

In Object Mode drag the **Key 1 Slider all the way to the right** (0.000 – 1.000) then return to 0.000. The Plane changes shape in the 3D View Editor,

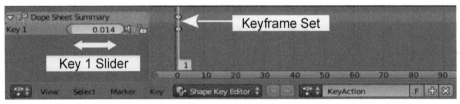

Figure 21.7

21.4 Inserting Keyframes

Dragging the slider in the Shape Key Editor and returning it to 0.000 automatically sets a **Keyframe** in the **Timeline**. The Keyframe is placed at the location of the Timeline Cursor (the blue line at Frame 1) and displays as little orange diamonds (Figure 21.7).

> **Note:** Dragging the slider moves the selected Vertex only within the limits that were set. The slider value is from 0.000 to 1.000, that is from the initial position to the maximum limit of the movement.

Inserting a Second Keyframe

To insert a second Keyframe move the blue line **Cursor** in the **Shapes Key Editor** to another Frame (Frame 50). Move Key 1 Slider until the Vertex in the 3D View Editor is where you want it (0.759). Release the mouse button (Figure 22.8). Leave the Slider at the chosen value of the second Keyframe. Return the blue line Cursor to Frame 1.

When you drag the blue line Cursor, the shape of the Plane in the 3D window changes with the corner (Vertex) moving from its initial rest position to where you positioned it at Frame 50.

Maybe you didn't get the position of the Vertex exactly where you intended. Dragging the Key Slider is a bit touchy when you want an exact location.

To delete a Keyframe and start over, place the blue Cursor in the Shape Key Editor at the Frame in the Timeline where you want to remove Keyframes. **RMB click on Relative Value bar** in the **Properties Editor, Data buttons, Shape Keys Tab** and select **Delete Keyframe**.

Note: The relative Value Bar replicates the Key 1 Slider.

Add a New Keyframe

You may add a new Keyframe by moving the Key 1 slider again. If you want an exact value double click the slider and type in a value.

Figure 21.8

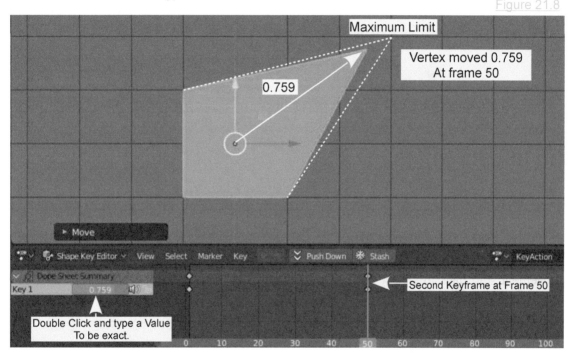

21.5 Inserting Multiple Keyframes

After placing a Keyframe you do not have to return the Timeline Cursor to frame 1. Move it to another Frame. Move the Key 1 Slider. Another Keyframe is added. Repeat the process for multiple Keyframes (Figure 21.9).

Figure 21.9

21.6 The Animation

To this point Keyframes have been added in the **Shape Key Editor Timeline**. You may scrub the Timeline (drag the blue line Cursor) to see the shape change in the 3D View Editor. To see an animation play open the **Timeline Editor** and press the **Play** button (Figure 21.10).

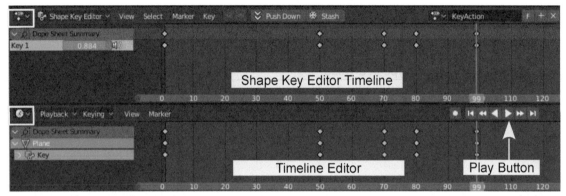

Figure 21.10

21.7 Additional Keys

Additional Keys are added in the Dope Sheet Summary for Animating other parts of the Mesh (other Vertices).

Move the cursor in the **Shapes Key Editor Timeline** to Frame 1. In the **Properties Editor, Data buttons, Shape Key Tab**, click on the plus sign again to add **Key 2** (Figure 21.5). In the 3D View Editor, Tab to Edit Mode, select a different Vertex, and move it somewhere to set the limit of movement. Tab back to Object Mode and you'll see that Key 2 has been added to the Dope Sheet Summary (Figure 21.11). Repeat the Keyframing process using Key 2 for the new Vertex.

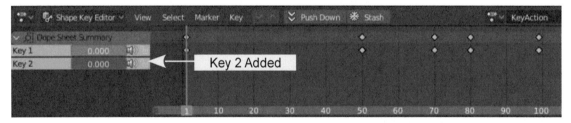

Figure 21.11

After inserting Keyframes for the new Vertex controlled by Key 2, scrubbing the Timeline Editor Cursor or playing the Animation will show both Vertices moving as the animation plays.

21.8 Action Editor

Figure 21.12

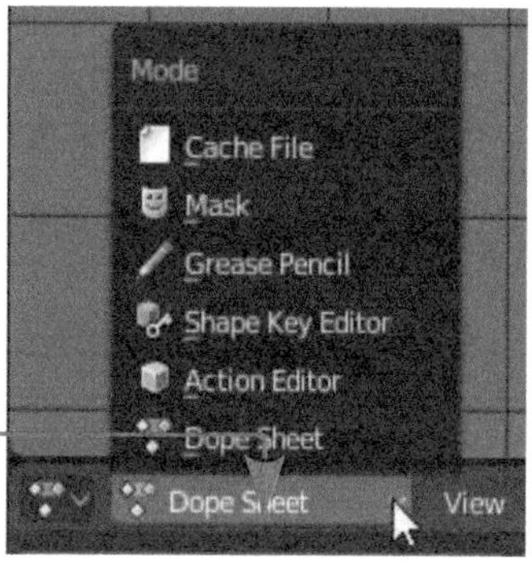

From the default Screen arrangement with the 3D View Editor and the Timeline Editor at the bottom of the Screen, change the Timeline Editor to the Dope Sheet Editor. To demonstrate the Action Editor change the Dope Sheet Editor to the **Action Editor** (Figure 21.12).

Select Action Editor ————

In the **3D View Editor** select the default **Cube**. With the Mouse Cursor in the 3D View Editor press the I Key and select **LocRotScale**. This inserts a **Keyframe at Frame 1** and enters **a Dope Sheet Summary** in the **Action Editor** with an **Object Transforms** summary. Click on the chevron preceding **Object Transforms** to display the Keyframe entries for **X,Y and Z, Location Rotation and Scale.**(Figure 21.13).

Figure 21.13

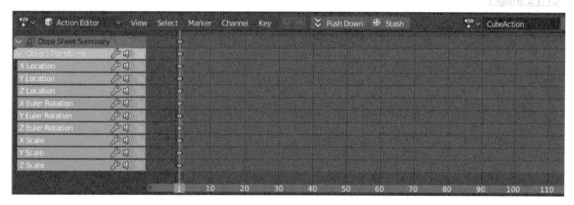

In the **Action Editor Header**, click on **View** and check (tick) **Show Sliders**; sliders display for each Keyframe component (Figure 21.14).

Figure 21.14

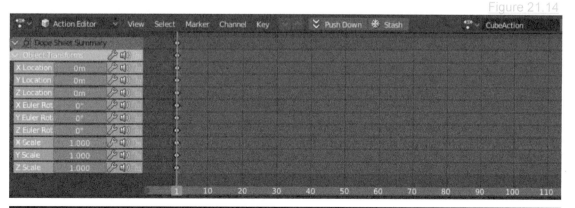

By repositioning the Cursor (blue line) in the Action Editor to a new Frame and moving the Sliders, you manipulate the Cube in the 3D View Editor (Figure 21.15). After moving the Slider, **RMB click** on the new value and select **Replace Keyframe**. When the Cursor is repositioned at a different Frame and slider values are changed, Keyframes are inserted, which produces an animation.

Figure 21.15

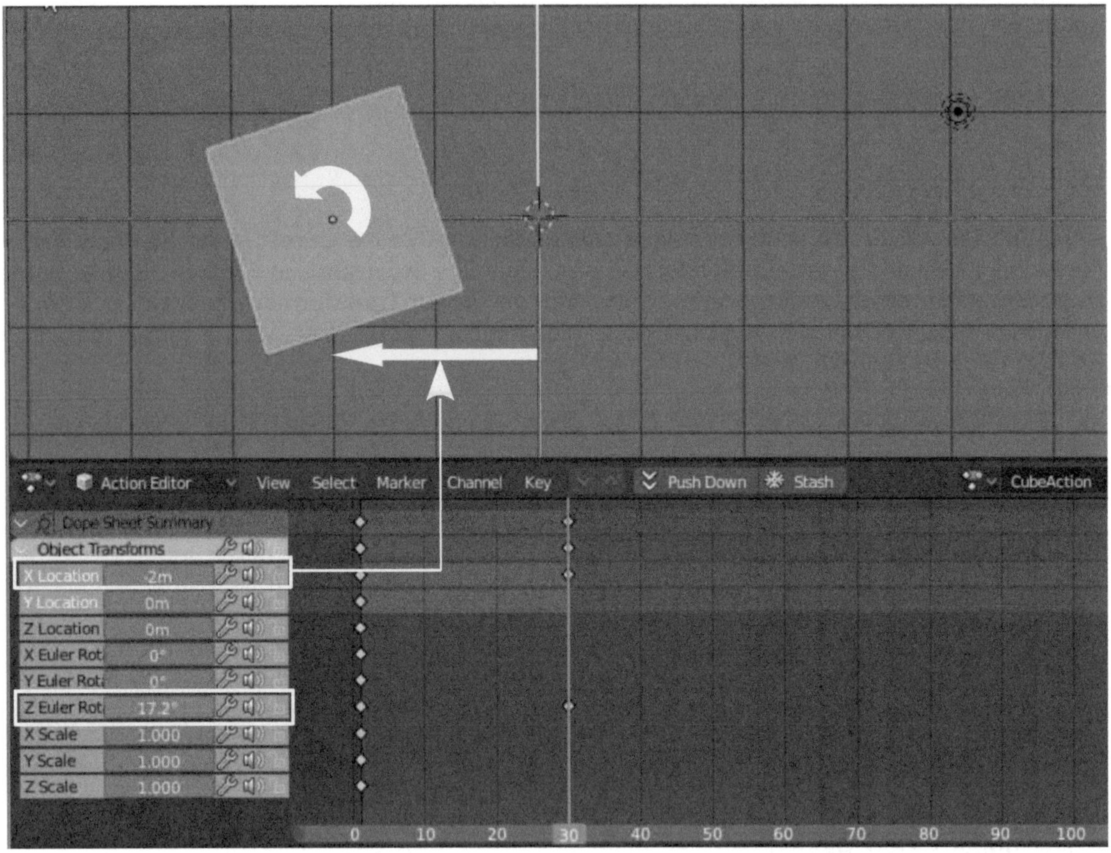

21.9 Shape Keys and Action Editor in Practice

The forgoing examples show you the fundamentals of the tools but they are not very exciting and you could be left wondering what to do with them in some practical application. To expand on the topics perform the following exercise:

Figure 21.16

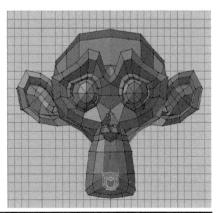

In a new Blender Scene delete the **Cube** and add a **Monkey Object**. Place the Scene in **Front Orthographic view** and zoom in to fill the 3D View Editor with Suzanne's head. **Tab to Edit Mode** and select the Vertices in the face as shown in Figure 21.16.

Change the Timeline Editor to the Dope Sheet Editor then to the **Shape Key Editor**. In the 3D View Editor position Monkey to have the mouth visible (Figure 21.16 -17).

Tab to Object mode.

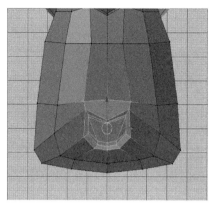
Figure 21.17

In the **Properties Editor, Data buttons, Shape Key tab** click on the plus sign to add a **Basis Key** which places a Dope Sheet Summary in the Dope Sheet, Shape Key Editor. Click the plus sign again to insert **Key 1**.

You are about to make Suzanne speak.

In the **3D View Editor** change to **Right Orthographic View** . Tab to **Edit Mode**. Use the widget and move the selected Vertices to the left making Suzanne's lips protrude slightly (Figure 21.18). Change to **Front Orthographic View** . Scale the selected Vertices up on the Z Axis and a little bit on the X Axis (Figure 21.19). Using the widget move the Vertices up. **Tab to Object Mode**. The Vertices revert to their original location.

Figure 21.18

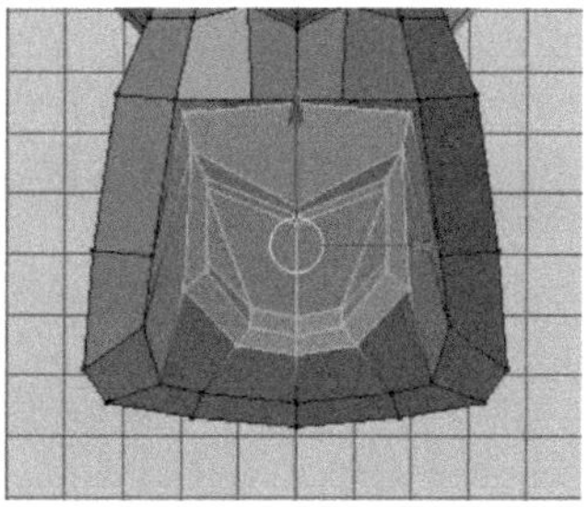

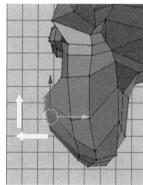

Figure 21.19

In performing the scaling and location operations you have set the limits of movement for Key 1 for each of the Vertices that were selected.

Move the Key 1 Slider and see Suzanne's mouth move. Remember, moving the Slider inserts a Keyframe at the Frame number in the Animation Timeline where the Timeline Cursor is positioned (Frame 1) (Figure 21.20). If you don't want Suzanne to start laughing at the start of the animation move the cursor down the track in the Timeline. Also remember that by default Blender has a 250 Frame animation set in the Timeline. If you place the Shape Key Editor Cursor beyond this it will have no effect unless you change the End Frame value in the Timeline Editor Header.

Place a series of Keyframes in the animation. Move the Cursor to Frame 10 and move the Key slider leaving it in position. This inserts a Keyframe at frame 10. Move the Cursor to frame 20 – move the slider. Move the Cursor to frame 30 – move the slider etc. (Figure 21.20). Go back to Frame 1 and play the animation. Monkey's mouth moves as the animation plays.

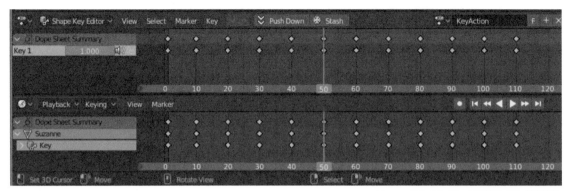

Figure 21.20

Change the Shape Key Editor to **Action Editor mode**. Zoom out on the 3D View Editor. With the Cursor at Frame 1, Press I Key and select LocRotScale to place action Keyframes (Figure 21.21). Move the Cursor to Frame 50 to coincide with the **Shape Key** animation and move the **Z Euler Rotation slider to 45 degrees** (Rotation in Blender is measured in Euler units). RMB click the Z Eular Rotation value and select Replace Keyframe.

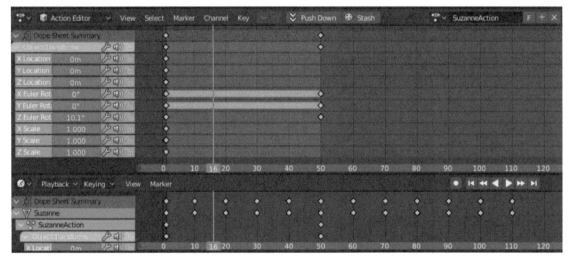

Figure 21.21

Place the 3D View Editor in Camera View and play the animation. Suzanne's mouth moves while turning to face the Camera.

This has been a very simple practical demonstration so use your imagination and experiment, experiment, experiment!

22

Particle Systems

Particle Systems are used to simulate large amounts of static or moving Objects, creating effects like fire, dust, clouds and smoke and for creating hair, fur, grass and other strand based Objects. Particles can be made to display as other Objects which means they can display as Models of Characters. For example, like an army of solders or a swarm of insects.

In Blender **Particles**, by default, appear as points or small circles on the computer screen, being emitted from an Object. To Emit Particles from an Object a **Particle System** is assigned (added) to the Object then an animation sequence is run.

Adding a Particle System to an Object creates a system with default settings which is ready to run by itself. To create Particle effects you modify the settings.

The best way to see how this is accomplished is to follow a few simple instructions and run the Particle System.

Before setting up a system, recap on the Screen arrangement, and in particular the **Properties Editor** which contains the controls for manipulating the display in the **3D View Editor**.

You also need to know how to play an animation in the **Timeline Editor**.

22.1 The Default Particle System

To set up a default **Particle System** open a new Scene in Blender. Delete the default Cube Object and add a **UV Sphere**.

Particles are emitted from the Vertices, the Faces or from the Volume of a mesh. Using a UV Sphere provides a reasonable number of Vertices and Faces from which to emit the Particles. Leave the default values for the Sphere as they appear in the Properties Editor. With the UV Sphere selected, go to the **Properties Editor, Particles buttons**. Click on **New** to add a Particle System (Figure 22.1).

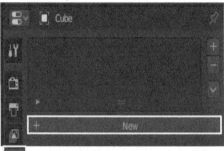

Figure 22.1

Properties Editor, Particle buttons

The **Particles buttons** open displaying the **Tabs** (panels)   that control the system. Blender has automatically created a default Particle System for the UV Sphere (Figure 22.2).

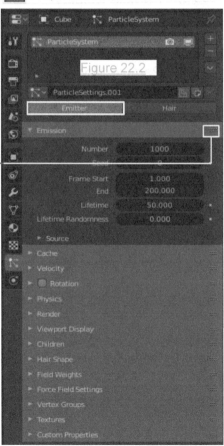

Figure 22.2

Note:
When a Particle System is created it is unique to the selected Object in the 3D View Editor.

The arrangement of the **Tabs** (panels) in the **Properties Editor** is purely a matter of convenience. There is no order of priority. The Properties Editor is arranged at the RHS of the Screen with the Tabs in a vertical stack. The Tabs (panels) may be moved up or down by clicking and dragging the dimpled area in the upper RH corner of each Tab.

Particles only display in the 3D View Editor when an animation sequence is run by activating Play in the Timeline Editor or scrubbing (dragging) the Timeline cursor (vertical blue line) to a Frame in the animation.

The default Particles display as small white circles.

Note the **Type: Emitter** under **Particle Settings.**

Figure 22.3

Clicking on the panel where the word **Emitter** is displayed will open a menu with two selection options, **Emitter** and **Hair** (Figure 22.3). Type: Hair is a unique system which will be discussed later in this chapter.

To see the default **Particle System** in action, with the Mouse Cursor in the 3D View Editor, press the **Play button** in the **Timeline Editor.** This runs an animation showing Particles being generated (Figure 22.4).

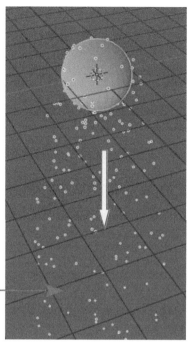

Figure 22.4

Note: The Timeline Editor is displayed across the bottom of the Screen (Figure 22.5). The blue line (Timeline Cursor) moves as the animation plays. With the Emitter Object selected (the UV Sphere), the animation will play showing Particles as small white circles being emitted and falling towards the bottom of the Screen.

The animation plays for 250 frames then repeats. Press **Esc** to stop the animation. Advance the animation to Frame 63 by pressing the right arrows on the Keyboard (**with the Mouse Cursor in the Timeline Editor**) or by clicking RMB, holding and dragging the blue line Cursor in the Timeline Editor or by RMB clicking on frame 63 in the Timeline Editor. The Particles will be displayed as they occur at Frame 63.

Timeline Editor Cursor

Figure 22.5

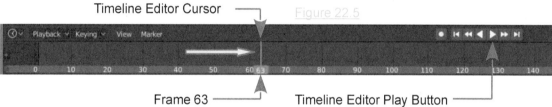

Frame 63

Timeline Editor Play Button

The example has demonstrated a simple Particle System being applied. The Particles emitted from the Sphere cascade down; this occurred since there is a **gravitational effect** applied (see the Scene buttons in the Properties Editor).

In the **Properties Editor, Scene buttons, Gravity Tab,** click on the tick next to **Gravity** (removes the tick) to remove the gravitational effect.

Set the animation in the Timeline Editor back to Frame 1 and replay the animation.

Figure 22.6

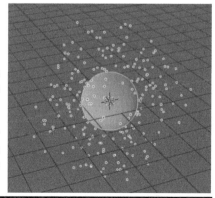

Replaying the animation shows Particles Emitted from the UV Sphere disperse in all directions away from the Sphere (Figure 22.6).

Note: The Particles move for a certain time and disappear before the end of the animation. The time that the Particles display is set in the **Particles buttons, Emission Tab (Lifetime).**

22.2 The Emissions Tab

Figure 22.7

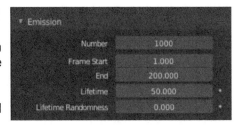

You control the Particle display in the 3D View Editor in the Emissions Tab by adjusting values as follows (Figure 22.7).

Number: The total number of Particles to be Emitted over the length of the animation.

Frame Start: The Frame number in the animation to start emitting.

End: The Frame number to stop Emitting Particles.

Lifetime: The number of Frames in the animation that Particles, **which have been Emitted**, will display for.

Lifetime Randomness: Gives **Lifetime** a random variation.

With the default settings 1000 Particles will be emitted over the length of the animation. The default animation length is 250 Frames (see the Timeline Editor). The Particles will begin Emitting at Frame 1 and end at Frame 200. The Particles display for a Lifetime of 50 Frames, therefore, the last Particle to be emitted (at Frame 200) displays for 50 frames, that is, to the end of the animation.

22.3 The Source Tab

Figure 22.8

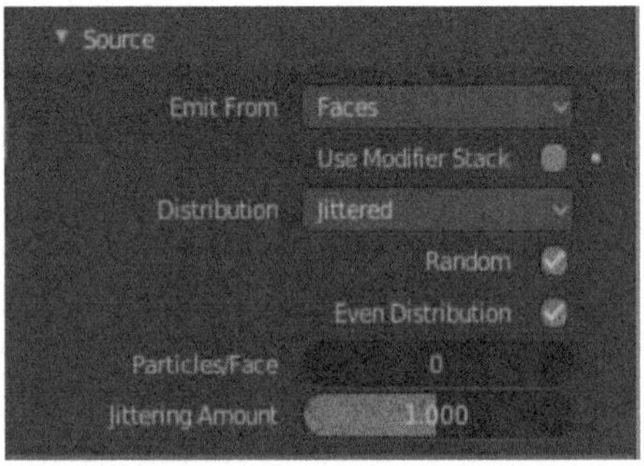

Emit From: Faces. The Particles Emit from the Faces of the Object's **Mesh**. The alternatives are from the **Verts** (Vertices) or from **Volume** (the body of the mesh). See 22.7.

The remainder of the settings in the Source Tab govern the order in which Particles are emitted (see 22.8).

22.4 The Cache Tab

Figure 22.9

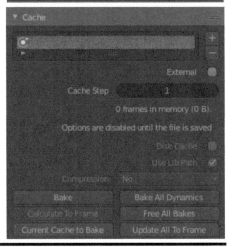

When a Particle System is played for the first time in the default Blender Scene the computer calculates the information required to display each Frame in the simulation (animation) and stores it in RAM (memory).

When the simulation is played a second time the computer recalculates the information with any changes made to the settings and again stores the information in RAM. If the Blender file is closed without being saved the information is lost.

With a complicated Particle Simulation, writing data to RAM can use a considerable amount of memory which in turn can influence the performance of the computer. It is, therefore, advisable to save the Blender file as early as possible. With the file saved you have the option to save the simulation to a Cache which frees up memory.

Note the statement in the **Cache Tab: Options are disabled until the file is saved**. This is basically saying you you can't save to the Cache until you have saved the Blender file. With the file saved check **Disk Cache** which will save the data to the Cache using the Library (Lib) Path.

Playing the simulation with Disk Cache checked creates a **blendcache_Cache** file and places it in the same directory as the .blend file. When Disk Cache is checked after saving the file you will see a red line at the bottom of the Timeline Editor indicating the data that has been saved. Playing the simulation with the default settings creates a solid line since data is recorded for each Frame of the default 250 Frames. In the directory where the Blender file is saved you will find the blendcache_Cache folder containing 250 BPHYS files. Figure 22.10

| blendcache_Cache | 14/10/2018 4:49 PM | File folder | |
| Cache.blend | 14/10/2018 4:47 PM | Blender File | 656 KB |

Name	Date modified	Type	Size
537068657265_000002_00.bphys	14/10/2018 4:49 PM	BPHYS File	1 KB
537068657265_000003_00.bphys	14/10/2018 4:49 PM	BPHYS File	1 KB
537068657265_000004_00.bphys	14/10/2018 4:49 PM	BPHYS File	1 KB
537068657265_000005_00.bphys	14/10/2018 4:49 PM	BPHYS File	1 KB
537068657265_000006_00.bphys	14/10/2018 4:49 PM	BPHYS File	1 KB
537068657265_000007_00.bphys	14/10/2018 4:49 PM	BPHYS File	2 KB
537068657265_000008_00.bphys	14/10/2018 4:49 PM	BPHYS File	2 KB
537068657265_000009_00.bphys	14/10/2018 4:49 PM	BPHYS File	2 KB
537068657265_000010_00.bphys	14/10/2018 4:49 PM	BPHYS File	2 KB
537068657265_000011_00.bphys	14/10/2018 4:49 PM	BPHYS File	2 KB
537068657265_000013_00.bphys	14/10/2018 4:49 PM	BPHYS File	2 KB
537068657265_000014_00.bphys	14/10/2018 4:49 PM	BPHYS File	2 KB
537068657265_000015_00.bphys	14/10/2018 4:49 PM	BPHYS File	3 KB
537068657265_000016_00.bphys	14/10/2018 4:49 PM	BPHYS File	3 KB
537068657265_000017_00.bphys	14/10/2018 4:49 PM	BPHYS File	3 KB
537068657265_000018_00.bphys	14/10/2018 4:49 PM	BPHYS File	3 KB
537068657265_000019_00.bphys	14/10/2018 4:49 PM	BPHYS File	3 KB
537068657265_000020_00.bphys	14/10/2018 4:49 PM	BPHYS File	3 KB
537068657265_000021_00.bphys	14/10/2018 4:49 PM	BPHYS File	3 KB
537068657265_000022_00.bphys	14/10/2018 4:49 PM	BPHYS File	4 KB

250 BPHYS Data Files, one for each Frame in the Simulation

Timeline Editor – Red Line indicates files saved.   Figure 22.11

With the default simulation (250 Frames) there are 250 BPHYS Files. The longer the simulation the more files are created. To save space in the Cache when you have a lengthy simulation you may elect to only save data for some of the Frames. To do this increase the Cache Steps value. Increasing the value to 10 means every tenth frame is recorded, therefore, the number of BPHYS files in the Cache for the default 250 frame simulation would be 26 (25 divisions – Frame at each end). Increasing the Cache Steps saves space on the Hard Drive at the expense of a lesser quality in the simulation.

22.5 The Velocity Tab

Figure 22.12

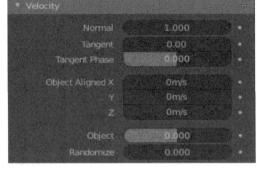

The settings in the **Velocity Tab** control the direction and speed of the Particle Emission (Figure 22.12).

Normal: Gives the Particles an initial Velocity normal (at right angles to) the point of origin.

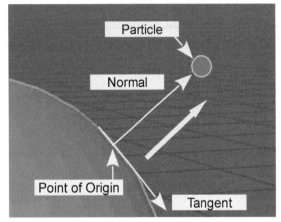

Object Alignment: Controls the Emission direction between Normal and Tangent.

Figure 22.13

The Particle is being emitted from the point of origin on the Face, normal to the Face (at right angles to the Face).

Tangent: Parallel to the Face.

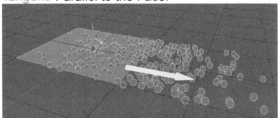

Normal: 0.000 – X: 1.000

Figure 22.14

Note: Gravity has been turned off in the Scene buttons.

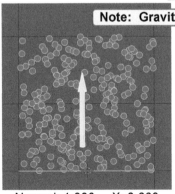

Normal: 1.000 – X: 0.000

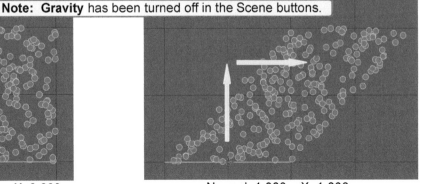

Normal: 1.000 – X: 1.000

Figure 22.14 shows Particles being emitted from the single Face of the Plane Object. By changing Face to **Verts** (vertices) in the **Source Tab**, with the default values (Normal: 1.000 – X: 0.000) the Particles are emitted from the four **Vertices** of the Plane, normal to the face of the Plane (Figure 22.15).

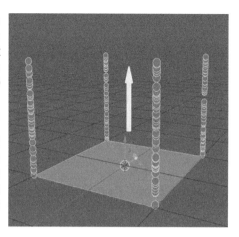

Figure 22.15

At this point you have just enough information to control the Emission of Particles but they are just Particles, little white circles, and not particularly interesting. The circles represent positions on the computer Screen for the display of other Objects with the objective being, to create visual displays.

22.6 Particle Display

A Particle will display as an Object which has been added to a Scene.

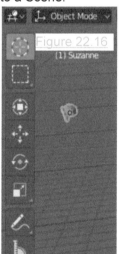

Figure 22.16
(1) Suzanne

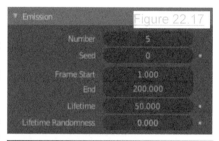

Figure 22.17

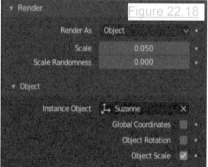

Figure 22.18

To demonstrate; have a Plain Object and a Monkey Object in a Scene. Scale the Monkey way down and park it off to one side (Figure 22.16).

Have the Plane selected in the 3D View Editor and apply a Particle System. **Turn off Gravity in the Scene buttons.**

In the **Emission Tab** (Figure 22.17) in the Particles buttons for the Plane decrease the Number to 5 (Emit 5 Particles only) and change the End value to 10 (the 5 Particles will be Emitted in 10 Frames). In the Render Tab (Figure 22.18) change **Render As** to Object. Selecting Object introduces an Object Tab. Click where you see Instance Object and select Suzanne (Monkey).

Figure 22.19

Figure 22.20

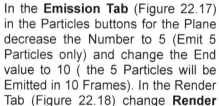

Play the animation in the Timeline Editor (you may stop at Frame 50 since the Particles will only display for 50 Frames). Position the Timeline Cursor at Frame 45 then zoom in on the Plane. If you look closely you will see five tiny Monkeys sitting above the Plane. In the Render Tab increase the Scale.

22.7 Particle Emission Options

Wireframe Display

The options for Particle Emission have been briefly mentioned when discussing the Source Tab in 22.3 and Emission from Vertices demonstrated in 22.5, Figure 22.15. To clarify the options look at the default Cube Object in the default 3D View Editor. Have the Cube displayed in **Wireframe Display Mode**. Click the button in the Header (upper RH side of Screen) (Figure 22.21).

Figure 22.21

The Particle Emission options are accessed in the Properties Editor, Particle buttons, Source Tab (Figure 22.22).

Figure 22.22

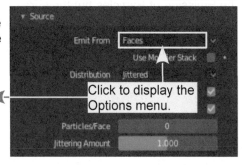

Click to display the Options menu.

Figure 22.23

Figure 22.23 shows the default Cube with the default Particle System applied at Frame 1 (One Particle Showing). The default **Emit From** value in the **Source Tab** is: **Faces** (Figure 22.22).

Wireframe Display Mode

Figure 22.24

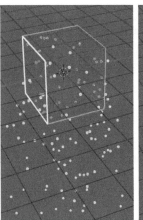

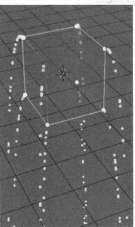

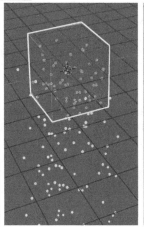

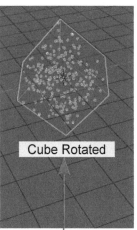

Cube Rotated

Emit From: **Faces**   Emit From: **Verts**   Emit From: **Volume**

Figure 22.24 shows particles being Emitted with the different options selected.

Emit From: Volume with Velocity Normal = 0.00 and Gravity turned off. The Particles accumulate inside the Volume of the Cube.

22.8 Order of Emission

Figure 22.25

To demonstrate the Order of Emission options, replace the default Cube in the 3D View Editor with a UV Sphere. The Sphere has significantly greater number of Vertices and Faces from which to Emit Particles.

Disable Gravity in the Scene buttons.

The Order Of Particle Emission is controlled in the Properties Editor, Particle buttons, **Emission Source Tab** (the Source Tab only displays when the Emission Tab is opened).

By default Particles are set to **Emit From: Faces** in a **Random Order** (Distribution).

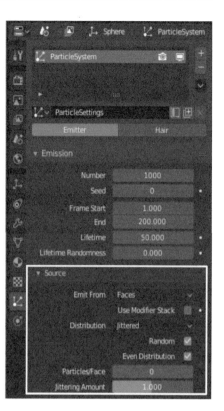

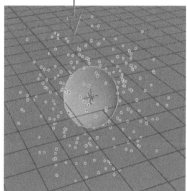

Figure 22.26

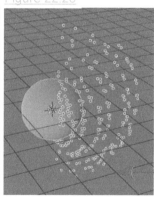

In the Source Tab **uncheck Random** and replay the animation.

The 3D View Editor, by default, is in **User Perspective View**, therefore, it is difficult to see what has been achieved by removing the Random tick. Change the view to **Top Orthographic View** (Figure 22.27) then to **Front Orthographic View** (Figure 22.28). With the Timeline Editor Cursor, advanced to Frame 50, you will see an ordered array of Particles.

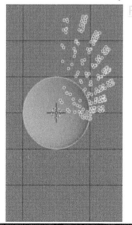

Figure 22.27

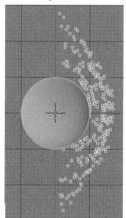

Note: In both views the Particles are being Emitted from Faces.

By changing Emit From to Verts in the Source Tab (figure 22.29) the array of Particles is even more ordered (Figure 22.30 over).

Figure 22.28

Figure 22.29

Particles Emitted from Vertices at Frame 50

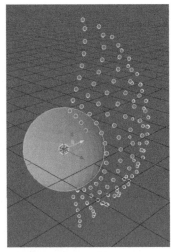 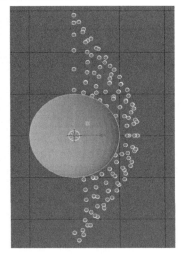 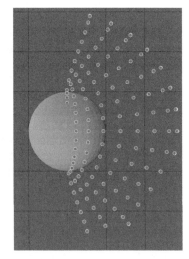

User Perspective View   Front Orthographic View   Right Orthographic View

Figure 22.30

Particles Emitted from Faces at Frame 50

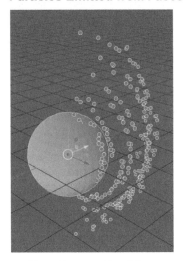 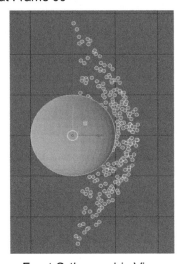 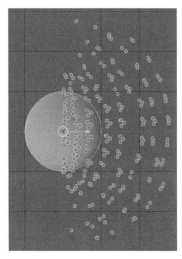

User Perspective View   Front Orthographic View   Right Orthographic View

22.9 Normals

Particle Effects may be created by using different shaped Objects as Particle Emitters and manipulating **Normal** values in the Particle buttons (see 22.5 The Velocity Tab – Normals). Understanding how to control Normals is a key factor.

Have a Plane Object in the 3D View Editor and apply a Particle System. When the animation is played in the Timeline Editor, Particles are emitted from the Face of the Plane and descend in the Scene due to the Gravitational force. In the **Velocity Tab** increase the Normal value to 5.000 and replay the animation.

You will observe that the Particles rise from the surface of the Plane before descending (Figure 22.31).

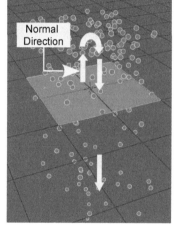

Figure 22.31

The Particles are emitted from the surface, Normal to the Face. In the default Particle System the direction of the Normal is upwards. Rotate the Plane 45° about the X Axis (R Key + X Key + 45).

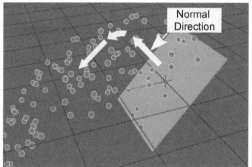

Figure 22.32

With the Plane rotated Particles continue to be emitted Normal to the Face of the Plane (Figure 22.32). The direction of the Normal is relative to the Face.

The direction of Normals for emission may be visualised in two ways:

In **Object Mode** click on **Overlays** in the Header and check **Face Orientation**. In the default Scene the upper surface of the Plane displays blue indicating the positive direction for Emission. By rotating the view you will see the underside of the Plane is displayed red (negative) (Figure 22.33). Bear in mind that you can enter positive and negative values in the Velocity Tab which change the direction of Emission. This does not change the color display on the surface.

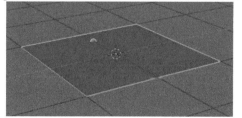

Top Side - Positive   Figure 22.33   Bottom Side - Negative

In **Edit Mode Overlays** (at the bottom of the panel) you will find **Normals** (Figure 22.34).

3D View Editor – Edit Mode

Figure 22.34

Overlays Panel

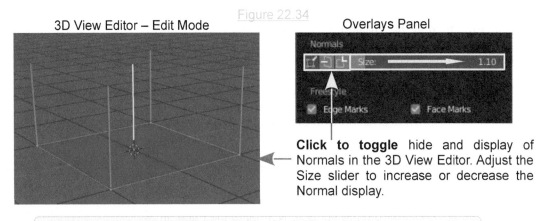

Click to toggle hide and display of Normals in the 3D View Editor. Adjust the Size slider to increase or decrease the Normal display.

Note: Adjusting the Size value does not change the Velocity for emission.

Knowing how Particles will be Emitted from an Object allows you to set up a Particle Display.

As an example, construct a flat disk Object as shown in Figure 22.35 by selecting a Circle Object in Edit Mode. Press the E Key (Extrude – DO NOT Move the Mouse). The Vertices are duplicated. Scale the duplicated Vertices in.

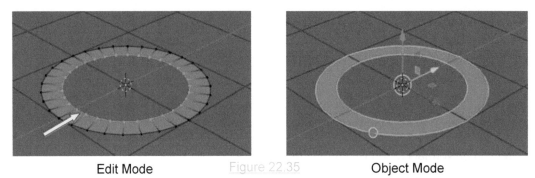

Edit Mode

Figure 22.35

Object Mode

Turn off **Gravity** in the **Properties Editor, Scene buttons, Gravity tab**.

With the Disk Object selected in the 3D View Editor, in Object Mode, add a **Particle System** leaving the default values in place. Play the animation in the Timeline Editor.

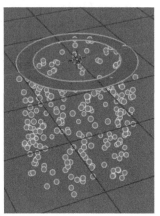

Particles will be Emitted from the Faces of the Disk and **fall** towards the bottom of the Screen despite Gravity being turned off. (Figure 22.36).

Figure 22.36

Particles are Emitted with a default starting velocity of **Normal = 1**. The velocity value is seen in the **Particle buttons, Velocity Tab**.

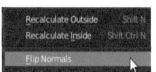

By turning on Normal visualisation as previously described you can see that the Normal direction is down, hence the descent (Figure 22.38).

You may quickly change direction in the Edit Mode Screen Header, Mesh Button by selecting **Normals, Flip Normals** (Figure 22.37).

Figure 22.37

Figure 22.38

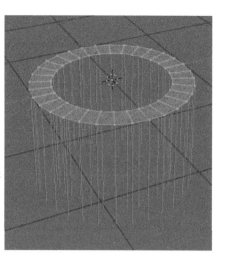

An example of creating a Particle Effect is as follows:

With the disk as shown in Figure 22.39, flip the Normals into the upward direction. In Object Mode change the Emit From: Faces to Verts in the Source Tab. Change the Lifetime value in the Emission Tab to 200.

When the animation is replayed the Particles are Emitted progressively around the disk from the mesh Vertices and rise up forming a spiral configuration (Figure 22.39). The Particles are grouped in short columns.

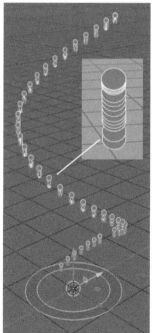

Figure 22.39

In the Velocity tab make the Emitter Geometry, **Normal: 0.000** and the **Emitter Object Y: 1.000**.

When the animation is replayed the Particles spiral on the Y Axis in the Scene (Figure 22.40).

Up to this point Particles have been displayed in the 3D View Editor as little white circles in Object mode.

Figure 22.40

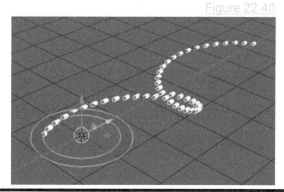

22.10 Particle Modifiers

In the Modifier selection menu you will find the **Particle System Modifier** and the **Particle Instance Modifier**. Having gained a little knowledge in respect to the Particle System it is appropriate to mention these two Modifiers.

Particle System Modifier

Adding a **Particle System Modifier** to a selected Object merely adds a default Particle System. This is the same as going to the Particle buttons and clicking the **New button**. With the Modifier added you manipulate settings to achieve the desired result.

Particle Instance Modifier

Figure 22.41

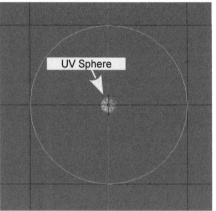

The **Particle Instance Modifier** allows you to create an array of Objects mimicking the array of Particles which are being Emitted.

To demonstrate set up a Scene in **Top Orthographic View** containing a Circle Object and a UV Sphere Object (scaled down) positioned as shown in Figure 22.41.

Turn Gravity off.

Have the Circle selected and add a Particle System with values as follows:

In the Emissions Tab:	Number: 10	
	Lifetime: 200	
In the Source Tab	Emit From: Verts	
	Uncheck Random Order	
In the Velocity tab:	Normal: 0.250	

Do not play the animation at this point.

Deselect the Circle and select the UV sphere.

In the Properties Editor, Modifier buttons, Add a **Particle Instance Modifier** and enter **Circle** as the Object (the Circle being the Object with the Particle System applied).

Figure 22.42

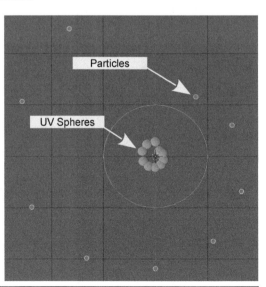

Play the animation in the Timeline window to see an array of Spheres generated in a spiral configuration mimicking the spiral of the Particles (Figure 22.42).

22.11 Particles Array

With the control of Particle Emission and the display of Particles as other Objects you can create arrays for effect when combined with the application of Materials and the addition of lighting (Lamps). The following is an example.

In the default Blender Scene delete the Cube and add a UV Sphere. The default Scene has a single Point Light. Add a second Point Light and a Sun Light and position above and spaced around the UV Sphere.

Figure 22.43

Add an Ico Sphere, set to smooth shading and scale 0.500. Park the Ico Sphere to one side of the Screen. You may hide the Ico Sphere from view by clicking the eye icon in the Collection in the Outliner Editor.

Select the UV Sphere (the Emitter Object) and add a Particle System. Increase the Emission Number to 30 000. In the Render Tab, Render as Object with the Ico Sphere as the Instance Object in the Object Tab. Deselect the UV Sphere.

Turn Gravity Off.

Add a Turbulence Force Field to the Scene (Shift + A Key – Force Field – Strength 5m) (set the Strength value in the Properties Editor, Physics buttons, Settings Tab).

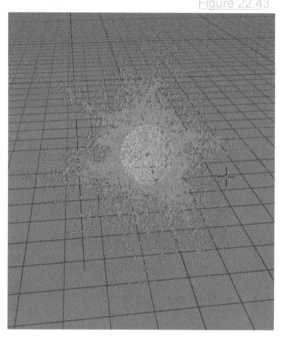

Play the animation to see the flow of Objects. Figure 22.43 shows the flow in LocDev Viewport Shading Mode with the 3d View Editor background (Gradient High/Off) color modified).

In the Particle buttons change Lifetime to 999 (forever) and the End value to 100. In the render Tab leave Scale: 0.050 but change Scale Randomness to 0.800.

Move the Timeline editor Cursor to frame 120 and rotate the Viewport to see the scatter of Ico Spheres.

Divide the 3D View Editor in two and have one in LocDev Viewport Shading Mode and the other as Rendered Viewport Shading (Figure 22.44 over).

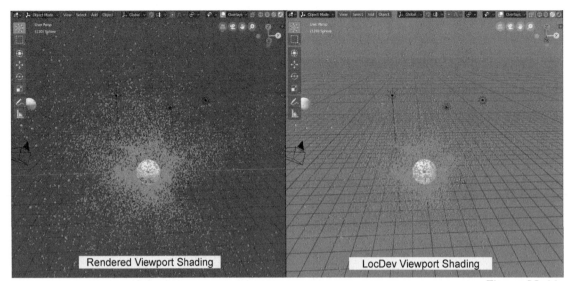

Figure 22.44

Select the UV Sphere and add a Material and set to Smooth Shading.
Select the Ico Sphere and add a Material using the Node Arrangement shown in Figure 23.45.

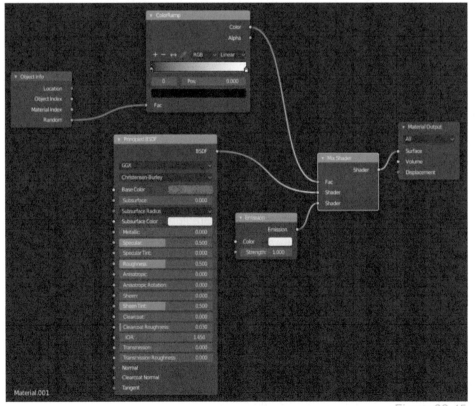

Figure 22.45

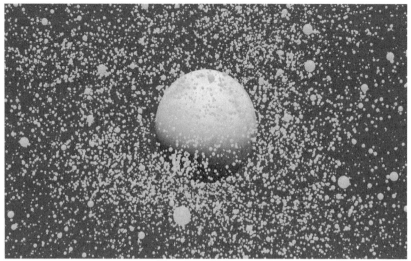

Rendered View

Figure 22.46

22.12 The Viewport Display Tab

Click for Display Options

How Particles display is controlled in the Properties Editor, Particle buttons Viewport Display Tab.

When multiple Particle Systems are in play it is advantageous to display Particles from one system differently to another. This is not to be confused with what takes place in a Rendered Image of a Scene. Particles themselves do not Render. In Figure 22.46 above, the Particles are Rendered as the Ico Sphere (the Instance Object). In the 3D View Editor the Particles display as white circles.

Figure 22.47

Cross

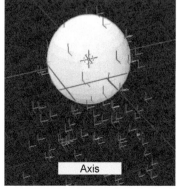

Axis

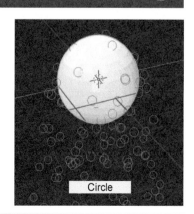

Circle

381

22.13 Particle Interaction

Figure 22.48

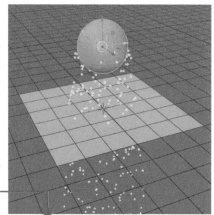

Particles can interact with other Objects and be affected by Forces like wind. Particles can bounce off other Objects and act like sparks or droplets. To show how these features work, set up a Scene with a UV Sphere positioned above a Plane as shown in Figure 22.48 (the Plane is scaled up three times).

With the UV Sphere selected, go to the **Properties Editor, Particle buttons** and add a **Particle System** (to the UV Sphere).

| Properties Editor Buttons shown Horizontal |

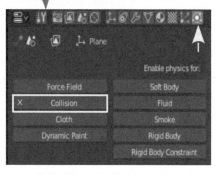

In the **Emission Tab**, set the **End** value to 100 and in the **Velocity Tab**, set the **Object Aligned: Z value** to –3.000 (Emitter Object gives the Particles a starting velocity -3 down).

Figure 22.49

In the Timeline Editor press the Play button . You will see the Particles fall and pass through the Plane (Figure 22.48).

To stop the Particles passing through the Plane, select the **Plane** and go to the **Properties Editor, Physics buttons** (Figure 22.49). Select **Collision** and replay the animation (**remember** you must be at frame 1 before you replay).

Figure 22.50

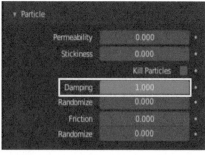

The Particles bounce up from the surface of the Plane (Figure 22.51).

By increasing the **Particle Damping: Factor** value in the **Particles Tab** to 1.000 (Figure 22.50), the Particles will land on the Plane but they will no longer bounce; they will just slide on the surface (Figure 22.51).

Figure 22.51   Figure 22.52

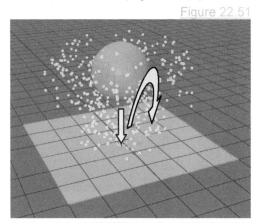

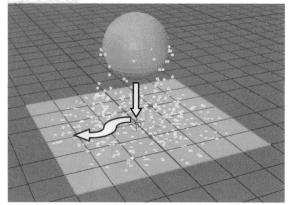

22.14 Wind Force Effect

Figure 22.53

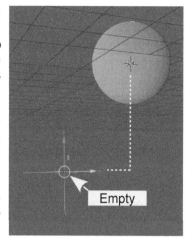

Particles can be influenced by a simulated **Wind Force**. To create a wind effect, you have to place an Object in the scene and assign a wind Force to it. The **Empty** Object is ideal for this since it doesn't render.

Set up a Scene with an Empty Object located below and off to the side (Figure 22.53). Add the default Particle System to the UV Sphere. The UV Sphere will emit Particles that will fall downwards since the Gravity box is ticked in the Scene tab.

With the **Empty** selected in the 3D View Editor, go to the **Properties Editor, Physics buttons** and click on the **Force Fields button** (Figure 22.54).

Figure 22.54

Select **Wind** from the **Type** selection menu.

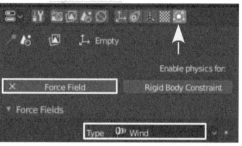

You will see the Wind Force field in the 3D View Editor attached to the Empty Object (yellow arrow) (Figure 22.55).

The Wind Force is acting along the Z Axis of the Empty Object as indicated by a yellow arrow, at a strength of 1.000 (disable the manipulation widget to see an orange arrow pointing up on the Z Axis).

You want the wind to blow the Particles falling from the Sphere along the global X Axis.

Figure 22.55

With the Empty selected, in Front Orthographic View, rotate about the Y Axis so that the Empty local Axis points in the same direction as the global X Axis.

Increase the **Strength** value to 10 and play the animation to see the Sphere's Particles being blown (Figure 22.55).

Wind strength is able to be animated, which creates a realistic wind effect.

Note: The Wind Force Strength is indicated by the displacement of the yellow and orange arrows.

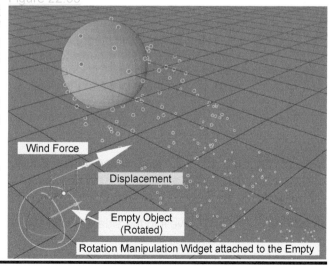

22.15 Boids Particles

Boids Particle Systems are used to simulate flocks, swarms, herds and schools of various kinds of animals or anything that acts with similar behaviour. **Boids** Particle Systems are of **Type: Emitter** with **Boids Physics** applied.

Boids Particles in one Particle System can react to Particles in another system or they can react to Particles within their own system.

Boids are given rules of behaviour, which are listed in a Stack. The rules at the top of the Stack take precedence over rules lower down, but the Stack is able to be rearranged once it is written.

Since only a certain amount of information is evaluated, if the memory capacity is exceeded, rules lower down the Stack are ignored.

The procedure for setting up **Boids Particle Systems** will be demonstrated with the following examples.

Example 1: A Flock of Birds

Since you are working with the basics, the Particles will act like a flock of birds but won't actually look like birds.

Open a new Blender Scene with the default Cube. The Cube will be the **Particle Emitter**. In the **Properties Editor, Particles buttons**, add a new Particle System. Leave all the button settings with their default values, except for the following:

- **Emission Tab**
    - Number: 300 (Have a small flock.)
    - Lifetime: 250 (The default animation length in the timeline.)
- **Physics Tab**
    - Select Physics Type:**Boids**.
- **Boid Brain Tab**
    - With **Separate** highlighted, hit the **minus** sign to delete it. Click on the **plus** sign at the RH side of the window to display a selection menu for **Boids rules** and select **Follow Leader**. Click on the up arrow below the minus sign to move Follow Leader to the top of the Stack.

You have instructed the Particles to follow the leader while flocking together. You will now give the Particles a leader to follow.

Deselect the Cube in the 3D window and add an **Empty Object.**

The Empty is a location point that can be animated to move in the Scene but does not render.

Select the Empty and move it to the side. Deselect the Empty and select the Cube.

In the **Boid Brain Tab** , make sure **Follow Leader** is highlighted.

Below the stack panel you will see the Object panel with a 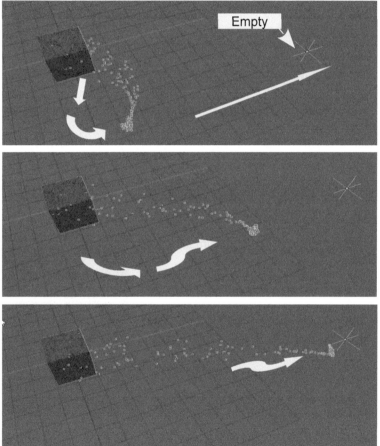 icon. Click in the panel and select **Empty** from the menu that displays.

You have instructed the Particles to follow the Empty.

Animate the Empty to move across the Screen (see Chapter 18 for a refresher on Animation. Say 12 grid spaces in 250 Frames-gives PS time to catch up).

When the animation is played Particles Emitted from the Cube, head towards the Empty, and attempt to follow it as it moves across the Screen (Figure 22.56).

Figure 22.56

Note: With a high Particle amount, Blender may crash due to overload when calculating data. This depends on the capability of your computer.

This example will demonstrate how to direct Particles to move from one object to another.

Start a new Scene and add a second Cube Object. Note that the default Cube is named **Cube** (see the upper left side of the 3D View Editor) and the new Cube is named **Cube.001**.

Position the Cubes as shown in Figure 22.57, and scaling the new Cube down.

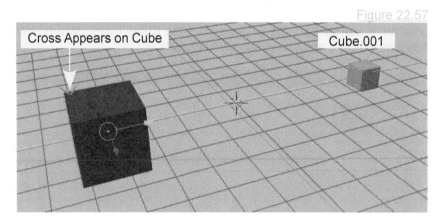

Figure 22.57

Cross Appears on Cube

Cube.001

Select the original Cube and add a Particle System with **Boids Physics**. In the **Emission Tab**, reduce the **Number** value to **10** and set the **Lifetime** value to **1500**; you want to keep the number of Particles low and have them visible for a fair amount of time in the animation.

Go to the **Timeline Editor** and set the animation **End** value to 1500 frames.

In this example a Particle will be displayed as a cross.

In the **Particles button, Viewport Display Tab**, select **Cross** and set the **Size** value to **1 px**; you will see a cross appear on the Cube (Figure 22.58).

Figure 22.58

In the **Boid Brain Tab**, remove **Separate** and **Flock** and add **Goal** (Figure 22.620).

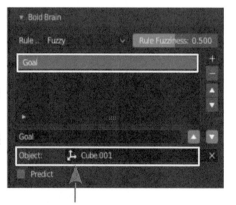

Click in the **Object Panel** below the Rule Panel and select **Cube.001** - this tells the Particles Emitted from the original cube to go and find the target which is Cube.001.

Play the animation to see the result. Crosses emitted from **Cube** migrate across the Screen and accumulate on the target Cube.001(Figure 22.59).

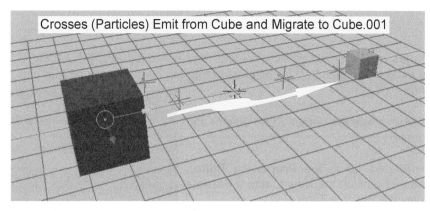

Remember that the location of either or both of the Cubes in the Scene may be animated at the same time. Animating the target Cube can cause the Particles confusion. They may head over to where the target Cube was originally located , have a think, then chase the target. Some Particles may take off in a completely different direction but in letting the animation play on they will eventually find out they have made a mistake and discover where they should be going.

Boids Example - Swarming

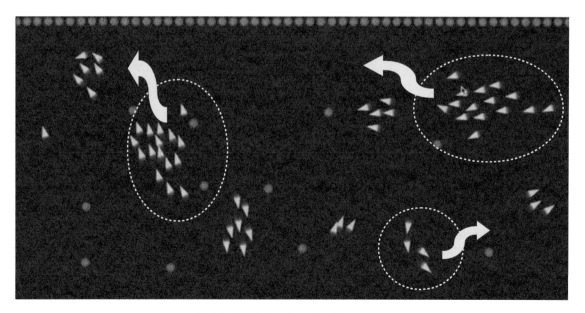

Boids Particles forming Swarms

22.16 Hair Particles

Type: Hair Particles are rendered as strands and may be edited in the 3D View Editor. Hair Particles may be used to represent such things as grass, fur, hair, or anything that has a surface with fibrous strands.

In the 3D View Editor, delete the default Cube object, add a Plane, and zoom in.

Figure 22.60

With the Plane selected, go to the **Properties Editor, Particles buttons** and click on the **New** to add a **Particle System** and display the **Particle Tabs**.

In the top panel of the Particles Editor, click where you see **Type: Emitter** and select **Hair** from the menu that displays (Figure 22.60).

The Plane in the 3D View Editor will show long strands sticking up from the surface. The **Hair Length** value in the **Emission Tab** allow you to adjust the length of the strands. (Figure 22.60).

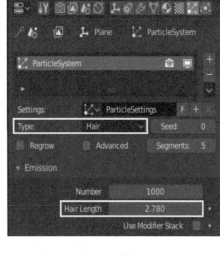

Figure 22.61

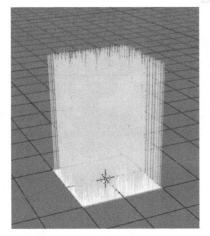

Hair Particles Emitted From Plane
Default Material

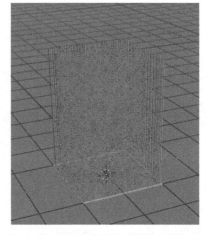

Hair Particles Emitted From Plane
Material Added
LocDev Viewport Shading

Adding Hair to a Character

Start a new Blender Scene, delete the Cube, and add a **Monkey Object**. Give Suzanne a head of hair and a beard.

If you add a **Hair Particle System** to **Suzanne** you will get a hairy-headed Monkey with hair sticking out in every direction (Figure 22.62).

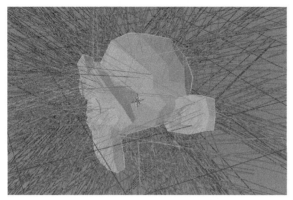

Figure 22.62

Try for a more clean-cut look. Remove the Particle System by clicking the minus button.

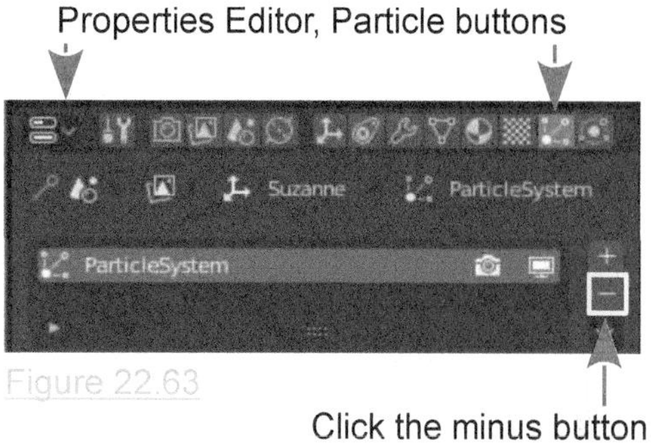

Properties Editor, Particle buttons

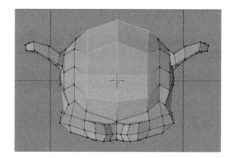

Figure 22.63

Click the minus button

You designate specifically where the hair is to grow by selecting a **Vertex Group** (Chapter 05 – 5.9 Creating Vertex Groups).

Create a Vertex Group on the top of Suzanne's head.

Name the Vertex Group **Hair.**

Figure 22.64

At this point you have nominated an area on the head by selecting a group of Vertices. **You do not have hair.** Go to the **Particles buttons** and click on **New** to add a new **Particle System**. Change **Type: Emitter** to **Type: Hair.** Nothing happens because you are in **Edit mode**.

Note: Blender has named the new Particle System simply, **Particle System** as before.

Tab to **Object Mode** in the 3D View Editor and you will see plenty of hair. In fact, there is hair everywhere.

To correct this look, in the **Hair Length box** in the **Emission Tab,** decrease the value until the hair strands look reasonable; say, about 0.820.

Still in the Particles buttons, go down to the **Vertex Groups Tab** and in the panel next to **Density** click and select **Hair** from the menu that displays (Figure 22.65).

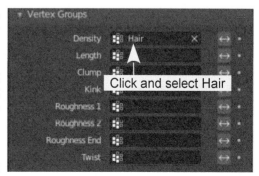

Figure 18.65

389

You will have hair only on the area selected. Press Num Pad 3 to get a side view (Figure 18.74). To fix the scrawny look, go to the **Children tab** and click on **Simple** to get a bushy, Mohawk (Figure 22.66).

Figure 22.66

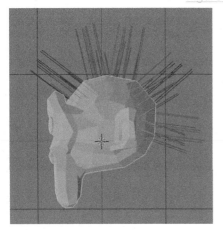 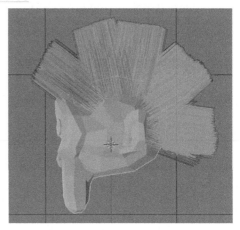

Adding a Beard

Continue on and add a beard. To make the process interesting , vary the procedure just a little. You previously created a Vertex Group, named it, then assigned selected Vertices to the Group.

With **Suzanne** selected in **Object Mode** in the 3D View Editor, go to **Properties Editor, Data buttons** and click on the plus sign in the **Vertex Groups Tab** to add a new Vertex Group. Blender names the new group **Group**. Rename this to **Beard** as you did before for the hair. You now select the Vertices to assign to the new group. You could use the procedures as outlined previously, but do it a different way.

Tab into **Edit Mode** and **deselect** all the Vertices. In the 3D View Editor Header, change to **Weight Paint Mode**. Suzanne turns blue in the 3D View Editor, which indicates that no Vertices are selected (Figure 22.67).

Figure 22.67

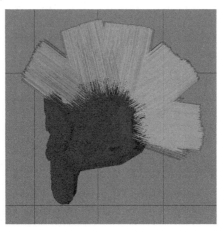

390

Note that **Beard** is high-lighted in the **Vertex Groups Tab**. Click on **Hair**. If you look closely amongst all that hair (it may help to rotate the view), you will see a red scalp; this is showing the area that was previously selected. Tab to Edit Mode and click on **Select** in the **Vertex Groups Tab** and you'll see the vertices that were painted for Hair.

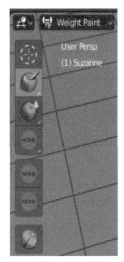

Press the **Alt + A Key** in the 3D View Editor to **deselect**, and click on **Beard** again in the **Data buttons, Vertex Groups Tab. Tab** to **Weight Paint Mode** in the 3D View Editor and look at the **Tools Panel** at the left hand side of the screen (Figure 22.68).

Figure 22.68

By default the Draw Tool is selected and the Cursor is a Circle. **Note; The Weight** value in the Header is 1.000. In the 3D View Editor, click LMB, hold and drag the Cursor (circle) over Suzanne's chin. You will see the color change as you drag.

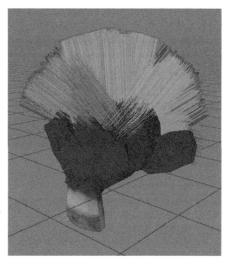

Keep dragging until the chin is all red (rotate the 3D View Editor as you paint). The red chin means that you have selected this area as the new Vertex Group for the beard (Figure 22.68).

Tab to **Edit mode**, making sure all Vertices are **deselected**, then in the **Vertex Groups tab,** with **Beard** highlighted (selected), click on **Assign** to assign the painted Vertices to the beard Vertex Group. Click **Select** to see them.

With the painted Vertices selected (you are in Edit Mode) go to the **Particles buttons** and add a new **Particle System** (click on the plus sign next to where you see **Particle System** highlighted).

Note that Blender names this new system **Particle System 2**.

Select **Type: Hair**, decrease the **Hair Length value** in the **Emission Tab** to 0.290, and go down to the **Vertex Groups Tab**, click in the **Density box**, and select **Beard**.

In the **Render Tab** check that **Path** is in the **Render As** panel. **Tab** to **Weigh Paint** mode in the 3d window.

You have scrawny hair on the Suzanne's chin. Go to the **Children tab** and click **Simple** for a hairy Beard (Figure 22.69).

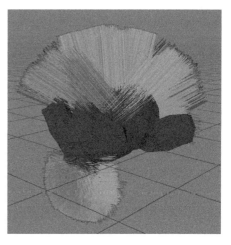

Figure 22.69

It doesn't matter in which order you do it, the procedure is the same: select Vertices to define the area, create a Vertex Group, assign Vertices to the Vertex Group, create a Hair Particle System and assign it to the Vertex Group.

> **Note:** If you elect to select Vertices, assign them to a Vertex Group then add a Hair Particle System you may find the Hair displaying as dots instead of strands. **In the Render tab click on Path**.

In Object Mode in the 3D View Editor you have a gray Monkey with a grey beard and hair (Figure 22.70). This is fine, but it isn't all that exciting in a render. Jazz it up by adding different **Materials** to Suzanne's surface and to the two Vertex Groups (Chapter 5 – 5.9).

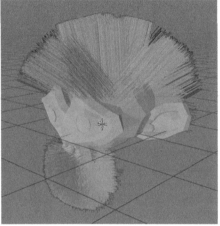

Figure 22.70

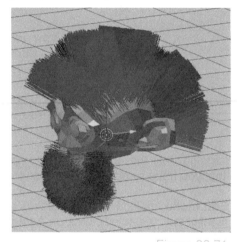

Figure 22.71

Final Note

Adding hair to an Object can add an awful lot of Vertices, which when rendering can take an awful lot of time and may even cause your computer to stall out. If you are not doing anything serious and have a slow machine to start with, keep the number of strands low.

22.17 Particles for Arrays

Particles emitted from an animated Object may be used to create interesting display Arrays.

To continue with the information obtained in the preceding examples have a Plane Object in the Scene as the Emitter Object with an Ico Sphere as the rendered Object.

When you add the Ico Sphere the **Add Ico Sphere panel** displays in the lower LH corner of the Screen. You will see Subdivisions: 2 as the default setting. Reduce this to Subdivisions: 1. This reduces the Vertex count on the surface of the Ico Sphere. This is not necessary here but is good practice when creating simulation where it's advisable to use a minimum number of Vertices.

Park the Ico Sphere off to the side of the Screen or you may place it in a separate Collection to hide it from view. Give the Ico Sphere a nice bright Material.

Have the 3D View Editor in LocDev Viewport Shading Mode.

Animate the Plane

Select the Plane Object in Top Orthographic View and animate it to Rotate 360° over 40 Frames (45° each 5 Frames).

Simple Procedure: With the Timeline Editor Cursor;
    At Frame 1, Press I Key - Select Keyframe type Rotation.
    At Frame 5, Press R+45, Press Enter, Press I Key– Rotation.
    At Frame 10, Press R+45, Press Enter, Press I Key-Rotation
            Repeat until F40.

Playing the animation will see the Plane Rotate 360° over the 40 Frames. To make the Plane continuously Rotate, change the graph for the animation to **Cyclic Extrapolation** in the **Graph Editor**.

Add a Particle System

Add a Particle System to the Plane with Particles being Emitted from the Verticies and rendering as the Ico Sphere Object. Increase the **Lifetime to 250** and in the **Source Tab** uncheck **Random Order.**

Figure 22.72

Playing the simulation (animation) in the Timeline Editor show Particles displayed as Ico Spheres being emitted and rising in spirals as the Plane rotates (Figure 22.72).

This is a relatively simple exercise demonstrating how an effect is created by combining the different Particle settings. There are no hard and fast rules which have to be obeyed. The way to create something is to experiment and when you produce a worthwhile result, save the file and record results for future use.

The following example incorporates more combinations.

22.18 More Arrays

Particle Arrays are only limited by your imagination and your knowledge of what tools to use and where the tools are located. This example will help you on your way.

In the default Blender Scene replace the default Cube with a **UV Sphere** as a **Particle Emitter** and add an **Ico Sphere** to be used as a rendered Object (Instance Object).

Give the Ico Sphere Smooth Shading and park it to one side of the Scene. Scale down to approximately 0.250. The Ico Sphere will be what is termed the **Instance Object**. When Particles are generated by the UV Sphere they will display as this Object.

Add Lamps to improve illumination in the Scene.

Figure 22.73

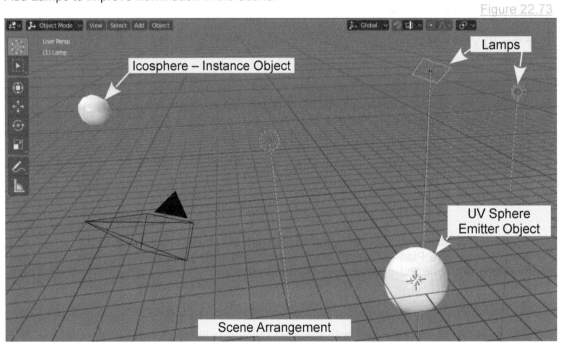

The objective in the exercise is to create an array of small Objects that could represent a swarm of insects hovering around the UV Sphere or a cloud of stars in a far off galaxy. This is where your imagination comes into play. For realism you would create a small model of what the Objects in the Array were to be but for simplicity, the Ico Sphere will be used.

Turn off **Gravity** in Scene buttons to make the Particles disperse in 3D Space.

Select the UV Sphere and add a Particle System.

Playing an animation in the Timeline Editor at this point with the default Particle System would see particles being emitted as small circles which float away from the UV Sphere and disappear after 50 Frames from their point of creation (Lifetime 50.000).

To generate something a little more exciting modify the Particle System.

In the Emission Tab

Increase **Number** to 30 000.

Change Lifetime to 999 (i.e. Forever).

Leave Start: 1 and End: 200.000.

Change Lifetime Randomness to 0.800

In the Render Tab

Change Render As from Halo to Object.

Leave Scale at 0.050

Change Scale Randomness to 0.080.

In the Render, Object Tab click where you see **Instance Object** and select **Ico Sphere.**

In the Timeline Editor play the animation then move the Timeline Cursor to Frame 120 and rotate the Viewport.

Figure 22.74 shows the Array generated in Rendered Viewport Shading Mode. The Array is ordered as seen by the Particles radiating out from the UV Sphere as scattered lines. By zooming in on the 3D View Editor you will see that each Particle is an Instance (copy) of the Ico Sphere parked in the Scene.

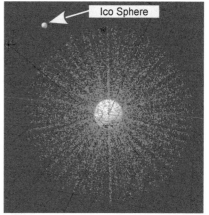

Figure 22.74

From this point you make further modifications to settings to alter the appearance of the Array.

Add a Material to the Ico Sphere. Figure 22.75

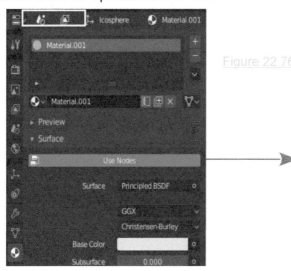

Figure 22.76

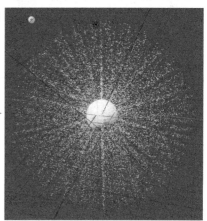

Deselect the UV Sphere and add an **Empty Object** and activate a **Force Field, Type Turbulence**, Strength 5 in Physics buttons (Figure 22.77 over).

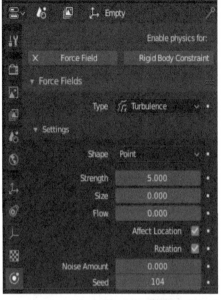

Figure 22.77

Play animation to see flow of Particles.

Particles Dispersed by Force Field Figure 22.78

Figure 22.78 shows a Screen Capture taken while playing the animation at approximately Frame 120

Select the **UV Sphere** and change the **Particle System to Emitter Type: Hair**. With the animation in the Timeline Editor at Frame 1 the UV Sphere displays as a red disk.

In the **Particle System, Render Tab**, change **Render As** to **Path**. In the Children Tab select Simple for a different sort of Array (Figure 22.79).

Figure 22.79

The possibilities are endless, therefore, experiment and record settings or save Blender files for future use.

22.19 The Assignment Panel

When a **Particle System** is first added to a Scene by clicking on the plus sign in the Particles buttons, Blender introduces data to the Scene that creates a default Particle System. Blender names this data block **ParticleSettings**, as seen in the **Settings panel**. The data block named **ParticleSettings** is automatically linked to the default Particle System that is named **ParticleSystem**. ParticleSystem is placed in the Assignment Panel where it is assigned to an Object in the 3D View Editor.

Figure 22.80

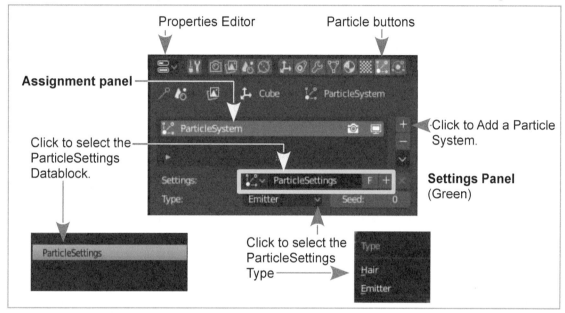

There is no **Assignment Tab** or **Assignment Panel** as such, but for the purpose of this discussion consider the **Settings Panel** marked in green as the Assignment Tab and the panel displaying **ParticleSystem** as the Assignment Panel (Figure 22.80).

Below the Settings panel there is a Particle Type selection menu with the two options, **Hair** and **Emitter**.

Type: Emitter is the default selection, which means that with the Particle System assigned to an Object in the Scene, that Object becomes the emitter of the Particles. In either case, the Object becomes an emitter with a Particle System assigned. **Type: Hair** may be viewed as a specialized static emitter.

In Figure 22.80, Particle System, Type: Emitter is selected for the ParticleSettings Datablock. This is assigned to the ParticleSystem which in turn is assigned to the Object which is selected in the 3D View Editor.

Note that the names **ParticleSettings** and **ParticleSystem** may be renamed by double clicking in the panels, deleting the name and retyping a new name. This is useful when there are multiple

Objects, Data Blocks and Particle Systems. Multiple Objects in the 3D View Editor can each have a different Particle System assigned, and each Object may have more than one Particle System.

When a new Particle System Data Block is added to the Scene, Blender creates a new name for the Data Block. The default particle settings Data Block is named **ParticleSettings** as previously stated. When a second Data Block is added, it is named **ParticleSettings.001**, a third would be named **ParticleSettings.002**, etc.

Renaming Data Blocks to something more relevant to Objects in the Scene would be an advantage. When new Data Blocks are created, they are stored in a cache for reuse by other Particle Systems.

When a new Particle System is added to the Scene, Blender assigns that system to the Object selected in the 3D View Editor. If no Objects are selected, the new Particle System is assigned to the last Object that was introduced to the Scene. Particle Systems added to a Scene initially have the default Particle Settings Data Block linked and a new name applied as described previously. At this point, the Data Block settings may be altered to create a new unique Data Block or a previously created Data Block may be selected and linked to the new Particle System. Clicking on the icon in front of the Particle Settings panel reveals a drop down menu showing the Cache, mentioned previously, with Data Blocks for selection.

The forgoing statements may seem confusing and not easily related to what has been labelled the **Assignment Tab.** The following exercise will attempt to clarify the statements and at the same time demonstrate the application of Particle Systems in practical terms.

18.20 Particle Exercises

Open a new Scene in Blender and delete the Cube from the 3D View Editor. Add three separate Plane Objects and position them at the center of the Scene so that they are all visible in Camera View . Add a diffuse Material color to each of the Planes. Make the colors red, green and blue. (Figure 22.81).

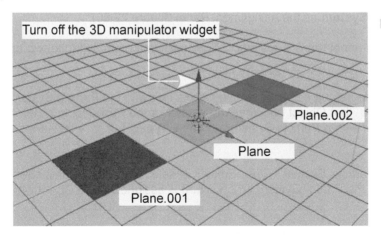

Turn off the 3D manipulator widget

Plane.002

Plane

Plane.001

Figure 22.81

Turn off the **Gravity** setting in the Properties Editor, Scene buttons, Gravity tab (untick).

Turn off the 3D Manipulator Widget in the 3D View Editor.

At this time, the three Plane Objects have been named **Plane**, **Plane.001**, and **Plane.002** by Blender, as seen in the upper left-hand corner of the 3D View Editor when each is selected. In the diagram the green Plane was entered first followed by the red Plane then the blue Plane.

This automatic naming is not all that relevant to what is in the Scene, therefore, the Planes will be renamed.

In the 3D View Editor, select the red Plane and go to the **Properties Editor, Object buttons**. At the top of the Editor you will see **Plane.001** in the Data Block ID name panel (Figure 22.82).

Figure 22.82

Click on the name to highlight it, hit delete, type in **Red_Plane** and press Enter. Select the green plane in the 3D View Editor and rename it **Green_Plane**, and then similarly for the blue Plane.

> **Note:** Renaming may be done in the Properties Editor, Object buttons, Datablock ID name panel or in the Outliner Editor (upper RH of the Screen)

It is time to add **Particle Systems** to the Planes. Select the red Plane and click on the **Particles button** in the **Properties Editor**. Click on **New** to add a Particle System. The Particle System panel displays with all the tabs and buttons for controlling the settings and has been set up with default values. Leave all the values as they are displayed except for the **Lifetime** and **Number** value in the **Emission Tab**. Change the value as shown in Figure 22.83. This will give you a better view of Particles being generated.

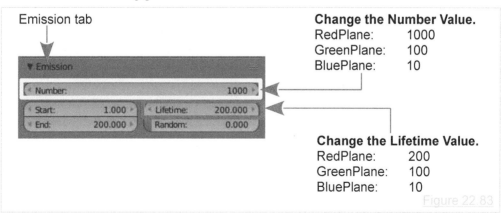

Emission tab

Change the Number Value.
RedPlane: 1000
GreenPlane: 100
BluePlane: 10

Change the Lifetime Value.
RedPlane: 200
GreenPlane: 100
BluePlane: 10

Figure 22.83

Do the same for the other two Planes. Shift select all three Planes in the 3D View Editor and play the animation in the Timeline Editor to show Particles being generated.

Cycle through the animation in the Timeline Editor (drag the Timeline Cursor) to frame 180 and observe the Particles (Figure 22.84). You have three different Planes with three different Particle Systems—RedPlane: 1000 Particles, GreenPlane: 100 Particles, BluePlane: 10 Particles.

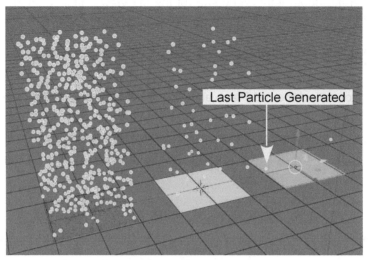

3D View Editor at Frame 180

Blender generates Particles beginning at Frame 1. The number of Particles set for each Plane is generated and spread over 200 Frames (200 is the End value in the Emission tab). The actual length of the Animation is 250 Frames. In Figure 22.84 BluePlane is selected showing the last of the 10 Particles being generated. For BluePlane the Particle Lifetime is set at 10 Frames, therefore, it disappears at Frame 190.

In the 3D View Editor select each Plane separately and note the names that display in the **Name** and **Settings** panels in the **Properties Editor, Particles buttons , Assignment tab**, (Figure 22.85).

- **Red_Plane**
  - Name: Particle System
  - Settings: Particle Settings
- **Green_Plane**
  - Name: Particle System
  - Settings: Particle Settings.001
- **Blue_Plane**
  - Name: Particle System
  - Settings: Particle Settings.002

Entries for the Red_Plane

It was previously stated that there were three separate Particle Systems, however, you see that the three names are all **Particle System**, but each one has a different **ParticleSettings** name. At this stage it's probably a good idea to do some renaming.

Change the names to the following:

- **Red_Plane**
  - Name: RedPSystem
  - Settings: RedPSettings
- **Green_Plane**
  - Name: GreenPSystem
  - Settings: GreenPSettings
- **Blue_Plane**
  - Name: BluePSystem
  - Settings: BluePSettings

After renaming, proceedings should be easier to follow.

To continue; In the 3DView Editor select the **Green Plane** to reassign some settings.

In the **Properties Editor, Particles button, Assignment Tab**, click on the button just in front of the name panel and next to Settings.

Browse Particles to be linked menu

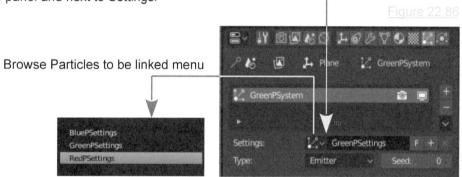

Figure 22.86

The menu that displays has the names of the three **Particle settings Data Blocks** (Figure 22.87). Whenever a new group of Particle Settings is created, Blender puts it into a cache for reuse. You can see these **Data Blocks** in the **Outliner Editor** in **Data API Mode**.

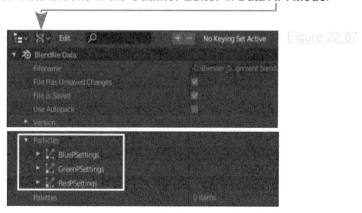

Figure 22.87

With the **GreenPlane** selected in the 3D View Editor, click on **BluePSettings** in the **Browse Particles to be linked menu.**.

You will have the **BluePSettings** assigned to the **GreenPSystem**.

If you replay the Particle generation animation, the green and blue Planes generate the same number of Particles.

Note that in the **Settings panel** for the green and the blue Planes, a number 2 has appeared; this tells you that **BluePSettings** is being used by two systems. The number of Particles Emitted is set by the Particle System settings.

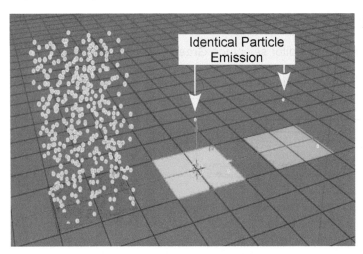

Figure 22.88

Identical Particle Emission

The forgoing has demonstrated that you can select any Data Block of settings and assign it to any Particle System.

Continue by clicking on the number 2, which makes the Data Block a single user. Blender does this by leaving the original as it is and creating a new Data Block, however, the new Data Block is identical to the original.

Figure 22.89

You can see that the settings name is **BluePSettings.001** (Figure 22.89).

In the **Emission tab** change the **Number** value to 10 and the **Lifetime** value to 30.

In the 3D View Editor, add a **UV Sphere** to the Scene and give it a yellow Diffuse Material color.

Note: Blender has named the Sphere simply, **Sphere**. Make sure it is off to one side in the Scene away from the planes.

Select the Green Plane in the 3D View Editor and then go back to the **Particle buttons** in the **Properties window**.

Change some data in this new Data Block (BluePSettings) which is assigned to the GreenPSystem for the green Plane.

In the **Render Tab** in the **Particles buttons** (scroll down a bit). In the bar labelled **Render as** click and select Type: **Object** (Figure 22.90).

Selecting **Type: Object** instructs Blender to Render (Display) Particles as an Object entered in the Scene.

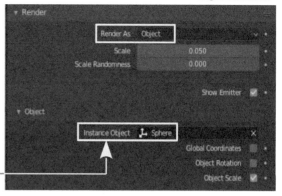

Figure 22.90

In the **Object Tab** that displays, click where you see Instance Object and select Sphere (the yellow UV Sphere).

You are telling Blender to display and render the Particles as replicas of the yellow Sphere entered in the Scene. Play the particle generation animation and you will see yellow Spheres being generated (Figure 22.91).

Yellow Sphere (Instance object) entered in the Scene Parked to one side

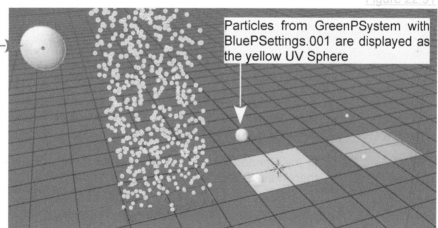

Figure 22.91

Particles from GreenPSystem with BluePSettings.001 are displayed as the yellow UV Sphere

The size of the Spheres generated is determined by the size of the yellow Sphere entered in the Scene and the Scale value in the Particle buttons, Render Tab .

This exercise has demonstrated how manipulating values in the Properties Editor controls the Emission of Particles in the 3D View Editor. This can be used to create visual effects in a Scene.

Note: An Object can have more than one Particle System in operation at the same time.

22.21 Multiple Particle Systems

Work through the following exercise to see how to apply **Multiple Particle Systems**. A Plane Object is entered in the 3D View Editor with a blue Material applied. The 3D View Editor is in LocDev Viewport Shading Mode.

A Particle System is added to the Plane in the Properties Editor, Particle buttons with the Emission values as shown in Figure 22.93 (default settings except Lifetime 200). Gravity has been turned off in the Scene buttons.

Playing the animation in the Timeline Editor produces the array of Particles shown in Figure 22.92.

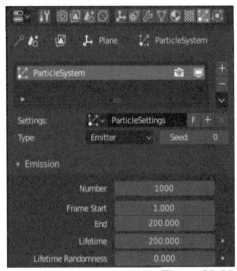

Figure 22.92

Figure 22.93

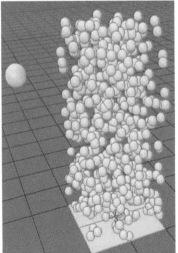

You may have the Particles display as another Object. Add a UV Sphere to the Scene. Give the Sphere a nice bright Material (color) and park it off to the side.

In the Render Tab change **Render As** to **Object** (Figure 22.94) then in the Object Tab select Sphere as the **Instance Object**.

Figure 22.94

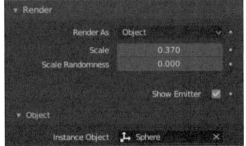

Figure 22.95

Replay the animation for a colorful display (Figure 22.95).

To add a second Particle System to the Plane click on the Plus icon adjacent to the Assignment Panel.

ParticleSystem2 is entered in the Assignment Panel. **Note;** Settings: Particle Settings.001.

Change the **Lifetime** in the Emission Tab to 200 so that the Particles remain visible when the animation is played.

Add a Monkey Object to the Scene with a Material and park it to one side.

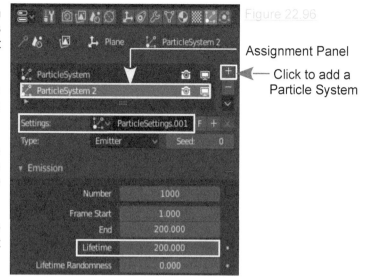

Figure 22.96

Assignment Panel

Click to add a Particle System

At this point a second Particle System is applied to the Plane with Settings: ParticleSettings.001. The Settings (at this point) are identical to the original ParticleSettings (Figure 22.96), therefore, playing the animation will produce two identical Particle displays (yellow spheres) and appear as if nothing has changed. To make it obvious that two systems are in play modify the settings for ParticleSettings.001.

With ParticleSystem2 selected (highlighted) change the values in the Render Tab as shown in Figure 22.97.

Change values in the Velocity Tab (Figure 22.99) as shown to change the direction of emission of the second set. Play the animation.

Instance Objects

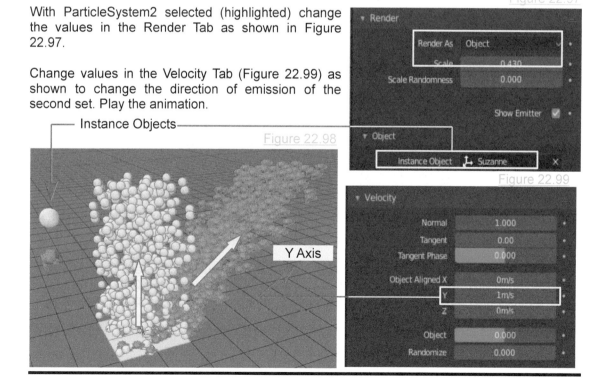

Figure 22.97

Figure 22.98

Y Axis

Figure 22.99

22.22 Keyed Particles

Keyed Physics is a way of controlling the movement of particles by directing them from the original Emitter Object to a second Target Object and onto subsequent Objects. The flow of Particles may be used as an animation or used to create a static image. The following procedure for setting up a keyed system will demonstrate the principles involved.

Open a new Scene in Blender and delete the default Cube. Add three separate Plane Objects and position them as shown in Figure 22.100. Note that in the **Outliner Editor** under **Collection** the first Plane will be named **Plane**. The second Plane named **Plane.001** and the third **Plane.002**.

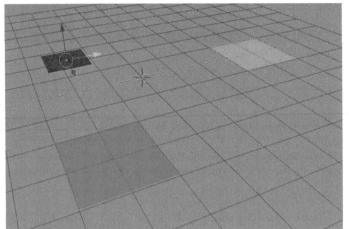

Figure 22.100

Figure 22.101

In the **Outliner Editor** rename the Planes, **Red_Plane**, **Green_Plane** and **Blue_Plane.**

> **Note:** You can go to the Properties Editor – **Object Data buttons** and edit the name in the **Name box** at the top of the panel or you can edit the names in the **Outliner Editor**. You could use any name you like but since the Planes are colored it's probably best to name per the colors assigned.

Select the first plane, **Red_Plane** and in the **Properties Editor, Particles buttons**, add a Particle System. In the **Physics Tab** change Physics Type: Newtonian to **Keyed.**

Figure 22.102

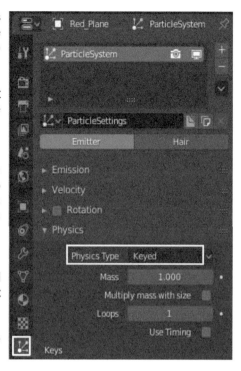

Deselect **Red_Plane** in the 3D window and select **Green_Plane** and **Blue_Plane** in turn, repeating the procedure for adding a **Keyed** type particle system.

Go back and select **Red_Plane**. At this point you are about to tell the Particles emitted from Red_Plane to migrate to Blue_Plane then on to Green_Plane. This is done by designating Blue_Plane and Green_Plane as Targets in the Physics, Keys, Relation Tab.

Click on the plus sign at the RHS of the Relations panel. This enters a Target Channel and inserts **Invalid target**. Below the relations panel click in the **Target Object** panel and select **Red_Plane**.

Click the plus sign a second time and repeat the process, this time entering **Green_Plane** as the Target. Repeat for **Blue_Plane**.

OK! You have the objects, **Red_Plan, Green_Plane** and **Blue_Plane** each with a **Keyed** particle system and you have told the particles generated from **Red_ Plane** to assemble.

When the animation is played Particles emitted from Red_Plane travel towards Green_Plane then turn and head over to Blue_Plane.

Figure 22.103

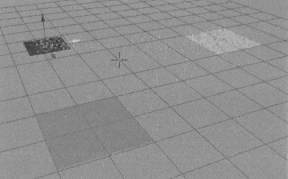

Figure 22.104

Remember: All the rules for number of particles, Lifetime, Start, End, and Normal velocity apply.

Physics and Simulation

Creating an animation is the process of simulating actions which take place in the real world and consequently involves applying or simulating the application of real world Physics.

When Objects and characters in a Scene move and interact they generally obey the rules of Physics which exist in the real world. Characters jump up and fall down obeying the law of gravity. They collide with with each other and with obstacles in the Scene. These actions may or not be exaggerated or strictly adhere to the laws of physics, depending on the story being depicted.

To simulate **Real World Physics** Blender incorporates Modifiers. The Modifiers are applied to Objects (Characters) from the Properties Editor, **Modifiers buttons** or from the Properties Editor, **Physics buttons**.

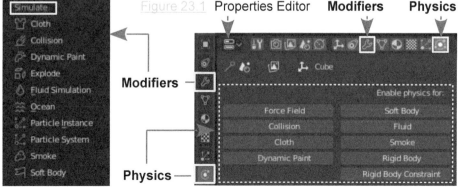

Figure 23.1 Properties Editor

23.1 Modifiers and Physics

Properties Editor, Physics buttons Figure 23.2

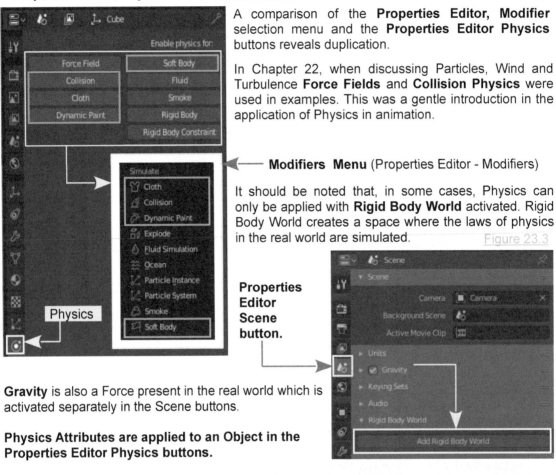

A comparison of the **Properties Editor, Modifier** selection menu and the **Properties Editor Physics** buttons reveals duplication.

In Chapter 22, when discussing Particles, Wind and Turbulence **Force Fields** and **Collision Physics** were used in examples. This was a gentle introduction in the application of Physics in animation.

Modifiers Menu (Properties Editor - Modifiers)

It should be noted that, in some cases, Physics can only be applied with **Rigid Body World** activated. Rigid Body World creates a space where the laws of physics in the real world are simulated. Figure 23.3

Properties Editor Scene button.

Physics

Gravity is also a Force present in the real world which is activated separately in the Scene buttons.

Physics Attributes are applied to an Object in the Properties Editor Physics buttons.

23.2 Force Field

Clicking **Force Field** in the Physics buttons opens the **Force Field Tab** where you select a Type.

Figure 23.4

Force Field Tab

Select the Force Type

Force Type: **Force** selected

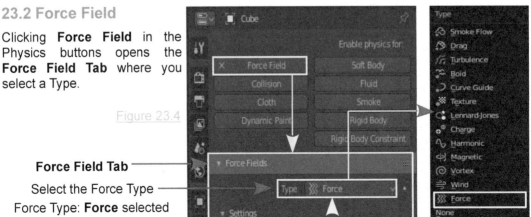

23.3 Collision Physics

Applying **Collision Physics** to an Object causes it to interact with other Objects in the Scene.

23.4 Cloth Physics

With **Cloth Physics** applied, an Object exhibits the characteristics of different types of fabric. With Cloth Physics activated, controls display in the Properties Editor (Figure 23.5). If you click on the Modifier button in the Properties Editor you will see that a Cloth Modifier has been added to the Plane referring you to the controls in the Physics buttons.

Consider a **Plane Object** in the 3D View Editor in Object Mode, Subdivided ten times (in Edit Mode). With the Plane selected in Object Mode, click **Cloth** in the **Physics buttons**.

Figure 23.5

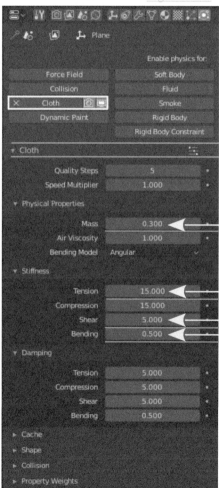

The default Cloth settings in the Physics buttons give the Plane the characteristics of a cotton fabric.

As a guide the following setting changes may be made for other **fabric materials**.

Default

	Cotton	Leather	Rubber	Denim	Silk
Mass	0.300	0.4	3.000	1.000	0.150
Tension	15	80	15	40	5
Shear	5	25	25	25	0.0
Bending	0.5	150	25	10	0.05

To see the Plane acting as a cotton fabric leave the default settings in place.

At this point playing an animation in the Timeline Editor will see the Plane exhibit the characteristics of a piece of cloth as if it had been released in space after being laid out perfectly flat. The cloth simply falls away under the influence of Gravity. There is no air resistance or other obstacle to impede its descent.

411

With the Plane selected in the 3D View Editor, Tab into Edit Mode, deselect all vertices then select two corner vertices and create a **Vertex Group** with just the two. The Vertex Group is names **Group.**

In the Properties Editor, Physics buttons expand the **Shape Tab** (Figure 23.6). You are about to fix (Pin) the two Vertices in space, something like pegging the corners of a sheet on a clothes line, without the line.

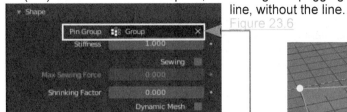

Figure 23.6

Imaginary Clothes Line Figure 23.7

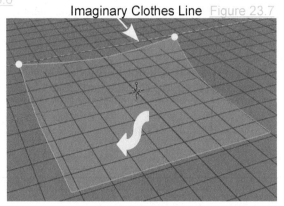

In the Shape Tab, click where you see **Pin Group** and select **Group** from the menu that displays.

Replay the animation in the Timeline. The Cloth swings down pinned at the corners (Figure 23.10).

To further demonstrate Cloth Physics, position a UV Sphere below the Plane before playing the animation. Create a second Vertex Group for the Plane, this time, including all Vertices on the Plane.

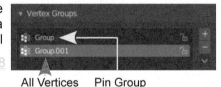

Figure 23.8

All Vertices   Pin Group

Properties Editor, Physics Buttons Figure 23.9

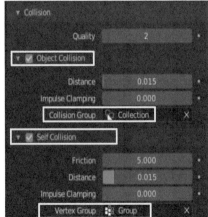

With the Plane selected, in the Cloth Physics buttons, Collision Tab, have **ObjectCollision** checked with **Collision Group: Collection** entered. Also have **Self Collision** checked with **Vertex Group: Group** entered. Replay the animation to see the Cloth droop over the Sphere (Figure 23.10).

Figure 23.10

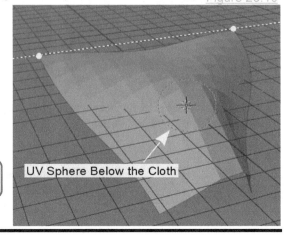

Note: Dynamic Paint is the next entry in the Physics list. This is explained in Chapter 24.

UV Sphere Below the Cloth

23.5 Soft Body Physics Figure 23.11

Soft Body Physics, when applied to an Object causes it to act like dough or clay or anything that is soft and pliable.

As an example, set up a UV Sphere Object above a Plane (Figure 23.11).

Select the UV Sphere and Tab to **Edit Mode**. With all the Vertices selected create a Vertex Group and set **Weight: 0.000.**

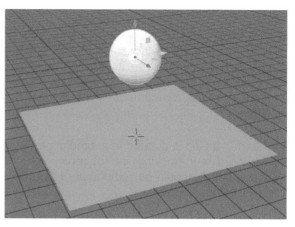

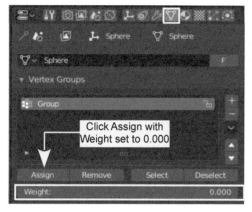

Figure 23.12

Tab to Object Mode and add Soft Body Physics to the UV Sphere.

In the Goal Tab enter the Vertex Group (Figure 23.13).

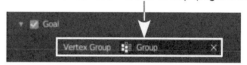

Figure 23.13

Select the Plane Object and add Collision Physics. Play the animation in the Timeline Editor.

Figure 23.14

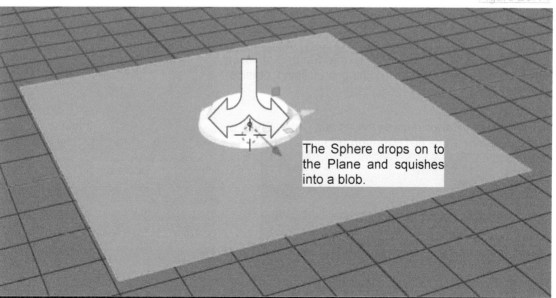

The Sphere drops on to the Plane and squishes into a blob.

23.6 Fluid Simulation

Fluid Simulation, as the heading describes, simulates how fluid behaves in the real world. How a fluid behaves depends on its environment which comprises physical obstacles and physical forces such as gravity and pressure. The physical composition of the fluid also has an effect on its behaviour. As you can guess the laws of physics have a great deal to do with how a fluid behaves.

In Blender, a fluid is created in a simulation. This means, a graphical display is generated on the computer screen tricking the observer into believing they are seeing a fluid react to an environment. It should be remembered that this is an illusion and what you think you see is a clever bit of trickery.

The Concept in Blender

To create a Fluid Simulation you create a mini world inside the artificial 3D World in a Blender Scene. The mini world is called the Domain and the simulated flow of fluid takes place entirely inside this space. The Domain contains a Fluid Emitter Object and other Objects which act as controls and obstacles. The Domain is shaped to fit in amongst other Objects in the Scene, therefore, creating the illusion that the Fluid Flow is moving in the Scene.

To demonstrate the basic concept work through the following exercise beginning with the default Blender Scene containing the Cube Object.

Place the 3D View Editor in **Wireframe Display Mode**.

Deselect the Cube and add a second Cube scaling it twice on the X and Y Axis and four times on the Z Axis. Both Cubes will be located at the center of the 3D World. Move the first Cube (the default) up towards the top of the second Cube. The second Cube will be the **Domain** (the mini artificial World). Note; it is very important to keep all Objects participating in the Fluid Simulation entirely inside the Domain (nothing protruding outside) (Figure 23.15).

In the **Outliner Editor** rename the default Cube, **Fluid** and the second Cube.001, **Domain** (Figure 23.16).

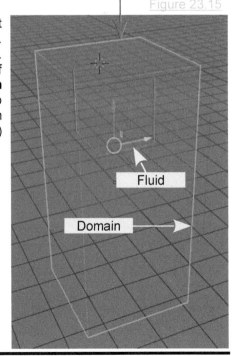
Figure 23.15

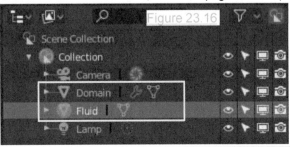
Figure 23.16

In the Properties Editor, Physics buttons, with the Domain Cube selected in the 3D View Editor, click on **Fluid** in the **Enable Physics Panel** and select **Type: Domain**.

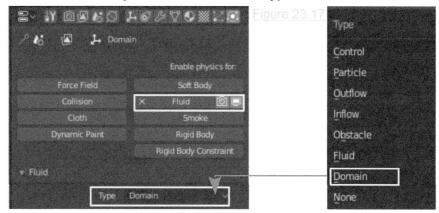

Deselect the Domain in the 3D View Editor and select the Fluid Cube. In the Properties Editor, Physics buttons, click **Fluid** and select **Type:Fluid**.

Go back and select the Domain in the 3D View editor then in the Properties Editor, Physics buttons go to the **Bake Tab. Click Bake**.

Domain appears to shrink

Figure 23.18

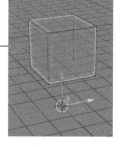

Since this is a very basic Fluid simulation the Bake process which converts data into a simulation will be almost instantaneous. For more advanced simulations the Bake can take a considerable time. The Domain appears to shrink to the size of the Fluid Cube. Play the animation in the Timeline Editor.

Figure 23.19

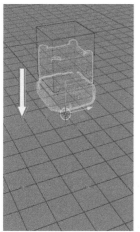
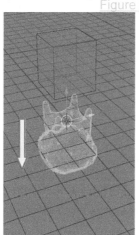
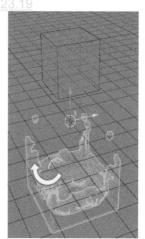
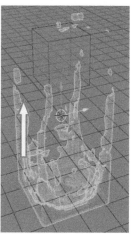

Playing the animation shows the Fluid created by the Emitter Object falling under the influence of Gravity into the area defined by the Domain. On hitting the bottom it splashes up then finally comes to rest in the bottom of the Domain (Figure 23.19).

The Bake process creates a series of animation frames. When the animation is played you see a simulation of the Fluid Flow.

Baking

Baking is the process of creating frames in an animation. With the Domain selected, at the bottom of the Fluid tab in the Properties Editor, Physics buttons, you will see the directory path showing where the animation frame files are stored. By default, on a Windows Computer this is in a temporary folder.

Figure 23.20

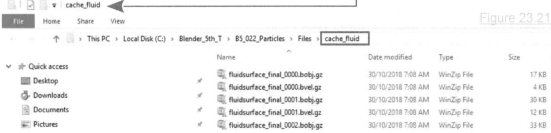

Figure 23.21

The Bake Cache show in Window File Exporer

The actual animation frame files are named :   fluidsurface_final_0002.bvel.gz
fluidsurface_final_0002.bobj.gz

With Start: 1 and End: 250 set as the animation length in the Timeline Editor, Blender will Bake 250 Frames for the simulation.

Note: This is a Temp (temporary) folder. When Blender is closed the simulation files are deleted even if you save the .blend file. You will have to re-bake and create new files for the simulation when the .blend file is reopened.

To keep the simulation files for future use, change the director path to a folder of your choice. They will not be deleted from there when Blender is closed.

The Domain

As you have seen the Domain defines the cubic volume of space in which a simulation takes place.

A Domain object is shaped to encapsulate other Fluid Objects in the simulation. Be aware that the size of the Domain and the included Objects affect the memory required for Baking and this affects the time it takes to Bake the simulation.

Also be aware, that following the Bake, the simulation may be Rendered to a video file. What is Rendered is what is seen in the Camera View. This may be only a portion of what you see in the 3D View Editor. For example, in the simple simulations demonstrated so far you may not wish to see the Cube which has generated the fluid. You may only want to see the fluid itself.

Remember, how a scene is rendered depends on the lighting arrangement (see Chapter 15).

Any of Blender's Primitives (Objects) may be used as a Domain but the shape of the Domain will always be calculated as a cubic volume. If you use a Cone object the Domain size will be a cubic volume equal to the diameter of the base, times the diameter of the base, times the height.

To demonstrate using an object other than a Cube as a Domain, construct the following simulation.

Open a new Blender Scene and delete the default Cube Object. Add a Monkey Object (Suzanne). Deselect the Monkey and add a Cube. Scale the Cube to fit inside the Monkey (be in Wireframe Viewport Shading Mode Figure 23.22).

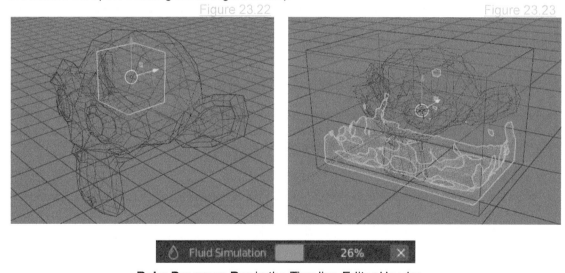

Figure 23.22   Figure 23.23

Bake Progress Bar in the Timeline Editor Header

After Baking the Fluid simulation and playing the animation you see the Fluid descend and splash, conforming to a cubic volume dictated by the overall shape of the Monkey Object (Figure 23.23).

Control and Obstacle Objects

As previously mentioned the Domain can contain Control Objects and Obstacle Objects.

As seen the Fluid Tab, Fluid Type selection menu contains the options.

Control: A Control object is used to influence the direction in which a fluid flows inside the Domain.

Figure 23.24

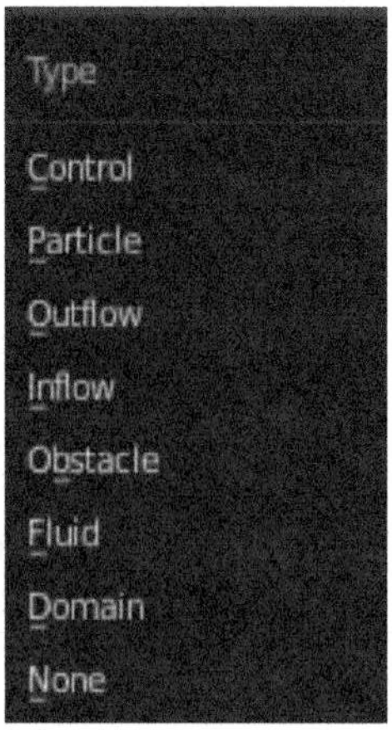

Particle: An Object designated as Type: Particle is also a Generator. Instead of producing Fluid it generates Particles in a continuous flow which is mixed in with the fluid (see 23.8 Fluid Particles).

Outflow: An Outflow Object acts as a drain hole in the Domain releasing fluid thus limiting accumulation.

Inflow: Generates a continuous flow of fluid

Obstacle: The Object interacts with the fluid obstructing flow or acts as a container.

Fluid: Generates a cubic volume of fluid.

Domain: The Domain defines the cubic volume of space in which the simulation takes place. All Objects included in the simulation must be totally inside the Domain.

Generators: This category is not included in the Fluid Object Type menu. In these discussions the convention of calling an Object a Generator has been adopted when it is used to create the Fluid in a simulation. The two Types are **Fluid** and **Inflow**.

Viscosity Presets

The Viscosity of the Fluid determines how the fluid flows. Water, oil, honey, lava and hot tar are all fluids and you will be aware that they each differ in the way they flow. Settings for Viscosity are found in the Properties Editor, Physics buttons, Fluid type Domain, Viscosity Tab (Figure 23.25). You must have the Domain selected before applying Viscosity.

Figure 23.25

The default Viscosity setting is: Fluid Preset with Base 1.000 (1.002 Water). Figure 23.25 shows settings for some fluids.

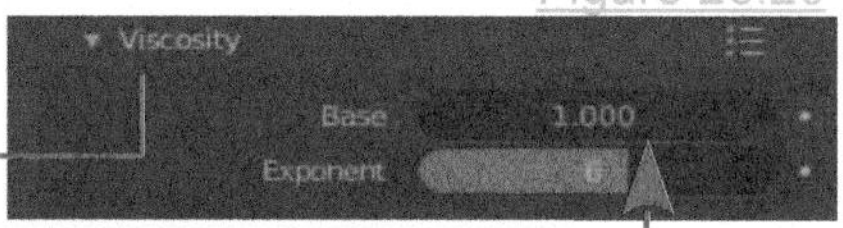

Fluid	Dynamic viscosity (in cP)	Kinematic viscosity (Blender, in $m^2.s^{-1}$)
Water (20° C)	$1.002×10^0$ (1.002)	$1.002×10^{-6}$ (0.000001002)
Oil SAE 50	$5.0×10^2$ (500)	$5.0×10^{-5}$ (0.00005)
Honey (20° C)	$1.0×10^4$ (10,000)	$2.0×10^{-3}$ (0.002)
Chocolate Syrup	$3.0×10^4$ (30,000)	$3.0×10^{-3}$ (0.003)
Ketchup	$1.0×10^5$ (100,000)	$1.0×10^{-1}$ (0.1)
Melting Glass	$1.0×10^{15}$	$1.0×10^0$ (1.0)

Blender viscosity unit conversion.

Inflow Example

Figure 23.26

Set up a Cube Object as a Domain with the Cube scaled twice on the X and Y Axis and four times on the Z Axis. Position a default Cube inside the Domain towards the top (Figure 23.26).

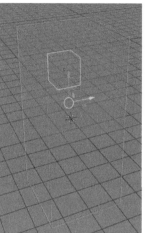

Select the **Cube** inside the **Domain** and assign Fluid Type: **Inflow Physics**. In the **Flow Tab** change the **Flow Velocity Y** value to **2.0** (Figure 23.27).

Reselect the Domain and Bake the simulation.

Play the simulation by pressing Play in the Timeline Editor.

Figure 23.27

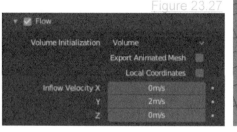

The Inflow Cube generates fluid directing it along the Y Axis where it splashes against the back wall of the Domain cascading down filling a cubic volume equal to the dimensions of the original Domain Cube

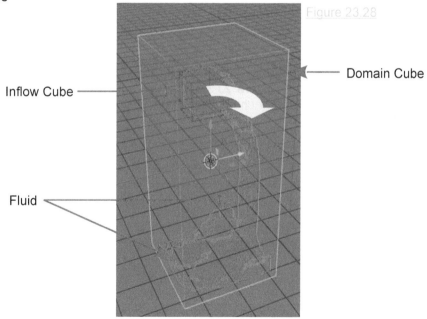

Figure 23.28

Inflow Cube

Domain Cube

Fluid

> **Note:** The size of the Domain has a significant effect on the Bake time. The bigger the Domain the greater the time.

23.7 Fluid Simulation Examples

Figure 23.29

In this example a volume of fluid will be generated to fill a cup.

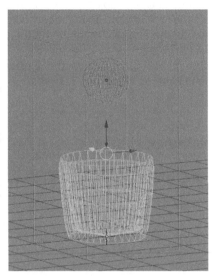

The arrangement in Figure 23.29 shows the 3D View Editor in Wireframe Viewport Shading Mode. The Scene has been constructed with a fluid emitter (UV Sphere), a Domain Cube (the default Cube scaled up), and an Obstacle Object (a Cup). For the Cup see Chapter 8 – 8.13 and 8.14.

Note: Providing you have saved a Blender file containing the Cup you will be able to append into a new Blender Scene.

Domain Object Setup

The Domain is a Cube that has been scaled to enclose the Sphere and the Cup.

Figure 23.30

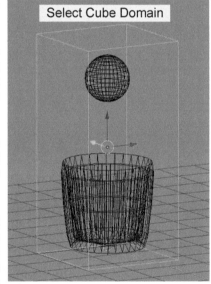

Select Cube Domain

Assign fluid simulation values to the Domain. Select the Cube in the 3D View Editor (Figure 23.30). Go to the Properties Editor, Physics buttons (Figure 23.31) and click on Fluid to display the Fluid Tab and change the Type to **Domain**.

In the Fluid Tab default values will be used, with one exception. In the **Fluid tab, Time** settings change the **End value to 6.000.** This reduces the Bake time for the demonstration.

When baking, Blender looks at the Start and End values set in the Fluid tab, calculates the time period, then computes how the volume of fluid would react to the environment during that time. In this example, the time period is 6.000 seconds. The Start and End values are in seconds and have no bearing on how many frames will be produced in the animation. The values are concerned with the physical force and the fluid viscosity—in other words, how the fluid will react to its environment in the given time period.

In the Properties Editor, Render button, Dimensions tab, the default animation length is set at 250 frames (Start frame: 1 – End Frame: 250). The display Rate is 24 Frames per second. The animation frame range is also displayed in the Timeline Editor. These values produce an animation of approximately 10 seconds, therefore, the behaviour of the volume of fluid in this example over 6.000 seconds will be spread over the animation time of 10 seconds. Imagine dumping a cup of water and observing its action over 6.000 seconds then stretching that behaviour over 10 seconds—a slow motion effect will result. A bake of 6.000 second will serve to demonstrate simulating a fluid flow, even though it does not produce a real-time animation.

What is real-time animation? Real-time animation with respect to fluid flow is an animation that shows precisely how the fluid reacts in real time as opposed to a slow motion effect. If you are interested in real time, set the Start and End values in the Fluid tab to match the length of the animation. For example, with the default animation of 250 frames at 24 frames per second equalling approximately 10 seconds, you would set the time values to provide a 10-second period. Be warned: there will be a long wait while your Blender Bakes. Varying the Start and End values of the fluid action therefore affects how the behaviour of the fluid is seen in the final animation. For now, leave all the values in the Physics, Domain Fluid tab set per the defaults, except for the End time setting.

Create a folder on your hard drive and enter the File Path in the Domain, Fluid tab (see **//cache_fluid** Figure 23.20).

Generator Object Setup

The fluid is emitted by the Sphere that has been placed in the Domain immediately above the Cup. The convention of calling this type of Object the **Generator** is adopted.

It is tempting to call the Sphere simply the Fluid Object, since it controls the fluid generation, but all Objects included in the simulation which have Fluid Physics applied, are Fluid Objects.

Figure 23.31

The size of the Generator (Sphere) relative to the Domain and the Cup determines the volume of the fluid in the simulation. For this demonstration, make sure the Sphere is smaller than the Cup or you'll have some mopping up to do. Select the Sphere in the 3D View Editor, go to the **Properties Editor, Physics buttons** and click on **Fluid**. In the Fluid tab select **Type: Fluid** (Figure 23.31). You may leave the settings as they are, but it is worth noting that the Initial Velocity values will give your fluid a kick start in whatever direction you set. In this instance the default Gravity force setting in the Properties Editor, Scene buttons, Gravity tab (Z: -9.81 Earth's Gravity) will be used.

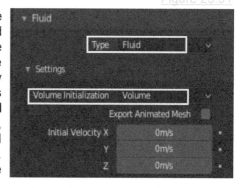

Tip: Objects in the 3D View Editor may be selected in the Outliner Editor, Collection when obscured.

Obstacle Object Setup

Figure 23.32

Objects included in the simulation which interact with the fluid are called **Obstacles**. The Obstacle to the fluid flow will be the Cup.

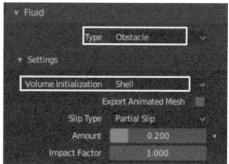

421

With the Cup selected in the 3D View Editor, go to the **Properties Editor, Physics buttons** and click on **Fluid**. In the Fluid tab select **Type: Obstacle** (Figure 23.32). Change the Volume Initialisation setting from Volume to **Shell**. With Volume, Blender considers the overall shape to be solid with no interior.

Baking

In the 3D View Editor in Wireframe Viewport Display mode, select the Domain Cube which at this point is displaying as a blob attached to the UV Sphere. The Domain Physics Properties Tabs will be displayed in the Properties Editor with the values that were previously set. Make note that Baking a simulation can take a long time depending on the complexity of the simulation, the resolution, the length of the animation and the speed of the computer. For the purpose of this example the default value of 250 frames in the animation, in the Timeline Editor has been used. At a display rate of 24 frames per second, this will produce an animation lasting approximately 10 seconds.

In the Properties Editor, Physics button, Fluid Tab, with the Domain Object selected in the 3D View Editor, click on the Bake button. The Bake progress can be observed at the bottom of the Timeline Editor in the fluid simulation progress bar; the bar only appears when you Bake. If you want to cancel a bake, click on the cross next to the bar. The Bake can take a considerable time; it is similar to creating an image for each frame of an animation, so be prepared to sit back and wait awhile. On my computer, in this example, the bake takes about 30 seconds.

If the Bake is not performing as expected, it can be terminated by pressing the Esc Key or the Cancel button in the Header. Settings can be adjusted to correct the action. To REBAKE the simulation, select the Domain (which is now the blob attached to the sphere) and press Bake a second time in the Domain, Fluid Tab.

Note: If the demonstration does not perform as expected you have probably made an error in the set up. Check your settings and change values accordingly, BUT Note; having changed a setting you will have to REBAKE the simulation to overwrite the data in the cache file. Simply changing settings will not correct the action.

Note: Before setting up a new Fluid Simulation clear the data from the Cache file or set a new location for saving the Bake. If data exists in the Cache when a new Domain is created, Blender will attempt to use use the existing data.

Play the Simulation

At the start of the Bake the Domain has disappeared and been replaced by a blob that attaches to the Sphere Object Playing the simulation shows the blob descending and splashing into the cup (Figures 23.32).

Figure 23.33

Animation Time and Speed

As previously stated, with the default Start: 1 and End: 250 values in the Timeline Editor the simulation will produce an animation time of approximately 10 seconds. The Bake process produces 250 Frames which will be played at the Frame Rate which is set in the Properties Editor, Render buttons, Dimensions Tab. The default value is 24 fps (frames per second). You could change the value to 25 fps in which case the animation would be exactly 10 seconds. You could change the End value in the Timeline Editor to change the number of Frames created. Changing values alters the Memory required for the Bake and the time it takes to perform the Bake.

Real World Properties

In the Properties Editor, Physics buttons, Fluid Tab, with the Domain selected, you will see **default values** of Start: 0.000 and End: 4.000 (Note: In the previous example the End value was changed to 6.000).

These values are in seconds of Real World Time.

The Start and End values tell Blender to calculate what the volume of fluid will do when released under the influence of gravity in 4.000 seconds.

The animation sequence for the simulation plays for 10 seconds, therefore, what occurs in 4.000 seconds is stretched out to 10.000 seconds producing a slow motion effect.

Another Real World factor to be considered in the simulation is size. In particular this is the size of the fluid volume in relation to other Objects included in the simulation.

If you appended the Cup model from Chapter 8 its Object Properties Scale Value is 1.000, since the model was created from a Circle Object one Blender unit in radius and this was not scaled.

The Cup's Object properties Dimensions are, therefore, X: 0, Y: 0, Z:0

In this example the Fluid Generating Object was made smaller than the Cup Obstacle Object. Small and Large are very loose terminologies but by and large suffice since you will only be concerned with proportion, not exact figures.

The rule is: A large Fluid Generating Object in proportion to a small Obstacle Object will produce a large Fluid Volume.

It's time to move on and explore more Fluid Generation techniques.

Exacting a Fluid Volume

When you want to fill a container with just the right amount of fluid you create a Fluid Generating Object of a specific size.

To demonstrate use the Cup you have previously created. Start a new Blender Scene, rebuild or Append the Cup.

Note: When the Cup was modeled, a Subdivision Surface Modifier was added at the end of the exercise. Before using the model in this example Apply the Modifier by clicking the Apply button in the Properties Editor, Subserf Modifier buttons.

The relative size and shape of the Generator dictates the volume of fluid produced. To fill the cup you create a shape which matches the inside of the cup. Have the cup selected in the 3D View Editor, in Edit Mode, in Top Orthographic View. Deselect the Vertices. Make sure **Limit Selection to Visible** is active (Chapter 5 – Figure 5.4) so that you only select Vertices that you actually see on the Screen. Use Circle Select to select the bottom inside Vertices of the cup (Figure 23.34).

Hold Ctrl and press Num Pad Plus to expand the selection capturing all the inner Vertices. (Figure 23.35)

Figure 23.34   Figure 23.35

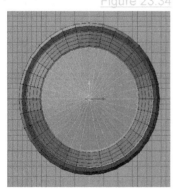
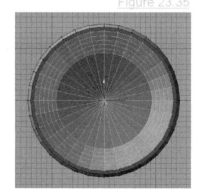

With the inside Vertices selected press Ctrl + D Key to duplicate the selection then press the P Key and select **Separate by Selection** in the menu that displays. This separates the selection from the Cup creating a new Object. Scale the selection down (in) slightly. (Figure 23.36)

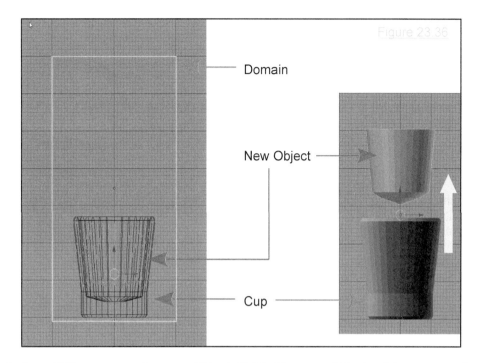

Figure 23.36

Domain

New Object

Cup

In the Outliner Editor rename the new Object **Fluid**. The new Object will be open at the top so add Vertices and fill it in.

With the new Fluid Object positioned inside the Cup and both Objects inside a Domain, set the Fluid Physics properties. Obviously the Fluid Object is Type: Fluid with Volume Initialization: Volume. The Cup is Type: Obstacle with Volume Initialization: Shell.

In the Domain Fluid properties set a File Path to a new folder to house the Cache.

Bake the simulation.

After Baking, with the 3D View Editor in Solid Viewport Shading Mode you will probably see that the Fluid partially breaks through the surface of the Cup. This is due to the Domain Resolution settings. The default Resolutions are set fairly low to limit Bake time and allow you to test the simulation. Increasing the Render Displays to something like 100 and re-baking will partially resolve the issue but with an increase in Bake time. For a flawless simulation you will have to increase the Resolution even more and scale the Fluid Object down but the settings described so far will be good to demonstrate the technique.

Note: If you experience the Bake producing a fluid which is off to one side and outside the cup, this will be due to the incorrect direction of Normals on the Fluid object.

A **Normal** is a line or vector that is perpendicular to a given Object. For example, the Normal line to a curve at a given point, is the line perpendicular to the tangent to the curve at that point. In Blender you have Normals perpendicular to Vertices, Edges and Faces which in Fluid Physics are used to calculate the displacement of the Fluid.

To display Normals for the Fluid Object, have the Object's Vertices selected in Edit Mode. The 3D View Editor, Overlays click on either of the display modes for Normals (Chapter 22 - 22.9). The Size value determines the display length of the Normal line.

To correct the direction of Normals, select the Fluid Object, Tab into Edit Mode. In the 3D View Editor Header click Mesh, Normals, Recalculate, Inside or Outside.

When the Bake is complete move the Fluid Object to a different Collection and hide from view.

Figure 23.37

Playing the simulation in the Timeline merely shows a volume of fluid sitting inside the cup (Figure 23.37) but suppose you drop an Object into the fluid. Add a UV Sphere Object to the Scene placing it above the Cup and inside the Domain (Figure 23.38). Animate the UV Sphere to drop from its initial position into the Cup in say, 30 Frames of the animation (Animation Chapter 18). Apply Fluid Physics to the UV Sphere, Type: **Obstacle**. Volume Initialization: Volume is OK.

Play the animation in the Timeline and see the UV Sphere drop and splash into the Fluid

Figure 23.38

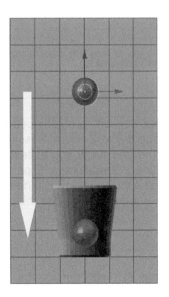

In this simulation a fluid flow will be generated which will cascade down a trough into a cup.

Note: Before setting up a new Fluid Simulation clear the data from the Cache file or set a new location for saving the Bake. If data exists in the Cache when a new Domain is created, Blender will attempt to use the existing data.

The arrangement in Figure 23.39 shows the arrangement of Objects in Wireframe Viewport Shading Mode. Figure 23.40 shows Solid Viewport Shading Mode with Material (color) applied to the trough and the cup.

Note: All Objects participating in the simulation must be within the confines of the Domain.

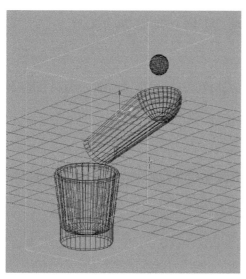

Figure 23.39

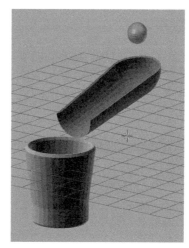

Figure 23.40

Domain Object Arrangement

The Domain is a Cube Object scaled to encapsulate a UV Sphere (Generator Type: Inflow), a trough and a cup. The cup is the same cup previously used. The trough is modeled from a UV Sphere by deleting and extruding Vertices.

In arranging the Objects, the Sphere's diameter should be less than the width of the trough, and the width of the trough at the outflow end, should be less than the diameter of the cup. These relationships are purely proportional and do not represent actual sizes.

To create a simulation using Real World sizes arrange the Objects as shown. Create a Domain to enclose the Objects. Have the Domain selected and apply Physics Fluid type: Domain. In the Properties Editor you will see the Fluid World Tab with a Real World Size setting. The default value is 0.500 Meters.

This size represents the dimension of the longest size of the Domain cuboid.

The size of Objects enclosed by the Domain is calculated in proportion to the size of the Domain. Therefore with a Domain approximately 7.5 Blender units long, 7.5 units = 0.500 Meters. If the cup is 2.25 Blender units in diameter it will be calculated as 2.25 x 0.5 / 7.5 = 0.150M (15cm or 150mm or 6 inches, which is a big cup or a small bucket).

Domain Object Set-up

Apply Fluid Physics to the Domain, leaving the default settings, but change the File Path for the Bake to a folder of your choice.

Generator Object Set-up

The Sphere is the Generator Type: Inflow with Volume Initialization: Volume. Set the Inflow Velocity Z value to minus 0.900 to give it a kick start in the downward direction.

Make sure the diameter of the Sphere is approximately 1/3 the width of the trough.

Obstacle Object Set-up

Position the Cup and the Trough as shown in the diagram. With both Objects make sure to set Volume Initialization as Type: Shell.

Adding Material Color

Coloring the Objects is simply applying a Material. To color the fluid you apply a Material to the Domain not the Inflow Sphere.

Finally: Bake the simulation, play or scrub through the animation in the Timeline Editor. (Figure 23.41)

 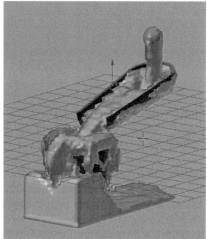

Figure 23.41

You will probably see that the fluid breaks through the surface of the trough and the sides of the cup. This is due to the default Resolution used in the Bake process. To get reasonable results set the Resolution in the Domain Physics settings above 100. This will resolve the break through issue but at the cost of more Memory being required for the Bake, and also a significant increase in the time for Baking.

Outflow and Control Objects

Outflow Objects act like a drain hole in the Domain where the Fluid exits. The height of the Control object sets a level for the Fluid in the Domain (Figure 23.42).

The height of the Control Object limits the depth of the Fluid in the Domain.

Figure 23.42

Control Objects attract Fluid causing it to flow towards the Object and attach itself to the Object. When used in conjunction with a Flow Generator the Control object influences the direction of the fluid flow (Figure 23.43).

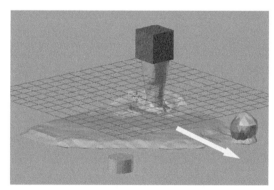

Figure 23.43

Figure 23.44

A Control Object which is animated to move will carry fluid with it.

Set a Scene with a Cube scaled down on the Z axis (Fluid Object) placed inside another Cube (the Domain) and with a Monkey Object positioned as shown (Figure 23.45 over). With the Domain selected reduce the Final and Preview Resolution settings to 40. In the Timeline Editor set the End Frame to 100. These settings produce a fairly quick render. Animate the Monkey to rise in the Domain.

Render the simulation to see fluid generated in the bottom of the Domain surrounding the Monkey. The fluid bulges up where it is displaced by the Monkey . Scrub the animation in the Timeline window. At first the Fluid billows up as it is displaced by the Monkey (Figure 23.46) then as the Monkey rises, Fluid attaches itself to the Monkey and is transported with the Monkey(Figure 23.47).

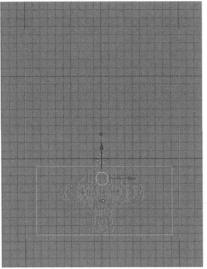
Figure 23.45

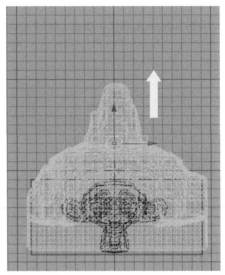
Figure 23.46

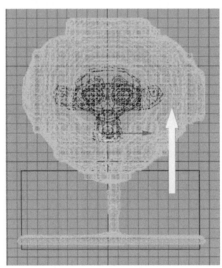
Figure 23.47

23.8 Fluid Particles

Particles can be introduced into a simulation to follow the Fluid Flow creating special effects.

Start a new Blender Scene. Leave the default Cube object in place to be used as the **Domain**.

Add two new Cube Objects and give them different Material colors. **Note: Do not duplicate the default Cube.** One Cube will be the **Fluid Generator**, the other will be the **Particle Generator**.

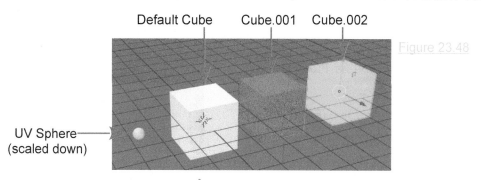

Default Cube   Cube.001   Cube.002

Figure 23.48

UV Sphere
(scaled down)

Add a UV Sphere to the Scene and scale down. Give it a Material color. The Particles in the simulation will be made to display as Spheres You can use any of the Primitives or an Object you have modeled. As an example; yellow model ducks could be made to float on water.

Place the 3D View Editor in Wireframe Display Mode and arrange the new Cubes and the UV Sphere inside the Domain Cube. Scale the Objects in proportion (Figures 23.49). Rotate the view and ensure that all Objects are totally inside the Domain.

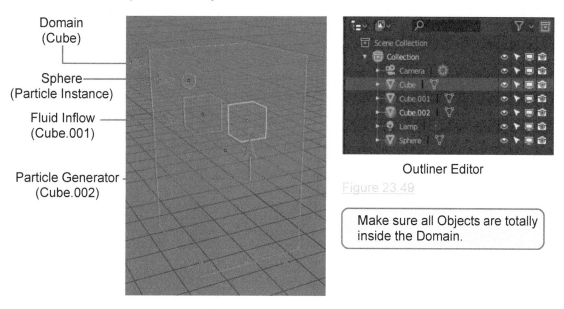

Domain
(Cube)

Sphere
(Particle Instance)

Fluid Inflow
(Cube.001)

Particle Generator
(Cube.002)

Outliner Editor

Figure 23.49

Make sure all Objects are totally inside the Domain.

Add **Fluid Physics** to the Objects amending the default values as follows: Figure 23.50

(Cube): Domain **Cube:** The Domain (Figure 23.50)

You may leave all the Domain settings as the default except for those in the Particles Tab. The default values here are: Tracer: 0 and Generate: 0.000

With these values set to 0 and 0.000 Particles **will not be generated**. In this example you can leave Tracer: 0 since you are not using tracers. For the Particle Generator you will be setting the Particle Type as **Float**, therefore, set the Generate value as 1. 000

(Cube.001): Inflow Fluid Generator (Figure 23.51)
  Fluid type: Inflow
  Volume Initialization: Volume
  Inflow Velocity: Y: 1.600 (Gives the fluid a starting velocity along the Y axis).

  Gravity is also in effect on the Z axis.

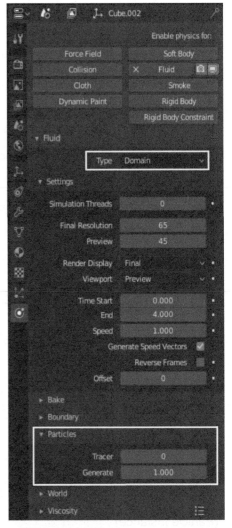

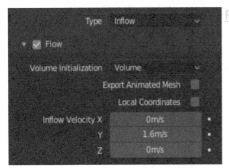

Figure 23.51

(Cube.002): Particle Generator (Figure 23.52)
  Fluid Type: Particle
  Influence: Size 1.000, Alpha: 1.000
  Particle Type: There are three options.
      Drops -   Show drop particles
      Float - Shows floating foam particles.
      Tracer- Shows tracer particles.

  For this example check (tick) the Float option.

Ensure that the File Path to the **Particle Cache** is to the same folder containing the **Domain Fluid Cache**.

Figure 23.52

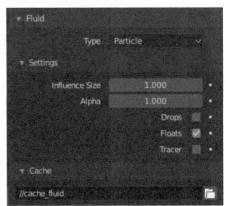

Particle System

Figure 23.53

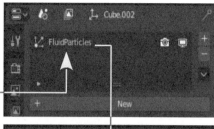

When **Fluid Physics Type: Particle** is applied to an Object a Particle System is automatically created. You can see this in the Properties Editor, Particle buttons with Cube.002 selected. **Click where you see FluidParticles** to display the **Render** tab with options for displaying the Particles.

The default display **Render As** option is **Halo**. In this example the Particles are to display as small spheres, therefore, change to Object. The **Object Tab** will display.

In the Object Tab enter the **Instance Object Sphere**. The Sphere is the Sphere Object you have placed in the Domain. The Particles will display as duplications of the Sphere. Since you selected the Particle type: **Float** the Spheres will float in the fluid.

Note: None of the above takes effect until the Bake is executed.

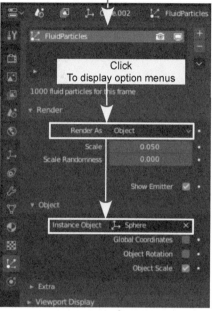

Bake the Simulations

Baking converts the data set in the Physics Buttons into an animation.

With the Domain selected the Physics buttons will display the Bake Tab.

Figure 23.54

Ensure that the File Path to the Fluid Bake Cache is identical to that of the Particle Cache.

With all settings in place, press **Bake** in the Domain Fluid tab. The Bake progress bar displays at the bottom of the Timeline Editor.

Figure 23.55

When the Bake is complete (note:The display in the 3D View Editor (Figure 23.56).

The Domain has consolidated to an orange cube attached to the Fluid Emitter.

Scrub the cursor or press Play the animation in the Timeline Editor.

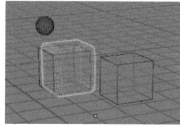

Figure 23.56

The animation shows Fluid being emitted from the Fluid Generator and cascading to the bottom of the volume created by the Domain. At the same time Particles are generated and displayed as yellow spheres floating on the Fluid (Figure 23.57).

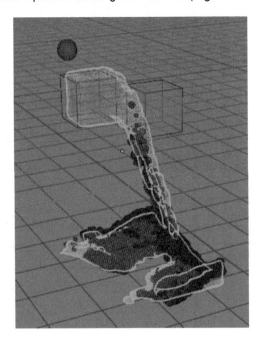
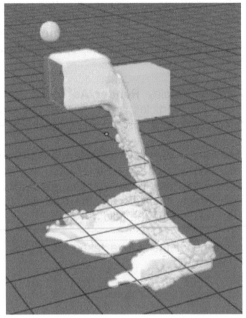

Particles display as yellow Spheres

Wireframe Display Mode   Figure 23.57   LocDev Display Mode

Experiment

Having completed the exercises continue to experiment with settings and see the different results. Go on the internet and find tutorials on Fluid Simulations. There are many many tutorials showing a variety of techniques and applications, including techniques for various effects. This chapter has but touched the tip of the iceberg but hopefully having worked through the examples you will be better placed to follow video tutorials.

24

Dynamic Paint

Introduction

Dynamic Paint is the process of using one Object to color or deform the surface of another Object.

When coloring the process is much like painting on a canvas using one Object as the Brush. The Object being painted on is the Canvas.

Although being called Dynamic Paint the process can also deform the surface of an Object by displacing Vertices in a permanent displacement or by simulating a wave formation in a dynamic effect as one Object moves through the surface of another Object.

24.1 Dynamic Paint - Painting

To demonstrate **Dynamic Painting** a UV Sphere Object will be used as a Brush to paint a Material Color onto the surface of a Plane Object representing the Canvas. You may use any Object for a Brush but a Plane gives a nice flat surface as a Canvas on which to work.

The word Dynamic in the title refers to the fact that, in this process, painting takes place when an animation sequence is being run in the Timeline Editor. The Brush is moved on the surface of the Canvas while the animation sequence is running. Actually, this introductory demonstration will employ **Format Type: Vertex** which means that where the Brush Object intersects with the Canvas Object, the Vertices of the Canvas at the intersection, will have color applied.

Set up a Scene as shown in Figure 24.1 with a UV Sphere Object at the center of a Plane Object. The Plane is scaled up six times and subdivided, in Edit Mode, eighteen times producing plenty of Vertices. Both the Plane and the UV Sphere have a Material applied.

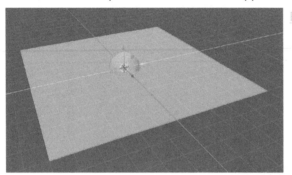

Figure 24.1

Figure 24.2

With the **Plane** selected in **Object Mode** go to the **Properties Editor, Physics buttons** and click on **Dynamic Paint** (Figure 24.2).

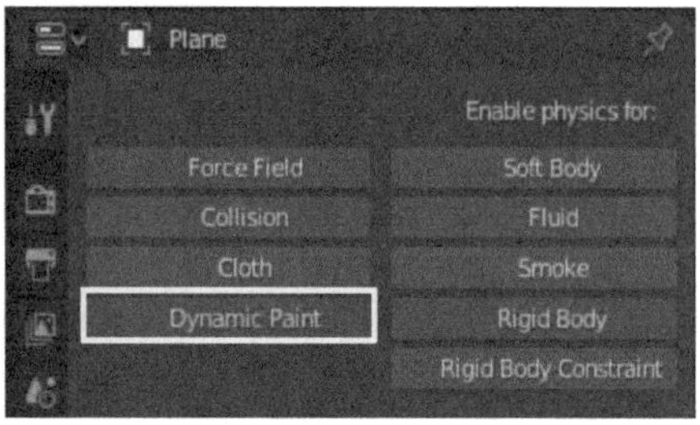

In the **Dynamic Paint tab**, note that by default, **Canvas** is active (Figure 24.3).

Click **Add Canvas**. You will be painting on the Plane, therefore, it will be the Canvas.

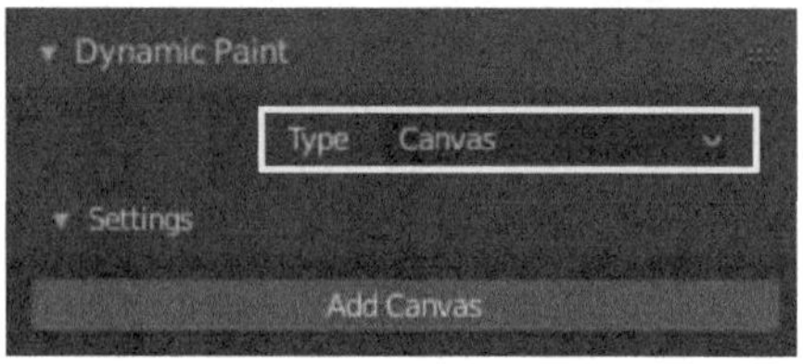

Select the **UV Sphere** and add Physics, Dynamic Paint but this time, change the Type to **Brush** (Figure 24.4).

Figure 24.3

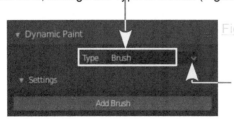

Figure 24.4

Click and select Brush

With the Dynamic Paint Type Canvas set for the Plane, select the UV Sphere and in the Physics buttons click Type and select Brush, then click Add Brush (Figures 24.6).

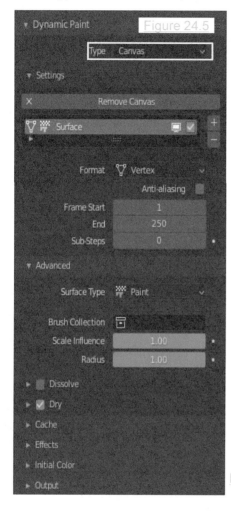

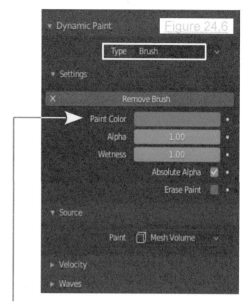

The default paint color is blue. You see this appear at the intersection of the Plane and the UV Sphere (Figure 24.7).

Figure 24.7

Have the Brush selected in the 3D View editor. Click Play in the Timeline Editor and drag the Brush in the surface of the Canvas (Figure 24.8).

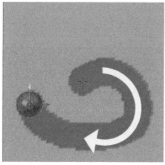

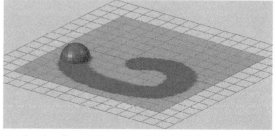

Figure 24.8   As the Brush is moved Material color is applied to the canvas as long as the animation plays.

The default animation in the Timeline window is set at 250 Frames and the default Frame rate is 24 Frames per second giving approximately 10.4 seconds of animation. You may increase the time for painting by increasing the **End** value in the Timeline Editor header. Once the animation reaches the end the Canvas is wiped clean. Before the end of the animation, pause the animation to Render an image.

The Dynamic Paint, Physics buttons allow a variety of paint application effects. You will have to experiment with the settings and record your findings but to get you started try the following.

> **Tip:** The simple Plane – Sphere Scene arrangement will provide a base for experimenting but it is tedious to restart the animation play, select and grab the Sphere each time you try a new setting. With the Scene in User Perspective view and the Sphere in Grab Mode the paint application stops when the Sphere goes above or below the surface of the Plane. This has the potential for an animation effect but to make life a little easier, set up a simple animation to have the Sphere move across the surface of the Plane as the Timeline animation plays. You can then change Dynamic Paint settings and simply press the Spacebar to play and to see results.

Brush Paint Source Options

The Brush can affect how the paint is applied to the Canvas in several ways. Paint options are found in the Physics buttons, Dynamic paint, Source Tab.

Figure 24.9

Besides applying color to a surface the Brush may also be used to deform the surface of the Canvas. Options are found in the Dynamic Paint Physics buttons for the Canvas in the **Advanced Tab** as **Surface Type**.

Figure 24.10

As an example: With the Plane selected create a wave effect on the surface by changing the **Dynamic Paint Advanced, Surface Type** to **Waves**. With the Sphere animated to move on the surface of the Plane the sphere appears to plough through water (Figure 24.11). Make the Sphere jump from below the Plane and splash down again (Figure 24.13).

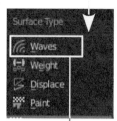

With the Sphere selected try the different options in the Properties window, Physics buttons, Dynamic Paint Waves tab (Figure 24.12).

Figure 24.11   Figure 24.12

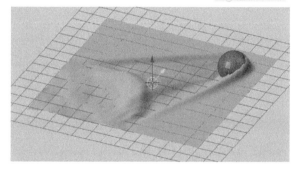

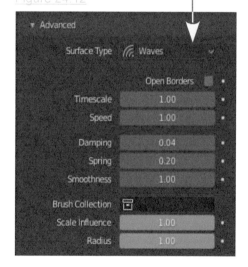

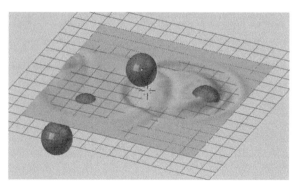

Figure 24.13

25

Installing Add-Ons

Introduction

Add-ons are additional Blender functions which you activate when required. Blender comes with a variety of Add-ons hidden away in the **Preferences Editor** and there are literally hundreds available for download from the Internet. Add-ons are pieces of computer code written the **Python** programming language (Python Scripts).

The Blender website contains a link to the scripts repository where a great number can be found.

When you download an Add-on (Python Script), you have to **install** it into Blender, then before you can use it, you have to **activate the script**. The best way to demonstrate this process is to provide an example.

At the time of writing there are a limited number of Add-ons available for Blender 2.80

One such script is named **Sculpting Sculpt Tools**. This example will show you how to download the compressed (.zip) file and install the script into Blender. This is an exercise in manipulating files to add functionality to Blender.

25.1 Blender FishSim Add-On

The tool does not come pre-installed in Blender, instead, it is one of many additions for the program that are available for download. The tool is download in a compressed file (zip file).

25.2 Finding the FishSim File

Go online, open a browser, and search for **FishSim-master.zip** and select the website shown in Figure25.1.

GitHub - nerk987/FishSim: Blender Addon - Fish Swimming Simulator   Figure 25.1
https://github.com/nerk987/FishSim ▼
Blender Addon - Fish Swimming Simulator. Contribute to nerk987/FishSim development by creating an account on GitHub.

The   GitHub   download
page will open where you download the Zip Add-on file (Figure 25.2).

Click **Clone or Download** (Figure 25.2).

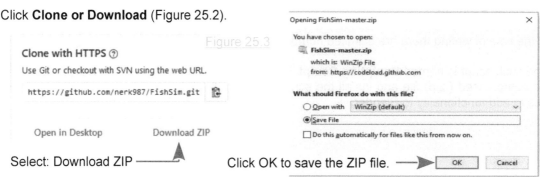

Download the Zip file and save to a place on the hard drive (Figure 25.4).

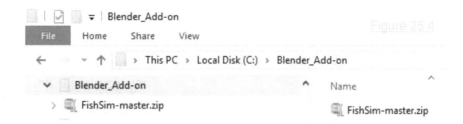

Figure 25.4

25.3 Installing the Add-on

In Blender, open the Preferences Editor and select the Add-ons Tab in the left hand column. To install the new Add-on click on **Install** in the Header (Figure 25.5).

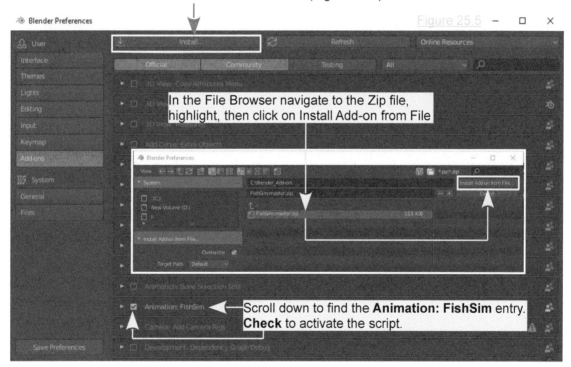

Figure 25.5

In the File Browser navigate to the Zip file, highlight, then click on Install Add-on from File

Scroll down to find the **Animation: FishSim** entry. **Check** to activate the script.

With the script activated **FishSim** will display as an entry under **Armatures** in the **Add menu** in the 3D View Editor.

Figure 25.6

The **FishSim Add-0n** is designed to be used in conjunction with an Armature constructed for a fish. A pre constructed Armature for a shark can be found in the Add menu when the **Rigging: Rigify** Add-on in the Preferences Editor is activated.

Figure 25.7

Figure 25.8

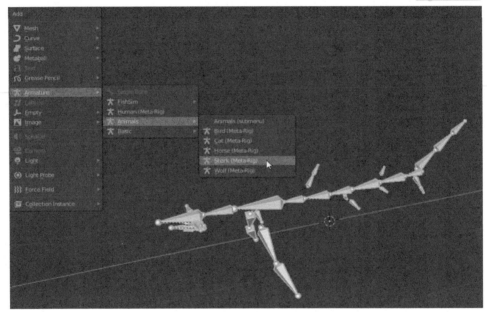

444

Grease Pencil – 2D Animation

26.1   Annotation

26.2   Grease Pencil Object

26.3   2D Animation

Introduction

The Grease Pencil provides 2D Animation tools within Blender's 3D Pipeline. 2D Animation creates characters, storyboards, and backgrounds in two-dimensional environments which may be may be used in advertisements, films, television shows, computer games, or websites.

The Animation Walk Cycle typifies a 2D Animation sequence where a drawing of a Character is animated to walk in a Scene. Each individual drawing is captured as an Animation Frame which when played in succession creates the illusion of motion.

The following instruction will introduce the Grease Pencil with reference to Blender's Graphical User Interface.

Blender's Grease Pencil may be considered as two separate components: **Grease Pencil Annotation** for simply adding freehand notations to a view and **Grease Pencil Objects** for advanced 2D Drawing and Animation.

26.1 Annotation

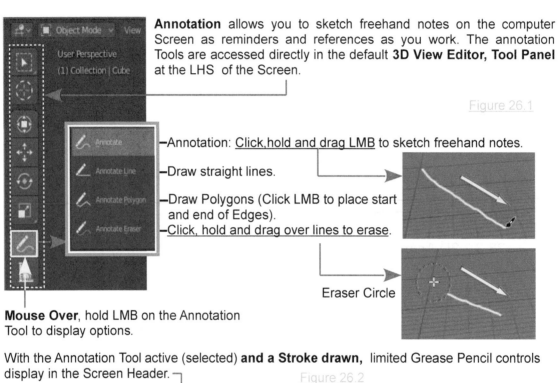

Annotation allows you to sketch freehand notes on the computer Screen as reminders and references as you work. The annotation Tools are accessed directly in the default **3D View Editor, Tool Panel** at the LHS of the Screen.

Figure 26.1

–Annotation: <u>Click,hold and drag LMB</u> to sketch freehand notes.

–Draw straight lines.

–Draw Polygons (Click LMB to place start and end of Edges).
–<u>Click, hold and drag over lines to erase</u>.

Eraser Circle

Mouse Over, hold LMB on the Annotation Tool to display options.

With the Annotation Tool active (selected) **and a Stroke drawn,** limited Grease Pencil controls display in the Screen Header.

Figure 26.2

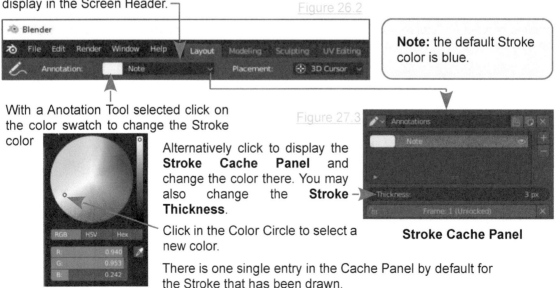

Note: the default Stroke color is blue.

With a Anotation Tool selected click on the color swatch to change the Stroke color

Figure 27.3

Alternatively click to display the **Stroke Cache Panel** and change the color there. You may also change the **Stroke Thickness**.

Click in the Color Circle to select a new color.

Stroke Cache Panel

There is one single entry in the Cache Panel by default for the Stroke that has been drawn.

Adding Strokes

You may add Strokes in the **Stroke Cache Panel** for future selection. Figure 26.1

Click the Plus sign to add a Channel.
Change the color and thickness.

Select a Channel (Stroke) in the Cache to draw
in the 3D View Editor.

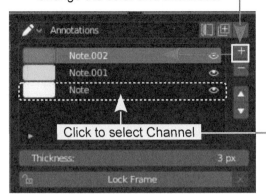

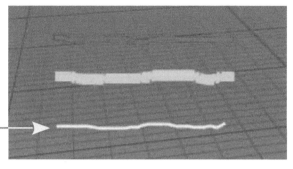

Strokes Drawn in the 3D View Editor

Figure 26.4

Erasing

> Note: Erasing: You can only Erase a Stroke when it is selected in Annotation Draw Mode.

For example; to erase the Green Stroke (named **Note.001** in the **Cache Panel**) select the
Note.001 Channel. In the 3D View Editor, Tool Panel, select one of the draw Tools. The controls
display in the Header indicating that the Channel is selected. You may now select the Erase Tool
and Erase any Stroke that has been drawn with the Note.001 Channel selected.

Renaming Stroke Channels

You may rename the Stroke Channels to make them relevant to what you are doing in the 3D
View editor.

Layers

When a Stroke is drawn on the Screen it is drawn on a Layer. The Stroke Cache Panel previously
described, is in fact, a Layer Panel. Each Channel created in the Panel is a separate Layer. This
explains why you can only erase a Stroke when a Channel Layer has been selected.

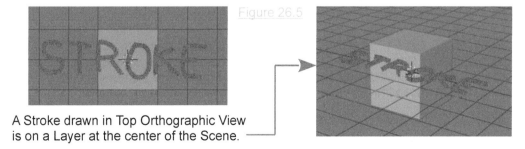

Figure 26.5

A Stroke drawn in Top Orthographic View
is on a Layer at the center of the Scene.

Hiding Strokes

A stroke Layer may be hidden from view by clicking the eye icon in the Stroke Layer panel.

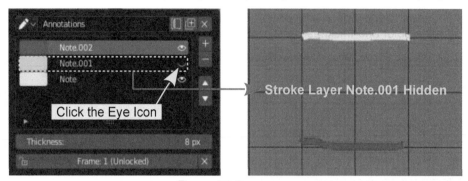

Figure 26.6

All Strokes may be hidden from view by unchecking Annotations in **Overlays** (Figure 26.7).

> **Overlays** – Upper RH Corner of the 3D View Editor.

Figure 26.7

26.2 Grease Pencil Object

For advanced 2D Animation, figures are drawn in the 3D View Editor where the Strokes are treated as an Object and, therefore, may be manipulated just like any Blender Object. Figures may be drawn and animated directly in the 3D View Editor but there is a dedicated 2D Screen Arrangement for 2D Animation.

Working in the 3D View Editor

To work in the 3D View Editor when creating 2D Animations you have to consider the computer Screen as your sketch pad or canvas. The General default Screen is presented in User Perspective View which could possibly lead to disorientation when figures are drawn and manipulated. If you wish to work in the 3D View it's best to arrange the Screen in Front Orthographic View in Camera View. What you see in Camera View will be what is eventually captured as an image and subsequently an Animation Frame. The Camera should be aligned such that it is square on to the 3D View presenting the equivalent to a flat canvas.

As a suggestion, the arrangement shown in Figure 26.8 may suit. This shows Camera Perspective View. The Camera location and orientation are shown in the Object Properties Panel.

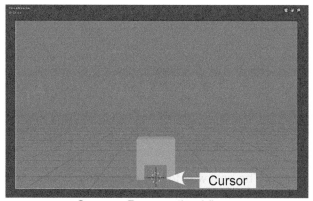

Camera Perspective View   Figure 26.8   Object Properties

In Figure 26.8 the default Cube Object has been scaled down and is positioned sitting on top of the Mid Plane Grid. The Cube merely shows you the perspective in the view. The Mid Plane Grid also provides perspective should you wish to move characters towards the back of the Scene.

Note: The 3D View Editor Cursor is located at the center of the 3D World.

Grease Pencil Access

The Grease pencil is accessed like any other Object in Blender, either from the Add button in the 3D View editor Header or by pressing Shift + A Key to display the Add menu (Figure 26.9).

Selecting Grease Pencil in the Add Menu displays three options.

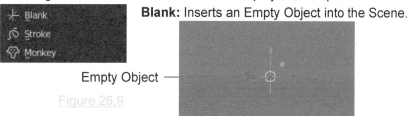

Blank: Inserts an Empty Object into the Scene.

Empty Object

Figure 26.9

Stroke: Inserts a pre-constructed Stroke.

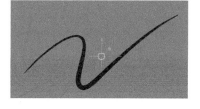

Monkey: Inserts a pre-constructed Figure.

Note: With each of the three options an Empty Object is placed at the center of the Scene.

With the selection of the **Stroke** and **Monkey** options, the pre-constructed Stroke and the Strokes forming the Monkey Figure are linked or parented to the Empty Object. Selecting Blank places the Empty Object in the Scene, then when you draw Strokes creating a Figure the Strokes, hence the Figure, is linked to the Empty. With the Empty selected the Figure (all Strokes drawn to create the Figure) may be Translated, Rotated and Scaled in the 3D Scene. This is manipulating the Layer (Scaling the Layer).

You select and manipulate the Layer by selecting the Empty Object in Object Mode. You draw individual Strokes in **Draw Mode**. The Strokes are drawn on the Layer linked to the Empty Object that is selected. You edit Strokes in Edit Mode and Sculpt Mode.

This information is, no doubt, somewhat confusing. The best way to understand the process is to step through a practical exercise and the best way to do this is to use the **2D Animation Workspace** which is built into Blender.

To access the Workspace click on **File** in the Screen Header and select **New, 2D Animation**.

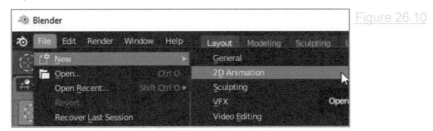

Figure 26.10

2D Animation Workspace   Figure 26.11

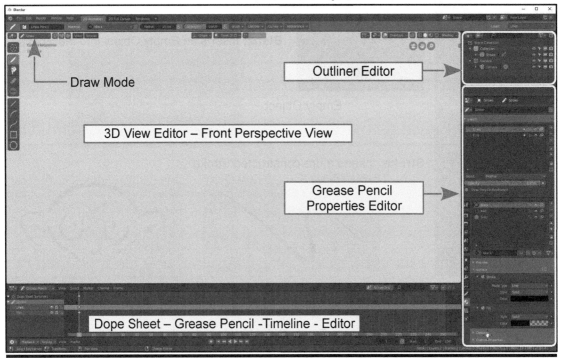

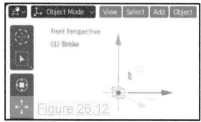

Figure 26.12

The 2D Animation Workspace, by default, opens with the 3D View Editor in Front Perspective View in **Draw Mode**. If you change to **Object Mode** you will see an Empty Object located at the center of the View. Figure 26.12 shows the Empty translated (Moved) to the upper LH corner of the Editor. The translation Widget is activated and the Cube shape of the Empty is seen in perspective (Front Perspective View).

In **Draw Mode** there is no indication that an Empty Object exists. In the Outliner Editor the Empty has been renamed **Stroke** (Figure 26.13).

Properties Editor ——▶

You will see that there is a special versions of the Properties Editor displayed with special buttons for the Grease Pencil (Figure 26.14).

The upper part of the Properties Editor has the Layers Tab activated displaying **Layers** and Fills.

Special Grease Pencil Buttons ———▶

The lower part of the Properties Editor has the Material button activated displaying **Material Slots**.

Remember: The Properties Editor, buttons and controls are for the selected Object in the 3D View Editor. The selected Object is the Empty Object that you see with the 3D View Editor in Object Mode, which in turn represents the drawing **Layer** in Draw Mode.

Special Grease Pencil Buttons ———▶
Materials activated

Figure 26.13

Figure 26.14

Drawing Strokes

To see what the buttons in the Properties Editor do, you will require something to be drawn in the 3D View Editor.

Have the Grease Pencil 3D View Editor in **Draw Mode**. Select the **Draw** Tool in the Tool Panel.

Click LMB in the 3D View Editor, hold and drag the Mouse to draw a Stroke. By default the Stroke is colored black. It has a Radius of 25px and the type of Stroke is **F Draw Pencil**.

Examine the Tool Header and the Grease pencil 3D View Editor Header.

Figure 26.15

Click for Stroke Types.

Tool Header

Click to see the **Stroke Cache**

Grease Pencil 3D View Editor Header

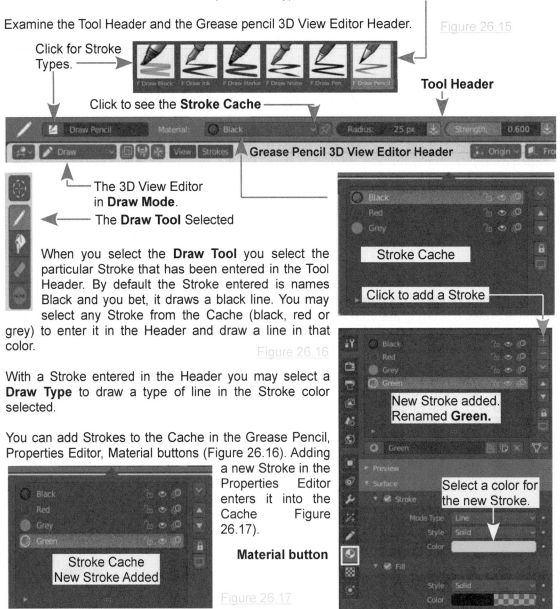

The 3D View Editor in **Draw Mode**.

The **Draw Tool** Selected

When you select the **Draw Tool** you select the particular Stroke that has been entered in the Tool Header. By default the Stroke entered is names Black and you bet, it draws a black line. You may select any Stroke from the Cache (black, red or grey) to enter it in the Header and draw a line in that color.

Figure 26.16

With a Stroke entered in the Header you may select a **Draw Type** to draw a type of line in the Stroke color selected.

You can add Strokes to the Cache in the Grease Pencil, Properties Editor, Material buttons (Figure 26.16). Adding a new Stroke in the Properties Editor enters it into the Cache Figure 26.17).

Material button

Stroke Cache

Click to add a Stroke

New Stroke added. Renamed **Green.**

Select a color for the new Stroke.

Stroke Cache New Stroke Added

Figure 26.17

With a Stroke selected from the Cache and a F Draw Type selected from the Header you select the different options in the Tool panel for drawing.

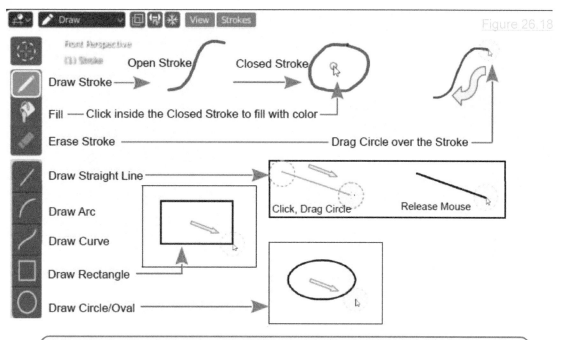

Figure 26.18

Front Perspective
(1) Stroke
Open Stroke
Closed Stroke
Draw Stroke →
Fill ── Click inside the Closed Stroke to fill with color ──┘
Erase Stroke ──────────────── Drag Circle over the Stroke ──┘
Draw Straight Line ──────────→
Click, Drag Circle   Release Mouse
Draw Arc
Draw Curve
Draw Rectangle ──┘
Draw Circle/Oval ──────────→

Note: Drawing Tablets may be used with the Grease Pencil to supplement Mouse Actions and give control when drawing Strokes. Tablet Pressure sensitivity may be toggled off/on in the Header as required when using a Tablet Stylus (Figure 27.19).

Toggle Stylus Pressure Sensitivity On/Off

Draw Pencil   Material: Black   Radius   25 px   Strength   0.600

Figure 26.19

Brush/Stroke Types

Different Brush/Pen Types may be selected in the Header and the Properties Editor. Active Tools.

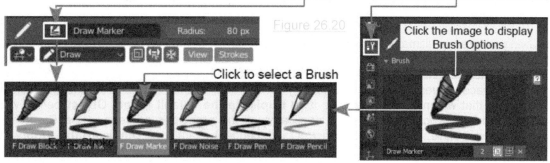

Draw Marker   Radius   80 px   Figure 26.20

Draw

View   Strokes

Click to select a Brush

Click the Image to display Brush Options

Brush

F Draw Block   F Draw Ink   F Draw Marker   F Draw Noise   F Draw Pen   F Draw Pencil

Draw Marker

In Figure 26.21 two types of Stroke are shown; Open Stroke and Closed Stroke. A Closed Stroke forms a closed loop which may be any shape defining an area. The area may be formed by closing a single Stroke or by different intersecting Strokes.

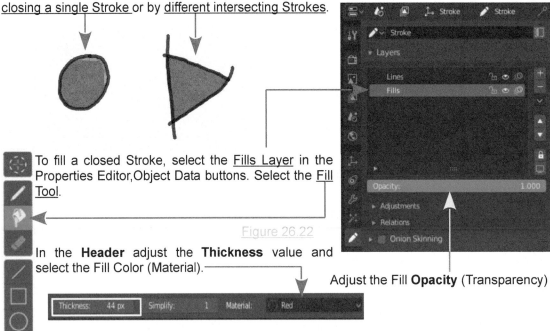

To fill a closed Stroke, select the Fills Layer in the Properties Editor,Object Data buttons. Select the Fill Tool.

Figure 26.22

In the **Header** adjust the **Thickness** value and select the Fill Color (Material).

Adjust the Fill **Opacity** (Transparency)

Place the Fill Tool Brush inside the Closed Stroke and repeatedly click LMB to fill.

Note: Creating a Fill on the **Lines Layer** may overlap the Stroke line depending on the Fill Thickness value.

Multiple Characters/Layers

Drawing Strokes is ultimately drawing Characters to enact a story. When you draw Strokes to create a Character, all the Strokes are linked to the one Empty Object that you see in the default Grease Pencil 2D Animation Workspace (in Object Mode). Consequently, moving one Stroke in the Workspace moves all Strokes. One way of overcoming this, if you know the number of Characters that will make up your cast, is to **Duplicate the default Empty Object** before you begin drawing. Duplicating the Empty, duplicates all the properties as seen in the Properties Editor and, therefore, allows you to construct independent characters. **Duplicate the Empty in Object Mode.** Note: Adding a **New Empty Object** (in Object Mode) does not reproduce the properties required for Grease Pencil drawing. **Duplicate the default Grease Pencil Empty**.

Strokes may be edited to refine their shape. They may be repositioned, rotated and scaled and have special effects applied. Repositioning is performed in Object Mode and Edit Mode. Refining the shape of the Stroke is performed in Sculpt Mode and special effects are applied with the Properties Editor, Special Effects buttons. There are also special Grease Pencil Modifiers.

Editing in Object Mode

Figure 26.23

Rotated and Scaled

In Object Mode, use the manipulation Tools to Translate, Rotate and Scale. All Strokes will be affected since they are linked to the Empty Object.

Figure 27.24

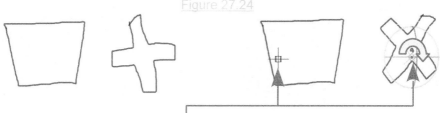

Drawing Strokes linked to separate Empty Objects (default Empty duplicated) allow individual manipulation.

Editing in Edit Mode

To edit an individual stroke in Edit Mode when multiple Strokes are drawn, use the **Select Box** to select the Stroke to be edited (click, hold and drag a rectangle over the stroke). The stroke will display orange when the Mouse button is released.

With the Stroke selected use the Edit Tools to affect the selected Stroke. Generally click LMB, hold and drag the Mouse. Press **Alt + A Key** to deselect.

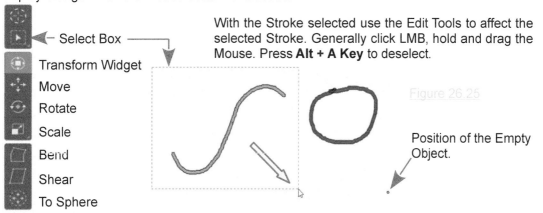

- Select Box
- Transform Widget
- Move
- Rotate
- Scale
- Bend
- Shear
- To Sphere

Figure 26.25

Position of the Empty Object.

In Edit Mode Strokes may be edited by applying special grease pencil Modifiers or Object Visual Effects from the Properties Editor.

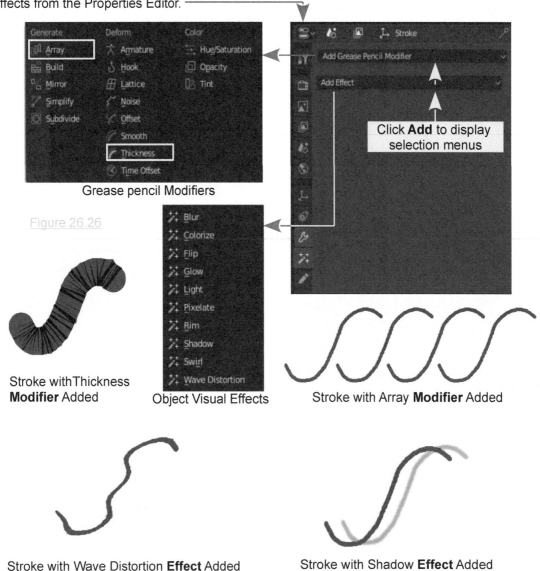

Grease pencil Modifiers

Figure 26.26

Stroke withThickness **Modifier** Added

Object Visual Effects

Stroke with Array **Modifier** Added

Click **Add** to display selection menus

Stroke with Wave Distortion **Effect** Added

Stroke with Shadow **Effect** Added

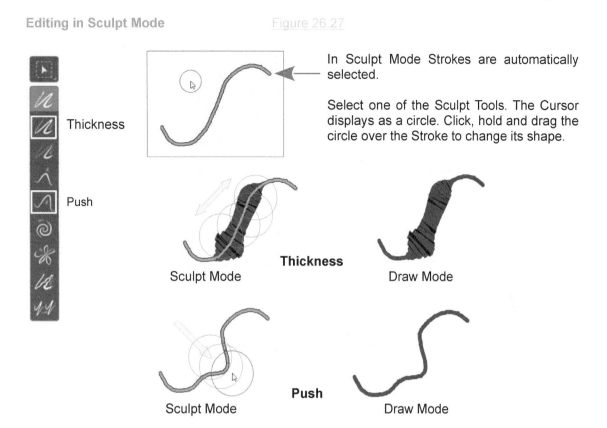

In Sculpt Mode Strokes are automatically selected.

Select one of the Sculpt Tools. The Cursor displays as a circle. Click, hold and drag the circle over the Stroke to change its shape.

Thickness

Push

Thickness

Sculpt Mode   Draw Mode

Push

Sculpt Mode   Draw Mode

26.3 Grease Pencil Animation

Grease Pencil Animation follows the rules of Animation as described in Chapter 18. Instead of Translating, Rotating and Scaling Objects to move in the Scene you draw, copy and modify Strokes at different Keyframes in the Timeline to create the illusion of motion. The Walk Cycle diagram in the introduction to this chapter typifies the process.

The following exercise will serve as an introduction to the Grease Pencil Animation process.

In Grease Pencil Draw Mode construct a simple character face (Figure 26.28).

Figure 26.28

Inserting a Keyframe

Drawing a single Stroke in the 3D View Editor inserts a Keyframe in the Dopesheet Timeline.

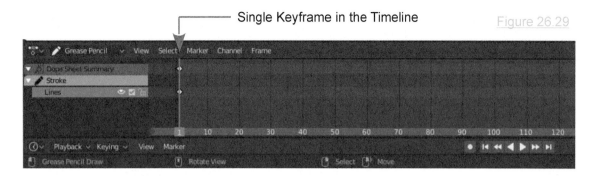

Single Keyframe in the Timeline

Figure 26.29

Onion Skinning

In the top version of the **Properties Editor, Object data buttons**, check **Onion Skinning**. By default Onion Skinning is also checked in the Overlays Panel. Onion Skinning draws a shadow of the original Stroke when the stroke is edited (modified). This enables a comparison between the modification and the original Stroke.

Inserting a Second Keyframe

Figure 26.30

Position the Timeline Cursor at the next Keyframe (Frame 10) and modify the Strokes making up the Character's Face. You may change the Editor Modes and use any of the modification Tool previously described.

Modifications only have to be slight. Look closely at Figure 26.27 to see the faint green shadow lines showing how the original Strokes were before modification.

Onion Skinning

Continue on changing Keyframe positions in the Timeline and altering the Strokes to change facial expression.

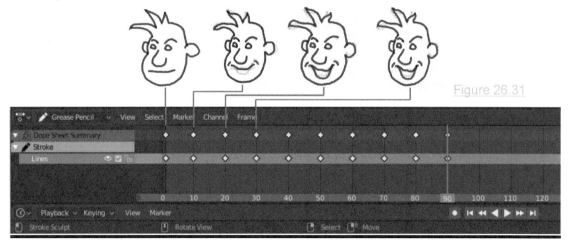

Figure 26.31

You may right click a Keyframe to select, press **Shift + D Key** to duplicate then move to another Frame. In Figure 26.28 Keyframes 50 to 90 have been duplicated from Keyframes 1 to 40 and placed in reverse order.

Drag the Timeline Cursor to scrub through the animation. You may select any Keyframe and adjust Stroked in the 3D View Editor. Press the Play button in the Timeline to view the animation.

At this stage playing the animation will show a jerky animated movement as each Keyframe is displayed. In the Timeline you may box select all the Keyframes then scale the group down. This produces a much smoother transition but also a much shorter animation.

Summary

The information in this chapter will obviously not turn you into a graphics artist but having a basic knowledge of procedures and tools in the Grease Pencil should make it easer to follow more detailed tutorials.

27

Video Sequence Editor

The Video Sequence Editor is where you compile a Video Sequences (Movie). **Movie** originated from the term Moving Pictures. Moving Pictures were developed to entertain and tell stories and this has developed into modern Communication Systems. The basic concept however, which is, to tell a story, remains .

Blender provides the tools which allow you to tell your story by using animated pictures (animations). You create Scenes in which actors move depicting events that you wish to communicate to an audience. The animated Scenes are recorded and rendered to movie files. The individual files are not necessarily produced in a sequence that tells the story, therefore, they need to be arranged in the correct sequence, hence the **Video Sequence Editor**.

Movies are made by piecing together short segments of video produced when you render animation sequences. Sound files and special effects are added to enhance the visual and audio presentation.

27.1 Making a Movie

Making a movie in Blender will be discussed in relation to producing a video from a series of short animations which have been rendered to video files. The animations may have been created in separate Scenes in a single Blender file or in different Blender files. In either case the animations must be pre-rendered into video file format and be saved to a folder on your hard drive. The files should preferably be named or numbered in relation to a sequence of events which will tell whatever story you are about to tell.

27.2 Storyboard

A movie is a visual way of telling a story or communicating a message. To effectively piece together a movie you must have at least an idea of how you want to tell your story. In other words you should have a plan or sketch to use as a reference. The plan is called a **Storyboard**. It is easy to become immersed in the technical detail of the process and lose the plot.

In the movie, in this demonstration, a submarine on the surface of the ocean, dives underwater and conducts a torpedo attack. The story has been broken down into five parts. Submarine on surface, submarine dives, two underwater views and firing torpedoes. Each part has been animated in a separate Scene in the same Blender file then rendered to an .AVI video file.

The video files are all rendered from 250 Frame animations which when combined, equals a movie of 1250 Frames. The movie will be rendered for PAL TV which plays at 24 frames per second, therefore, the movie will play for approximately 52 seconds. It is a long way from being a feature film but will give you the idea.

To demonstrate the process of compiling a movie work through the procedure as follows. The demonstration will combine the five video files and a sound file.

Sound file? Sound files can be background music, recorded voice, sound effects, in fact anything to enhance the video. For the purpose of the demonstration a sound file has been compiled in **.wav** format. As with video files there are many types of sound files. You are probably familiar with **MP3**, **MP4** etc. Blender supports WAV (.wav) files best although you can enter MP3.

27.3 The Video Files

Figure 27.1

Five .avi Video Files saved in the Folder: BDemo_Submarine

27.4 The Sound File

For this demonstration a series of sounds, downloaded from Free Sounds at **www.freesound.org**, have been combined (Figure 27.2) using the free program **Audacit**

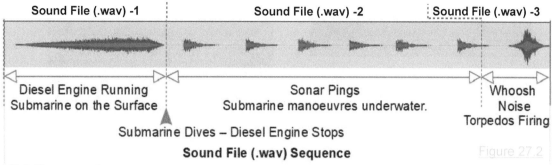

Sound File (.wav) -1   Sound File (.wav) -2   Sound File (.wav) -3

Diesel Engine Running   Sonar Pings   Whoosh
Submarine on the Surface   Submarine manoeuvres underwater.   Noise
    Torpedos Firing

Submarine Dives – Diesel Engine Stops

Sound File (.wav) Sequence   Figure 27.2

27.5 Preparation

File Definition: In this demonstration the five **.avi files** saved to the hard drive will be referred to as **Video Files**. When combined the final output will be called the **Movie File**.

Before attacking the Video Sequence Editor some preparation is required. Open a new Blender file. Leave the Cube, Lamp and Camera in the default Scene.

Set the File Path for Saving   Figure 27.3

The first step in the movie making process is to set the file path to the location where you want your **Movie File** saved and to define the **Video Output Format**.

By default Blender sets the file path for saving files to the **tmp** (temporary) folder on your hard drive. This can be seen in the **Properties Editor, Output buttons, Output tab** (Figure 27.3).

You change this setting by clicking on the **Browse Folder** button (Figure 27.3) and navigating to a new folder in the **File Browser Editor**. Select the folder then click on the **Accept button** at the top right hand side. For convenience and simplicity create a new folder. In this demonstration the folder is named **A_Submarine_Movie** and the file path to the folder is: **C:\A_Submarine_Movie** (Figure 27.4).

Figure 27.4

Set the Video Format

Set the Movie Video output format (see File Type in Chapter 17 - 17.9 Video Codecs). To demonstrate the movie making process the **AVI Raw** codec (.avi) will be used from the **Movie** list in the **Properties Editor, Output buttons, Output Tab** selection menu (Figure 27.5 over).

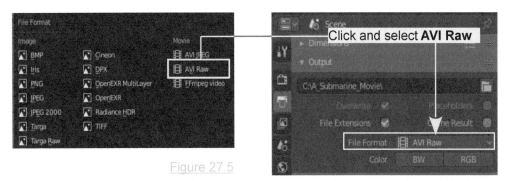

Figure 27.5

Since the **Video Files** (clips) being compiled into a **Movie File** are also **.avi file format** you are, in fact, simply assembling the files into a single file. If you select either the AVI JPEG or FFmpeg video options then the output after assembling would undergo a conversion.

Figure 27.6

27.6 Video Editing Workspace

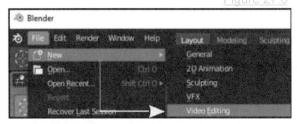

Video assembly is performed in the Video Sequence Editor but to assist, Blender has a **Video Editing Workspace** hidden away. In the Screen Header click on File, then New and select **Video Editing** (Figure 27.6).

The **Video Editing Workspace** contains five Editors (Figure 27.7).

Figure 27.7

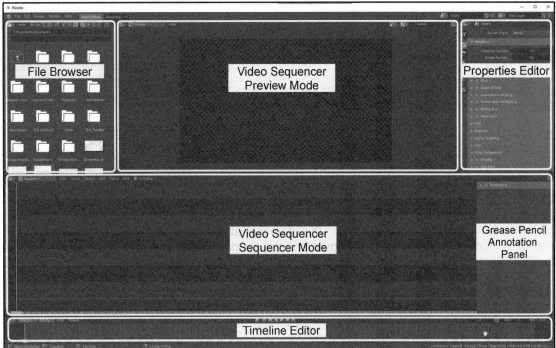

File Browser

Video Sequencer
Preview Mode

Properties Editor

Video Sequencer
Sequencer Mode

Grease Pencil
Annotation
Panel

Timeline Editor

File Browser Editor: Where you navigate and select files.
VSE Preview Mode: Where you see the video playing.
Properties Editor: Controls relevant to the VSE.
VSE Sequencer Mode: Where you combine Video Files (clips).
Timeline Editor: Provides control of how the video sequence plays.

GP Annotation: Grease Pencil Annotation panel for writing notes.

In this basic instruction you will be concerned with the **File Browser Editor** and the **two versions of the Video Sequencer**

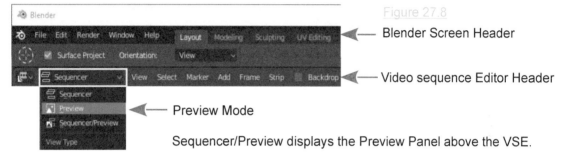

Figure 27.8

◀—— Blender Screen Header

◀—— Video sequence Editor Header

◀—— Preview Mode

Sequencer/Preview displays the Preview Panel above the VSE.

27.7 File Browser Editor

The File Browser Editor was discussed in Chapter 3 – 3.5 but a point to remember is, the Editor will show files in a variety of ways. The default display in the **Video Editing Workspace** shows thumbnail images of the first Frame in the video file. You can change this to display the file names if you wish. Click on the button shown in the diagram (Figure 27.9).

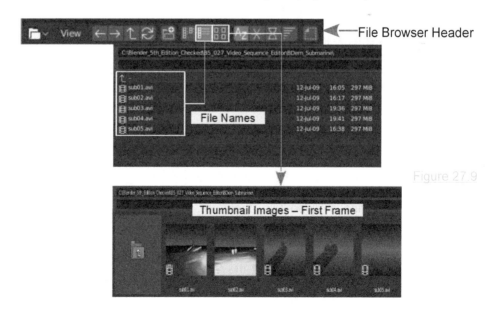

◀——File Browser Header

File Names

Figure 27.9

Thumbnail Images – First Frame

27.8 Video Sequence Editor

Preview superimposed in the VSE

Figure 27.10

VSE Editor Cursor

Movie File Entered in the VSE.

The main panel in the Video Sequence Editor (VSE) is divided into Channels (horizontal strips), numbered at the left hand side. In Figure 27.10 a Video File named **sub01.avi** has been entered in Channel 1. A preview panel has been superimposed in the diagram showing the first Frame of the animation. When a Video File is entered in the Video Sequence Editor the first Frame of the animation displays in the Video Sequencer Preview.

To enter a file, click the file in the File Browser, hold and drag into the Sequencer. Position over a Channel and release the Mouse button.

When a Video File is entered in the VSE, what was originally the Annotation Panel changes to an Editing Panel for the Video File. Note: In this case the Video File is by default selected, therefore, the controls in the editing Panel relate to this file. With multiple files entered in the VSE the controls will relate to the file that is selected.

Placing Files in the VSE

Figure 27.10

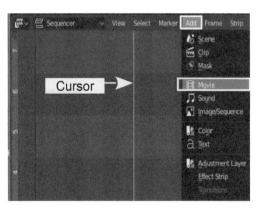

Cursor

Various types of files may be entered in the VSE and combined with video files. Click on Add in the VSE Header (Figure 27.10) and select what you wish to enter (the File Browser Editor opens). In this instance you are entering a Video File, therefore, select **Movie**. Navigate to the folder containing your Video Files and select a file. This is an alternative to the method previously described. By default the File is entered in **Channel 1**. Note: By default the VSE Editor Cursor is located at position 0+00 in the **Playback Timeline** along the bottom of the VSE. When Files are entered in the VSE they are located at the position of the Cursor.

To see Video Files in action click the Play button in the Timeline Editor at the bottom of the Screen. You may also click, hold and drag the VSE Cursor to scrub through the Video Files.

Video Files in upper Channels take precedence and play over lower Channels.

Selecting in the VSE

You select a File in a Channel by clicking RMB. Press G Key and drag R or L to reposition. RMB click on a file, hold and drag up or down to place the file in a different Channel.

Note: When repositioning horizontally, click RMB, hold and drag then you may release RMB. The file remains in Drag Mode until you click LMB to locate the file. When positioning horizontally you will see a Frame Number appear at the beginning and end of the Video File giving you the exact location in the Timeline.

Figure 27.11

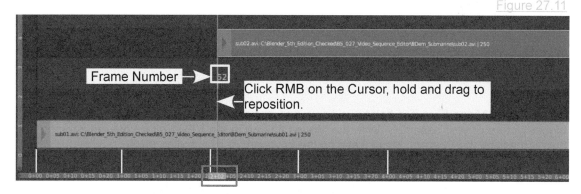

Timeline Graduations / Positions

Example: File named sub02.avi is positioned at Frame 52. In the Timeline the position is given as 2+02. The horizontal divisions (faint vertical lines) are located at:

0+00 = Frame 0.00   1+00 = Frame 25   2+00 = Frame 50

Frame 52, is therefore 2 +02

$(2 \times 25) + 2 = 52$

Erasing (Deleting) a File

LMB click on the File in the VSE (border highlights white), press the X Key, select **Erase Strips**.

The Add Button

The **Add button** in the VSE window header has several options.

Scene: Adds a strip containing information about a Scene in the Blender file.

Mask: If a mask has been created it can be added to the VSE to hide or alter the appearance of parts of the video.

Image: A still image or a series of images may be inserted into the video much like adding individual frames of an animation or a slide show.

Sound: Sound files can be inserted in the VSE to enhance video.

Effects Strip: Effects to provide enhancement, background and transition

Figure 27.12

With the forgoing information you are in a position to proceed and compile the Movie File.

Adding Video Files

When adding Video Files it is helpful to scale and pan the VSE Editor. This allows you to get a bigger picture of your assembly. With the Mouse Cursor in the VSE Editor you can zoom in and out by pressing the Plus and Minus keys on the keyboard or by scrolling MMB.

In the Timeline Graduation bar, click LMB on the light gray area, hold and drag to the right. You will observe a dot at the end of the light gray section and a darker section being displayed.

Click, hold and drag the dot.

Figure 27.13

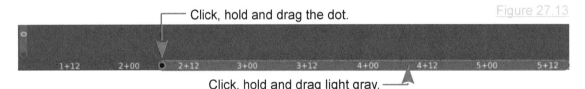

Click, hold and drag light gray.

By clicking LMB and dragging the light gray you pan the view left and right. By clicking on either of the dots at each end of this panel and dragging left or right you zoom the scale . As you do this the scale values expand and contract accordingly. This is the same as zooming in the VSE Editor.

As you have seen you add Movie Files by clicking **Add** in the **VSE Editor header** (Press Add – Movie – navigate in the **File Browser window** – select etc.).

The first file was entered by default in Channel 1 with the VSE cursor located at 0+01. To add a second file, position the cursor where you want it to start and repeat the Add process. A second file is entered in Channel 2. The files can be moved to different channels as you wish and repositioned horizontally.

> **Note:** If the VSE Cursor is placed at the end of the first Movie File the second file will be placed in the same Channel as the first, end to end.

Each successive file addition is entered in the Channel above the preceding Channel except when the VSE Cursor is positioned at the end of the preceding file. To have two Movie Files play end to end as a continuous sequence, position the start of the second file horizontally at the end of the first file (they do not have to be in the same Channel). With the second file selected, press the **G Key** and drag the Mouse. You will see Frame Numbers display at the beginning and end of each file which makes it easy to align exact Frames. You can purposely overlap files since a file in a higher Channel will take precedence over a file in a lower Channel when playing.

> **Note:** If you shift select multiple Video Files in the File Browser Editor they will be automatically placed end to end in a single Channel.

Playing the Video File

No matter where the file is located you can view different Frames in the file by dragging the Cursor along the Timeline. You play the file by pressing the **Start button** in the **Timeline Editor**. Press **Esc** to quit or Pause, Fast Forward etc. by using the play controls (Figure 27.14).

To mention some more obvious information about playing consider this; the Video Files used in the demonstration are 250 Frames long. With the first located with the **Start Frame** at 0+01 it will play in its entirety then repeat until you press **Esc**. This only occurs since, in the **Timeline Editor**, **Start: 1** and **End: 250** are set. If **End: 100** was set the file would only play for 100 Frames then repeat, or if the start Frame of the file was positioned on the VSE Timeline other than at Frame 1 then only part of the file will play.

Figure 27.14

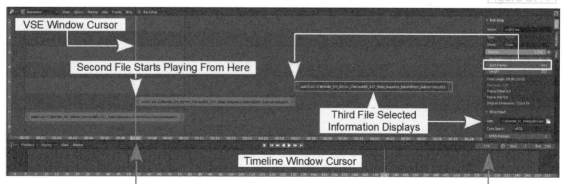

VSE Window Cursor at position 6+25 (6 x 25 FPS + 24 = 174)

Cutting Video Strips

Another feature is the ability to select only part of a video strip for playback. You can cut the strip into segments. There are two ways to do this which are; a **Soft Cut** and a **Hard Cut**. In either case, position the Cursor at the Frame where you wish to make the cut. For a **Soft Cut** press the **K Key**.

For a **Hard Cut** press **Shift + K key**. In either case you finish up with two separate segments of clip which you can reposition or move to a different Channel in the VSE. The difference is, with a **Soft Cut** both segments of the clip retain the data for the other part. With a **Hard Cut** the data is not retained (Figure 27.15).

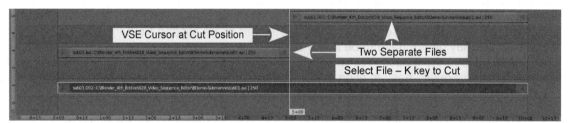

VSE Cursor at Cut Position

Two Separate Files

Select File – K key to Cut

Figure 27.15

Window Scene Background

In the VSE Editor header click Add – Scene – Scene to add a Scene strip (Figure 27.16). Shift select a movie file strip plus the Scene strip (RMB click) then click **Add - Effect Strip - Add** . The Scene in the **3D View Editor** will superimposed and display as a background to the Video File.

Inset showing the 3D View Editor Scene superimposed on the Movie File

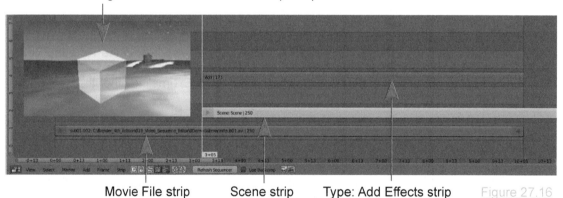

Movie File strip   Scene strip   Type: Add Effects strip   Figure 27.16

Adding Sound Files

Sound files such as MP3 and WAVE are entered by selecting **Sound** instead of **Movie** and then manipulated the same as a Video File.

With all your strips aligned and edited you can press the **Play button** in the **Timeline Editor** to preview the final movie.

27.9 Rendering the Movie File

When all the specifications have been set for your Movie output File it is time to render the final movie.

In the **Screen Header** click the **Render button** and select **Render Animation**. Be prepared to wait a considerable time. Even a short movie will take awhile depending on the speed of your computer. Long movie sequences are often uploaded to websites called **Render Farms** which will perform the render process for you (at a cost).

Once the render is complete you find the file in the output folder and give it a test run in a media player.

27.10 Summary

The Blenders Video Sequence Editor allows you to introduce transitional effects between video clips, to render a Video File into a series of Image Files so that you can manipulate images (Frames) within any one clip, then render the reconstructed Frame back to a Video File. Video Files can be cut and edited and combined to produce the most sophisticated animated Movies.

Drivers

Drivers are functions or scripts which use properties (values) to affect other properties. This is particularly applicable when animating. Drivers are used to control the animation of one property based on the value of another.

For example, the Translation (movement) of one Object may be used to control the Rotation of another Object. This means that the Object's animated value is not controlled by the Frame number interpolated from Keyframes, but rather by the data in a specified animation channel. Drivers can take their effects from single properties, differences in rotation or scripted Python expressions which may be edited inside the User Interface controls.

Drivers are not limited to simple animated movements. You may use the X location of a Driver of an Object to control the Material color (RGB curves) of another Object's material, or use the rotation of a Driver to control the scale of an Object, or use the scale of a Driver to control the shape (through shape keys) of a mesh/curve/etc., use a Python function to control a constraint's influence, and much much more.

One key usage of Drivers is in character animation: for example, you can add Object drivers to the relative shape keys of a face. Then, you manipulate the expressions of your character just by moving these Drivers' Objects.

To explain Drivers in detail would require a dedicated publication. This chapter will simply demonstrate, in practical terms, what a driver is and where the controls are located in the interface. This will provide a starting point for a detailed study.

28.1 Blender Drivers - Introduction

As an example of using Drivers, work through the following example:

Open Blender with the default Scene containing the Cube object. Deselect the Cube and add a Monkey Object. Move the Monkey to one side as shown in Figure 28.1.

Split the 3D View Editor in two and make one part the **Drivers Editor** . With the cursor in the Driver Editor window press **N key** to display the **View Properties Tab** expanded.

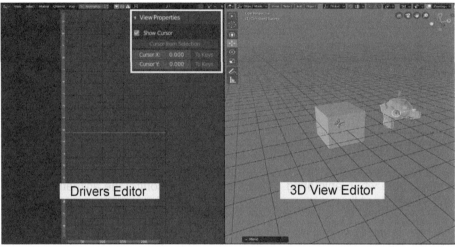

Drivers Editor

3D View Editor

Figure 28.1

A Driver will set up to Rotate the Monkey on its Z Axis when the Cube is Translated on its Y Axis.

With the Mouse Cursor in the 3D View Editor, press the **N Key** to display the **Object Properties Panel**. You now have a Properties panel in the 3D View Editor and in the Driver Editor. In the 3D View Editor, press the **T Key** to close the Tools panel and remove clutter from the scene.

3D View Editor, Object Properties (N Key)——▶

With the Monkey Object selected right click on the **Z Axis Rotation** slider in the **3D View Editor Object Properties Panel** (press N key). Select (click) **Add Drivers**. The slider will turn purple showing that a driver has been added (Figure 28.2).

RMB Click select Add Driver

In the **Driver Editor** at the upper LHS, you will see that a <u>Driver has been added</u>.

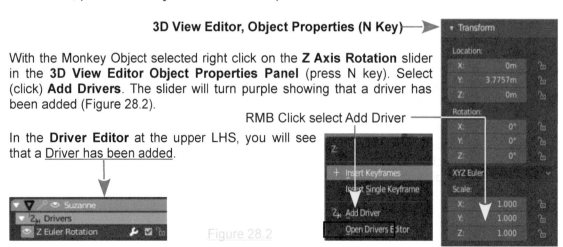

Figure 28.2

In the **Driver Editor** click on **Z Euler Rotation** .

A **Properties Panel** displays at the RHS of the Driver Editor with the **F-Curve Tab** open. Tabs are displayed at the RHS of this Properties panel. Click on the **Drivers Tab**.

Figure 28.3

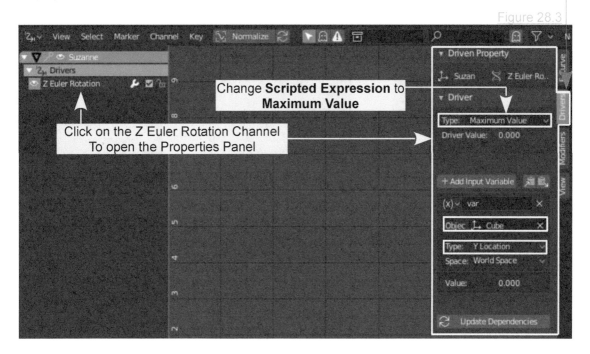

In the **Driven Properties Panel** change **Driver Type: Scripted Expression** to **Maximum Value**. Click where you see **Object** and select **Cube**. Just below the Cube entry change Type: **X Location** to **Y Location**.

You have set the Driver for the Monkey to be controlled by the Y Axis movement of the Cube.

In the 3D View Editor select the Cube and translate it along the Y axis. The monkey rotates on its Z axis (Figure 28.4).

Figure 28.4

28.2 Understanding Drivers

The example previously described explains the basic concept of applying Drivers but understanding Drivers in relation to Blender's interface will allow you to use them for a variety of applications. Look at the Object Properties, Panel, Transform Tab in the 3D View Editor (N Key to display) and the Driver Property in the Driver Editor.

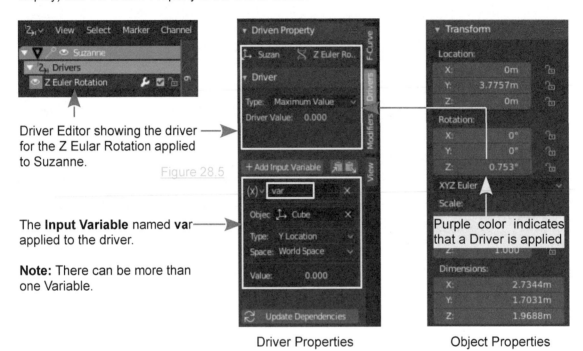

Driver Editor showing the driver for the Z Eular Rotation applied to Suzanne.

Figure 28.5

The **Input Variable** named **var** applied to the driver.

Note: There can be more than one Variable.

Purple color indicates that a Driver is applied

Driver Properties   Object Properties

RMB clicking on the Z Axis Rotation Slider in the Object Properties in the 3D View Editor and selecting Add Driver adds a Driver (purple color). The Driver is displayed in the Driver Editor. In the Driver Property Tab you see the driver for the Z Euler Rotation of Suzanne (the Monkey Object). The Driver has one **Variable** named **var**. This is where values are entered to control what the driver does.

The values entered in this particular example are:

Figure 28.6

Object: Cube (the controlling Object).

Type: Y Location (the Y Axis location of the Cube determines the Rotation of Suzanne).

Space: (Transform Space):World Space

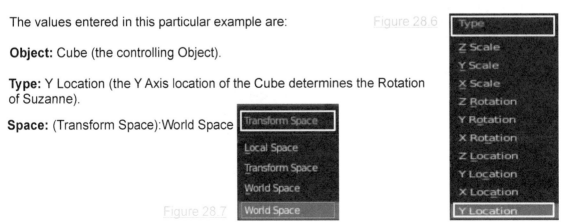

Figure 28.7

476

Take a step back and in a new blender file add a Driver to the X Axis Transform Location slider.

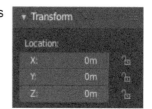

With the Driver added the X Location slider in the Transform Tab is ineffectual. The control is passed over to the Driver.

Delete Expression: var+0.0 and enter 2 →
The Cube moves + 2 Units on the X Axis.

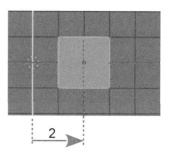

Instead of 2 enter 2*2 (2 x 2)
The Cube moves 4 Units'

Entering 3*4/6 (3 x 4 ÷ 6) the Cube locates at + 2 Units.

This is demonstrating that maths can be performed in the Expression panel to set values for the Driver.

Figure 28.8

Multiple Variables

Clicking +Add Input Variable adds a new Variable named var_001.

Graph Editor Figure 28.9

Clicking on the Eye icon in the Driver editor, Driver Channel displays a Graph in the Graph Editor section of the Driver Editor.

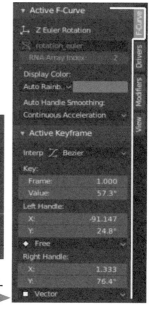

Properties for the Graph are displayed and controlled by clicking the F-Curve Tab in the Driver Editor, Properties panel. ————————————▶

Figure 28.10

Multiple Drivers

You may have Drivers for any or all of the Transform Channels in the Object Properties Panel as well as many of the Properties in the Properties Editor.

28.3 Randomize Object Properties

To lead you on, into the world of Drivers the following exercise is offered as encouragement to pursue this topic.

The objective is to set up a Blender file which may be used to create random properties. To begin the default Cube will randomly Rotate when it is repositioned in the Scene.

The following instructions will demonstrate how to set up the **Blender file** including a **Python Script** which may be used with **Drivers**.

Create a Python Script

The first step is to create the Python Script which you then register in a Blender file.

A **Python Script** is a piece of code written in the **Python Computer Language** and is simply a text file. The script shown in Figure 29.11 will be used.

```
import bpy                              Figure 28.11
import random

# Random floating point number between lo and hi

def randf(lo, hi):
        return random.uniform(lo, hi)

bpy.app.driver_namespace["randf"] = randf
```

Type the text shown in the diagram into a Text Editor such as Notepad or Wordpad and save the text file. Name the file **Random.py**. You will copy and paste this into a Blender file. You can type it directly into the Blender text editor but having it saved as a text file gives you a back up.

Note: Make sure the text is copied **exactly** as shown. The slightest error will cause an error when running the script.

The Python script will be used in conjunction with the **Blender Drivers Function**.

In simple terms **Drivers** are functions which affect the attributes or properties of an Object. Refer to the demonstration at the beginning of this chapter where the translation of one Object controls the rotation of another. In that instance the position of one Object in the Scene controlled the rotation of the other. Instead of using the translation of an Object, the **Python Script** will be introduced to the Driver to control properties of Objects.

The first step is to enter and register the **Python Script** in a Blender file. This will create a Blender file which you can save for future use.

Open a new Blender file and open the Blender **Text Editor**. Create a new **Text Block** by clicking **New** in the window Header or by clicking Text - Create Text Block.

The default name of the new Text Block is shown simply as **Text** (center of the Text Editor Header). Rename this to something more significant. Since you are about to work with random properties and a Python Script, **ran.py**. is appropriate. Note the suffix **.py** is very important, therefore make sure you include this in the name.

With the Text Block created go get your Python Script. That is, go to the text file you previously created. Open the file in the Text Editor you used (Word Pad or Notepad) and select (highlight) the text and copy it to the clipboard. Paste the text into the newly created Text Block in the **Blender Text Editor** (Figure 28.12).

In the Blender **Text Editor Header** click **Run Script** (upper RHS of the Editor) then check **Register**. Run script will make the functions contained in the script available to the Driver. The function in the Python Script is named **randf**. **Register** means, the next time you open the Blender file it will run the script and register automatically.

Rename **Text** to **ran.py**   Figure 28.12   Run the script then check Register

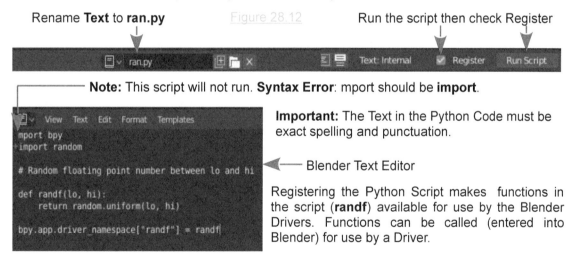

Note: This script will not run. **Syntax Error**: mport should be **import**.

Important: The Text in the Python Code must be exact spelling and punctuation.

— Blender Text Editor

Registering the Python Script makes functions in the script (**randf**) available for use by the Blender Drivers. Functions can be called (entered into Blender) for use by a Driver.

Saving the **RandomPy.blend** file means you now have a Blender file available for generating random properties. How the **randf (lo, hi)** part of the Python Script works will be demonstrated. To understand this statement you will have to undertake a study of the Python programming language.

Have the **RandomPy.blend** file opened. You can close the **Text Editor** and return the **3D View Editor**.

With the mouse cursor in the 3D View Editor press the **N key** to display the **Object Properties Panel** at the RHS. **Note:** This Properties Panel is distinct from the **Properties Editor** displayed at the RHS of the Screen.

Note that some values display in both i.e. in the **Properties Editor, Object buttons Transform Tab** there are **Location, Rotation and Scale** sliders. Identical sliders for the same Transform properties are displayed in the Object Properties panel of the 3D View Editor.

Split the **3D View Editor** in two and change one part to the **Drivers Editor** (Figure 28.1).

The driver Editor by default comprises two panels. An empty Driver panel at the LH side and a Graph panel on the right.

With the Mouse Cursor in **either panel** press the **N Key** to display the **View Properties Tab** at the top of a new **Properties** panel. The Graph part of this Editor will not be used in this exercise, so you can arrange the Editor to only show the **empty Driver panel** and the new **Properties Panel** (Figure 28.13).

Figure 28.13

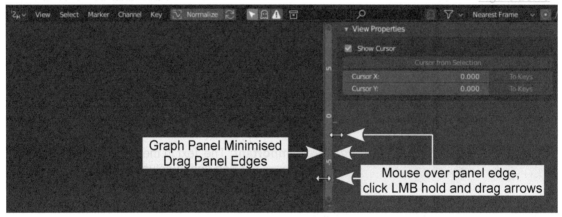

Drag edges of panels leaving the Graph display as a narrow strip.

In creating the file you have registered a **Python Script** in the file and configured the 3D View Editor.

With the mouse cursor in the **3D View Editor** press the **T key** to remove the Tool panel to save space.

At this point you have three Properties panels displayed. There are Properties panels in the Driver Editor and the 3D View Editor and also the Properties Editor at the RHS of the Screen.

Save the Blender file for future use. Name it, **RandomPy.blend**. (You can name the file anything you like. Just remember what the name is and where you save it.)

28.4 Using The RandomPy.blend File

It is assumed the file has been saved and Blender has been closed. Open Blender and open the **Random.py** Blender file.

Rotation Driver Properties

RandomPy will be used to make the default Cube Object randomly Rotate when the Cube is moved.

Begin by setting a Driver for the X Rotation Property of the default Cube Object. Make sure the Cube is selected. In the **Object Properties Panel** of the **3D View Editor**, right mouse click on the **X Rotation slider** and select **Add Driver** (Figure 28.14).

Figure 28.14

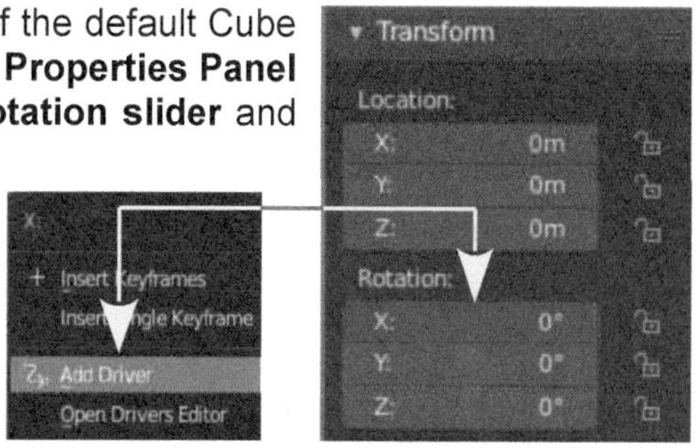

The slider turns purple indicating a driver has been added and the driver channel displays in the **Driver Editor** (Figures 28.15).

Figure 28.15

At this point all that displays in the **Driver Editor, Properties panel** is the **View Properties Tab**. Minimal information is displayed in the Properties panel since the **Driver Channel** is not selected.

Click on the **X Euler Rotation Driver Channel** and more properties display in the panel (Figure 28.16)

Select the Drivers Tab

Enter **randf(-pi, pi)**

Enter the Python Script Function

Figure 28.16

You will be using a **Scripted Expression** (Python Script) and calling the **randf** function. Enter the function from the script as **randf(-pi, pi)** and hit Enter.

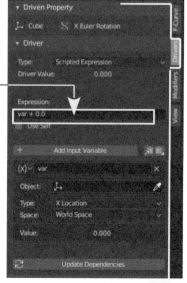

You enter this in the **Driver Editor, Properties Panel, Drivers Tab**, just below the Scripted Expression selection button where you see **Expression: var+0.0.** Delete and enter **randf(-pi, pi)** in the **Expression:** panel (Figure 28.16).

Note: Warning: Python expressions limited for security (ignore).

Note: If you save the Blender file and open it at a later date you may see the warning message in Figure XXX. This is saying Blender doesn't trust the script. Providing you know the script is OK, click **Allow Execution**.

Figure 28.17

Entering the function is in effect telling Blender to use **randf** expression of your Python script with the arguments **-pi** and **+pi** to recalculate a random value of rotation about the Cube's X Axis within the range **minus π** to **pluss π**. In other words pick a rotational value about the X Axis between 0° and 360° since there are **2 π** radians in a circle (**Arguments** are values that an expression uses in its calculation).

Immediately you enter the expression, Blender will re-evaluate the X Rotation value and you will see the Cube in the 3D View Editor rotated. Every time you click **Update Dependencies** the rotation values will be recalculated and the cube randomly rotated.

Note: Translating the cube in the 3D View Editor will also Update Dependencies and randomly Rotate the Cube.

Note: When using scripted expressions you can delete the **Variable data-block** in the Driver Editor driver properties.

The set up is ready to go. By clicking on **Update Dependencies** in the Driver Editor Properties or by **Translating the cube** in the 3D View Editor, the Cube is automatically Rotated.

Driver Alternative Method for Activating

There is an alternative method for **activating Drivers**. First add Drivers to the X, Y and Z Rotation sliders in the Properties Editor, Object buttons, Transform Tab, by right clicking on each of the sliders and selecting **Add Driver**. This adds a Driver to the X, Y and Z slider values. Left click on each of the Driver Channels in turn in the **Driver Editor,** then in the **Driver Property Panel**, **Drivers Tab** delete the **Expression value**. In place type the Python expression **randf(-pi, pi)**. When done press **Enter**. Do this for all three Channels.

Re-evaluating Drivers

With Drivers set , in the 3D View Editor Solid Shading Display Mode, press **G key** (grab) drag the mouse and move the object in the 3D Editor. Blender constantly re-evaluates the driver and produces random values for the properties values. Note; this will affect any driver which has the **randf**, Python expression inserted. This is just another method of updating randf(-pi, pi) dependencies.

Material properties can be randomized using Python Script just as you did with the rotation and scale properties. For the Rotation you used a value range of **-pi** to **pi** (2π radians in a circle, therefore -π to +π) .

Consider the **randf(min value, max value)**. What do you use here for Material color? Take a look at the Base Material color sliders in the color picker in the **Properties Editor**. There are three sliders for the red, green and blue color channels, each with a minimum value of 0.000 (black) and a maximum value of 1.000 (white) (Figure 28.18).

Figure 28.18

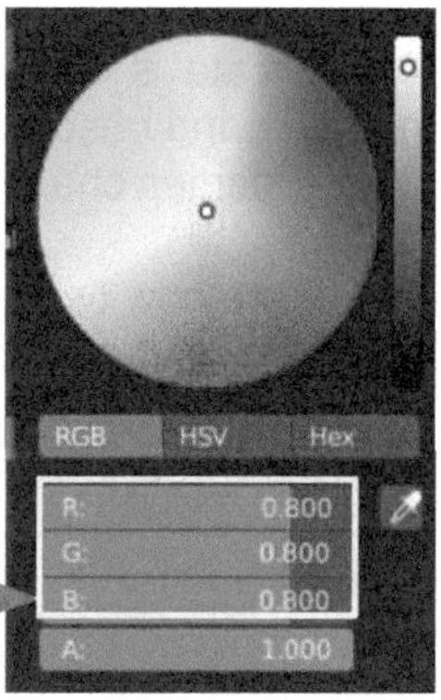

The values between the maximum and minimum produce the spectrum of visible color between white and black. To randomize Material within the spectrum, all that is required is to use the expression **randf(0.000, 1.000)**.

Slider Values Min 0.000 (black) Max 1.000 (white) ──────▶

Right click on the **Base Color** bar and select **Add Driver**. A Material Drivers Channel is displayed in the Driver Editor, Driver panel. Click on the expansion button (triangle) to display the RGB Base color Drivers (Figure 28.16).

Clicking on each driver entry will display the driver properties where you replace the default Expression value var+**0.800** with the **randf(0.000, 1.000)** expression. In the variable data block **(var)** change **World Space to Transform Space**, click on the cube icon and select **Cube** as the ID data block. Do this for all four drivers (Figures 28.19).

Figure 28.19

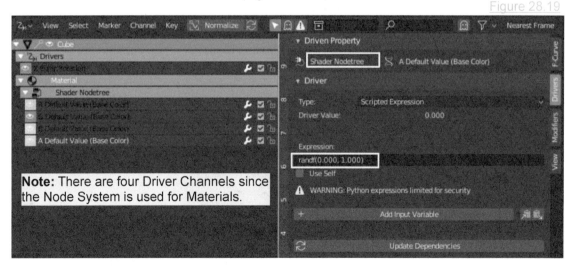

Note: There are four Driver Channels since the Node System is used for Materials.

Clicking **Update Dependencies** or translating the cube in the 3D window re-evaluates the Material, Scale and Rotation values changing the Diffuse color of the Cube in the 3D window.

Duplicating the Object

In the 3D View Editor you only have a single Cube in the Scene. Remember, at the beginning of the chapter, the objective was to create a group of cubes scattered about the Scene.

All you do is simply duplicate the Cube. With the Cube selected press **Shift + D key** to duplicate.

A duplicate is created and placed in grab mode ready to be translated. Drag the mouse to relocate and observe that the original and the duplicate are both re-evaluated by the drivers and the properties change.

There are now two Cube objects in the Scene which are identical and appear to be separate. The duplicate Cube (Cube.001) is, however, linked to the original (Cube) in that it is sharing properties data-blocks of the original. If you translate **Cube.001, Update Dependencies** is activated and the properties of the cube change. If you translate **Cube**, the properties of both cubes are changed. Shift select both cubes and you will see two sets of drivers in the Driver **Editor** (Figure 28.20).

Figure 28.20

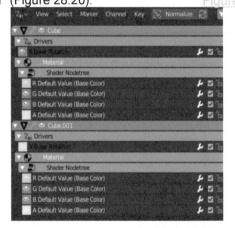

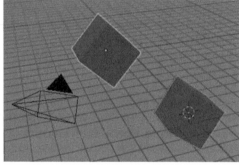

Tip: When working with Materials have the 3D View Editor in LocDev or Reneere Viewport Shading Mode.

3D View Editor Header

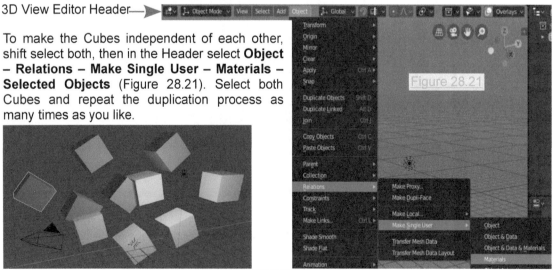

To make the Cubes independent of each other, shift select both, then in the Header select **Object – Relations – Make Single User – Materials – Selected Objects** (Figure 28.21). Select both Cubes and repeat the duplication process as many times as you like.

Figure 28.21

29

Cycles Render

The Cycles Render Engine

The Cycles Rendering system built into Blender is designed to produce photo realistic images and to provide an interactive workspace where you see a rendered view as a Scene is created.

Photo realism and high definition in images, including animation frames comes with a demand on computer power and render time.

The Eevee Render Engine gives an excellent result but there are situations where Cycles will provide added benefit.

All the Blender tools and controls for generating a Scene are applicable to both Render processes although there is a slight difference in the Node systems.

Creating Scenes and Rendering using Cycles, possibly, demands a dedicated publication, therefore, this chapter is limited to how to start Cycles, obtain the best results from your computer and providing a brief example of its application.

29.1 Cycles Render

Cycles Rendering simulates many effects that have to be specifically added to other methods of rendering such as soft shadows, depth of field, motion blur, caustics, ambient occlusion and indirect lighting.

The **Cycles Render Engine** is described as being a raytracing based engine with support for interactive rendering. Being interactive means you see a rendered view of your work as it progresses in the 3D View Editor in **Rendered Viewport Shading Mode**. Cycles incorporates a Shading Node system, a different material and texture work flow and it utilises **GPU** acceleration.

Computer Specifications for Cycles

Before using Cycles, be aware that you will require a reasonable computer processor and a graphics card which meets the specifications to handle this advanced process (refer to the Blender Wiki – Hardware Requirements).

In essence, to fully utilise **Cycles** you need a fast processor, heaps of memory (RAM) and a graphics card with **Open GL** (graphics card with built in memory **GPU** and **CUDA** enabled).

> **Note:** Cycles Rendering is activated from the main Blender interface but CUDA and GPU acceleration require a secondary activation similar to an Add-on.

If you are new to Blender these terminologies and specifications may be slightly on the technical side but just be aware that, to utilise the full effects of **Cycles** you computer has to meet the requirements. The following will show you how to activate Cycles and discover if your system is up to speed.

29.2 How To Start Cycles

Figure 29.1

To activate Cycles change **Eevee** to **Cycles** in the Properties Editor, Render buttons (Figure 29.1).

To demonstrate Cycles Rendering set up a Scene in the 3D View Editor as shown in Figure 29.2.

Figure 29.2 shows a UV Sphere positioned just above a Plane (ground plane). A second Plane (Plane.001) is placed above and behind the UV Sphere opposite the Camera. The ground plane is scaled to fill the Camera aperture as shown in the Camera View inset, while Plane.001 is positioned outside Camera View. The UV Sphere is scaled up and set to Smooth. There is a single Point Lamp in the Scene.

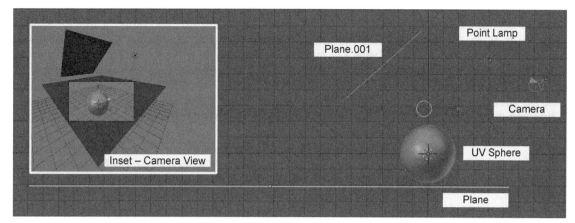

Figure 29.2

To activate the **Cycles Render Engine** click on the selection button in the Properties Editor, Render buttons as shown in Figure 29.1. From the menu select **Cycles Render**. With the 3D View Editor in **Rendered Viewport Shading Mode** you see a rendered view of the Scene.

You will note that some of the options in the **Properties Editor** change. Leave all the settings just as they are for this demonstration.

Figure 29.3

The 3D View Editor will change showing the Objects with a dark gray background (Figure 29.3). If you rotate the Scene you will see the Objects being re-rendered as you rotate.

Unless you have a reasonably fast processor the render will be very blocky and grainy and can take a considerable time. With Rendered Viewport Shading the 3D View Editor re-renders at each change made to the Scene. The longer you wait the clearer the render becomes, up to a point. You wouldn't want your computer stuck in an infinite rendering loop so Blender incorporates a time-out setting to limit the render.

When the Scene is altered e.g. rotated, the **Render** process is activated. In the upper LH corner of the 3D View Editor you will see a progress display giving the number of render Samples. When a Render is completed this displays, **Rendering Done**.

In the **Properties Editor, Render buttons, Sampling Tab** see **Render 128 – Viewport 32**. These are the default Render Pass settings. The render it limited to 32 Passes for the view in the viewport and 128 Passes for a Rendered View when you press F12.

Increasing the Pass settings produces a better result, bearing in mind that an increase in Samples incurs an increase in time to perform the Render.

The content of the Scene also affects the Render time. For example, on a machine, with the **Default Blender Scene** containing the single **Cube** Object the elapsed time for the 32 Sample preview is 00.02.20 seconds. The full image Render, pressing F12 with 128 samples takes 00.09.51 seconds. Scaling the **Cube** X 2 increases the preview time to 00.03.43 seconds and a full render is 00.24.89 seconds.

The 3D View Editor view is very dark since the default Lamp provides only a limited illumination. Changing the Lamp type or providing additional Lamps will improve the illumination, but in Cycles you can use Objects as a light source. More on that later.

What to expect from Cycles will depend on your computer and operating system, your display adapter (Graphics Card) and the drivers (Software) that have been installed for the card.

Before proceeding it will help to understand some terms.

NVIDIA graphics: NVIDIA is one of many suppliers of graphics chipsets used in graphics cards. At the time of writing Blender is configured to use NVIDIA with Open GL and CUDA enabled for GPU rendering.

Open GL is a set of graphics standards used world wide which is designed to give maximum performance on the GPU.

GPU (Graphics Processing Unit) is the processing device built into the graphics card which performs computations in parallel with the computer's central processing unit (CPU).

CUDA™ (Computer Unified Devise Architecture) is a parallel computing platform and programming model that enables dramatic increases in computing performance by harnessing the power of the graphics processing unit (GPU).

To summarize, the GPU performs computations in conjunction with the CPU which significantly speeds up the changing graphics display that is required for **On the Fly** graphics rendering. BUT! whether the GPU is faster than the CPU depends on your computer configuration. It could be your CPU is faster for some aspects of the process.

Another factor in this technicality is the **Compute Capability** rating of your graphics card. Cards are rated through a range something like 1.1 to 3.0. At the time of writing, Blender only supports graphics cards rated at 1.3 and above for GPU processing (Rendering), so again, unless your system meets the requirements you will not realize the full capability of **Cycles**.

OK! Cycles has been turned on and there is a display on the Screen but at this point the CUDA architecture and GPU processor are not activated. As previously stated CUDA and GPU require a secondary activation.

Also be aware that what you see in the Blender controls will depend on your system configuration. Blender takes a look at your system and displays controls accordingly.

To activate CUDA, in the **Blender Screen Header** click on **Edit** and open the **Preferences Editor**. Select **System** in the LH column to see **Cycles Render Device** (Figure 29.4).

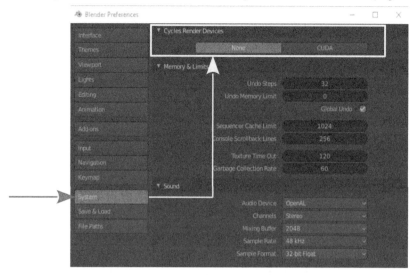

Figure 29.4

If you do not have a NVIDIA graphics chipset or your drivers for the card are outdated then you will see a message stating **No compatible GPUs** found and, therefore, the Cycles rendering process will be performed entirely by the CPU.

Providing you have the correct graphics chipset you may click on CUDA and the Cycles Render Devices Tab will show the name of your graphics card (Figure 29.5).

Figure 29.5

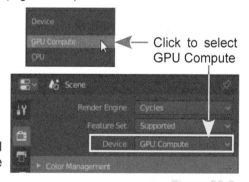

Click to select GPU Compute

In the **Properties Editor, Render buttons** you will have the option to select **GPU Rendering** (Figure 29.6).

Figure 29.6

With Cycles activated it's time to see what it can do.

29.3 Create an Object Light Source

With the demonstration Scene previously created (Figure 29.2) select the elevated Plane Object (Plane.001).

Figure 29.7

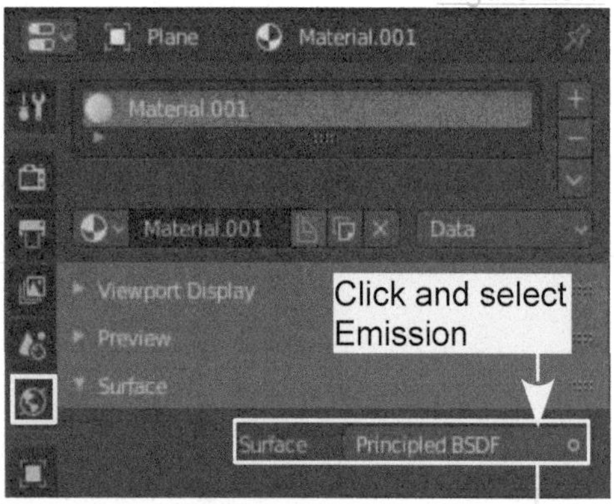

Go to **Properties Editor, Material buttons**. **Note:** When the **New button** has been pressed the Materials buttons will show the **Surface Material** (color) being controlled by the **Principled BSDF Node**. You may verify this by opening the Shader Editor where you will see the Principled BSDF Node connected to the Material Output Node.

In **Surface bar** where you see **Diffuse BSDF** click and select **Emission** from the menu that displays. This changes the plane into a light source (Figure 29.9). Note the **Strength** value is 1.000 (alter to increase the light intensity).

Figure 29.8

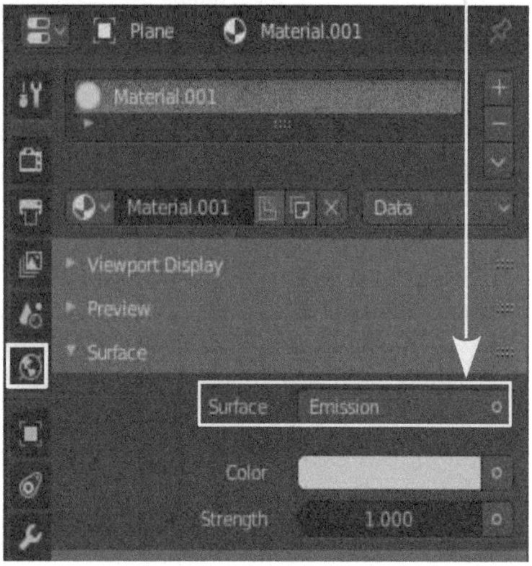

In the **Surface Tab** click on the **Color bar** and in the color picker that displays, select a bright yellow color.

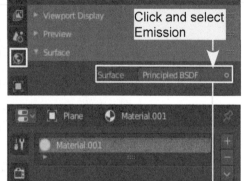

Click and select Emission

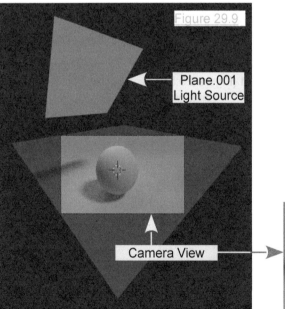

Plane.001 Light Source

Camera View

Plane.001 Light Source – Yellow Light

Figure 29.10

Rendered Image

Plane.001 emits light casting it in the Scene where it reflects off the UV Sphere and ground Plane (Figure 29.10).

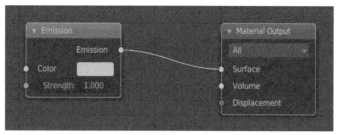

Figure 29.11

Figure 29.11 shows that the Principled BSDF Node has been replaced by an Emission Shader Node.

Note: The Node system in Cycles is different from that used with Eevee Render. The Emission Shader does not work in Eevee.

If you care to compare the Nodes available in the Add Menu you will find Cycles has a larger selection.

To demonstrate the Node system, start a new Blender file and place the **3D View Editor** in **Cycles Render** mode with **Viewport Shading – Rendered**. Change the **Timeline Editor** to the **Shader Editor**. Click on the **Material buttons** in the **Properties Editor**.

At this point you will have the gray Cube in the 3D View Editor and the Principled BSDF Node connected to a Material Output Node in the Shader Editor.

The Shader Editor Header has Material Nodes activated by default with Use Nodes checked.

Note: You are working with the **Material buttons** in the **Properties Editor,** therefore, the **Material Node button** in the **Shader Editor** is active.

The Nodes displayed are a Principled BSDF Node and a Material Output Node (Figure 29.12).

The Principled BSDF Node is a replica of the **Surface Tab** in the Properties Editor and note, this node is connected to the **Surface** input socket on the **Material Output** Node. In other words the Base Color is being mapped to the surface of the selected Object.

Clicking on the Base Color bar in the **Diffuse BSDF Node** displays a color picker where a new color may be selected, the same as the Base Color bar in the **Properties Editor** (Figure 29.12).

Figure 29.12

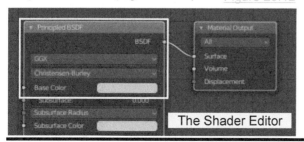

The Shader Editor

Properties Editor Materials

29.4 Cycles in Practice

To view **Cycles Render** in perspective and demonstrate its practical application, work through the following demonstration which will show you how to create and illuminate a scene.

Arrange a UV Sphere and a Monkey **inside** the default Cube in a new Blender Scene as shown (Figure 29.13 and 29.14). The UV Sphere and the Monkey have smooth shading applied and the Cube has been scaled up and elongated and subdivided with several faces deleted on the back side creating a window. A **Solidify Modifer** has been applied to the modified Cube to create wall thickness.

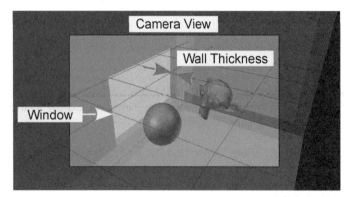

The objective is to place the Sphere and Monkey inside a room next to a window.

The Camera and single Point Lamp are also inside the room.

The Sphere, the Monkey and the window are positioned in Camera View.

Figure 29.13

With the 3D View Editor in **Solid Viewport Shading** mode all you see is the Cube. To see Objects inside the room change the 3D View Editor to **Wireframe Viewport Shading**.

At this stage the scene is illuminated by the default point lamp which is inside the room. Pressing F12 renders an image of the Camera view in Figure 29.15.

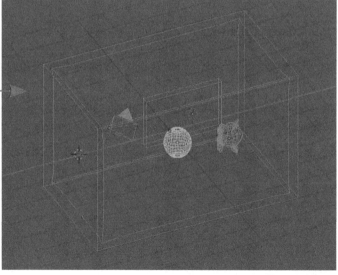

More Set Up Stuff

You may hide an Object temporarily to unclutter a Scene. In Solid Viewport Shading mode select the Cube (the room). Press the **H key**.

Figure 29.14

To reinstate the Cube press **Alt + H key**. This is not particularly useful in this instance but is worth remembering.

In the Properties Editor, Render button, change **Eevee Render** to **Cycles Render.** Have the 3D View Editor in Camera Perspective View and change to Rendered Viewport Shading Mode. This will allow you to see rendered results as you progress.

If you have GPU rendering available and it is faster than CPU rendering it's time to turn it on.

You may go to the **Properties window, Render buttons, Sampling tab** and change the Preview Samples value. The default is 32 which doesn't allow a fantastic result (Figure 29.15). Remember: Increasing the value will increase the render time.

Figure 29.15

By comparison a full render (F12) at 128 Samples is shown in Figure 29.16.

Figure 29.16

Figure 29.17

Select the Monkey in the 3D View Editor. Remember: The monkey is named **Suzanne** as you can see in the upper left hand corner of the **3D View Editor** and in the **Outliner Editor**.

In the **Properties Editor, Material buttons**, click on the **New** button. As previously explained the Material Nodes for Cycles Render are different to Eevee Render.

The default settings show the **Principled BSDF** Node active. The Color (the white color bar/picker) is showing Blender's default gray, RGB 0.800. Click on the **Surface** button where you see Principled BSDF and select **Glass BSDF (**Figure 29.17).

This gives Suzanne a gray glass like effect. Change the color and reduce the Roughness value to 0.000. The effects of the Surface Shader and color are immediately seen in the Camera view (Figure 29.18 – **Note:** Render Sample 200 and Time taken to complete the render 2 minutes, 8.68 seconds).

You will have to decide if the wait is worth it.

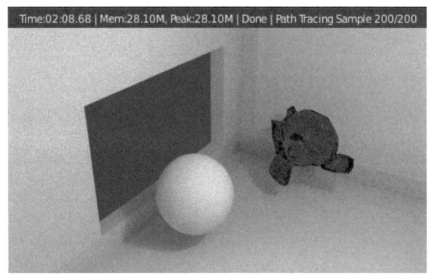

Figure 29.18

This procedure has applied a **Material** to the Monkey by using the **Properties Editor, Materials buttons**.

Remember: The application of Materials using Cycles Render is using the **Cycles Node System**. You may use the Properties Editor or the Shader Editor to apply Materials.

Materials in the Shader Editor

Deselect Suzanne and select the **UV Sphere**. Change the Timeline Editor at the bottom of the Screen to the Shader Editor and drag the top edge up. Place the 3D View Editor at the top of the Screen in Rendered Viewport Shading mode.

In the Rendered View the UV Sphere displays with Blender's default gray Material color even though a Material has not been applied. With the UV Sphere selected the Shader Editor is empty. By default Blender applies the default gray color to the UV Sphere. Click on the New button in the Shader Editor Header to activate the Node System. In the Shader Editor the Principled BSDF Node displays connected to the Material Output Node. The Properties Editor, Material buttons show Principled BSDF in the Surface Tab.

With the Mouse Cursor in the **Shader Editor** press **Alt + A Key** to deselect all Nodes then LMB click on the Principled BSDF Node to select. Press the X Key to delete the Principled BSDF Node. The UV Sphere displays black in the 3D View Editor.

Click Add in the Shader Editor Header and select Shader – Diffuse BSDF to enter a Node. Connect the Diffuse BSDF Node output socket to the Surface input socket of the Material Output Node.

In the **Shader Editor** the **Diffuse BSDF**. This Node is the graphical representation of the data in the **Properties Editor**. The **Material Output** Node is the graphical representation of data sending the Diffuse material color to the surface of the UV Sphere.

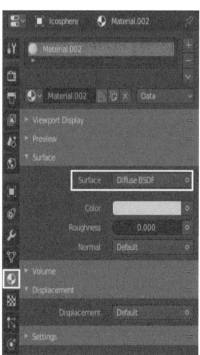

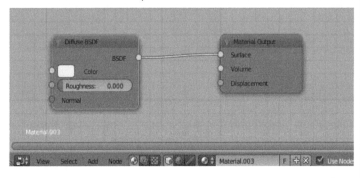

Figure 29.19

The display in the 3D View Editor, Rendered Viewport Shading, Camera view is as shown previously in Figure 29.15.

To discover the power of using Nodes in Cycles Render, select the UV Sphere and perform the following:

Add a Glossy BSDF Node (click Add in the header – Shader - Glossy BSDF). Add a Mix Shader Node (click Add in the header – Shader – Mix Shader). Arrange and connect the Nodes as shown in Figure 29.20.

In the Glossy BSDF Node click on the Color button to display the color picker and select a soft pastel color. The UV Sphere in the 3D View Editor will immediately render showing a glossy surface.

In the Diffuse BSDF Node select a bright vivid color. The 3D View Editor re-renders, mixing the two Shaders together. The Roughness sliders in the Shader Nodes vary the intensity of the colors while the Fac: slider in the Mix Shader Node adjusts the ratio of the mix.

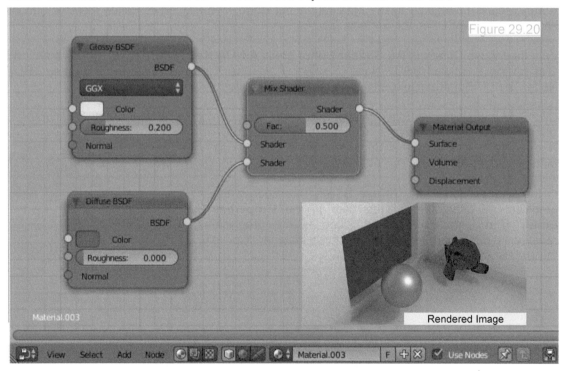

There are numerous combinations of Nodes available and it is impossible to cover everything but this simple demonstration shows the potential of one aspect of Nodes in Cycles.

What you see in the rendered view has been reliant on the default single point lamp for illumination. This can be vastly improved in Cycles.

The Scene that has been created shows the Monkey and UV Sphere placed next to a window. This is in Camera View. The effect of Sky Lighting is to create an ambient light which is the overall lighting from the sky in the natural world. Since the Camera is positioned inside the room Camera View would only show this through the window.

To have a better understanding of the effect, select the Cube in the Scene (the room) and press the H key to hide the room (this is temporary).

In the **Properties Editor, World buttons, Surface tab**, click at the end of the **Color bar**, click on the button and select **Sky Texture** from the menu (Figure 29.22). Voila! you have blue sky in the window background. In the **Color bar** you will see **Sky Texture**.

Click, hold and drag the mouse on the **Sky Ball** to adjust shadow effect in the Scene. You may also adjust the **Turbidity** value between 1.00 and 10.00 for a variation. The Strength value also changes the sky effect. Sky Lighting sets the lighting for outdoors.

Figure 29.21 shows Sky Lighting with the values in Figure 29.22.

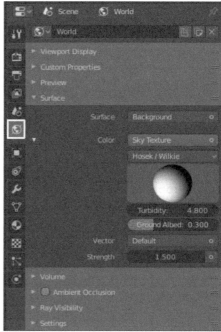

Figure 29.21   Figure 29.22

You can see the Node Arrangement for the Sky effect produced by the values set in Figure 26.22 in the Shader Editor with World Shader Nodes active (Figure 26.22 – Editor Header only).

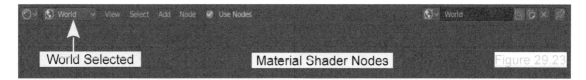

Figure 29.23

It is time to go back indoors.

Reinstate the Room: With the Mouse cursor in the 3D View Editor, press Alt + H key.

The rendered Scene reverts to being illuminated by the single point lamp positioned inside the room. With the **Top** and **Side Orthographic** Views in **Solid Display** mode all you see is the outside of the room. Change to **Wireframe Display Mode** to see what's inside. Select and delete the Point Lamp. The rendered window turns very dark. There is no light inside the room but there is light coming from outside (Figure 29.24).

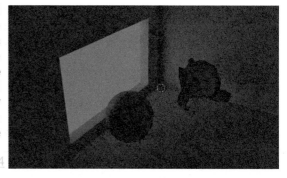

Figure 29.24

Object Lighting

The Point Lamp will be replaced by an Object acting as a light source.

Figure 29.25

Add a Plane and position as shown in Figure 29.25. You want the Plane above and angled towards the Objects. Think of it as a mirror which will reflect light onto the Objects.

Make sure the Plane, when in Camera view, is not in the aperture.

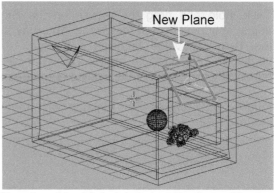

New Plane

In the **Properties Editor, Material buttons**, click **New** to add a Material. Select **Surface, Shader** type, **Emission**. This makes the plane a light source (Figure 29.26).

Figure 29.26

With the **Camera View** in **Rendered mode** you see the inside of the room illuminated (Figure 29.27). The light Color can be changed and the Strength value adjusted. The position and scale of the light source affects the rendered view. You may add more than one light source.

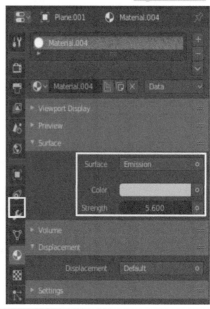

Time:00:46.70 | Mem:27.74M, Peak:51.72M | Done | Path Tracing Sample 32/32

Figure 29.27

29.5 Texture in Cycles

Textures in Cycles can produce spectacular effects. The simple process of using one Texture to color an Object's surface and another to deform the surface will serve as a demonstration. The following exercise may be performed with either Cycles or Eevee Render active.

In the default Blender Scene replace the Cube Object with a Plane scaled up five or six times. To deform the Plane's surface Subdivide making the number of Cuts 20 (plenty of Vertices).

With the Plane in Object Mode add a Material. The default gray will do since a Texture will replace the Material color. The Textures to be used will be Image Textures which have to be saved on the hard drive of the computer. In this demonstration the Image Textures are named: Art_Stains.jpg (used to deform the surface) and Art-Paint.jpg (to color the surface).

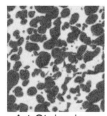 

Figure 29.28

Art-Stains.jpg   Art-Paint.jpg

Figure 29.29

Art-Stains is used to deform since it has two contrasting colors. Any image may be used as a Texture and the first step in the process it to enter the images in Blender as a Texture. In the Properties Editor, Texture buttons, click **New** to add a Texture.

Figure 29.30

The Texture buttons display with a Texture Datablock entered in the Texture Slot. The Datablock is named **Texture** and at this point contains no data.

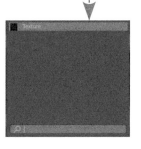

Texture Cache

In the Image Tab under Settings click Open and navigate to one of the .jpeg images (Figure 29.30).

The image entered, shows in the preview and its data is entered in the **Texture datablock**.

Figure 29.31

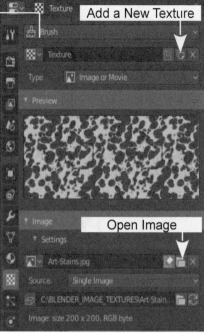

Add a New Texture

Open Image

Click on **Add a New Texture** and a new datablock is created named Texture.001. Open the second image. The second image will display in the preview and its data is entered into the new datablock. In the Cache you will see Texture and Texture.001. You may rename if you wish.

At this point the two images are entered as Textures in Blender but nothing has occurred in the 3D View Editor even though the Plane Object has been selected.

In the Properties Editor, Material buttons, click on the button at the end of the Base Color bar and select Image Texture in the menu.

Clicking the **Browse Material to be linked** button allows you to select either of the two Texture Images. Clicking here shows the images with their original names.

Browse material to be linked

Figure 29.32

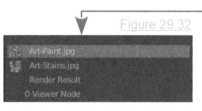

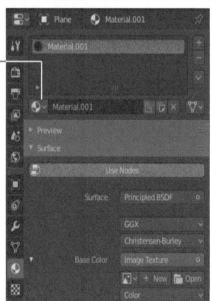

To color the Plane, select (click on) Art-Paint.jpg (the image with the bright colors). With the 3D View Editor in Rendered Viewport Shading Mode you see the image mapped to the surface of the Plane (Figure 29.33).

Figure 29.33

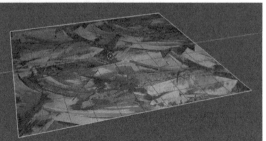

To deform the surface, use a **Displace Modifier**. In the Properties Editor, Modifier buttons, click Add Modifier and select Displace. With the Modifier opened click on Texture and select **0 Texture.**

Texture 0 is the Art-Stains.jpg Texture

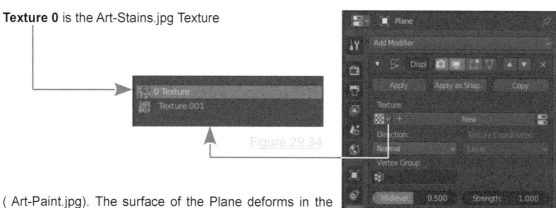

Figure 29.34

(Art-Paint.jpg). The surface of the Plane deforms in the 3D View Editor.

3D View Editor – Eevee Render   Figure 29.35   3D View Editor – Cycles Render

Camera View – Eevee Render   Camera View – Cycles Render

29.6 Summary

What has been shown in this chapter is merely an introduction. The Cycles Render system is capable of fantastic effects.

30

Internet Resources

The Complete Guide to Blender Graphics opens the door to a fantastic world of computer creativity and once you have entered the portal you will want to learn more. The following website links are resources for information which will expand and enhance that which is is provided in this book.

CGMasters

https://cgmasters.net/free-tutorials/blender-2-8-tutorial-overview-eevee-more/

CG Tutorial

http://tutorials.cgrecord.net/

Blender Nation

https://www.blendernation.com/2018/06/07/sci-fi-corridor-blender-2-8-eevee-tutorial/

Blender 3D Architect

https://www.blender3darchitect.com/

Tufts University – Neal Hirsig:

In previous versions of The Complete Guide to Blender Graphics references were given to a series of video tutorials presented by Neal Hirsig. Neal was a senior lecturer at Tufts University in Boston USA who conducted classes in Blender.

Neal has retired from teaching but his tutorials remain available from **EMG-Mediamaker** at:

http://www.emg-mediamaker.com/tutorials-blender-3d-design.php

Neal's Tutorials and Course Material have been recognised as an excellent source for learning Blender being a self paced and well structured source of information. The Tutorials are based on the previous versions of Blender but remain an excellent reference.

Sardi Pax: Basics of Animation – Learning Blender

Beginners **Tutorials:**

http://learningblender.com/tutorials/beginner

Site Homepage:

http://learningblender.com/

Blender Education:

Blender Website Tutorials:

https://www.blender.org/support/tutorials/

What You Need To Get Started:

b3d101.org/en/learn/

CG Cookie:

Blender Basics Tutorial:

https://cgcookie.com/course/blender-basics/

Blender Guru:

https://www.blenderguru.com/tutorials/blender-beginner-tutorial-series/

Blender Nation:

Video Tutorials:

https://www.blendernation.com/category/education/tutorials/

Blender 3D: Noob to Pro

https://www.slant.co/topics/1761/viewpoints/6/~best-online-resources-for-learning-blender3d~blender-3d-noob-to-pro

Blender Stack Exchange

https://blender.stackexchange.com/questions/15355/resources-for-blender/15376#15376

The Blender Manual

https://docs.blender.org/manual/it/dev/

The Blender Website

https://www.blender.org/

Appendix - A

Basic Blender Commands

This is a partial list of Blender commands. Please visit www.blender.org for more details.

A Key: Press to **select All Object** in the Scene.

Alt + A Key: Press to deselect Objects.

B Key: In Object Mode and Edit Mode, press to activate **Box Select** cross hairs; Position the cross hairs with the Mouse, click LMB, hold and drag the Mouse Cursor to create a window around an Object or multiple Objects to be selected. Release the Mouse button to select the Objects.

C Key: In Object Mode and Edit Mode press to activate **Circle Select**; Creates a circle around the Mouse Cursor. Scroll MMB to adjust the diameter. Click LMB, hold and drag the circle over multiple Objects or Vertices to select. Press Esc to cancel leaving the Objects or Vertices selected..

E Key: Extrude; While in Edit mode, selected Vertices, Edges, or Faces, drag Mouse, extrude.

G Key: Grab; press the **G Key** and drag the mouse to freely move a selected Object or selected Vertices. Click LMB to set in position.

I Key: Press to **insert** an animation **Keyframe**.

M Key: Press, with the Mouse Cursor in the 3D View Editor, to display the **Move to Collection** panel.

N Key: Toggles between showing and hiding the Object Properties Panel containing numeric data relating to the selected Object or Vertices.

O Key: In Edit Mode, toggles Proportional Vertex Editing (On - Off).

P Key: In Edit Mode, press to opens the **Separate** menu in order to separate .

R Key: Rotate; Press the R Key and drag the mouse to rotate an Object or selected Vertices.

S Key: Scale; Press the S Key and drag the Mouse to Scale an Object or selected Vertices.

T Key: Toggles the **Tool Panel** display on - off.

U Key: In Edit mode, press to open the **UV Mapping** menu.

W Key: Toggles the Selection Tools – Cursor Select, Box Select, Circle Select, Lasso Select.

X Key: Delete Key. Press to display O.K. Delete menu.

Z Key: Toggles display of Shading option Pie Menu. Click LMB to select an option.

Arrow Keys: Used to advance Frames in an animation: left and right arrows = 1-Frame increments, up and down arrows move to the First and Last Frames.

Ctrl + A Key: Opens the **Apply** menu; this can reset the Object data.

Ctrl + J Key: Joins two selected Objects.

Ctrl + S Key. Opens the **File Browser** window to save a Blender file.

Ctrl +Z Key: The global **undo command**; with each press, one step will be undone (up to 32 steps are possible by default). If you are in Edit Mode, it will only undo editing steps on the selected Object.

Esc: **Cancels** an action or ends an animation.

F2: Opens the **File Context** menu.

F3: Opens the **Search Panel**.

F4: Opens the **Window Context Menu**.

F11: Opens the **Image Editor**.

F12: **Renders an image** of the Camera view.

LMB: Left Mouse Button . Click to select an Object. Click an empty space to deselect Objects. Click to manipulate the 3D Manipulator Widget, to activate functions, to enter values, etc.

RMB: Right Mouse Button . Click to display the Object Context menu.

MMB: Middle Mouse Button (MSW) . Click to manipulate specified options.

MSW: Mouse Scroll Wheel. Zooms in and out and scrolls to expand/contract selection options.

NumPad: (Number Pad) Controls the view.

7:........ Top	5:......... Toggles User Perspective – User Orthographic View
1:........ Front.	+ and – : Zoom in and out and control the vertex size in
3:........ Side.	proportional vertex editing
0:........ Camera.	

Shift Key: Hold down while clicking the LMB to make multiple selections.

Shift + A Key: Displays the **Add** menu to add Objects to the Scene.

Shift + D Key: Duplicates or copies selected Objects or Vertices.

Shift + S Key: Displays the **Snap** pie menu for Selection and Cursor.

Shift + Space Bar: Displays **Tool Panel** options.

Shift + LMB Click: Selects multiple Objects or Vertices.

Shift + RMB Click: Locate the 3D View Editor Cursor.
                                    Note: No Objects selected.

Space Bar: Toggles Play / Stop Animation.

Tab: Toggles between Edit Mode and Object Mode.

Many shortcuts are listed in the menus accessed in the Editor Headers

3D View Editor Header

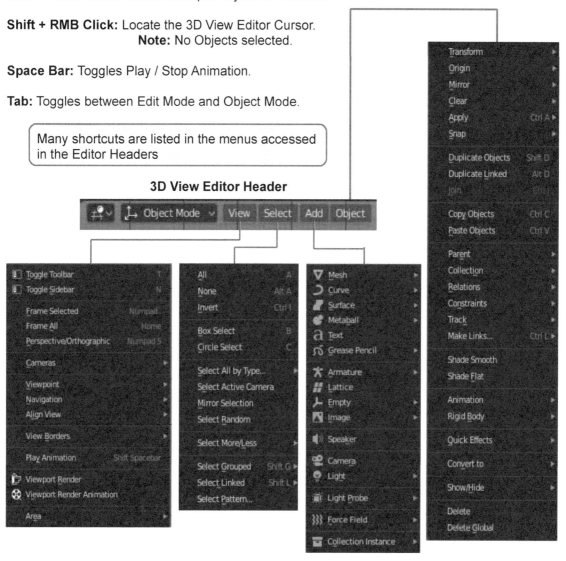

Index

R

Radians 51, 482
Radius slider 165, 166
Random.py 473, 478, 481
Randomize Object Properties 473, 478
Real World Properties 423
Real World Time 423
Relationship Constraint 307, 312
Relative Offset 102, 103
Remesh Modifier 99, 111, 112
Remove Double Vertices 88
Renaming a Node Group 252
Render 17, 255, 256, 260-264, 485
Render Layers 254
Render Animation 255, 262, 263
Render Buttons 249, 255, 256, 262
Render Demonstration 17
Render Farm 264, 471
Render Format 269
Render Preset 259
Render Result 253
Render Options 256
Rendered Image 253
Rendered Viewport Shading 89, 189, 190,
    196, 225, 255, 256,
Rendered Image 255, 260
Rendering 3, 255, 256
Rendering Systems 255
Rendering a JPEG Image 255, 260
Rendering a Movie File 255, 261
Repositioning the Keyframe 284, 300
Resizing Editors 21
Resolution 257
Rig 317
Rigging 317, 354
Right Orthographic View 71
Rigid Body World 410
Rip Region (Tool) 79, 92, 108
Root Bone 343, 344, 345
Rotate 47, 49, 291
Rotation Using F-Curves 265, 292
Rotation or Angle 51
Roughness 229, 243
Ruler/Protractor 41, 51

S

Samples 256, 257
Save 6, 35
Save As 6, 35
Save As Image 260
Save Blender File 29, 35
Save User Settings 14
Save a Copy 35
Saving Changes 14
Saving Work 27, 35
Scale 47, 49
Scale Units 49
Scaling 47
Scaling in the Dope Sheet 286
Scaling the Frame Bar 279
Scaling the Graph Editor 279
Scene Collection 25, 56, 174, 175
Scene Arrangements 203, 215, 229
Scene Background 211, 215, 470
Scene Controls 11
Scene Illumination 247
Scene Lighting 190, 191, 197, 199, 200,
    209, 211
Scene Lighting Modes 190
Scene Lighting and Cameras 199
Scene Lights 197, 200, 225
Scene Manipulation 1, 10, 14, 16, 18
Scene Manipulation Widget 18
Scene World 11, 197, 200
Screen 3
Screen Header 5
Screw 79, 91, 99, 113
Screw Modifier 113
Screw Tool 91
Scripted Expression 475, 481, 482
Scroll MMB 45
Scrubbing the Animation 272
Sculpt 157, 164, 166, 167
Sculpt Mode 164, 166
Sculpt Mode Tools 165
Sculpt Tool 111
Sculpting 164, 166
Selecting Keyframes 284
Selecting Vertices, Edges and Faces 64
Selecting and Deselecting Objects 44
Selection Circle 45
Selection option 62